THE WEST POINT ATLAS
OF AMERICAN WARS

Volume II   1900-1918

Compiled by

THE DEPARTMENT OF MILITARY ART
AND ENGINEERING
THE UNITED STATES MILITARY ACADEMY

WEST POINT, NEW YORK

Chief Editor

BRIGADIER GENERAL
VINCENT J. ESPOSITO, USA (RET.)

FORMER PROFESSOR AND HEAD OF THE DEPARTMENT
OF MILITARY ART AND ENGINEERING
THE UNITED STATES MILITARY ACADEMY

With a prefatory letter by DWIGHT D. EISENHOWER
Foreword by EDWARD M. COFFMAN

HENRY HOLT AND COMPANY · NEW YORK

Henry Holt and Company, Inc.
Publishers since 1866
115 West 18th Street
New York, New York 10011

Henry Holt ® is a registered trademark
of Henry Holt and Company, Inc.

Published in Canada by Fitzhenry & Whiteside, Ltd.,
195 Allstate Parkway, Markham, Ontario L3R 4T8.
Originally published in 1959 by Frederick A. Praeger, Inc., Publishers.

Library of Congress Cataloging-in-Publication Data

United States Military Academy. Dept. of Military Art and Engineering.
The West Point atlas of American wars / compiled by the Department
of Military Art and Engineering, the United States Military Academy;
chief editor Vincent J. Esposito; with prefatory letter by Dwight D. Eisenhower;
foreword by Edward M. Coffman. — 1st ed. 1997. [rev. and updated from 1959 ed.]
        p.   cm.
Originally published: New York: Praeger, 1959.
Contents: v. 2. 1900–1918.
1. United States—History, Military—Maps.   I. Esposito. Vincent
J. (Vincent Joseph), 1900–1965.   II. Title.
    G1201.S1U5   1997 <G&M>   95-6753
    912.73—dc20   CIP
                                                 MAP

ISBN 0-8050-5305-0

Henry Holt books are available for special promotions and premiums.
For details contact: Director, Special Markets.

First Revised and Updated Edition—1997

Printed in Hong Kong
All first editions are printed on acid-free paper. ∞

10 9 8 7 6 5 4 3 2 1

ACKNOWLEDGMENTS

The editors of this new edition have not sought to rewrite completely the original text. Instead, we have sought to revise the contents by incorporating some of the latest scholarship and modifying those portions that were clearly out of date. We owe a debt of gratitude to the original editors, authors, and cartographers of this venerated volume, who are identified in the Introduction and whose work has made our task an especially easy one. It is with great sadness that we must note the passing of Mr. Edward J. Krasnoborski, the master cartographer whose work has made these atlases recognized classics. We dedicate this revision to his memory. We also wish to express our appreciation to Major James T. Seidule, Professor Eugenia C. Kiesling, Professor Frederick Kagan, Major Mark Gerges, and Captain Kevin W. Ferrell, each of whom contributed to the rewriting of portions of the text. To Jim Charlton, whose belief in the importance of the project was instrumental in its completion, goes our special thanks.

COLONEL ROBERT A. DOUGHTY
LIEUTENANT COLONEL CONRAD C. CRANE

West Point, New York

Americans do not remember World War I very well. Armistice Day, which we used to commemorate with a minute of silence at the eleventh hour of the eleventh day of the eleventh month is now Veterans Day. The Civil War and World War II demanded much more from this nation and are naturally better remembered. Then, the United States took part in World War I for just 19 months, and large numbers of American troops were in action only six of those months.

The Europeans called it the Great War, and it left them with an indelible memory. Their war lasted longer and exacted devastating cost in blood and treasure. Dynasties fell, and the shapes of countries changed. The proportion of approximately ten percent of the maps in this atlas devoted to the American campaigns is thus proper. The suffering of the Europeans was enormous. One indication is that the 250,000 American battle casualties were less than 60 percent of those suffered by the British in the Somme campaign during 1916. Yet, what is little known is that there were more American than British troops in France, and they held a longer stretch of the Western Front in the closing days of the war. Nor are many aware that, despite the greater American role in World War II, the cemetery at Romagne for those who died in the Meuse-Argonne campaign is the largest of the American military cemeteries in Europe.

The story the maps do not tell is the tale of the tremendous mobilization that multiplied the American peacetime forces by some 22 times to 4.8 million and the logistical effort that got two million of those men to France. The American economic support of the Allies was also crucial, but it was the sheer weight of the American Expeditionary Force that won the victory in 1918.

******

In 1959, military historians who were not graduates of the Military Academy welcomed the publication of *The West Point Atlas of American Wars*. At last, we had access to the excellent maps that had helped cadets better understand those battles over the years. With ever increasing interest in military history over the years, it is time to make this atlas available to those readers who have not been able to obtain copies of the older volumes.

This atlas is a classic. Vincent J. Esposito, assisted by able soldier-historians John R. Elting and Thomas E. Griess, provided the concise, descriptive text to complement the maps that the master cartographer Edward J. Krasnoborski prepared. While the atlas stands alone, a reader will find it also useful to help explain other works on the various battles and campaigns.

All of us interested in military history are grateful to the Military Academy's Department of History for revising and reissuing this work.

EDWARD M. COFFMAN
PROFESSOR EMERITUS

University of Wisconsin—Madison.

THE WHITE HOUSE

WASHINGTON

April 22, 1959

TO THE CORPS OF CADETS, UNITED STATES MILITARY
ACADEMY

I am glad to learn of the forthcoming publication of The West
Point Atlas of American Wars, for use in cadet instruction -- and
indeed for use by all military personnel in the study of military
history.

Through a careful and objective study of the significant campaigns
of the world, a professional officer acquires a knowledge of military experience which he himself could not otherwise accumulate.
The facts of a given battle may no longer serve any practical purpose except as a framework on which to base an analysis; but when
the serious student of the military art delves into the reasons for
the failure of a specific attack -- or soberly analyzes the professional qualities of one of the responsible commanders of the past --
he is, by this very activity, preparing for a day in which he, under
different circumstances, may be facing decisions of vital conse-
quence to his country.

The "principles of war" which this atlas will assist you in studying
are broad.   They apply to air and naval warfare as well as to land
combat.   They are not, in the final analysis, limited to any one
type of warfare, or even limited exclusively to war itself.   But
principles as such can rarely be studied in a vacuum; military
operations are drastically affected by many considerations, one of
the most important of which is the geography of the region.   Thus,
it is important that these campaigns be studied in conjunction with
the very best available in clear and accurate maps.

I am confident that The West Point Atlas of American Wars will
prove a tremendous aid in instructing -- and inspiring -- the minds
of those whose profession it will be to defend the frontiers of the
Free World against all enemies.

Dwight D. Eisenhower

The Origin and Purpose of the Work

This atlas is especially designed for the cadets of the United States Military Academy as an aid in their initial studies in the History of the Military Art. It is equally appropriate for the civilian student of military history, while the advanced and experienced reader will find the text accompanying the maps to be valuable summations and the abundance of maps to be a boon. In a sense, this combined text and atlas is revolutionary in the field of military writing. Here the theme is carried along by the maps and the narrative is supplemental; in the normal work the reverse is generally the case.

The first step in the study of any military operation is to ascertain precisely what occurred and what factors influenced the course of the action and its outcome. These factors include: the quality of the leadership; the plans, the preparations, the training, and the morale; weather and terrain conditions; armament and equipment differentials; tactics and battle techniques; and contemporary political, economic, and sociological considerations. With this background clearly in mind, one can then proceed to the more exciting task of analysis, criticism, and, perhaps, speculation. The many splendid works on military history generally combine such background material with discussion and analysis as events progress, and this arrangement is excellent for the experienced reader who is able to relate the many factors and proceed without loss of continuity. Unfortunately, however, such is not the case with the new student. He must pause frequently for reflection and comprehension; many questions arise. Soon he begins to be confused as to the exact sequence of events described and is forced to go back to establish their continuity. In so doing, he encounters formidable obstacles. Military works are almost universally lacking in adequate maps. Many have the maps interspersed with the text so that, since many pages relate to one map, a constant turning of pages becomes necessary if the reader is to achieve any correlation. More frequently, the novice will find it necessary to work back through the narrative in order to pick up the lost strands. The new student eventually masters these problems, but initially they are time-consuming and at least somewhat frustrating.

The time available to the cadets of the United States Military Academy for study is severely budgeted. That allotted in the Academy curriculum to the Course in the History of the Military Art is limited, and the subject matter of the course covers an extensive field which expands constantly. It is therefore necessary to make sure that the cadets derive maximum benefit from the limited time at their disposal, and to this end, the course material has been progressively modified to facilitate study. In 1938, this department began the development of a series of atlases to accompany the several historical works used as texts. The first of these to deal with American wars was compiled in order to supplement *American Campaigns,* by Matthew Forney Steele (which, though published more than fifty years ago, remains one of the best works on American military operations prior to 1900). The maps of this first atlas covered the Colonial and Revolutionary Wars, the War of 1812, the Mexican War, the American Civil War, and the Spanish-American War. Revised throughout the years, these maps now form the content of Volume I of this publication. Another atlas was compiled to accompany a department text on World War I. During World War II, pamphlets were hastily prepared on operations as they progressed; and these were provided with fold-in maps at the back. Eventually, the pamphlets and maps were revised, corrected, and incorporated into a formal text and atlas comparable to the others of the series. With the advent of the Korean War, a department pamphlet was compiled, including appropriate maps. The maps of the atlases on World War I and World War II and of the Korean pamphlet comprise the content of Volume II of this work.

The title of these volumes—*The West Point Atlas of American Wars*—may mislead some into believing that only engagements in which Americans participated are considered. This is not the case. Though emphasis may be given to American actions, wars are treated as a whole. For example, most of the maps in the World War I section cover events prior to the entry of the United States into that war, and, in the World War II section, many of the maps concern engagements in which United States forces did not participate, while others portray operations undertaken jointly with our allies.

With few exceptions, the maps depict operations of the land forces. There is no intention to slight the splendid achievements of the air and naval forces; these are given appropriate recognition in the narrative. Air and naval operations are intricate and highly specialized; and since they do not lend themselves to the type of map portrayal employed in this general work, they must perforce be the subjects of separate detailed studies. Our Army,

Navy, and Air Force (and their individual components) can be proud of their traditions and accomplishments in defense of the United States and its ideals; each can prove itself to have been *a* decisive force in operations in which it has participated. But which was *the* decisive force is sometimes the subject of controversy that will long endure.

In the present work, every effort has been made to eliminate or reduce time-consuming processes and inconveniences to study. The narrative pertaining to each map is specially "tailored" to fit on the blank page opposite the map. Thus, side by side, text and map are most conveniently arranged for joint study; only on rare occasions will it be necessary to turn back to another map. The narrative is carefully designed to avoid involving the reader in a fruitless search for material not included on the map. Similarly, where places on the map are difficult to locate, the narrative includes direction guides.

The text is made brief not only for convenience in map-text reference but also for another highly important educational purpose. The novice engaged in the study of a standard work stands in awe of the author and is likely to accept his views and analyses without question. Eventually, with greater experience and broader background, he is able to evaluate the author's case properly; but, initially, his efforts do not go far beyond an exercise in memory. It is our purpose at the Military Academy to develop in the cadets an intellectual curiosity—the facility to question, to analyze, and to arrive at their own conclusions. The text is designed with this end in view. Its brevity permits the application of much of the cadets' limited study time to reflection rather than to reading. It is recognized that they will encounter difficulty at first in ascertaining which elements are worthy of consideration. Accordingly, they are provided with a list of pertinent subjects, illustrated by the particular campaign under study, for discussion. At the classroom sessions, which are conducted in round-table fashion with the instructor acting as moderator, the cadets express their views and contest those with which they are in disagreement. At times, compromises are reached (though more often they are not).

The study of a military campaign is not an end in itself; rather, it is a vehicle which introduces the student to the contemplation of many facets of the military art. For example, the German invasion of Flanders in 1940 presents for consideration a great number of subjects. The list of study topics for this campaign, if reduced to simple subject statements, would read: Military Geography and Topography, Military Organization and Doctrine, The Influence of Political Factors on Military Planning, The Role of Permanent Fortifications in Modern Warfare, The Influence of Technological Advances, The Influence of Naval Power in War Strategy, The Relationship of Time and Space Factors, The Conduct of Airborne Operations, The Attack of Fortified Strong Points, Mobility as a Factor in Operations, Air Support of Ground Operations, Tactics and Techniques of River Crossings, The Command Structure in Combined Operations with Allies, Analysis of Principal Military Leaders, Advances in Submarine Warfare, and The Influence of Present-Day and Future Weapons Systems. It is, of course, impossible to cover fully all of these subjects in a single classroom session, but these, and many others, arise again and again as different campaigns are studied. In the end, a fairly comprehensive field of knowledge has been assimilated.

A Guide to Study

The reader will find his study much easier if he will first become acquainted with the symbols employed to depict information on the maps. Most of the basic symbols are similar for all wars, but there are others peculiar to particular periods. There is a page of symbols in the front of Volume I which is applicable to the maps of the entire volume; Volume II contains a page of symbols pertaining to World War I and another for use with the World War II and Korean War maps.

The narrative accompanying a map will be easier to follow if a few moments are first spent examining the map to ascertain what is represented and, most important, the timing. The title block of each map contains a summation of this information. The troop dispositions at the specific time indicated are shown on the map in solid lines. On some maps, actions and movements, as shown by appropriate route lines and symbols, will lead to the positions shown in solid lines; on others, the solid lines indicate an initial location, and route lines emanating therefrom signify subsequent movements.

On the first map of most campaigns, numerals appear in parentheses under the names of commanders. These signify the numerical strength of the commanders' units. Their strengths are not shown on each map, but they are shown where significant changes from the initial strength have taken place.

The conduct of every campaign is strongly influenced by the topography of the area involved. Frequently, this topography dictates the course of action, and it often introduces significant hazards. An initial study of the ground over which the campaign or battle was fought—rivers, mountains, roads, railroads, vegetation—will prove most helpful in understanding the reasons for many of the actions.

Some of the first sixteen maps of Volume I, which contain much more than the average amount of material, will require special concentrated study.

Charts of chronology are provided for events of each of the major wars: the Civil War, World War I, and World War II. These charts are valuable in correlating events in other areas with those in the particular area under study. We have found from experience that the best way to study wars which are extensive in scope is to study by campaign areas rather than by chronology of events. Consequently, the maps in this atlas are grouped according to campaign areas. However, if the reader desires to study events by time sequence, he can do so by following the charts of chronology and referring to the appropriate maps.

After a period of study, the novice will develop confidence in his ability to master standard works in military history. He may wish to expand his investigation of a particular aspect of this work or to delve into related fields. To assist him, there is provided at the end of each volume a comprehensive list of books, conveniently arranged, which are recommended for further reading.

Acknowledgments

This department is deeply indebted to the many officers who, throughout the years, participated in preparing the material incorporated in this work. Some have passed on, others have retired from active service, and the remainder are expecting grade changes; for these reasons, the grades of those hereafter mentioned are not indicated. All are, or were, officers of the United States Army—except for those whose names are given in italics to indicate that they are members of the United States Air Force.

Research and preparation of the initial drafts of the maps were accomplished by the following: the Civil War section—Allen F. Clark, Jr., Ellsworth I. Davis, John C. B. Elliott, Clayton S. Gates, Lawrence J. Lincoln, Theodore M. Osborne, Alfred D. Starbird, David H. Tulley; all other maps of Volume I —John R. Elting; the World War I section—*Richard C. Boys,* Charley P. Eastburn, Philip L. Elliott, Walter J. Fellenz, Ralph R. Ganns, Earl F. Holton, Cecil E. Spann, Jr., *Daniel F. Tatum,* George P. Winton, Jr.; the World War II section—Raymond W. Allen, Jr., Allen F. Clark, Jr., Edmund K. Daley, Thomas Q. Donaldson, 4th, Charley P. Eastburn, John R. Elting, Clayton S. Gates, Ronan C. Grady, Jr., Charles L. Hassmann, Robert A. Hill, Max S. Johnson, Lawrence J. Lincoln, John J. Outcalt, William H. Roedy, Alfred D. Starbird, Harrison G. Travis; the Korean War—Philip L. Elliott, Cecil E. Spann, Jr.

The text is the product of the collaborative efforts of John R. Elting, Thomas E. Griess, and the undersigned, with the burden of research, initial manuscript drafting, and review of final manuscript falling to the first two mentioned. Many sources have been used in the preparation of the text, particularly official histories. For the World War II and Korean War text, the splendid publications prepared to date by the Office of the Chief of Military History, Department of the Army, have been drawn on heavily as primary sources.

Special acknowledgment is made of the contributions of: T. Dodson Stamps, former head of the department, who initiated the department atlas project; Robert A. Hill, formerly assistant professor, who supervised the preparation of the maps in most of the initial department pamphlets of World War II operations from which the corresponding maps in this work were developed; John R. Elting and Thomas E. Griess, who, in addition to bearing the major burden of text preparation, assisted in the many tasks incident to publication; Edward J. Krasnoborski, department cartographer, who so competently translated the final drafts of the maps into production copy; and James Glover, department secretary, who performed the tedious task of typing the manuscript.

Though many hands have labored in the production of the material which eventually has found its way into this work, the undersigned planned, supervised, and nurtured the original component atlases from their inception, and he either approved or prepared the final drafts of text and maps alike. He must therefore assume full responsibility for any deficiencies which may exist in these volumes.

VINCENT J. ESPOSITO

West Point, New York
June, 1959

TABLE OF CONTENTS

		PAGE
ACKNOWLEDGMENTS		III
FOREWORD		IV
PREFATORY LETTER		V
INTRODUCTION		VI
CHRONOLOGY OF EVENTS OF WORLD WAR I		XII
TABLE OF SYMBOLS		XV

		MAPS
Plans and Forces of the Major Powers		1–3
The Batttle of the Frontiers		4–10
The Battle of the Marne		11–14
Operations in East Prussia	1914	15–21
The Eastern Front to the End of 1915		22–27
The Dardanelles Campaign		28–31
Verdun-Somme Operations	1916	32–35
The Eastern Front	1916–18	36–41
The Campaigns in Italy and the Balkans		42–50
The Campaigns in Mesopotamia and Palestine		51–57
The Western Front	1917	58–61
The First Three German Drives	1918	62–64
United States Preparations and the Fourth and Fifth German Drives		65–67
The St. Mihiel and Meuse-Argonne Operations		68–71

RECOMMENDED READING LIST	*(follows map 71)*

1914	WESTERN FRONT	EASTERN FRONT	SERBIAN AND SALONIKAN FRONTS	ITALIAN FRONT	TURKISH FRONTS		
					DARDANELLES	MESOPOTAMIA	PALESTINE
AUG.	Battle of the Frontiers	Tannenberg	1st Invasion of Serbia				
SEPT.	Battle of the Marne; First Battle of the Aisne	1st Masuria; Galician Battles	2d Invasion of Serbia				
OCT.	Race to the Sea; First Battle of Ypres	German Operations in S.W. Poland					Defense Behind the Suez Canal
NOV.		Battle of Lodz	3d Invasion of Serbia		Initial Naval Bombardment	Landing and Establishment of Bridgehead	
DEC.							
1915 JAN.							1st Turkish Attack on the Canal
FEB.		Winter Battle of Masuria			Naval Attack		
MAR.	Stabilized Front with Limited Attacks on Noyon Salient in Champagne and Artois					First British Advance	
APR.							
MAY		Gorlice-Tarnow Breakthrough			1st Landing Helles		
JUNE				1st Isonzo			Defense Just East of the Canal and Minor Raids
JULY		Russian Withdrawal					
AUG.				2d Isonzo	2d Landing Suvla Bay		
SEPT.						First Battle of Kut	
OCT.			Final Invasion	3d Isonzo			
NOV.			Serbia Eliminated; Salonikan Front Established	4th Isonzo		Battle of Ctesiphon	
DEC.					Evacuation Begun	Siege of Kut	

1916	WESTERN FRONT	EASTERN FRONT	SALONIKAN FRONT	ITALIAN FRONT	TURKISH FRONTS		
					DARDANELLES	MESOPOTAMIA	PALESTINE
JAN.					Evacuation Completed		
FEB.						Siege of Kut	
MAR.		Lake Narotch Operations		5th Isonzo			
APR.						Fall of Kut	
MAY	Battle of Jutland			Asiago Offensive			British Advance and Clearing of the Sinai Desert
JUNE							
JULY	Battle of Verdun	Brusilov Offensive					
AUG.				6th Isonzo			
SEPT.	Battle of the Somme	Rumanian Offensive		7th Isonzo			
OCT.				8th Isonzo			
NOV.		Rumania Eliminated	Fall of Monastir	9th Isonzo			
DEC.						Second British Advance	
1917 JAN							British Arrive at Turkish Border
FEB.	German Withdrawal to the Hindenburg Line					2d Battle of Kut	
MAR.	U.S. Declares War	Russian Revolution				Capture of Baghdad	1st Battle of Gaza
APR.	Allied Offensives (Arras and 2d Aisne)		Limited Operations and Advance to the Greek Frontier				2d Battle of Gaza
MAY				10th Isonzo			
JUNE	Battle of Messines						
JULY		Kerensky (2d Brusilov) Offensive					
AUG.				11th Isonzo			
SEPT.	Third Battle of Ypres	Riga Operation					
OCT.							
NOV.	Battle of Cambrai			Battle of Caporetto			3d Battle of Gaza
DEC.		Russian Armistice					Battles of Junction Station and Jerusalem

1918	WESTERN FRONT	SALONIKAN FRONT	ITALIAN FRONT	TURKISH FRONTS	
				MESOPOTAMIA	PALESTINE
JAN.					
FEB.					
MAR.	**THE GERMAN DRIVES** Somme Offensive (1st German Drive)				
APR.	Lys Offensive (2d German Drive)	Defensive Operations			
MAY	Aisne Offensive (3d German Drive)				
JUNE	Noyon-Montdidier Offensive (4th German Drive)		Battle of the Piave		
JULY	Champagne-Marne Offensive (5th German Drive) **THE REDUCTION OF THE SALIENTS** Aisne-Marne Offensive				
AUG.	Reduction of the Amiens Salient The Lys Salient Evacuated				
SEPT.	St. Mihiel Offensive **THE FINAL OFFENSIVE**	Allied Offensive Bulgarian Armistice			Battle of Megiddo Pursuit
OCT.	French and British Offensives Meuse-Argonne Offensive		Battle of Vittorio-Veneto	Advance on Mosul	Armistice
NOV.	Armistice				

TABLE OF SYMBOLS

BASIC SYMBOLS:

Regiment	III	Infantry	⊠
Brigade	x	Cavalry	⊘
Division	xx	Cavalry covering force	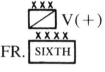
Corps	xxx	Trains	
Army	xxxx	Artillery	
Army Group	xxxxx		

Examples of Combinations of Basic Symbols:

Small infantry detachment

Third Reserve Division

Mackensen's XVII Corps

 3R MACKENSEN

Fifth Cavalry Corps with other units attached

French Sixth Army

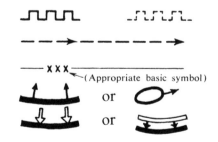 V(+)

FR. SIXTH

OTHER SYMBOLS:

	Actual location	Prior location
Troops on the march		
Troops in position		
Troops in bivouac or reserve		
	Occupied	Unoccupied
Field works		

Strong prepared defenses

Route of march

Boundary between units — x x x — (Appropriate basic symbol)

Troops displacing and direction   or

Troops in position under attack   or

THE WEST POINT ATLAS
OF AMERICAN WARS

Volume II   1900-1918

As a result of the Franco-Prussian War, the German Empire became the dominant nation on the continent of Europe. The technical advances of the Industrial Revolution, fully exploited by the hard-working Germans, made possible an enormous increase in industry and trade. This expansion led to a desire for colonies which could serve as markets and sources of raw materials. The acquisition of a colonial empire, in turn, made a strong navy necessary. Consequently, in the 1890's, Germany began the construction of a fleet. England, hitherto on good terms with Germany, considered this a direct challenge. Naval superiority was vital to England's existence as a great power—indeed, as a guarantee to feed her people.

France, suffering under the stigma of her defeat in 1870 and the attendant loss of her valuable provinces of Alsace and Lorraine, meditated a war of revenge. Her recovery was rapid; by the early 1900's, she was second only to Germany on the Continent.

In eastern Europe, there was a constant clash of Russian and Austro-Hungarian ambitions. Compounding this situation were the ferocious national aspirations of the smaller Balkan states. The most aggressive of these was Serbia, which had claims to several provinces ruled by Austria-Hungary (hereafter referred to simply as Austria). Russia, anxious to free her "little Slavic sisters" from all foreign domination except her own, supported Serbia. Russia longed to dismember Turkey and gain control of the Dardanelles. Turkey seethed with hatred of Russia—and of the Balkan states, which had driven her out of most of her European provinces in 1913.

These antagonisms, ambitions, and conflicts of interest kept the nations of Europe under the shadow of an impending general war. Seeking some measure of collective security, they therefore grouped themselves into alliances. By 1914, Germany, Austria, and Italy—the last irritated over French expansion in North Africa—had formed the Triple Alliance; England, France, and Russia, the Triple Entente. In each alliance, the members pledged that if one were attacked, the others would come to her assistance.

These powers set about diligently preparing themselves for war. Plans for general mobilization and initial operations were kept up to date. The impact of general mobilization on the national life and economy obviously would be so profound that it became universally accepted that general mobilization meant war. It was equally apparent that, if one nation mobilized, its neighbors must do likewise or risk being caught unprepared.

By 1914, tensions had tightened to the point where the slightest overt act would plunge all Europe into war. The bloody deed which actually did this was the murder of the Austrian Archduke Franz Ferdinand and his wife by a Serbian terrorist on 28 June.

Austria, having long wanted an excuse to suppress her troublesome little neighbor, confronted Serbia with a harsh ultimatum. Hoping to frighten the Austrians, Russia began partial mobilization. Austria, however, had secured promises of German backing and, when Serbia did not submit, declared war. Russia thereupon ordered general mobilization. Germany gave Russia twelve hours to halt this; when the Russians ignored the demand, the Germans declared war on them and—knowing that France intended to honor its alliance with Russia—on France as well. Great Britain was pledged, along with other European nations, to protect Belgian neutrality. When the Germans entered Belgium on 3 August, Great Britain declared war.

Thus, by 4 August, Germany and Austria were at war with Belgium, Britain, France, Russia, and Serbia. The first two were soon termed the Central Powers; the latter group, the Allies. Italy, announcing that the Triple Alliance was valid only if her allies were *attacked*, remained neutral. As the war continued, other nations entered it. Turkey and Bulgaria joined the Central Powers. Many countries took the part of the Allies; of these, only Greece, Italy, Japan, Montenegro, Portugal, Rumania, and the United States participated actively.

GENERAL MAP
EUROPE IN 1914

Germany's master war plan was the Schlieffen Plan of 1905, the final work of Count Alfred von Schlieffen, Chief of the German General Staff, before his retirement. In the West, its purpose was to crush France before Russia could mobilize completely.

Schlieffen felt that rough terrain and French fortifications would check an attack against France's eastern frontier. An envelopment through Switzerland seemed impossible. He therefore decided to make his main effort in the north.

For this offensive, Schlieffen proposed to concentrate the German ground forces, grouped into seven armies, on the Western Front. The right wing would consist of five armies (thirty-five corps), the left wing of two armies (five corps)—giving the right wing a preponderance of seven to one. The two northernmost armies were to be especially strong. Six "ersatz corps," formed from untrained reservists of military age, would follow those two armies, protect their communications, and besiege bypassed strongholds. Only local defense forces would defend eastern Germany against Russia. After the defeat of France, Schlieffen expected to move overwhelming forces to the East.

The left wing, though strategically on the defensive, was to attack immediately to lure the French into a major offensive in Alsace-Lorraine (*lower right*). Meanwhile, the right wing, pivoting on the Metz-Thionville fortress area (*center, right*), would move without warning and in overwhelming force across neutral Belgium and Holland. It would break into France as shown, the First Army swinging west and south of Paris, and strike the rear of the main French armies, by then engaged with the German left. The plan was subtle: the harder the French pushed against the left wing, the more thoroughly they would entangle themselves in Alsace-Lorraine, and the more rapid and decisive would be the German right wing's drive.

It must be noted, however, that the German Reichstag never authorized all the forces that Schlieffen considered essential. Nevertheless, his plan is outstanding in its attainment of maximum concentration of combat power in the decisive right wing through economy of force elsewhere.

Schlieffen's successor, General Helmuth von Moltke, faced a changing balance of international power. Russia, France, and England improved their armies. Italy's adherence to the Triple Alliance weakened. The Saar coal mines and the Rhineland industrial area became essential to Germany, and the five corps allotted by Schlieffen for their protection seemed inadequate.

Moltke accordingly attempted to modify the Schlieffen Plan. He decided not to violate Dutch neutrality, hoping that England would not fight for Belgium if Holland were spared. However, this decision would make it necessary to crowd the First and Second Armies through Liège (*upper right*).

Moltke also increased the forces on the Eastern Front by taking troops from the right wing. When new units were authorized, he assigned them to the left wing. Finally, he took the ersatz corps from the northernmost armies. These changes reduced the ratio of troops between the right and left wings to a bare three to one. This was largely due to Moltke's desire to be strong everywhere; but, in part, it was probably also a dim reflection of Schlieffen's advocacy of the double envelopment as the most decisive form of warfare. (In 1912, Schlieffen had recommended similar modifications to his original plan, *provided that* the army were greatly strengthened.) In the end, it was not so much Moltke's modifications of the plan as the faulty execution of it that caused its failure.

The French Plan XVII concentrated forces on the northeastern frontier. Though the French commander, Joseph Joffre, kept his intentions to himself, the plan expressed a willingness to attack, and identified two options: one, north of Verdun-Metz, and the other east of Toul. With the First, Second, Third and Fifth Armies along the frontier, the Fourth Army remained in the second line and prepared to move north or east in response to the anticipated German attack. Unfortunately for the French, they underestimated the willingness of the Germans to use their reserve corps in the front line and thereby extend their forces for a deep, sweeping envelopment through Belgium west of the Meuse River (*upper center*).

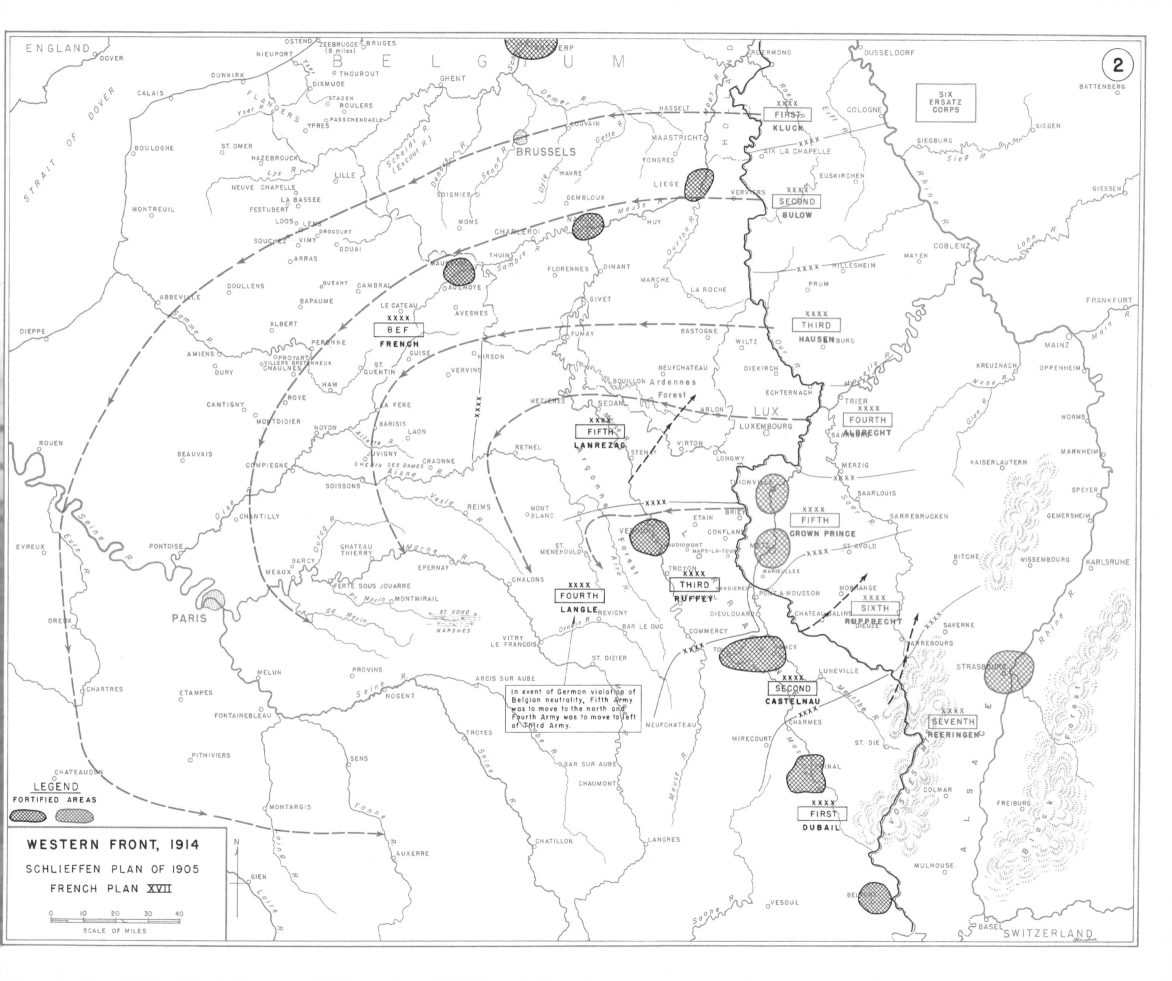

ENGLAND

BELGIUM

STRAIT OF DOVER

SIX ERSATZ CORPS

XXXX FIRST KLUCK

XXXX SECOND BULOW

XXXX THIRD HAUSEN

XXXX FOURTH ALBRECHT

XXXX BEF FRENCH

XXXX FIFTH LANREZAC

XXXX FIFTH CROWN PRINCE

XXXX FOURTH LANGLE

XXXX THIRD RUFFEY

XXXX SIXTH RUPPRECHT

XXXX SECOND CASTELNAU

XXXX SEVENTH HEERINGEN

XXXX FIRST DUBAIL

Ardennes Forest

ST. GOND MARSHES

In event of German violation of Belgian neutrality, Fifth Army was to move to the north and Fourth Army was to move to left of Third Army.

LEGEND
FORTIFIED AREAS

WESTERN FRONT, 1914

SCHLIEFFEN PLAN OF 1905

FRENCH PLAN XVII

0   10   20   30   40
SCALE OF MILES

SWITZERLAND

The strategy on the Eastern Front and the attendant army concentration areas were largely dictated by terrain features. The most dominant of these was the Polish salient—the part of Russia outlined in blue surrounding Warsaw and its vicinity (*sketch* a). This area—230 miles long and 210 miles wide—led directly into Germany. Its western extremity was only 180 miles from Berlin and abutted the rich mining and industrial areas of Silesia. Furthermore, no natural defensive barriers separated it from Germany. The broad, sluggish Vistula River traversed the salient; located thereon was the fortress city of Warsaw. Here the Russians had established a huge base, fed by six railroads from the interior of Russia. This base had considerable defensive value, and was also a fine point from which to launch a drive into Silesia.

But the Polish salient also posed problems for Russia. Its flanks were weak. If the Germans (in East Prussia) and the Austrians (in Galicia) launched converging attacks across the base of the salient against Brest Litovsk (*center*), Russian forces west of the Vistula could be isolated. To prevent such attacks, the Russians established a system of fortresses (useful also as bases for offensives) along the Niemen and Narew Rivers (*upper center*) and around Lublin and Kholm (*center*). Furthermore, the territory to the west of this fortress system was kept devoid of railroads, roads, and built-up areas, and no Russian forces were stationed west of the Vistula.

But if East Prussia threatened the Polish salient, the former was also vulnerable to attack from Warsaw. Hence the Germans had established fortified cities along the Vistula and made it their main line of defense. A forward line ran through the lake system near Lötzen (*upper center*). The other flank, in Galicia, was traversed by the Carpathian Mountains, running from Cracow to Rumania, which afforded Austria a defensive barrier. On the northern slopes, the Austrians likewise had fortified cities—Cracow, Przemysl, and Lemberg (*center*)—which could support an offensive into Russia.

East of the Polish salient, Russia was divided by the Pripet Marshes, a region of primeval bog, forests, and few roads. To the north, south, and east stretched vast spaces which could swallow entire armies (*sketch* b).

As we have seen, the Schlieffen Plan of 1905 accepted war on two fronts, but allotted minimum forces to the Eastern Front. Reliance was placed upon the fortress system to slow any enemy advance. Anticipating a slow Russian mobilization and a speedy German conquest of France, Schlieffen planned to create a strong force in East Prussia only after the defeat of France. But Moltke's plan took cognizance of Russian revitalization, and provided for mobilization of the Eighth Army in East Prussia (*sketch* a). It was given a defensive mission, and was authorized to withdraw behind the Vistula, if necessary.

Austria and Russia each had two war plans, depending upon how hostilities developed. Austria's Plan B assumed war with Serbia alone and its invasion by three armies, while the other three armies watched Russia from Galicia. Her Plan R assumed war with both Serbia and Russia, and called for offensives on both fronts, but here the Second Army would operate against Russia instead of Serbia. Russia's Plan G assumed that Germany—assisted by Austria—would make her main effort in the East, and therefore was defensive. In this plan, the Fourth Army was to be on the north flank, and both army groups would retire eastward until strength for a counteroffensive could be marshaled. Plan A was offensive in concept (envisaging the main German effort directed against France); it provided for simultaneous advances into East Prussia and Galicia, designed to clear the flanks of the Polish salient preparatory to an advance into Silesia. In this plan, the Fourth Army was to be in the south. Both France and Russia expected Germany to make her main effort in the west and conducted staff talks for several years before the war to ensure almost simultaneous offensives against their common enemy.

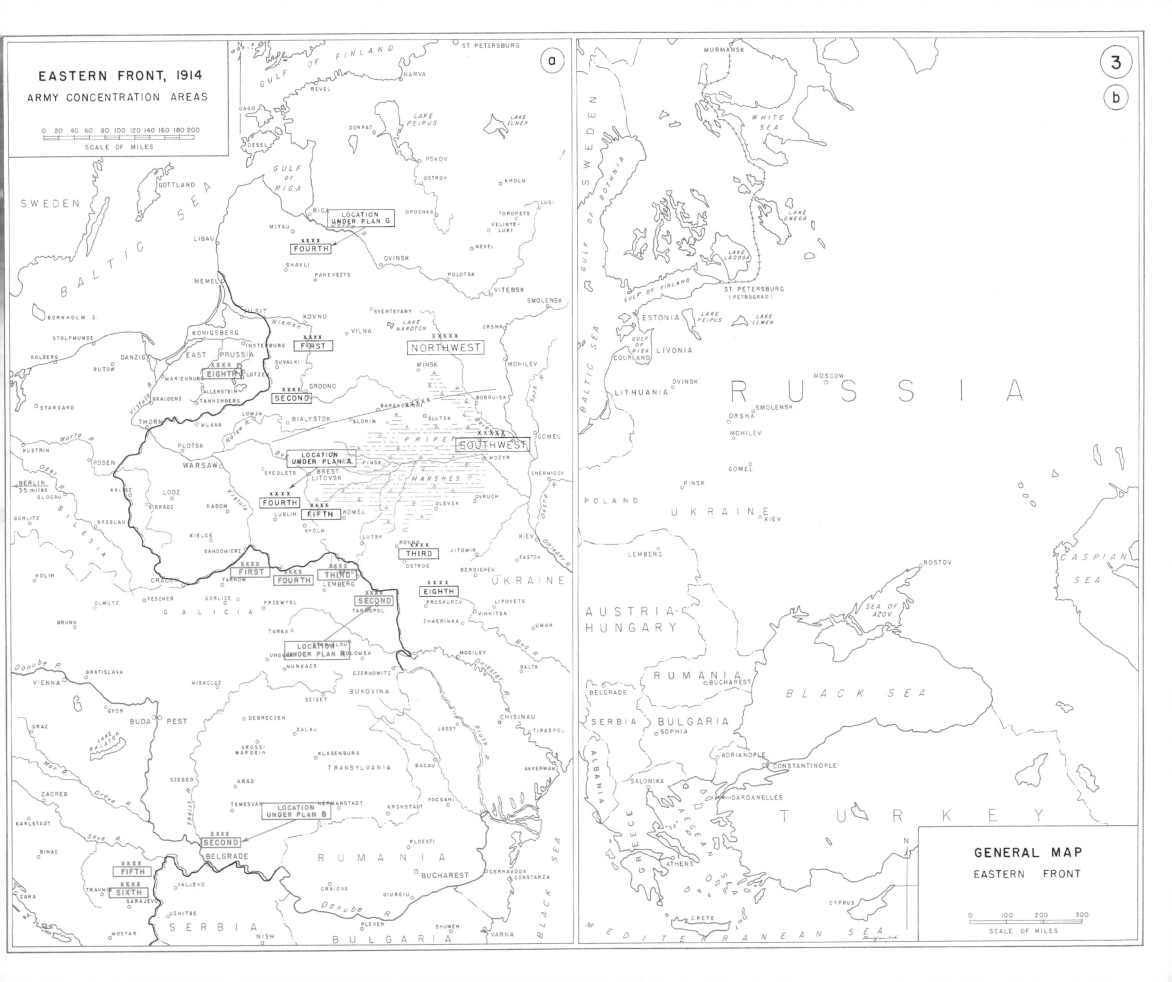

EASTERN FRONT, 1914
ARMY CONCENTRATION AREAS

0 20 40 60 80 100 120 140 160 180 200
SCALE OF MILES

③

ⓐ

ⓑ

GENERAL MAP
EASTERN FRONT

0 100 200 300
SCALE OF MILES

Most of southern Belgium is flat and open, forming a natural corridor into northern France. Entrance to this plain from Germany, however—without violating Dutch neutrality—must be through the Liège "bottleneck" (*right center*). Liège lies astride the Meuse River. A few miles to the north is Limbourg, the southernmost province of Holland; just south of Liège rise the rugged hills of the Ardennes Forest (*not shown*), a considerable barrier to rapid, large-scale troop movements. Liège, with its ring of forts, was considered one of the strongest places in Europe. Before the German First and Second Armies could advance, this fortress had to be captured.

The Germans required about two weeks to complete their mobilization. While this went on, they intended to take Liège. A special task force, kept at full strength and trained for this one mission, had been stationed near the Belgian border for years. On 3 August, its cavalry crossed the frontier; on the 4th, the rest of the force followed; the next day, its commander demanded the surrender of Liège. The commander of the garrison, General Gerard Leman, refused, whereupon the attack began.

Belgium's strict interpretation of her neutrality had kept her from making, plans for military cooperation with friendly neighbors, and her armed forces had been neglected. King Albert had intended to assemble his army along the west bank of the Meuse, anchoring it on Liège and Namur, and attempting to hold that position until French and British reinforcements reached him. It was a bold plan which might have stopped the German right wing in its tracks; but the Belgian Army was incapable of executing it, the influx of untrained reservists having destroyed its cohesion and discipline. The Belgians therefore decided to reorganize their troops behind the Gette River (*upper center*), sending one division to reinforce Leman's 40,000 fortress troops. Leman was ordered to "hold to the end."

The German tactical plan (*not shown*) was to penetrate between the Liège forts, capture the city with its important bridges, isolate the forts, then reduce them individually. Meanwhile, German cavalry would cross the Meuse north of Liège and move to encircle that city.

Despite long planning, the first German attack failed, Leman having connected the forts with hasty entrenchments. The German cavalry, however, crossed the Meuse, and Leman—knowing he would soon be cut off—sent his infantry division back to the field army the night of 6 August, choosing to fight it out with his fortress troops alone. That same night, the Germans again attacked, but still made no appreciable headway. Their leading units were disorganized and near panic when the chief of staff of the Second Army, General Erich von Ludendorff, went forward, rallied them, and bluffed the Belgian troops in Liège itself into surrendering. Leman and his forts still held out; it took three German corps and 420-mm. siege artillery to destroy them one by one, the last fort falling on 16 August. Leman's gallant defense delayed the German right wing two or three days, at a time when hours were precious.

The First and Second Armies then poured through Liège in an effort to cut the Belgian Army off from Antwerp. Albert, however, withdrew in time. By 20 August, the Belgian Army—except one division which had reinforced the Namur garrison—was in Antwerp on the flank of the German advance. General Alexander von Kluck had to detach one corps to watch it. (Moltke had just given the ersatz troops, which Schlieffen had intended for such missions, to the left wing.)

By 7 August, General Charles L. M. Lanrezac had warned General Joseph J. C. Joffre, the French commander in chief, that the Germans were moving into Belgium in unexpected strength. After several reports of German activity around Liège arrived, Joffre, on 15 August, ordered the French Fifth Army northward toward Namur and Charleroi.

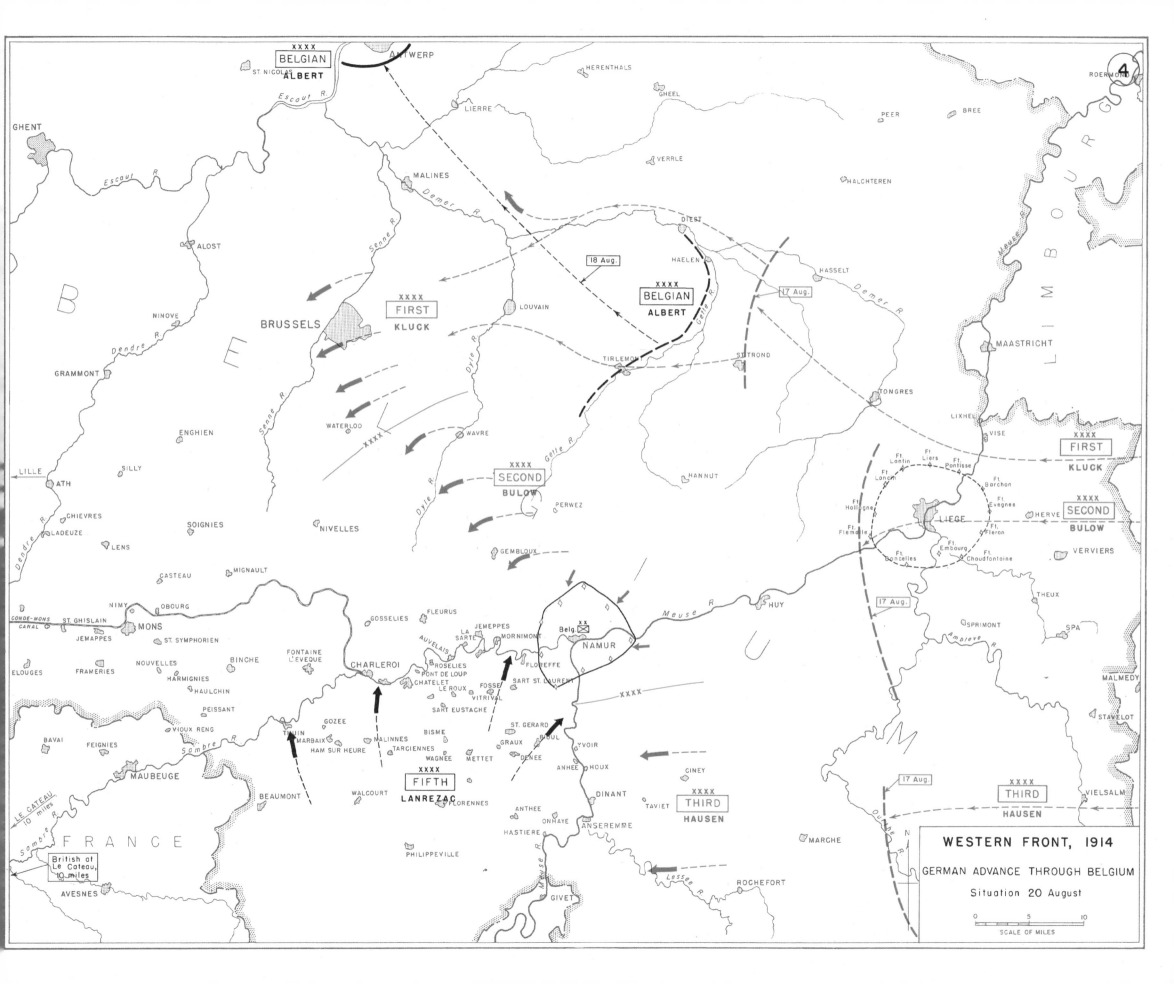

④

BELGIAN
ALBERT

GHENT

ST. NICOLAS

Escout R.

ANTWERP

ROERMOND

HERENTHALS

GHEEL

PEER

BREE

LIERRE

MALINES

Demer R.

VERRLE

HALCHTEREN

MAASTRICHT

ALOST

Senne R.

LOUVAIN

18 Aug.

DIEST

HAELEN

BELGIAN
ALBERT

HASSELT

17 Aug.

Demer R.

BRUSSELS

FIRST
KLUCK

TIRLEMON

ST. TROND

TONGRES

NINOVE

Dendre R.

Dyle R.

LIXHEL

VISE

GRAMMONT

WATERLOO

WAVRE

Gette R.

FIRST
KLUCK

Ft. Liers

Ft. Lontin

Ft. Pontisse

ENGHIEN

SILLY

LILLE

ATH

SECOND
BULOW

HANNUT

Ft. Lonch

Ft. Barchon

Ft. Hollogne

Ft. Evegnes

SECOND
BULOW

HERVE

VERVIERS

CHIEVRES

LADEUZE

Dyle R.

PERWEZ

Ft. Flemalle

LIEGE

Ft. Fleron

LENS

NIVELLES

Ft. Boncelles

Ft. Embourg

Ft. Chaudfontaine

SOIGNIES

GEMBLOUX

CASTEAU

MIGNAULT

FLEURUS

Meuse R.

HUY

THEUX

SPRIMONT

SPA

NIMY

OBOURG

GOSSELIES

LA
SARTE

JEMEPPES

MORNIMONT

Belg.

NAMUR

Amblève R.

CONDE-MONS
CANAL

ST. GHISLAIN

MONS

AUVELAIS

ROSELIES

FLOREFFE

MALMEDY

JEMAPPES

ST. SYMPHORIEN

FONTAINE
L'EVEQUE

CHARLEROI

PONT DE LOUP

CHATELET

LE ROUX

SART ST. LAUREN

XXXX

ELOUGES

FRAMERIES

NOUVELLES

BINCHE

FOSSE

VITRIVAL

SART EUSTACHE

STAVELOT

HARMIGNIES

HAULCHIN

PEISSANT

GOZEE

BISME

ST. GERARD

YVOIR

CINEY

BAVAI

FEIGNIES

VIOUX RENG

Sambre R.

THUIN

MARBAIX

HAM SUR HEURE

MALINNES

TARCIENNES

WAGNEE

METTET

GRAUX

BIOUL

DENEE

ANHEE

HOUX

THIRD
HAUSEN

VIELSALM

MAUBEUGE

WALCOURT

FIFTH
LANREZAC

FLORENNES

ANTHEE

ONHAYE

DINANT

TAVIET

MARCHE

LE CATEAU
10 miles

BEAUMONT

ANSEREMME

17 Aug.

THIRD
HAUSEN

F R A N C E

PHILIPPEVILLE

HASTIERE

Sambre R.

AVESNES

British at
Le Cateau,
10 miles

GIVET

Meuse R.

Lessee R.

ROCHEFORT

Ourthe R.

WESTERN FRONT, 1914

GERMAN ADVANCE THROUGH BELGIUM

Situation 20 August

0   5   10

SCALE OF MILES

While the Germans took the Liège forts, the French armies completed their mobilization and concentration according to Plan XVII. In a minor operation (*not shown*), designed to inspire public morale, elements of the French First Army took Mulhouse (*bottom right*) on 7 August; on 9 August, the Germans retook it. After this reverse, Joffre reorganized his forces, creating the Army of Alsace to cover his right flank.

On 8 August, Joffre issued his "General Instructions No. 1": the French First and Second Armies were to advance northeast into Alsace-Lorraine on 14 August, with Sarrebourg as their initial objective. Joffre and his staff were undisturbed by continuing reports of masses of German troops moving into Belgium. They were positive that the Germans did not have sufficient men on the Western Front for such extensive operations. In this assessment, they overlooked two important possibilities: first, that the Germans would gamble on the slowness of the Russian mobilization, and leave only a skeleton force in East Prussia; and second, that the German reservists would be so well trained that they could be employed immediately as first-line troops. Consequently, the Germans were able to mass approximately 2,000,000 men in the West, against 1,300,000 French, plus the small British and Belgian contingents. Had even part of the forces Joffre launched so blindly into Alsace-Lorraine been rushed by railroad to reinforce the Belgians along the Meuse (*center*), the history of the war might have been different.

This French offensive was opposed by the German Sixth and Seventh Armies. To unify the operations of his left wing, Moltke placed the Seventh Army under the control of the Sixth. Schlieffen had planned a fighting withdrawal in Alsace-Lorraine, designed to draw the French deeper into his trap. But the efficient and ambitious General Krafft von Dellmensingen—chief of staff to Prince Rupprecht of Bavaria, and the actual commander of the left wing in everything but title—browbeat Moltke into giving him the six ersatz corps for a counteroffensive. The Germans now planned first to fight a delaying action back to the line Morhange–Sarrebourg–Vosges Mountains; then, once the French had committed themselves to an attack against this line, they would launch a converging counterattack. The operation went much as planned, the French advancing to the line shown. On 20 August, the Germans struck. After a hard day's fighting, the French broke contact by a forced night march. The First Army maintained comparatively good order, but the Second was almost routed. During the 21st and 22d, the French fell back to the heights around Nancy and behind the Meurthe River.

In the north, Joffre unleashed his main offensive. Though he recognized the Germans were sending large forces across Belgium, he did not comprehend the size of those forces or the presence of two armies west of the Meuse. Consequently, on 15 August he sent Lanrezac's Fifth Army forward into the angle formed by the Sambre and Meuse Rivers (*upper left*), and on 20 August he ordered the Third and Fourth Armies to advance into Belgium toward Arlon and Neufchâteau (*center*). He also activated the Army of Lorraine, consisting primarily of reserve units, to cover the right flank of the Third and Fourth Armies. Joffre expected the Third and Fourth Armies to strike relatively small forces of the enemy's center while the Fifth Army engaged the enemy's main attack farther west.

Joffre's expectations proved false. On the 22d, the French Third and Fourth Armies, which were marching toward Arlon and Neufchâteau, stumbled into much stronger enemy units than they expected and were crushed. That same day, Fifth Army failed in its attempt to drive back strong German forces that had crossed the Sambre west of Namur.

Meanwhile, the British Expeditionary Force had disembarked and had concentrated at Le Cateau (*upper left*). On the 21st, Joffre requested that it cooperate with Lanrezac; Field Marshal Sir John French, its commander, moved it to the line shown.

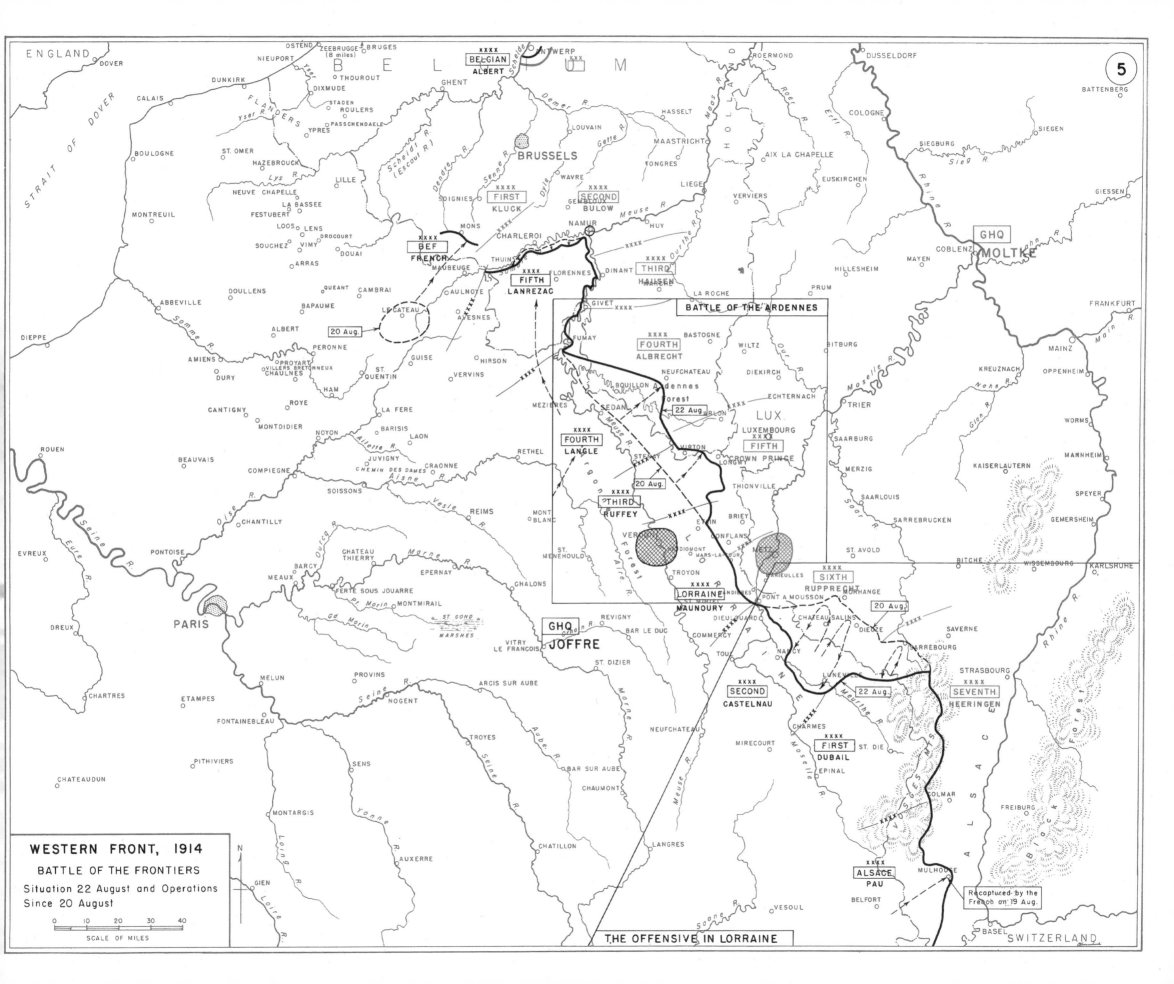

ENGLAND

BELGIUM

HOLLAND

SWITZERLAND

STRAIT OF DOVER

FLANDERS

ARDENNES

VOSGES MTS

ALSACE

Black Forest

BATTLE OF THE ARDENNES

THE OFFENSIVE IN LORRAINE

GHQ MOLTKE

GHQ JOFFRE

XXXX BELGIAN ALBERT

XXXX FIRST KLUCK

XXXX SECOND BULOW

XXXX THIRD HAUSEN

XXXX FOURTH ALBRECHT

XXXX FIFTH CROWN PRINCE

XXXX SIXTH RUPPRECHT

XXXX SEVENTH HEERINGEN

XXXX BEF FRENCH

XXXX FIFTH LANREZAC

XXXX FOURTH LANGLE

XXXX THIRD RUFFEY

XXXX LORRAINE MAUNOURY

XXXX SECOND CASTELNAU

XXXX FIRST DUBAIL

XXXX ALSACE PAU

20 Aug.
22 Aug.
20 Aug.
22 Aug.
20 Aug.

Recaptured by the French on 19 Aug.

WESTERN FRONT, 1914

BATTLE OF THE FRONTIERS

Situation 22 August and Operations
Since 20 August

0 10 20 30 40
SCALE OF MILES

Joffre's order of 15 August had sent Lanrezac's Fifth Army into the angle between the Sambre and the Meuse (*right inset sketch*). On 18 August, Lanrezac received instructions to attack either north or east—depending upon the direction of their advance—against the northern German armies. His cavalry, however, could not penetrate the German cavalry screen to locate the advancing German infantry. By the 21st, Joffre realized that the Germans were west of the Meuse in Belgium in considerable strength; he then ordered an attack when Lanrezac thought the "opportune" moment had arrived, and arranged for the British Expeditionary Force to join in this offensive.

Moltke, in an effort to coordinate the actions of his First and Second Armies, had subordinated Kluck to General Karl von Bülow. This was a mistake. Kluck was an aggressive and capable commander, while Bülow had few qualifications beyond his family name. In addition, he was a selfish individual, able to see only those matters that benefited his Second Army. General Freiherr von Hausen's Third Army was approaching from the east; Bülow decided that it should join him in his attack on Lanrezac. Hausen, subservient to nobility, agreed to a joint attack on the 22d. At the same time, Bülow ordered Kluck to change the First Army's direction of march from southwest to south (*left inset sketch*).

On the 21st, though ordered to attack, Lanrezac decided to defend his position south of the Sambre. However, he failed to establish strong bridgeheads on the north bank to protect the vital bridges over that river. The German advance guards, finding the bridges weakly defended, attacked on their own initiative and won a foothold on the south bank (*dashed blue line*). Next morning, the French corps commanders—also on their own initiative—counterattacked to drive the Germans back across the Sambre, but were unsuccessful. About noon, Bülow decided to attack Lanrezac without waiting for Hausen and gained considerable ground (*dotted blue line*).

During the 22d, Lanrezac withdrew most of the I Corps from the line along the Meuse, planning to use it to envelop Bülow's left flank the next day. He also tried, without success, to persuade Sir John French to turn east against Bülow's right flank. On the 23d, Bülow again attacked; the French resisted vigorously. General Louis F. M. F. Franchet d'Esperey's I Corps was about to attack Bülow's flank, when Hausen's advance guards crossed the Meuse. Realizing the danger to the Fifth Army, Franchet d'Esperey countermarched. Part of his corps returned to the right of the French line; the remainder checked Hausen's advance across the Meuse, but could not wipe out the German bridgeheads.

That night, Lanrezac made the decision—extremely difficult in the offensive-minded French Army—to withdraw. The Belgian division in Namur had retreated into his lines; obviously, the fortress would fall soon, releasing more German troops. His right flank was turned; the English, on his left, were under heavy pressure. Joffre concurred in his decision.

On the German side, Bülow planned a converging attack for the 24th: Hausen was asked to attack straight west; Bülow would continue south; Kluck now was ordered to turn southeast against the French left.

Kluck knew only that British troops had been reported some thirty miles northwest of Mons. Actually, Sir John French had occupied a defensive position at Mons (*left inset sketch, dashed blue line*) by the 22d. His airplanes reported masses of Germans moving to his front; consequently, he refused Lanrezac's request to turn eastward against Bülow's flank. At 0930, 23 August, Kluck struck the British. After several bloody repulses, he finally drove them back to the position shown (*solid blue line*). If Bülow had not ordered him to change his direction of march on 21 August, Kluck would have enveloped the British left flank. Sir John French organized his new position that night and prepared to fight again on the 24th. British morale was high. But, learning that Lanrezac was withdrawing, Sir John French—now highly distrustful of his French colleague—decided to do likewise.

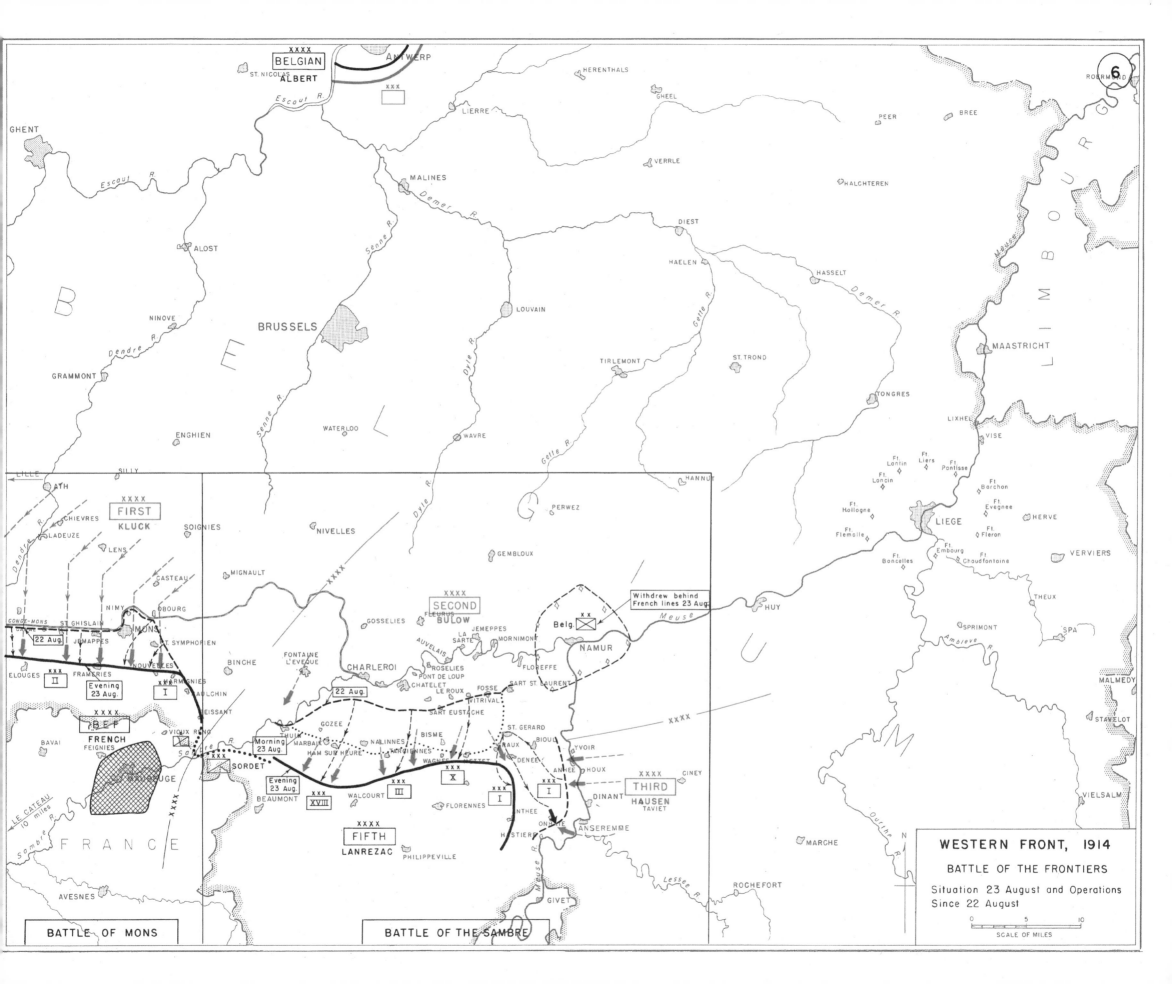

BELGIAN
ALBERT

ANTWERP

ROERMOND

6

GHENT

FIRST
KLUCK

SECOND
BÜLOW

THIRD
HAUSEN

BEF
FRENCH

FIFTH
LANREZAC

Withdrew behind
French lines 23 Aug.

Belg.

NAMUR

LIEGE

BRUSSELS

MAASTRICHT

LIMBOURG

WESTERN FRONT, 1914

BATTLE OF THE FRONTIERS

Situation 23 August and Operations
Since 22 August

0   5   10
SCALE OF MILES

BATTLE OF MONS

BATTLE OF THE SAMBRE

The over-all situation on the Western Front, as shown, looked extremely unfavorable for the Allies. Joffre's grand offensive had collapsed, with over 300,000 casualties. Moltke's version of the Schlieffen Plan was driving forward; but the inherent flaws, both in his plan and in Moltke himself, were already sapping the strength of the German offensive.

In the south, the French First and Second Armies had rallied along a natural defensive line, and in three days had made the position extremely strong. On the German side, Dellmensingen was convinced that his counteroffensive of the 20th had shattered the two French armies. He therefore cajoled Moltke into allowing him to attack their new position, promising he would destroy them and turn the right flank of Joffre's line. Moltke's assent abruptly converted the Schlieffen Plan into an attempted double envelopment. It also killed the last chance that his right wing could expect reinforcements, and placed a double drain on the German supply system.

Farther north, the French Third and Fourth Armies had suffered a great defeat in the confused Ardennes fighting, but not so bad a defeat as the Germans believed. Though retreating, their organization was still intact. During the 26th, the Army of Lorraine was dissolved. Two of its divisions went to Amiens (*upper left*) to serve as the nucleus of the French Sixth Army, which Joffre planned to activate there; the rest were transferred to the Third Army.

On the French Fifth Army's front, Lanrezac had begun withdrawing before daylight of the 24th. Bülow's converging attack that morning therefore struck thin air—especially since Hausen had advanced due west from Dinant. If Hausen had followed his original intention and moved to the southwest, he might have cut off Lanrezac's retreat.

The British Expeditionary Force, however, faced the iron-willed Kluck, who carried his men forward in a driving pursuit. Sir John French had a momentary temptation to throw his weary troops into the fortified city of Maubeuge, but resisted it. The roads by which he had to withdraw were clogged with civilian refugees and wandering French cavalry. On the early morning of the 26th, General Sir Horace L. Smith-Dorrien, commanding the British II Corps, was preparing to fight a desperate rear-guard action.

On the Allied left, Joffre had hastily improvised the Group d'Amade. (These French Territorial troops were second-line reserve troops—men from thirty-seven to forty-eight—similar the German Landwehr.)

The French Army, as a whole, was unbeaten, though tired, but many senior officers were demoralized by the complete failure of their cherished offensive. Joffre was far from a military genius, but he remained calm. Though the German plan was now obvious, the Fifth Army and the British alone could not halt the German right wing; the Allied left wing had to be strengthened. On 25 August, Joffre issued his "General Instructions No. 2." The First and Second Armies were to hold in place. The Third, Fourth, and Fifth Armies and the British were assigned zones of withdrawal to the general line Somme River–Verdun: they were to be prepared to counterattack upon reaching this line. Meanwhile, Joffre would draw troops from his right wing to form the French Sixth Army near Amiens for an eventual major counteroffensive against the tip of the German right flank.

While Joffre dealt realistically with hard facts, Moltke inhabited a fool's paradise. His headquarters remained far to the rear and his communications with his troops were extremely limited, yet neither he nor the senior members of his staff made any effort to visit the front. Instead, misled by fragmentary and overly optimistic reports of victory, he persuaded himself that the French Army was already practically destroyed. News from the Russian front being bad, he decided he could spare two corps from the West to reinforce it—and, for some unknowable reason, took them from his Second and Third Armies. These armies had already been weakened by detachments left to besiege bypassed towns. Moltke's three right-wing armies had entered Belgium with a total of sixteen corps; at this critical moment, they had only eleven left in contact with the retreating Allies.

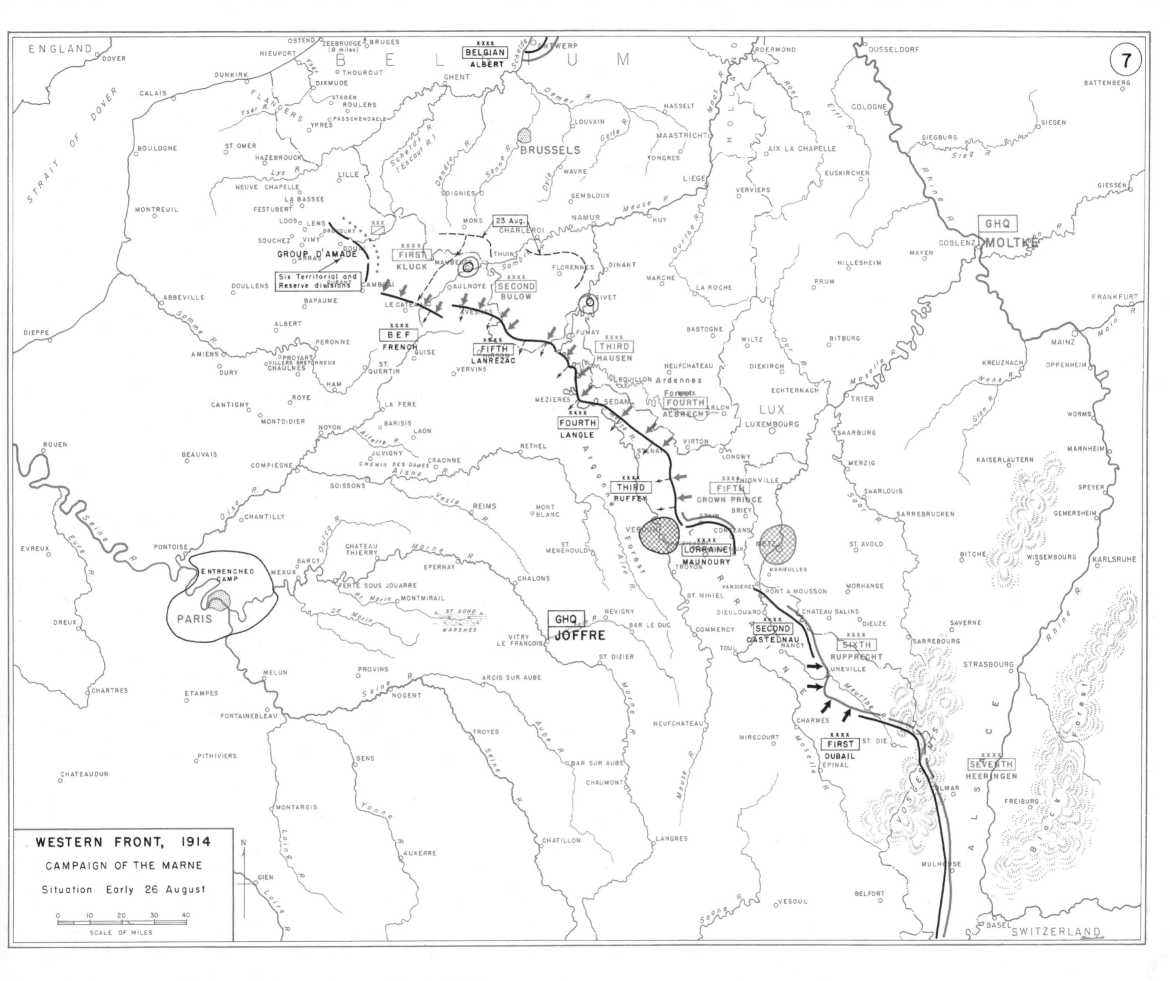

WESTERN FRONT, 1914

CAMPAIGN OF THE MARNE

Situation Early 26 August

0   10   20   30   40
SCALE OF MILES

Kluck was under the impression that the British were based on the Channel ports (*off map, northwest*). After the Battle of Mons, therefore, he directed his pursuit to cut them off from the Channel. Smith-Dorrien's II Corps, which bore the heaviest pressure, finally, on the night of 25 August, halted along the line shown (*upper sketch*). Its men were worn out by three days of marching and fighting, and the roads behind it were still encumbered by refugees and General C. C. Sordet's French horsemen.

Sir John French's orders for the 26th called for a continuation of the retreat southward. General Sir Douglas Haig's I Corps, which had been less heavily engaged at Mons than the II Corps and had been under less pressure since, was able to comply. Smith-Dorrien, who received this order sometime after midnight, felt that he could not. He would have to start before daylight to avoid a fight with the Germans, and his men were too tired to go on without rest; some of his units, in fact, had just reached his position. He therefore decided to stand his ground through the 26th, and withdraw that night. Sir John French was so informed, but his reaction was equivocal—he did not flatly order Smith-Dorrien to continue the withdrawal, and he did order the independent 4th Division to cover the II Corps' left flank. However, he made no changes in Haig's orders. The I Corps withdrew, as planned, leaving Smith-Dorrien's right flank open.

Kluck attacked as soon as he reached the British position at Le Cateau. The British held firmly in their center, but the Germans overlapped them on both flanks. By 1400, Smith-Dorrien's right-flank division was forced to retreat, losing most of its artillery. Somewhat later, the 4th Division was outflanked, but, in the nick of time, Sordet brought his worn-out cavalry forward. The Germans paused to reconnoiter this unexpected threat, darkness intervened, and the retreat went on. Both sides lost heavily, British casualties being 7,800 out of 40,000 troops engaged. By the morning of the 27th, the British

had completely broken contact. and Kluck was in considerable doubt as to which way they had retired.

Exaggerated reports concerning the British defeat at Le Cateau soon reached Joffre. He realized that he must do something quickly to take the pressure off the British, if they were to remain intact as an effective combat force. He needed time and secure east-west railroad communications in order to redeploy troops from his right wing to his left for his planned counteroffensive. Only by maintaining a cohesive, if elastic, front before the German right wing could he do this. If the British were overwhelmed, the whole front would collapse. Accordingly, on the 27th, he ordered the Fifth Army to attack westward against the flank of the German First Army.

Lanrezac was shaken by this development. He was withdrawing, and Bülow was following him closely; consequently, his new orders would be difficult to execute. He would have to turn his whole Fifth Army ninety degrees to the west and attack, thus exposing his own right flank to Bülow. Unwillingly, he prepared his plan. On 29 August, before his attack to the west could get under way, Bülow's Second Army came onto the field (*lower sketch*). After several hours of hard fighting, the French right flank was driven in, while the left flank fell back without becoming seriously engaged. At 1300, Lanrezac ordered his I Corps to attack to the north. Franchet d'Esperey, its commander, took the time to prepare a coordinated attack. Delivered at sundown, it was highly successful, though the Germans managed to hold a line south of the Oise. Lanrezac now wisely requested permission to withdraw, since his army was exposed to a converging attack by Kluck, Bülow, and Hausen. Joffre approved. Bülow halted for a day and a half, allowing both the Fifth Army and the British to withdraw unmolested.

This action—the Battle of Guise—can hardly be considered a French victory, though it did greatly improve the Fifth Army's morale.

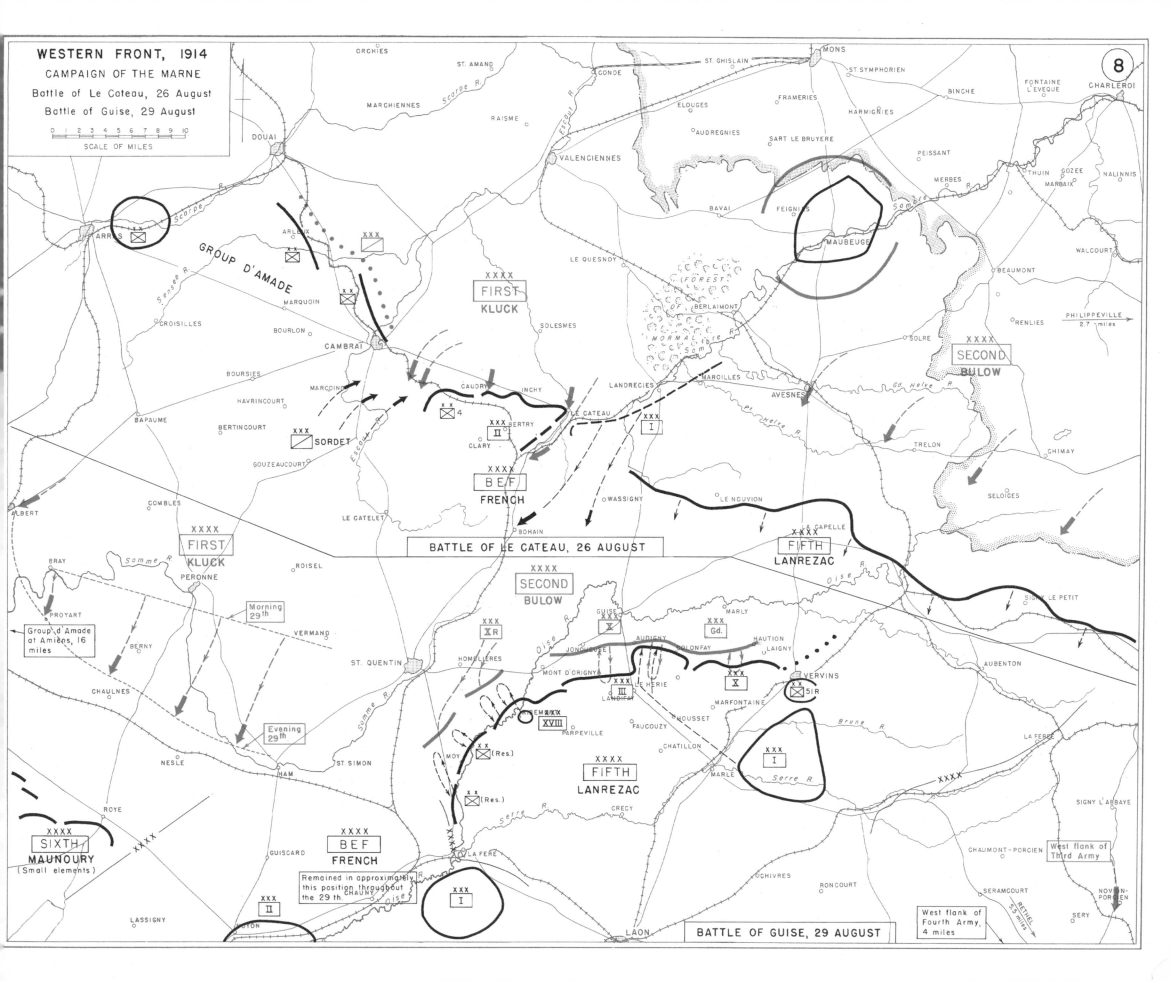

WESTERN FRONT, 1914
CAMPAIGN OF THE MARNE
Battle of Le Cateau, 26 August
Battle of Guise, 29 August

0 1 2 3 4 5 6 7 8 9 10
SCALE OF MILES

GROUP D'AMADE

XXXX
FIRST
KLUCK

XXX
SORDET

XXXX
BEF
FRENCH

XXXX
FIRST
KLUCK

BATTLE OF LE CATEAU, 26 AUGUST

XXXX
SECOND
BULOW

XXXX
FIFTH
LANREZAC

XXXX
SECOND
BULOW

Group d'Amade
at Amiens, 16
miles

Morning
29th

Evening
29th

XXX
IX R

XXX
X

XXX
Gd.

XXX
III

XXX
X

XX
5 IR

XX
5 IR

XVIII

XX
(Res.)

XX
(Res.)

XXXX
FIFTH
LANREZAC

XXX
I

XXXX
SIXTH
MAUNOURY
(Small elements)

XXXX
BEF
FRENCH

Remained in approximately
this position throughout
the 29th.

XXX
II

XXX
I

West flank of
Third Army

West flank of
Fourth Army,
4 miles

PHILIPPEVILLE
2.7 miles

RETHEL
5.5 miles

BATTLE OF GUISE, 29 AUGUST

8

On 27 August, at Coblenz (*upper right*), 200 miles behind the battle, Moltke—ignorant of the actual course of events—concluded that the French were trying to gain time and engage as much German strength as possible, in order to aid the Russian offensive in East Prussia. He now ordered a rapid advance on Paris, designed to destroy the French Army.

The First Army was to advance down the west bank of the Oise toward the lower Seine, protect the right flank of the German offensive, be ready to aid the Second Army, and prevent the formation of new Allied units within its zone of advance. The Second Army was to move on Paris; the Third Army, on Château Thierry (*center, left*); the Fourth Army, through Reims on Epernay (*center, left*). The Fifth Army had a multiple mission: to invest Verdun, protect the left flank of the German right wing, and march toward the line Châlons–Vitry le François. The mission of the left wing, now unsuccessfully attacking the new French line, was considered basically defensive, but the Sixth Army could advance if the French retired. Moltke stipulated one major, over-all reservation: if the Allies resisted stubbornly along the Aisne and the Marne, the direction of the right wing's advance might have to be changed from southwest to due south.

This change of direction came sooner than Moltke had anticipated. Kluck had renewed his advance on the morning of 27 August. That day, and the next two, he fought a series of successful actions against British rear guards, the Group d'Amade, and elements of the assembling French Sixth Army. These troops were driven westward or dispersed, and Kluck considered his mission of preventing the formation of new French units substantially accomplished. Apparently believing that the British were retreating toward the Channel ports, he now turned his thoughts to finding the French flank, enveloping it, and forcing the French armies eastward away from Paris. In fact, he had urged Bülow (to whom he was no longer subordinated) to join him in turning more directly south.

Now, on 30 August, he received a message from Bülow announcing a "decisive victory" at Guise and asking that Kluck help exploit this success by turning eastward toward the line La Fere–Laon. This request placed Kluck in a quandary. He could not both advance to the lower Seine, as ordered, and still support Bülow. It would be useless to ask Moltke for instructions—communications with his headquarters were atrocious, and it might take several days to get through. Kluck decided—under the circumstances, probably correctly—to help Bülow, but instead of turning east he moved southeast on the 31st, toward Compiègne and Noyon, hoping to intercept the Allied retreat. Bülow, however, remained in position during the 31st.

By Joffre's order, the French Fifth, Fourth, and Third Armies continued to fall back. The German Fourth Army forced the crossings of the Meuse and swung south. Moltke and his army commanders became increasingly convinced that the Allies were beaten. Moltke therefore issued an order on 30 August directing the center armies to pursue the French to their front rapidly, giving them no chance to rally. (Later, he approved Kluck's change of direction.) In a general sense, this order told the right-wing armies to close in and guide on the Third Army. Moltke, however, did not mention to Bülow and Kluck the important news of large troop concentrations around Paris.

Unlike Moltke, Joffre had kept in intimate touch with the situation, visiting all critical sectors of the front. He was shifting troops from his right to build up the French Sixth Army and the Foch Detachment, and had turned Paris into a huge entrenched camp. However, he now knew that it would be impossible to counterattack, as planned, from the Somme River–Verdun line, for his troops were not ready. Finally, the German right wing appeared to be changing the direction of its advance, thus altering, the whole strategic problem. Though Joffre had hoped to hold the Germans along a line running between Compiègne, Reims, and Verdun, strong pressure from the Germans compelled him to designate a new limit of retreat (*dashed blue line*).

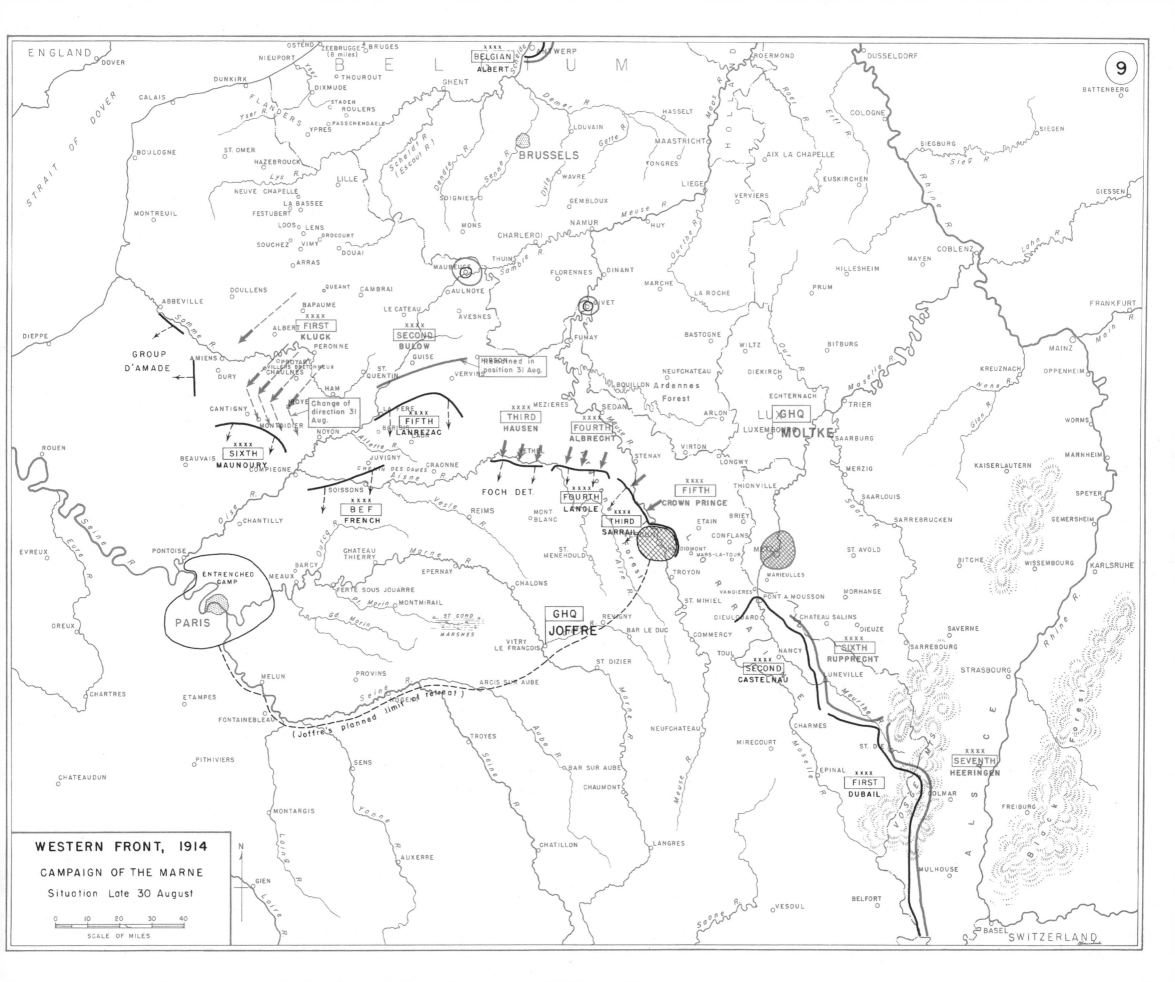

WESTERN FRONT, 1914

CAMPAIGN OF THE MARNE

Situation Late 30 August

On 31 August and 1 and 2 September, Kluck drove southeast with all possible speed, determined to fix and destroy the left flank of the French Fifth Army, which he believed to be the left-flank unit of the entire French front. As previously noted, he had lost track of the British after Le Cateau, and Moltke had not told him of the growing French strength in and around Paris. However, had Kluck not been so intent on his pursuit, he might have reconnoitered and discovered for himself the true situation at Paris.

Bülow, because of his halt after the Battle of Guise, was at least a good day's march behind Kluck. Their converging advances promised to trap the French Fifth Army, thereby accomplishing the decisive envelopment planned by Schlieffen. On the evening of 2 September, Kluck's left-flank corps reached the Marne River at Château Thierry. Farther east, the German Third, Fourth, and Fifth Armies continued to gain ground.

That night, Kluck received a radiogram from Moltke, changing the entire German plan of operations. The German Second, Third, Fourth, and Fifth Armies were to shift their advance from southwest to directly south; the Sixth Army was to penetrate the line of French forts (*not shown*) on its front and cross the Moselle between Toul and Epinal. The First Army was to follow in echelon behind the Second Army, with the mission of protecting the German right flank. Thus, the spearhead of the Schlieffen Plan was to be merely a security detachment!

This order was based on Moltke's sudden grasp of the fact that his right-wing armies were too weak to swing west of Paris without becoming dangerously overextended. Therefore, he would content himself with enveloping the left flank of the French field armies, the mass of which appeared to be between Paris and Verdun (*center*). If his Sixth Army were successful, a double envelopment would complete the task. Moltke realized that the French forces around Paris had become formidable, but apparently did not know that they included the new Sixth Army.

Consequently, he seems to have concluded that the troops concentrating there were merely reinforcements for the Paris garrison, and that, at any rate, Kluck should be able to deal with them until the French field armies were destroyed. But, having given Kluck this mission, he still failed to provide him with any information concerning the French forces around Paris.

Joffre still prepared for his counterattack, but there were two problems that he could not immediately solve. Kluck might once more change the direction of his advance, attempting to pass to the west of Paris, or even to advance directly against it from the north. Also, it was not yet certain that Sir John French would be able—or willing—to take part in the counterattack, for the British commander had lost confidence in the French and had opened a gap in the Allied lines by pulling his forces to the rear.

Consequently, Joffre's orders of 1 and 2 September were somewhat vague. The Sixth Army was to assemble within the entrenched camp of Paris. The retirement would continue until the Fifth Army was out of immediate danger of envelopment from the west, a situation which had been worsened by the British withdrawal toward the south. Then the Third, Fourth, and Fifth Armies would counterattack—joined, depending on the situation at that time, by the Sixth Army and the British. The Third Army was to be reinforced by two corps drawn from the First and Second Armies, even if this meant abandoning the high ground along the Meuse south of Verdun—and the possible isolation of that fortress city. All available cavalry was to be massed on the Allied left, near Melun (*lower left*). Every effort was to be made to replace casualties.

The operational concept of drawing the Germans into a pocket between Verdun and Paris and then cutting them off with an attack from the French capital coalesced slowly in Joffre's mind. Not until late on 2 September did he order French forces in Paris to prepare to attack east.

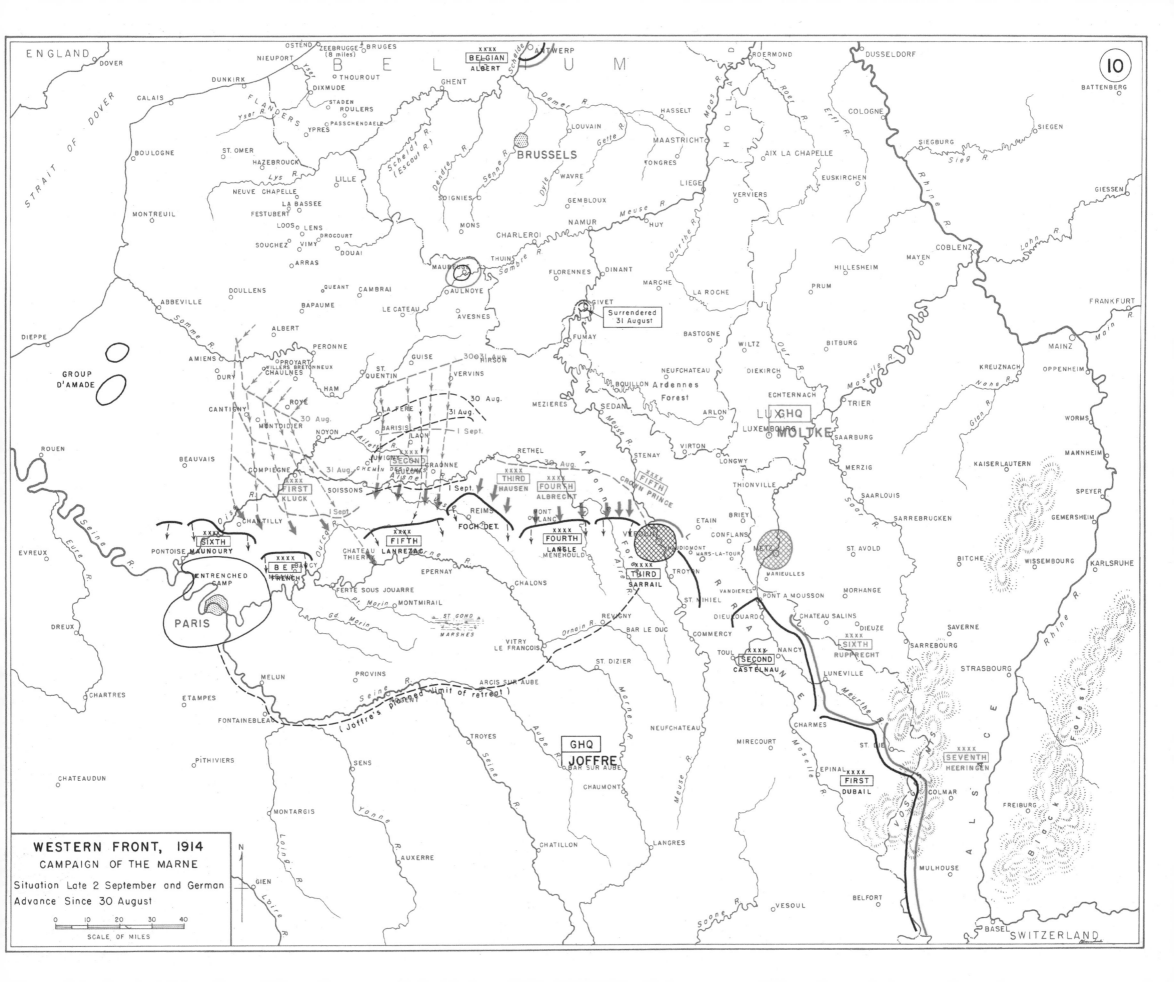

ENGLAND

STRAIT OF DOVER

BELGIUM

HOLLAND

10

GROUP D'AMADE

Surrendered 31 August

LUX GHQ
MOLTKE

XXXX
BELGIAN
ALBERT

XXXX
SECOND
BÜLOW

XXXX
FIRST
KLUCK

XXXX
THIRD
HAUSEN

XXXX
FOURTH
ALBRECHT

XXXX
FIFTH
CROWN PRINCE

FOCH DET.

XXXX
SIXTH
MAUNOURY

XXXX
FIFTH
LANREZAC

XXXX
FOURTH
LANGLE

XXXX
BEF
FRENCH

ENTRENCHED CAMP

PARIS

ST GOND
MARSHES

XXXX
THIRD
SARRAIL

XXXX
SIXTH
RUPPRECHT

XXXX
SECOND
CASTELNAU

(Joffre's planned limit of retreat)

GHQ
JOFFRE

XXXX
SEVENTH
HEERINGEN

XXXX
FIRST
DUBAIL

SWITZERLAND

WESTERN FRONT, 1914
CAMPAIGN OF THE MARNE

Situation Late 2 September and German
Advance Since 30 August

0   10   20   30   40
SCALE OF MILES

N

Early on 3 September, while studying Moltke's latest order, Kluck received word that his troops had seized the Marne River bridges at Château Thierry. This news deepened Kluck's quandary; it appeared that he now had two conflicting missions. To follow Bülow "in echelon" meant that he must halt for two days, to allow Bülow to catch up; meanwhile, the French forces he was pursuing would escape or rally. On the other hand, Moltke also wanted the French driven away to the southeast of Paris. Whereas Bülow was lagging behind, Kluck—as he saw it—was ideally situated to envelop the Allied left flank. His communications with Moltke were still poor; he must make his own decision. Kluck elected to continue across the Marne.

One of Joffre's major problems was the attitude of Sir John French, who—thoroughly disillusioned with his French colleagues—was continuing his withdrawal and showing no inclination toward further combined operations. Here, however, Joffre had the complete support of Lord Kitchener, the British Secretary of State for War. Alarmed by French's reports, Kitchener visited his discouraged subordinate. Thereafter, French cooperated with Joffre.

That problem solved, Joffre turned to his own armies. Their retreat had brought them nearer their depots. Troop transfers from the Lorraine front had given him numerical superiority on his left flank. Finally, Joffre had mercilessly weeded out all generals whom he considered unfit.

The large-scale troop movements required to set up Joffre's counteroffensive could not be concealed. Even Moltke recognized their implications. On 4 September, he therefore issued a new order. The German First and Second Armies were to face west and oppose any Allied attack from the Paris area. The First Army would establish a front between the Oise and Marne Rivers; the Second, between the Marne and the Seine. The Third Army would attack south toward Troyes; the Fourth and Fifth would continue driving the French forces opposing them to the southeast; the Sixth and Seventh were to attack westward

"as soon as possible." Moltke had finally wrecked the Schlieffen Plan; the troops needed by his right wing were on the Lorraine front, where smaller French forces, aided by rough terrain and fortifications, could easily contain them.

In issuing this order, Moltke again included no information as to the French concentration at Paris. Kluck, insubordinately dismissing it as based on erroneous information, continued his advance. But, late on the 5th, an officer from Moltke's staff reached Kluck and explained the situation. Kluck immediately realized that he had led his army into a trap; he began planning a move back across the Marne, where he had left only his weak IV Reserve Corps (*map symbol:* IV R) under General von Gronau to cover his right flank.

Meanwhile, also on 4 September, Joffre had issued orders for his counteroffensive. It was to begin on 6 September. The French Sixth Army would attack eastward across the Ourcq River toward Château Thierry; the British would advance northeast on Montmirail; the French Fifth Army would stand ready to join this advance. Foch's new Ninth Army would cover the right flank of the Fifth, holding the line of the St. Gond Marshes; the Fourth Army would halt its withdrawal and hold in position, ready to join in the offensive; and the Third Army would attack westward. The Second and First Armies would stand fast. Joffre thus planned a double envelopment of the German right wing.

On 5 September, the French Sixth Army moved eastward into its assembly areas. Simultaneously, Gronau's IV Reserve Corps was moving south as shown across the Sixth Army's front. His cavalry reported increasing French activity to the west, but a line of wooded hills and strong French patrols blocked their efforts to obtain further information. Convinced that something important was developing on his right, Gronau made a prompt and soldierly decision. Facing his entire corps westward, he attacked, surprising and defeating the leading French divisions.

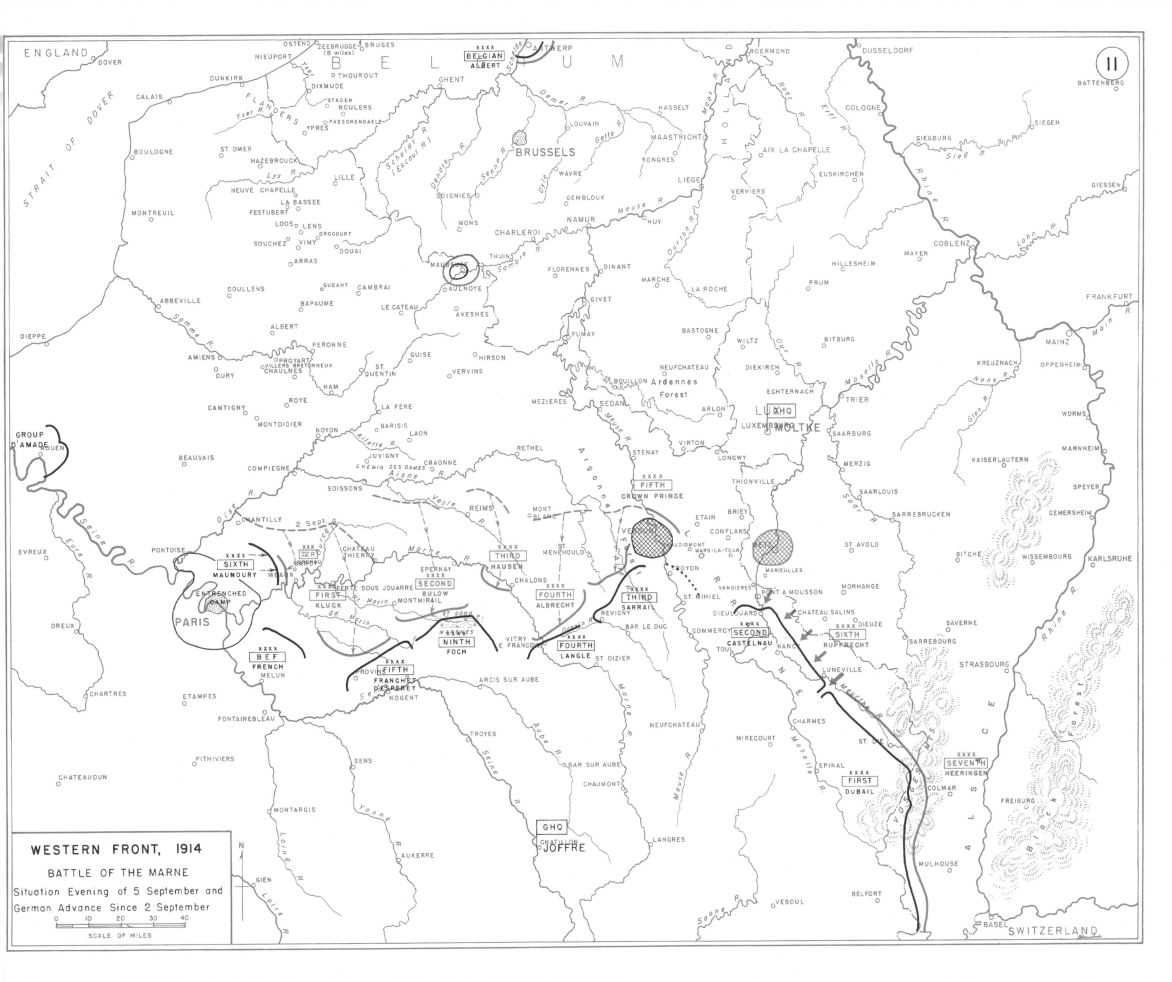

ENGLAND

BELGIUM

HOLLAND

XXXX
BELGIAN
ALBERT

BRUSSELS

LUXEMBOURG

XHQ
MOLTKE

XXXX
FIFTH
CROWN PRINCE

XXXX
THIRD
HAUSEN

XXXX
SECOND
BULOW

XXXX
FIRST
KLUCK

XXX
IV C

XXX
FERTE SOUS JOUARRE

XXX
SIXTH
MAUNOURY

ENTRENCHED
CAMP

PARIS

XXXX
BEF
FRENCH

XXXX
NINTH
FOCH

XXXX
FOURTH
ALBRECHT

XXXX
THIRD
SARRAIL

XXXX
SECOND
CASTELNAU

XXXX
SIXTH
RUPPRECHT

XXXX
FOURTH
LANGLE

XXXX
FIFTH
FRANCHET
D'ESPEREY

GROUP
D'AMADE

XXXX
SEVENTH
HEERINGEN

XXXX
FIRST
DUBAIL

GHQ
JOFFRE

SWITZERLAND

WESTERN FRONT, 1914

BATTLE OF THE MARNE

Situation Evening of 5 September and
German Advance Since 2 September

0   10   20   30   40
SCALE OF MILES

Gronau's judgment matched his courage. Realizing that he had defeated only an advance guard, he withdrew eastward to a stronger defensive position (*solid red line*) during the night of 5 September. The French did not pursue. About 0100, 6 September, Kluck started his II Corps to reinforce Gronau; Joffre had lost any chance of achieving surprise.

On 6 September, the French Sixth Army attacked. Kluck, hoping that this was merely a spoiling attack, designed to impede his march south, reinforced the II and IV R Corps with his IV Corps.

The British and the French Fifth Army likewise advanced on 6 September. Both—especially the British—had to make a considerable advance to regain contact with the enemy. Part of the Fifth Army encountered Kluck's III and IX Corps, which promptly attacked, halting the superior French forces until nightfall and then retiring behind the Grand Morin River. The right flank of the Fifth, meanwhile, advanced unopposed through Charleville (*lower center*), but was suddenly driven in by the German Second Army, which was attempting to carry out Moltke's order to face westward between the Marne and Seine Rivers. Bülow, however, now grew nervous about his own right flank and ordered it back of the Petit Morin River. Farther eastward, Foch—despite the defensive mission assigned him by Joffre—had moved aggressively north of the St. Gond Marshes. A skillful attack by Bülow's left wing threw him back.

On 7 September, Moltke warned Kluck that a captured copy of Joffre's orders indicated that the French Sixth Army was the major threat. Kluck thereupon ordered his III and IX Corps north of the Marne, and turned savagely on the Sixth Army. This created a gap between Kluck and Bülow, filled only by two weak German cavalry corps and some infantry rear guards.

The British were still out of contact; Moltke, Kluck, and Bülow alike considered them too crippled to constitute a serious threat. The French Fifth Army advanced slowly and overcautiously. It failed to maintain contact with Bülow's withdrawing right wing; furthermore, Foch's predicament—he was barely withstanding attacks by elements of the German Second and Third Armies—pulled it increasingly eastward.

Having suffered from French artillery fire during 7 September, Hausen delivered a large-scale night attack at 0300 on the 8th, driving Foch's right back some three miles. But Hausen's men were too exhausted to exploit their success, and he had no reserves, having sent large forces to aid the German Fourth Army (*off map, east*). Nevertheless, Foch's position was critical. Bülow continued attacking; the counterattacks Foch continually ordered were feeble, at best. To the west, the French Fifth Army battered vainly at the Petit Morin line. The British, delayed by the skillfully led German cavalry, were still south of the Marne. Kluck had stopped the French Sixth Army, and was preparing a coordinated attack on its north flank for the 9th.

On the night of 8 September, Franchet d'Esperey launched a surprise night attack across the Petit Morin, capturing Marchais-en-Brie. Bülow thereupon pulled back his right flank, widening the gap between himself and Kluck. This probably was the turning point of the battle.

During 6-8 September, Moltke issued no orders; his army commanders largely ignored him. Intercepted radio messages finally gave him an inkling of the dangerous gap between Kluck and Bülow. He rose to the emergency by sending a junior staff officer, Lt. Col. Richard Hentsch, to the right-wing armies. Hentsch's exact instructions remain unknown; he did have authority—if one army were already retreating—to issue the necessary orders to coordinate the withdrawal of the others. After sending back favorable reports from the Fifth, Fourth, and Third Armies, Hentsch found Bülow personally defeated. Early on the 9th, Bülow ordered his Second Army to retreat. Hentsch acquiesced, and proceeded to Kluck's headquarters. Kluck's enveloping attack against the north flank of the French Sixth Army was advancing rapidly, but his left flank was being forced to draw back before the slow British advance across the Marne. Bülow's retreat having left the German First Army isolated, Hentsch ordered Kluck to withdraw.

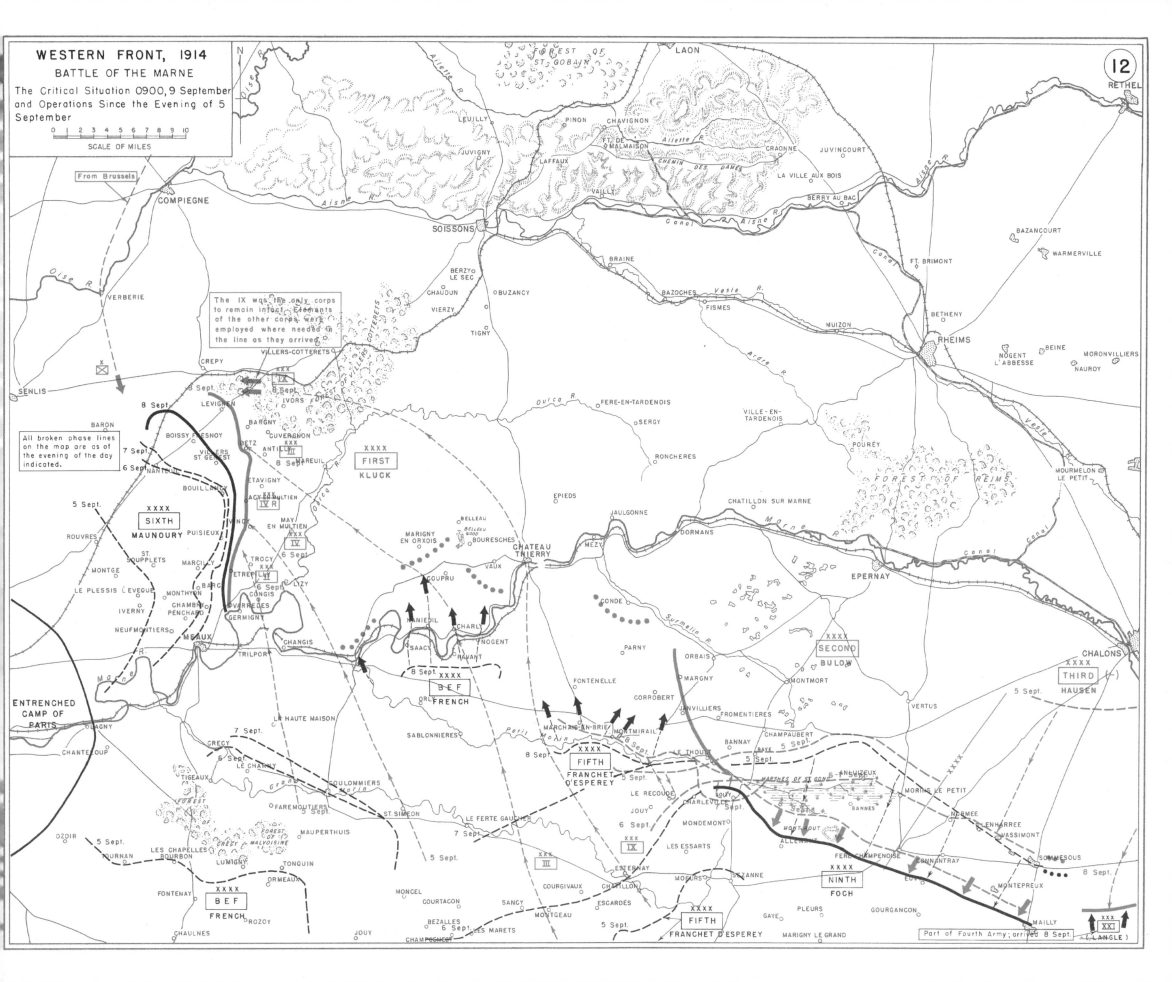

WESTERN FRONT, 1914
BATTLE OF THE MARNE
The Critical Situation 0900, 9 September
and Operations Since the Evening of 5
September

0 1 2 3 4 5 6 7 8 9 10
SCALE OF MILES

12

From Brussels

COMPIEGNE

The IX was the only corps
to remain intact. Elements
of the other corps were
employed in the line as they arrived.

All broken phase lines
on the map are as of
the evening of the day
indicated.

VERBERIE

SENLIS

BARON

CREPY

LEVIGNEN

VILLERS-COTTERETS

IX

FOREST OF VILLERS COTTERETS

8 Sept.

IVORS

BARGNY

CUVERGNON

BETZ

ANTILLY

III

MAREUIL

8 Sept.

FIRST

KLUCK

IV R

LACY EN MULTIEN

ETAVIGNY

MAY
EN MULTIEN

IV

ACY

6 Sept.

SIXTH

MAUNOURY

PUISIEUX

VINCY

TROCY

6 Sept.

ETREPILLY

LIZY

CONGIS

8 Sept

BEF

FRENCH

OISE R.

Oise R.

Aisne R.

SOISSONS

BERZY
LE SEC

CHAUDUN

VIERZY

OBUZANCY

TIGNY

Ourcq R.

FERE-EN-TARDENOIS

SERGY

RONCHERES

EPIEDS

MARIGNY
EN ORXOIS

BELLEAU

BELLEAU
WOOD

BOURESCHES

GOUPRU

VAUX

CHATEAU
THIERRY

MEZY

MANIEUIL

SAACY

CHARLY

NOGENT

SAVANT

CONDE

Surmelin R.

PARNY

FONTENELLE

CORROBERT

MARCHAIS-EN-BRIE

Petit Morin

MONTMIRAIL

8 Sept.

FIFTH

FRANCHET
D'ESPEREY

FOREST OF

St. GOBAIN

LAON

RETHEL

PINON

CHAVIGNON

FT. DE
LA MALMAISON

LAFFAUX

CHEMIN DES DAMES

CRAONNE

JUVINCOURT

LA VILLE AUX BOIS

LEUILLY

JUVIGNY

VAILLY

BERRY AU BAC

Aisne R.

BRAINE

BAZOCHES

FISMES

Vesle R.

MUIZON

Canal

Aisne

FT. BRIMONT

BAZANCOURT

WARMERVILLE

RHEIMS

BETHENY

NOGENT
L'ABBESSE

BEINE

NAUROY

MORONVILLIERS

Ardre R.

POUREY

VILLE-EN-
TARDENOIS

CHATILLON SUR MARNE

JAULGONNE

DORMANS

Marne R.

FOREST OF REIMS

MOURMELON
LE PETIT

Vesle R.

EPERNAY

Canal

Canal

SECOND

BULOW

THIRD

HAUSEN

5 Sept.

ORBAIS

MARGNY

MONTMORT

VERTUS

JANVILLIERS

FROMENTIERES

LE THOULT

BANNAY

CHAMPAUBERT

BAYE

5 Sept.

ENTRENCHED
CAMP OF
PARIS

CLAGNY

CHANTELOUP

OZOIR

TOURNAN

FONTENAY

ROZOY

CHAULNES

ROUVRES

MONTGE

ST.
SOUPPLETS

MARCILLY

LE PLESSIS L'EVEQUE

IVERNY

MONTHYON

CHAMBRY

PENCHARD

NEUFMONTIERS

MEAUX

TRILPORT

Marne R.

LA HAUTE MAISON

SABLONNIERES

LE FERTE GAUCHER

MONDEMONTO

LE RECOUDE

JOUY

CHARLEVILLE

Petit Morin

5 Sept.

BARGNY

ETREPILLY

GERMIGNY

CHANGIS

CRECY

LE CHARNY

TIGEAUX

FAREMOUTIERS

ST. SIMEON

MAUPERTHUIS

LES CHAPELLES
BOURBON

LUMIGNY

TONQUIN

ORMEAUX

FOREST
OF
CRECY

FOREST OF
MALVOISINE

MONGEL

COURTACON

BEZALLES

SANCY

MONTGEAU

6 Sept.

LES MARETS

CHAMPCHICOT

JOUY

COURGIVAUX

CHATILLON

ESCARDES

MOEURS

SEZANNE

GAYE

PLEURS

MARIGNY LE GRAND

GOURGANCON

BEF

FRENCH

FIFTH

FRANCHET D'ESPEREY

III

IX

LES ESSARTS

ESTERNAY

MARSHES OF ST GOND

ANEUIZEUX

MORINS LE PETIT

CHARLEVILLE

ALLEMANT

MONTGIOUT

BANNES

FERE-CHAMPENOISE

CONNANTRAY

NINTH

FOCH

NORMEE

LENHARREE

VASSIMONT

EUY

MONTEPREUX

SOMMESOUS

MAILLY

CHALONS

Part of Fourth Army; arrived 8 Sept.

XXX
XXI

(LANGLE)

While the Allied armies on the left launched their highly successful counterattack at the Marne, the others turned back the German attacks on their fronts—but not without violent fighting. Hausen's Third Army had Foch's Ninth Army at the breaking point on 9 September (*lower center, dashed lines*), but, despite poor French tactics, Foch's fighting spirit prevented a disastrous German breakthrough. Several attacks on Verdun (*center*) by the Crown Prince failed, though the last (on 24 September) created a troublesome salient around St. Mihiel, from which German artillery could shell the main Paris-Nancy railroad. In the south, two offensives by the German Sixth and Seventh Armies failed against strong French positions—as Schlieffen had always predicted they would. Moltke then shifted the Seventh Army to the right flank.

When Hentsch returned on the afternoon of the 10th, Moltke gained his first true picture of the situation of his First and Second Armies. He ordered these—and the Third—to withdraw; the others were to hold in place. On the 11th, he made his first visit to the armies at the front. His impressions being unfavorable, he ordered a general retreat to the line Noyon-Verdun. This line was to be fortified and defended. The withdrawal was conducted with little interference from the slow and poorly directed Allied advance. By 14 September, the Germans were organizing their new positions; that same day, the Kaiser replaced Moltke with General Erich von Falkenhayn.

The German position, along the crest of the plateau about two miles north of the Aisne (*center, left*), was very strong; a series of spurs running from this high ground to the Aisne allowed them to enfilade its banks. The Allies began crossing the Aisne without serious opposition on the 13th, and on the 14th started a general advance. The main effort was made by the British in the general direction of Laon, supported by an attack of the French Fifth Army on the Craonne plateau to its front. Allied attacks continued from the 14th to the 18th, but the German combination of field fortifications, coordinated modern firepower, and counterattacks turned back these assaults with heavy losses. It was a grim preview of the coming warfare in the West.

On the 18th, Joffre admitted a stalemate along the Aisne, and moved to envelop the German right. Falkenhayn attempted to do likewise on the Allied left. Repeated attempts (*small dated arrows*) by both the Germans and the Allies to envelop each other's north flank-known as the "Race to the Sea"-were bloody and indecisive. Eventually, the front became roughly stabilized as shown. During this maneuvering, the British were shifted from the Aisne to Flanders in the north.

Meanwhile, recognizing the Belgian Army at Antwerp (*top center*) as a possible threat to his communications, Falkenhayn had ordered the reduction of that city. Fearing that his army would be bottled up in Antwerp, King Albert withdrew westward on 6 October, accompanied by the British Naval Division which had reached Antwerp. Two other British divisions destined for Antwerp landed at Ostend and Zeebrugge (*top left*), but only in time to join the retreating Belgians. Antwerp fell on 9 October. Albert took over the Allied line north of Ypres; the British, the line from Ypres south to La Bassée.

Falkenhayn realized that any victory in the West would require a prompt attack before the Allied positions were fully organized. With the flanks on the sea, a penetration was the only recourse. The German Fourth and Sixth Armies moved north and struck the Allies on the front from the Lys River to the sea. From 12 to 20 October, the British held, but the Belgians could halt the Germans only by flooding the area from Dixmude to the sea. The Allies counterattacked from 20 to 28 October, but suffered frightfully and gained little. Falkenhayn, after careful preparations, renewed his attack on the Ypres front on the 29th, and pressed it until 11 November. At one point, he actually broke through, but was halted by the last available Allied reserves. Winter weather now set in and ended the First Battle of Ypres.

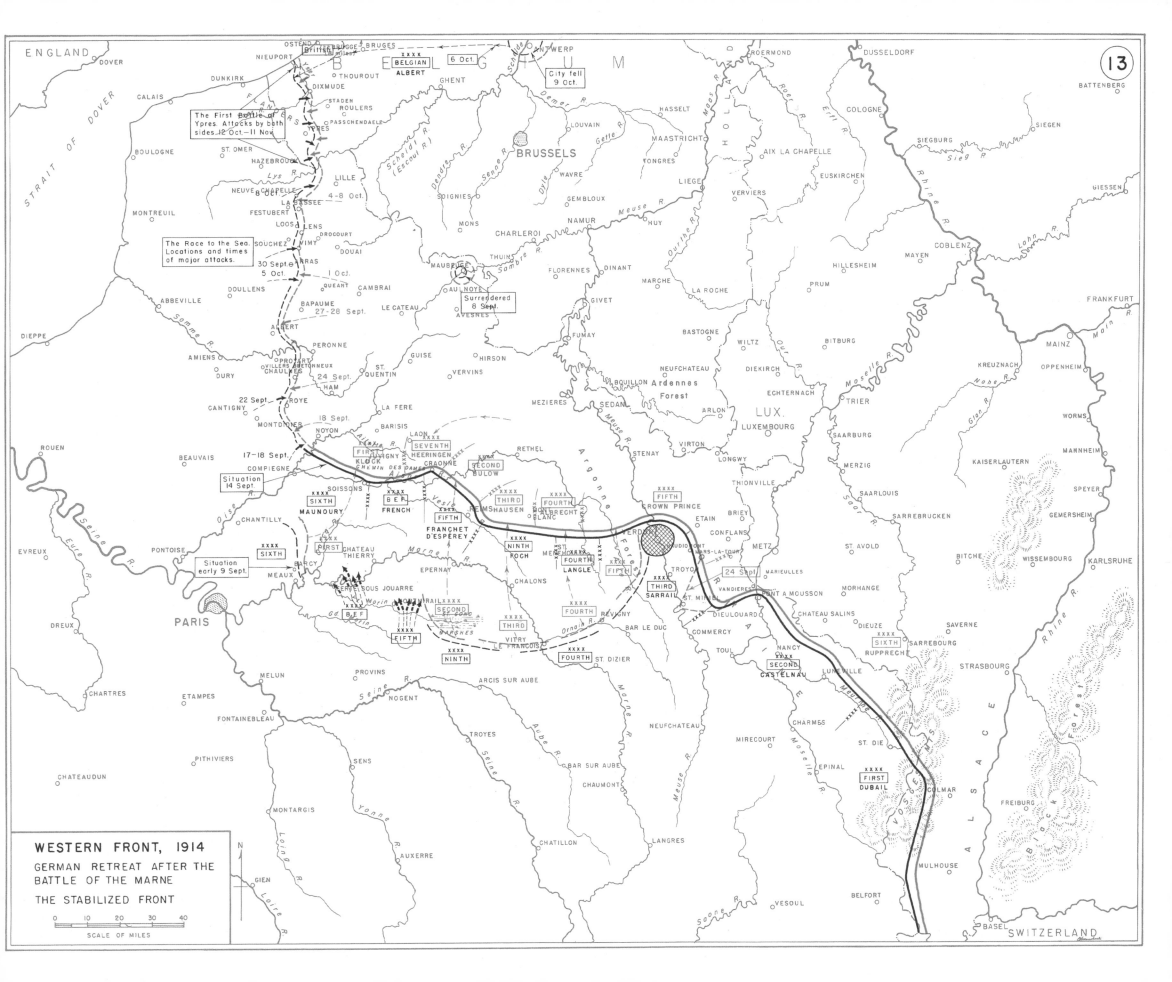

ENGLAND

STRAIT OF DOVER

13

The First Battle of Ypres. Attacks by both sides 12 Oct.–11 Nov.

The Race to the Sea. Locations and times of major attacks.

XXXX BELGIAN ALBERT

6 Oct.

City fell 9 Oct.

Surrendered 8 Sept.

BRUSSELS

LUX.
LUXEMBOURG

Ardennes Forest

Situation 14 Sept.

Situation early 9 Sept.

PARIS

XXXX SIXTH MAUNOURY

XXXX B.E.F. FRENCH

XXXX FIFTH

XXXX FIRST KLUCK

XXXX SEVENTH HEERINGEN

XXXX SECOND BÜLOW

XXXX THIRD HAUSEN

XXXX FOURTH ALBRECHT

XXXX FIFTH CROWN PRINCE

XXXX FIRST SIXTH

CHATEAU THIERRY

XXXX B.E.F.

XXXX FIFTH

XXXX SECOND

XXXX NINTH

XXXX NINTH FOCH

XXXX FOURTH LANGLE

XXXX THIRD SARRAIL

24 Sept.

XXXX SIXTH RUPPRECHT

XXXX SECOND CASTELNAU

XXXX FIRST DUBAIL

SWITZERLAND

WESTERN FRONT, 1914
GERMAN RETREAT AFTER THE BATTLE OF THE MARNE
THE STABILIZED FRONT

0 10 20 30 40
SCALE OF MILES

In contrast to the land fighting, naval operations in 1914 amounted to little more than cautious sparring. The British Navy in 1914 was by far the strongest in the world. Naval strength at that time was reckoned in terms of "dreadnaughts" (a relatively new type of battleship carrying eight or more heavy guns of the same caliber) and battle cruisers (warships armed like the dread-naughts, but carrying less armor, and therefore speedier). Britain had twenty-nine of these ships to Germany's seventeen. The submarine was still an unproven weapon.

British naval strategy was simple: the Grand Fleet would be kept in the North Sea (*center*), where it could blockade German ports and prevent the German High Sea Fleet from leaving its bases. If the Germans did come out, they would be engaged, provided that conditions made victory nearly certain for the British. This conservative strategy was based on the simple fact that, as long as the Grand Fleet remained intact, England controlled the seas for all practical purposes, regardless of minor operations. But, should some English admiral allow the fleet to be caught divided or at a disadvantage, a good proportion of its big ships might be lost, and Germany might gain control of the seas. This would, in Churchill's words, "lose the war in a single afternoon."

The German Navy was strong, but its commanders knew that it was, as yet, unable to meet the English in open battle. Their strategy was to remain at their bases, making occasional sudden sorties in the hope of whittling away the British superiority. These bases, along the German seacoast between Holland and Denmark, were covered by mine fields, shoals, coastal batteries, and the heavily fortified island of Heligoland. The whole complex, the so-called the "Wet Triangle," was too strong for direct attack. The Germans derived a further advantage from the Kaiser Wilhelm Ship Canal (now the Kiel Canal), through which they could shift their largest ships between the Baltic (*not labeled; southeast of Sweden*) and the North Sea. The British, on the other hand, were not able to get into the Baltic because the narrow channels between Denmark and Norway and Sweden had been mined by the neutral Danes as soon as war began.

The French Navy was chiefly concerned with safeguarding the transfer of colonial troops from North Africa to France. The Austrian Navy, unready for war, remained in the Adriatic (*not labeled; south of Austria*).

Ten German warships were caught at sea by the declaration of war. In the Mediterranean, the battle cruiser *Goeben* and the light cruiser *Breslau* escaped into the Dardanelles; Turkey, though neutral, gave them sanctuary. Besides these two ships, there were five German cruisers (under Admiral Maximilian Graf von Spee) in the Far East, one off East Africa, and two near the West Indies. These fast ships were a threat to British commerce and troop convoys from the dominions, but—in the days before long-range aircraft—the problem of intercepting them was extremely difficult. The British began by sending expeditions against German overseas naval bases in Africa. Australia and New Zealand occupied German-ruled islands in the Pacific.

When Japan entered the war in August and captured Tsingtao (*right center*), the German base in China, Admiral Spec sailed for South America. Detaching the *Emden* en route, and being joined by one cruiser from the West Indies, he reached the coast of Chile in September. On 1 November, he defeated a weaker British squadron. Receiving orders to return to Germany, he rounded Cape Horn and decided to raid the minor British base on the Falkland Islands. Here, he was intercepted by a stronger and faster British squadron. Only one of his cruisers escaped—to be destroyed later, in March, 1915.

Of the remaining cruisers, one was blockaded in an East African river, and one was destroyed off the West Indies. The *Emden* carried out a destructive raid across the Indian Ocean, until sunk by an Australian cruiser.

In European waters, each belligerent undertook minor operations, including two hit-and-run German bombardments of English seacoast towns. Possibly the most significant incident occurred on 22 September, when a single German submarine torpedoed three old British cruisers off the Dutch coast.

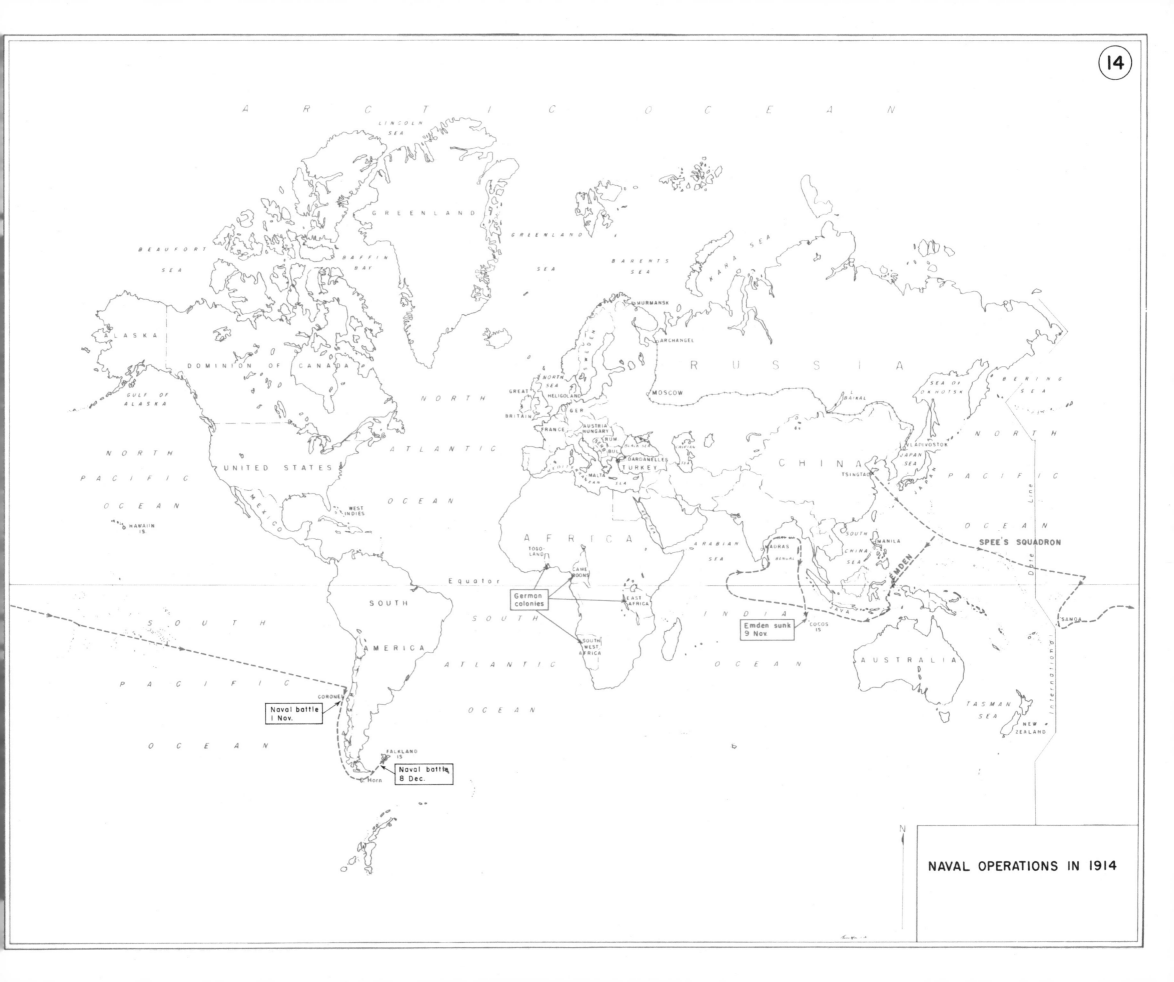

NAVAL OPERATIONS IN 1914

(Before studying the Tannenberg campaign, the reader should review the belligerents' war plans and the geographical considerations discussed in the text of map 3.)

By 1914, the Germans had developed an excellent system of railroads in East Prussia; the road net had also been given comparable attention. Thus, troop movements both into and within East Prussia could be made very quickly—a capability upon which German strategy in the East was largely based. On the other hand, the Russians had purposely left their communications systems near the border in an underdeveloped condition to handicap an invader. Now, this neglect was to prove a distinct disadvantage to them in their offensive operations.

Though East Prussia could be assailed from the east and the south, it held certain advantages for a defending army. The fifty-mile-long chain of lakes (the Masurian Lakes) extending from Angerburg to Johannisburg (*upper center*) formed an excellent barrier; the only major gap in the chain—at Lötzen—had been sealed by the construction of Fort Boyen. The lakes had steep, soggy, heavily wooded banks, and were patrolled by armed steamboats. From Johannisburg west, the country was thickly forested and studded with many small lakes, a condition that existed to a lesser degree as far west as Strasbourg (*lower left*). Thus, lateral communications and maneuver room for a force advancing north into the area would be severely restricted. Between Angerburg and Insterburg (*upper center*), the terrain was flat and generally open. This area, called the Insterburg Gap, afforded the best approach into East Prussia. However, the Angerapp River, which traversed its width, though fordable, could be organized into a suitable defensive position. To the west, the fortresses of Thorn, Graudenz, and Danzig (*lower left*) guarded the Vistula. In the north was the fortress of Königsberg, protected further by an extensive fortified area.

For several years before 1914 the Russians promised the French they would launch an offensive if war broke out with Germany, and in August 1913 they pledged to attack fifteen days after mobilization. Even if the entire Russian army could not be mobilized in such a short period, military leaders recognized the advantages of coordinated Russian and French offensives against Germany. The Russians planned on launching their earliest offensive into East Prussia, but when the French urged an attack west of Warsaw toward Berlin, General Ianushkevich, the Russian chief of staff, modified plans in the early days of the war and began preparations for making this attack with a new army to be formed at Warsaw. Though the formation of this new army diverted forces from the advance into East Prussia, General Zhilinskii, commander of the Northwest Army Group (First and Second Armies), launched a converging attack on East Prussia on 13 August from the east and southeast. The Russians expected First and Second Armies to clear East Prussia and then advance west until they came on line with the army forming at Warsaw. By the 17th, the campaign had progressed as shown.

German General Max von Prittwitz arrived at his headquarters near Allenstein (*center*) on 8 August, and ordered his four corps disposed as shown (*four large red circles*). He had authority to withdraw to the Vistula, if necessary, but he also knew that his superiors expected him to make use of the terrain and railroads to mass his strength against first one and then the other of the anticipated Russian advances. Prittwitz was well informed as to Zhilinskii's movements, through spies and intercepted radio messages. He decided, on the 14th, to leave the XX Corps at Allenstein, to protect the south flank, while he moved to defeat the Russian First Army; then he would turn south to oppose the Second. However, he did not know that his fiery I Corps commander, General Hermann K. von Francois, had exceeded his orders and moved forward to Stallupönen (*upper right*), where he was about to plunge the army into battle earlier than expected.

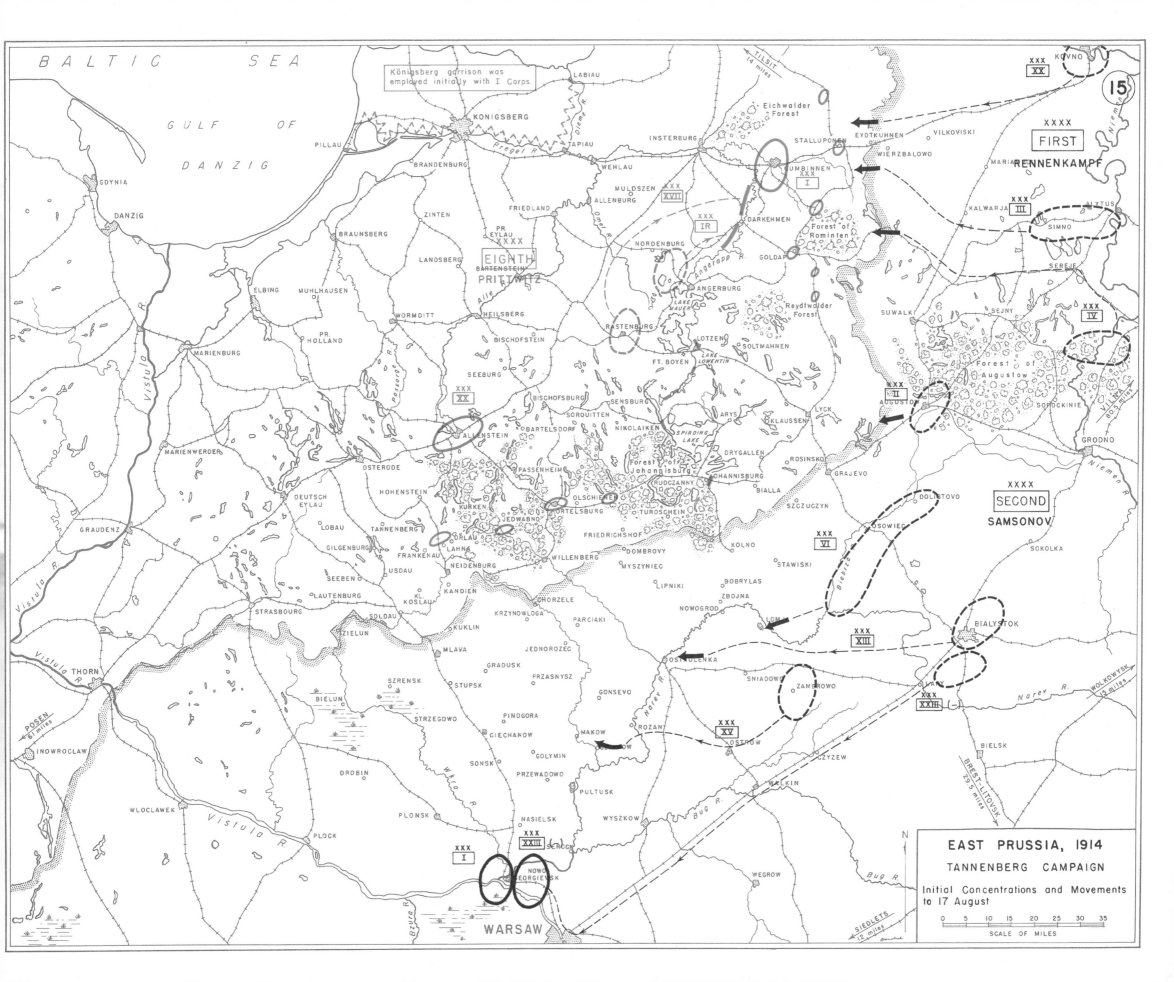

BALTIC SEA

GULF OF DANZIG

Königsberg garrison was
employed initially with I Corps.

EIGHTH
PRITTWITZ

FIRST
RENNENKAMPF

SECOND
SAMSONOV

EAST PRUSSIA, 1914

TANNENBERG CAMPAIGN

Initial Concentrations and Movements
to 17 August

0 5 10 15 20 25 30 35
SCALE OF MILES

General Paul V. Rennenkampf's First Army crossed the East Prussian border on 17 August (*sketch* a). There was a notable lack of liaison between the various columns, no cavalry screen to the front, and—worst of all—a sizable gap between the III and IV Corps. Furthermore, Rennenkampf, completely uninformed as to German dispositions, had not weighted his north flank in compliance with his orders to drive Prittwitz away from Königsberg (*off map, west*). Plainly, he did not expect much opposition until the army reached the Angerapp River (*left center*). He knew that his army was several days in advance of the Second Army and that if trouble developed, General Alexander V. Samsonov could probably not provide assistance before the 22d. Zhilinskii, too, had been aware of this fact, but had still ordered the advance. He expected the First Army to entice the Germans eastward while Samsonov got astride their rear.

On the German side, the headstrong Francois—unable to condone Russian violation of Prussia's "sacred soil"—had insubordinately disposed his I Corps well to the east of Gumbinnen (*left center*). His tactical dispositions were good— each of his forward elements was a balanced force, in constant communication with Francois' headquarters in Gumbinnen. But his aggressive intentions were in direct disobedience of Prittwitz's orders. Prittwitz intended to fight to the west (at the Angerapp River); Francois clearly planned to fight at the border. Thus, when the Russian III Corps struck his detachment at Goritten, he immediately reinforced it and launched a counter-stroke. Then the detachment commander at Tollmingkehmen moved the bulk of his force north and took the enemy III Corps in the rear. The Russian force suffered 3,000 casualties, became disorganized, and withdrew to the frontier. That night, 17 August, Francois withdrew his corps to Gumbinnen. His impetuous attack was tactically commendable but strategically deplorable, for he had upset the finely balanced German strategy. Time was important to Prittwitz: he had only about five days to dispose of Rennenkampf before it would be necessary to move south to face Samsonov. By his action, Francois had retarded the Russian advance to the contemplated battlefield at the Angerapp. It now appeared that the Eighth Army might be forced to advance eastward in order to fight the decisive action.

But Rennenkampf rectified the German error by continuing his advance the next two days—still without an adequate screen to his front—believing that his enemy's main force was well to the west. The dispositions of the opposing forces on the night of 19 August were as shown (*sketch b, dashed lines*). Francois continued to urge his chief to attack Rennenkampf to the east of the Angerapp. German cavalry successes on the 18th and 19th, and Rennenkampf's order to halt on the 20th—sent by radio in the clear and intercepted by the Germans—reinforced his argument. Prittwitz finally succumbed and—despite the protests of his staff—ordered an attack for 20 August. Unfortunately for the Germans, Prittwitz's order did not allow time for I R and XVII Corps to move forward so that a coordinated attack, in full strength, could be made.

Attacking piecemeal on the 20th and engaging the enemy corps one at a time, the Germans were successful only in the north. There, the I Corps attacked at 0400, achieved surprise, and forced the Russian XX Corps back five miles. This was followed by a cavalry attack which created panic among the Russian transport at Schwirgallen (*top right*). But the XVII and I R Corps, having marched all night, arrived tired and disorganized. At 0800, the XVII Corps attacked frontally, piecemeal, and without an artillery preparation; it encountered an entrenched foe and was driven back in complete disorder. The attack of the I R Corps at noon was also repulsed. The battle might be called a draw, but Prittwitz's immediate need was for a decisive victory. He was now faced with a major decision: should he renew the attack or withdraw?

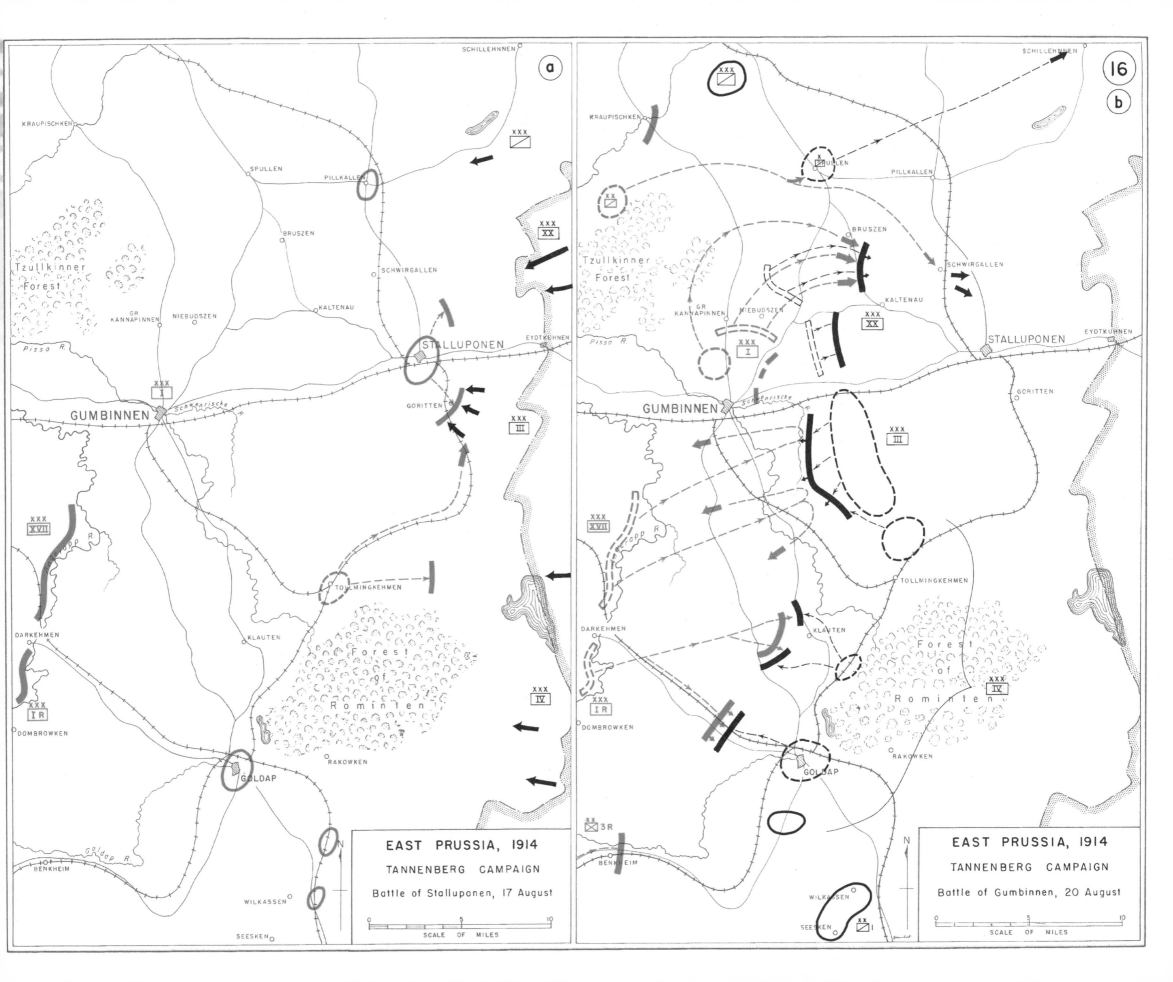

a

SCHILLEHNNEN

KRAUPISCHKEN

SPULLEN

PILLKALLEN

BRUSZEN

SCHWIRGALLEN

KALTENAU

Tzullkinner Forest

GR KANNAPINNEN

NIEBUDSZEN

XXX
I

Pissa R.

STALLUPONEN

EYDTKUHNEN

GUMBINNEN

Schwenrische

GORITTEN

XXX
III

XXX
XVII

Goldap R.

TOLLMINGKEHMEN

KLAUTEN

Forest of Rominten

DARKEHMEN

XXX
IR

DOMBROWKEN

XXX
IV

RAKOWKEN

GOLDAP

Goldap R.

N

BENKHEIM

WILKASSEN

SEESKEN

EAST PRUSSIA, 1914

TANNENBERG CAMPAIGN

Battle of Stalluponen, 17 August

0   5   10
SCALE OF MILES

b

16

SCHILLEHNNEN

XXX

KRAUPISCHKEN

X
SPULLEN

PILLKALLEN

XX

BRUSZEN

SCHWIRGALLEN

Tzullkinner Forest

GR KANNAPINNEN

NIEBUDSZEN

KALTENAU

XXX
XX

XXX
I

Pissa R.

STALLUPONEN

EYDTKUHNEN

GUMBINNEN

Schwenrische

GORITTEN

XXX
III

XXX
XVII

Rominten R.

TOLLMINGKEHMEN

DARKEHMEN

KLAUTEN

Forest of Rominten

XXX
IV

XXX
IR

DOMBROWKEN

RAKOWKEN

GOLDAP

N

XX
3R

BENKHEIM

WILKASSEN

SEESKEN

XX
I

EAST PRUSSIA, 1914

TANNENBERG CAMPAIGN

Battle of Gumbinnen, 20 August

0   5   10
SCALE OF MILES

Prittwitz, at his headquarters some seventy miles west of Gumbinnen, had no firsthand knowledge of the battle fought there. The rout of General August von Mackensen's XVII Corps weighed heavily on his mind, and served to confirm his apprehension that he had extended his left too far. At 1730, 20 August, he received news that Samsonov's Second Army had crossed the border that day. It seemed that all his fears were being realized. Despair and panic now seized the Eighth Army commander. Without consulting his staff, he telephoned Moltke at Coblenz and informed him that the Eighth Army would retreat to the Vistula and that he doubted his ability to hold even that river line unless reinforced.

Moltke's reaction was immediate. The weak-willed Prittwitz was relieved, and General Paul von Hindenburg (called from retirement) was placed in command. General Erich von Ludendorff, the hero of Liège, was appointed his chief of staff. By 1400, 23 August, they had arrived at Marienburg (*upper left*) to be met and briefed on events by the Eighth Army staff.

In the meantime, Prittwitz's staff was aghast when he informed them of the planned withdrawal. His capable operations officer, Lt. Col. Max Hoffman, pointed out that Samsonov was already eighty miles closer to the Vistula than the bulk of the Eighth Army. Regaining his composure, Prittwitz listened to his staff and approved a shift of the army to the south to fight Samsonov. No one informed Moltke of this new offensive concept. He fully expected the Eighth Army to withdraw to the Vistula, but hoped Hindenburg could breathe new life into it. Also, under the mistaken belief that affairs were going well on the Western Front, he decided to withdraw some troops from there to bolster the Eastern Front.

At Marienburg, on 23 August, Hindenburg and Ludendorff accepted the changes made by Prittwitz on the night of the 20th. The I Corps and 3 R Division were now en route by rail to reinforce the XX Corps. The XVII and I R Corps were moving westward, and were to turn south if Rennenkampf showed no inclination to press the advance. Only the 1st Cavalry Division and the garrison brigade assigned to the lake region remained to delay Rennenkampf. The Russian commander had not moved for sixty hours, and only now, on the 23d, did he resume his dawdling advance.

To the south, Samsonov had not moved much farther from 20 to 23 August. The inadequate railroad and road nets had begun to break down, and his hastily improvised system of logistical support had failed completely. He had been ordered by Zhilinskii to move north to the line Passenheim-Rudczanny (center), but had decided that an advance to the northwest would be more likely to intercept the Germans. He had ordered that the line Soldau-Ortelsburg (*center, line of blue arrowheads*) be reached by the 23d, and his orders, uncoded and broadcast in the clear, had been heard by the Germans. There now followed a controversy between Zhilinskii and Samsonov as to the direction of advance of the Second Army. The latter finally compromised and ordered seizure of the line Hohenstein-Sorquitten (*center*) by the 25th, while the I Corps remained at Soldau to protect the left flank. This line was in the general direction of Samsonov's movement, but farther to the east.

Samsonov advanced his army—as Rennenkampf had—without cavalry to the front. On 24 August, his XV Corps ran directly into the entrenched German XX Corps. It was somewhat of a surprise, for the Germans were presumed to be fleeing westward. The XV Corps moved clumsily to the attack; severe fighting raged all day, but the XX Corps could not be dislodged. Meanwhile, Samsonov made no effort to bring adjacent corps to the aid of the XV Corps. That night, his radio publicly announced that the 25th would be a day of rest for his troops.

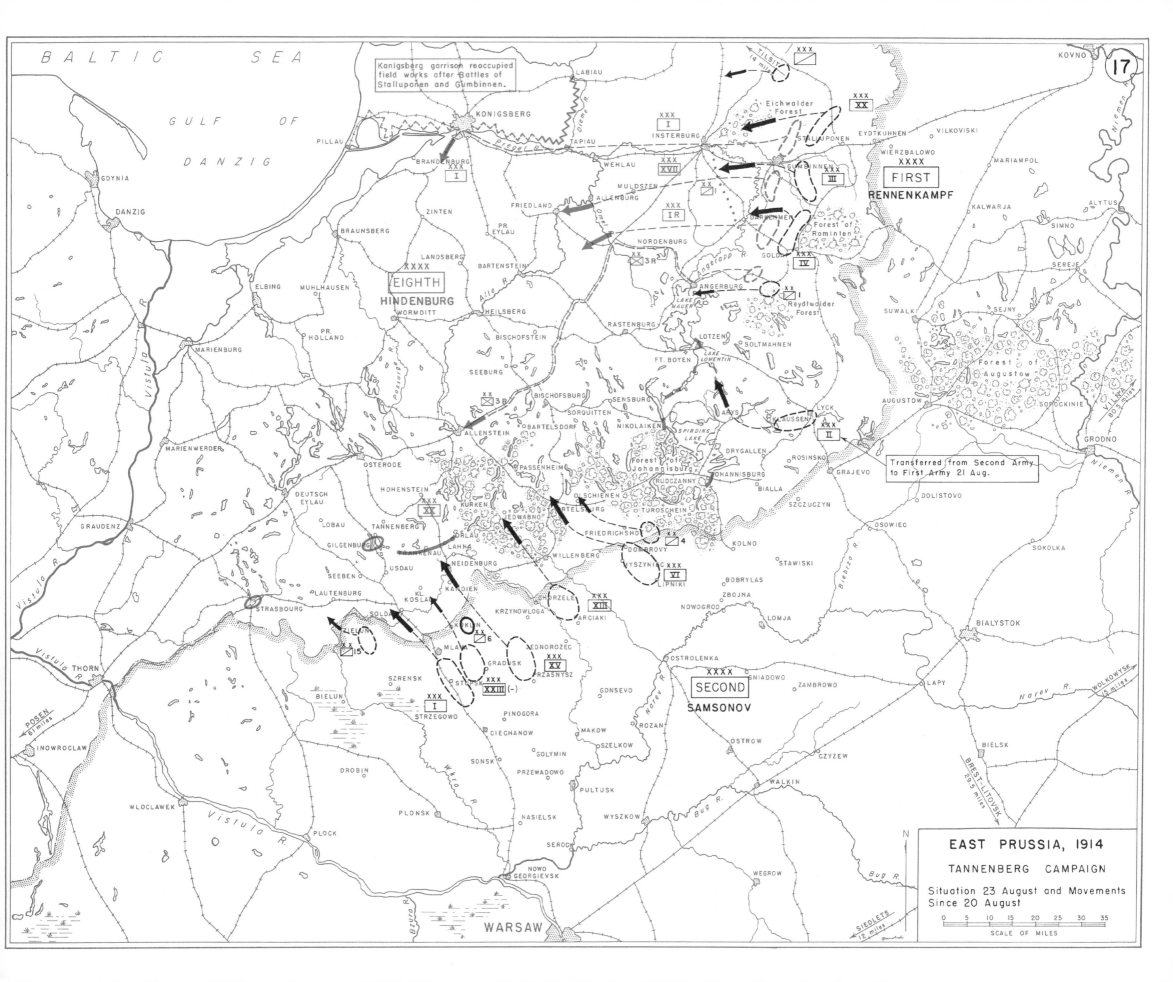

BALTIC SEA

GULF OF DANZIG

Konigsberg garrison reoccupied field works after Battles of Stalluponen and Gumbinnen.

KONIGSBERG

Transferred from Second Army to First Army 21 Aug.

EIGHTH
HINDENBURG

XXXX
FIRST
RENNENKAMPF

XXXX
SECOND
SAMSONOV

N

EAST PRUSSIA, 1914

TANNENBERG CAMPAIGN

Situation 23 August and Movements Since 20 August

0 5 10 15 20 25 30 35
SCALE OF MILES

WARSAW

17

Rennenkampf reached the line shown (*dashed blue line*) on 25 August, all the while unaware of the weakness of the German opposition on his front. That day, his radio announced his intention to reach a line through Allenburg by the night of the 26th. This was welcome news to the Germans, for it now appeared they would have time to concentrate against Samsonov before Rennenkampf could interfere.

To the south, the XX Corps had withdrawn from Frankenau after the fight on the 24th, to the position shown at Tannenberg. Meanwhile, Samsonov received permission to move to the line Osterode-Allenstein, but Zhilinskii insisted that the VI Corps and a cavalry division move to the Bischofsburg-Sensburg area (*center*) to protect the right flank. Thus, by late 25 August, the Second Army was spread along a seventy-mile arc from Zielun (*lower left*) to Sensburg, with a corps isolated on each flank. Samsonov's orders had also been broadcast, so that, on the 25th, the Germans knew the future plans of both Russian armies.

While the Russians blundered along the road to catastrophe, Ludendorff was busily making plans. On 23 August, the I Corps was ordered to detrain at Deutsch Eylau (*lower left*) and take position on the right of the XX Corps; the 3 R Division was ordered to move to the left of the XX Corps. On the night of the 24th—before learning of Rennenkampf's proposed slow advance—Hindenburg made the momentous decision to leave only the 1st Cavalry Division and a garrison brigade in front of the Russian First Army, and to move the I R and XVII Corps South to attack the Russian VI Corps at Bischofsburg. But he had no assurance that Rennenkampf would not suddenly veer southward against the German rear. (Actually, there was little to fear. Zhilinskii, instead of coordinating the operations of his two armies against the German Eighth Army, would order Rennenkampf, on the 26th, to move directly west with half of his army, while the remainder laid siege to Königsberg.)

On 26 August, one division of the Russian VI Corps moved toward Allenstein, while the other advanced north of Bischofs-burg. The 4th Cavalry Division was fifteen miles to the east at Sensburg. The division advancing north encountered Mackensen's XVII Corps and, underestimating its strength, attacked. It was severely repulsed. The second Russian division reversed its march and sought to assist. The German I R Corps now arrived, and the Russian VI Corps fled in rout. The way was open for a German envelopment of Samsonov's north flank.

Meanwhile, Francois' I Corps had arrived near Seeben by the night of the 25th. Ordered to attack the Russian I Corps the next day, Francois argued vehemently against the attack because he would not have his full complement of artillery until the 27th. Hindenburg insisted, and Francois launched the attack as planned—but not very energetically. The advance succeeded in taking only Seeben. On the 26th, too, the XX Corps repulsed strong attacks by the XV Corps, and even forced the XXIII Corps to withdraw somewhat. Two matters require clarification: the Russian radio difficulties and the German command system.

Although the Germans also failed to encode some of their messages, the Russians' lack of properly trained code and communication personnel resulted in their frequently sending radio messages in the clear. Their sending messages in the clear also stemmed from their having failed to bring sufficient telephone wire for communications and their lines often being cut by the East Prussians.

Above, we say: "Ludendorff was busily making plans." Hindenburg, the commander, might have been expected to make the plans. However, since the days of the elder von Moltke (1870), the German practice had been for the commander to make the broad basic decision, the staff to develop a plan, and the subordinate field commanders then to fight the battle in accordance with the plan. The over-all commander frequently exercised no battlefield direction. As the war progresses, it will be seen that Ludendorff begins to exercise more and more control on the battlefield; but even he leans heavily on a detailed plan prepared by the staff, which is held to as firmly as is practicable.

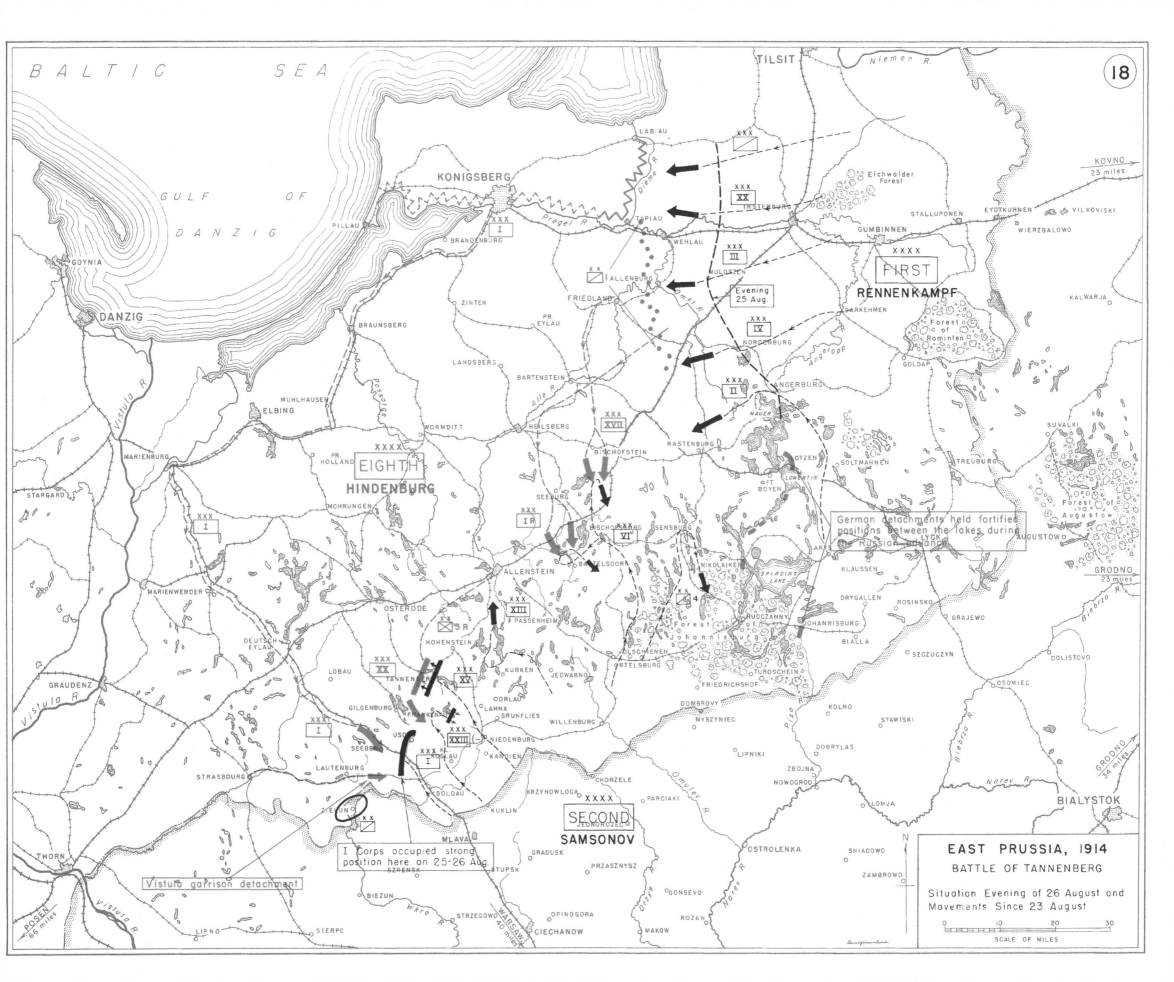

BALTIC SEA

GULF OF DANZIG

TILSIT

Niemen R.

KOVNO
23 miles

KONIGSBERG

FIRST

RENNENKAMPF

Evening 25 Aug.

German detachments held fortified positions between the lakes during the Russian advance

EIGHTH

HINDENBURG

SECOND

SAMSONOV

I Corps occupied strong position here on 25-26 Aug.

Vistula garrison detachment

EAST PRUSSIA, 1914

BATTLE OF TANNENBERG

Situation Evening of 26 August and Movements Since 23 August

0   10   20   30

SCALE OF MILES

18

The remnants of the fleeing Russian VI Corps (*dashed blue oval*) arrived south of Ortelsburg by nightfall, 27 August; the next day, they withdrew across the border. Had Ludendorff permitted the XVII and I R Corps to pursue, it is likely that none of the VI Corps could have escaped destruction or capture. But the chief of staff was worried about Rennenkampf, and ordered the victorious corps to move toward Allenstein (*center*) on the 27th, in order to protect the left flank of the XX Corps. On the 28th, he regained his confidence and directed Mackensen to march his XVII Corps to Jedwabno.

If Francois lacked enthusiasm in his attack on the 26th, he was in deadly earnest on the 27th. Reinforced by troops and heavy artillery from the Thorn fortress (*bottom left*), he delivered a devastating artillery bombardment on the poorly prepared enemy trenches. The Russian I Corps suffered heavy casualties, broke under the weight of the artillery fire alone, and fled. That night, thoroughly disorganized and beaten, it retired south through Soldau, thus exposing the left flank of the Russian center.

About noon on the 27th, Samsonov had finally learned of the disastrous defeat of his VI Corps, and the following morning he was informed of the withdrawal of his I Corps. But he apparently failed to appreciate the great peril now facing his center, for he ordered a continuation of the attack on the 28th. Fatalistically accepting the earlier reverses, he rode forward to the XV Corps area, expecting the tide to turn. The XIII Corps had reached Allenstein on the 27th, but before it could return to join the XV Corps in the attack, the German XX Corps—reinforced by the 3 R Division and a fortress division from the Vistula—launched an attack on the XV Corps that forced it to withdraw. By the morning of the 29th, the withdrawal had become general. During the day, confusion set in, and the retreat became disorganized as the Germans forced the three Russian corps into an ever-shrinking pocket.

Meanwhile, to the south, the advance elements of Francois'

I Corps had reached Niedenburg on 28 August. There, he received orders from Ludendorff directing him to turn north to aid the XX Corps. Seeing that Russian resistance was collapsing, the intractable Francois ignored the order and drove eastward. By nightfall, he had formed a thin line of pickets—twenty-five battalions stretched over thirty-seven miles—blocking the Russian southern escape route. Had he moved north from Niedenburg, as Ludendorff had directed, the result would have been a shallow envelopment and the likely escape of large bodies of enemy troops.

On the 30th and 31st, the now thoroughly confused Russians strove to break through Francois' line, but were turned back in every instance. The Russian I Corps launched a relieving attack and succeeded in taking Niedenburg on 30 August, but Francois' countermeasures forced evacuation of the town the following day. (Fortunately for Francois, his independent exploits had all turned out well.) On the 31st, the Russians succumbed to the inevitable. The Germans captured 125,000 men and 500 guns; their own losses were between 10,000 and 15,000 for the entire campaign. Accurate figures on Russians killed and wounded are not available. The despondent Samsonov took his own life, deep in the forest.

Not until the 27th had Zhilinskii ordered Rennenkampf to come to the aid of the Second Army. But by then it was too late, for, on the 30th, having reached the positions shown, Rennenkampf learned of Samsonov's defeat and turned back.

The Tannenberg campaign had ended in a dazzling German triumph, but since Rennenkampf's army was still intact, it was not decisive. A well-led German force, making excellent use of a central position, had defeated a greatly superior but poorly led Russian force. The resolute and bold handling of the German troops was the chief factor in the ultimate victory. Lack of intelligence, violations of communications security, slowness, indecision at high levels, and inadequate logistical support had all contributed to the Russian debacle.

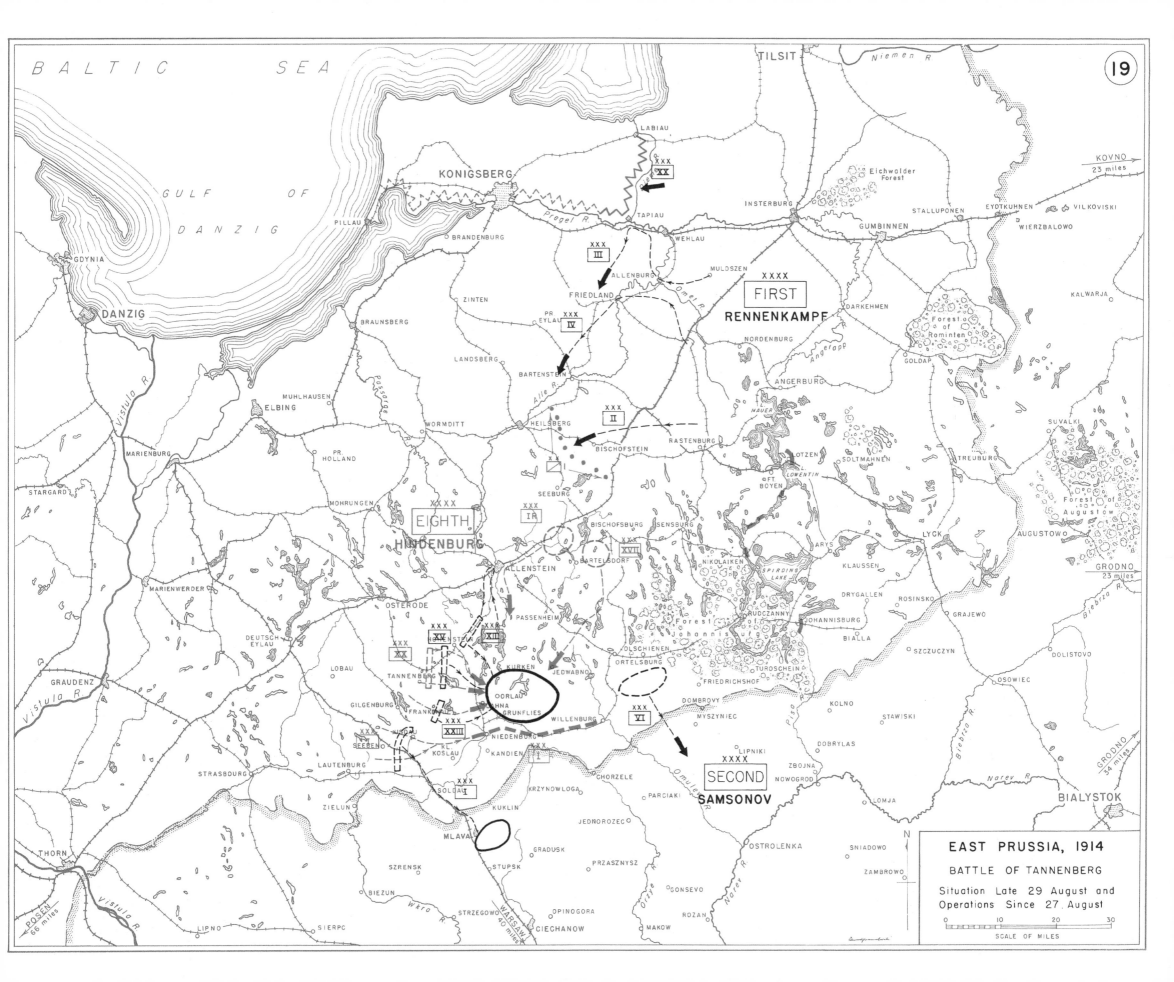

19

BALTIC SEA

GULF OF DANZIG

TILSIT
Niemen R

KOVNO
23 miles

LABIAU
XXX
XX

KONIGSBERG

INSTERBURG
STALLUPONEN
EYDTKUHNEN
VILKOVISKI
WIERZBALOWO

Pregel R.
TAPIAU
WEHLAU

MULDSZEN

XXXX
FIRST
RENNENKAMPF

GUMBINNEN

KALWARJA

Eichwalder
Forest

PILLAU
BRANDENBURG

ZINTEN

XXX
III

ALLENBURG

Omel R.

DARKEHMEN

Forest of
Rominten

GDYNIA

DANZIG

BRAUNSBERG

LANDSBERG

FRIEDLAND

PR
EYLAU
XXX
IV

NORDENBURG

ANGERBURG

Angerapp

GOLDAP

Passarge R.

MUHLHAUSEN
ELBING

WORMDITT

PR.
HOLLAND

HEILSBERG

Alle R.

BARTENSTEIN

Mauer

SOLTMAHNEN

TREUBURG

SUVALKI

MARIENBURG

STARGARD

BISCHOFSTEIN

RASTENBURG

L
LOWENTIN

FT
BOYEN

Lotzen

ARYS

LYCK

Blebro R.

Forest of
Augustow

AUGUSTOW

Vistula R.

MARIENWERDER

MOHRUNGEN

SEEBURG

XXX
II

XXX
I

XXXX
EIGHTH
HINDENBURG

XXX
IR

BISCHOFSBURG
SENSBURG

NIKOLAIKEN

SPIRDING
LAKE

KLAUSSEN

DRYGALLEN

ROSINSKO

GRODNO
23 miles

GRAJEWO

DEUTSCH
EYLAU

OSTERODE

BARTELSDORF

XXX
XVII

ALLENSTEIN

PASSENHEIM

*Forest of
Johannisburg*

RUDCZANNY

JOHANNISBURG

BIALLA

SZCZUCZYN

DOLISTOVO

OSOWIEC

GRAUDENZ

LOBAU

XXX
XX

XXX
XV

XXX
XIII

TANNENBERG

KURKEN

JEDWABNO

OLSCHIENEN

ORTELSBURG

FRIEDRICHSHOF

KOLNO

STAWISKI

Narev R.

GILGENBURG

FRANKEN

OORLAU
OHNA
GRUNFLIES

WILLENBURG

DOMBROVY

MYSZYNIEC

XXX
VI

Omulew R.

KOLNO

DOBRYLAS

THORN

NADRU

SEEBEN

XXX

KL.
KOSLAU

NIEDENBURG

KANDIEN

XXX
I

LIPNIKI

XXXX
SECOND
SAMSONOV

ZBOJNA
NOWOGROD

OSOWIEC

Brebza R.

GRODNO
34 miles

Narev R.

BIALYSTOK

LAUTENBURG

STRASBOURG

SOLDAU

XXX
I

ZIELUN

KUKLIN

KRZYNOWLOGA

CHORZELE

PARCIAKI

LOMJA

SNIADOWO

OSTROLENKA

MLAVA

GRADUSK

JEDNOROZEC

PRZASZNYSZ

GONSEVO

ROZAN

ZAMBROWO

POSEN
66 miles

LIPNO

SIERPC

BIEZUN

SZRENSK

STUPSK

STRZEGOWO
WARSAW
40 miles

CIECHANOW

OPINOGORA

MAKOW

Wkro R.

Orzyc R.

N

EAST PRUSSIA, 1914

BATTLE OF TANNENBERG

Situation Late 29 August and
Operations Since 27 August

0   10   20   30
SCALE OF MILES

Having eliminated Samsonov's Second Army, the Hindenburg-Ludendorff team immediately and earnestly went about the task of disposing of Rennenkampf's First Army. For this endeavor, the Eighth Army was stronger than heretofore, having been reinforced on 2 September by the XI and Guard Reserve Corps and the 8th Cavalry Division from the Western Front. It was noted earlier that these units—and a third corps, later withheld—had been designated for movement eastward when Moltke received Prittwitz's call for aid on 20 August. On the 27th, Ludendorff had informed the German GHQ that the reinforcements were not essential; nevertheless, they were dispatched. Thus, considering the critical situation in France from 1 to 10 September, it has been claimed by some authors that the outcome of the Battle of the Marne might have been different had Moltke accepted Ludendorff's recommendation. It is doubtful, however, that two corps could have ensured victory for Germany in the West. (It should be remembered that Hindenburg and Ludendorff acted as one, so that when the text states that Ludendorff made a decision, Hindenburg's concurrence is implied.)

On 30 August, Zhilinskii informed Rennenkampf of Samsonov's defeat and cautioned him to protect his southern flank. Rennenkampf decided to withdraw to the line shown with his right flank on the sea and his left on the lakes. Mindful of the Lötzen Gap, he stationed most of the II Corps to block that route around his flank. The partially formed XXII Corps—part of the Russian Tenth Army—occupied key localities to the south of Lötzen. The Russian First Army troops formed in line, with only two divisions in reserve, thus taking up almost a cordon defense. Rennenkampf placed no cavalry covering force to the front to develop the situation, but he did see that the position was well entrenched.

Zhilinskii expected that, while the First Army held its position, he would rebuild the Second Army, complete the forming of the Tenth, and then resume the offensive. But when General Rudiger Count von der Goltz—commanding three divisions of garrison troops from the Vistula fortress line—seized Mlava

(*lower center*) on 4 September, Zhilinskii jumped to the conclusion that the Germans were about to initiate a drive on Warsaw. Anxious to forestall such a move, he planned to launch an offensive on 14 September, using all three armies. Indeed, the Austrians—in trouble in Galicia—were pleading with the Germans to launch an attack on Warsaw, but Ludendorff was determined to dispose of Rennenkampf first.

Hindenburg finished regrouping by 4 September, and on the following day his advance began. The German plan envisioned an envelopment of the Russian south flank by the I and XVII Corps, the 3 R Division, and the two cavalry divisions (*not shown*)—while the other four corps executed the secondary attack against the main part of Rennenkampf's position to hold him in place. At first glance, it might appear that the secondary attack was too strong. However, Ludendorff was fearful of a Russian attack toward Friedland (*upper center*), and knew that his enveloping force would be beyond supporting distance. Furthermore, maneuver room in the south restricted the number of troops that could be used there. Von der Goltz's force was to prevent any interference by the Russian Second Army.

On 7 September, the 3 R Division seized Bialla (*lower right*), and the following day the capable Francois occupied Arys. On the 9th and 10th, the 3 R Division fought a spirited battle for Lyck, finally driving the Russians toward Augustow (*right center*) and securing the German south flank. Meanwhile, on 8 September, the German XVII Corps, attempting to break out of the Lötzen Gap, was repulsed by the Russian II Corps. In this battle, Rennenkampf committed his entire reserve of two divisions. In the north, the secondary attack was launched against the Russian line on 9 September, but was unable to achieve any gain. This same day, however, Francois' I Corps struck the Russian II Corps a savage blow in flank and rear, causing it to retire in disorder. The way was open now for the enveloping force to strike for Gumbinnen (*upper right*). Rennenkampf, having no reserves, realized the gravity of the situation and ordered a general withdrawal.

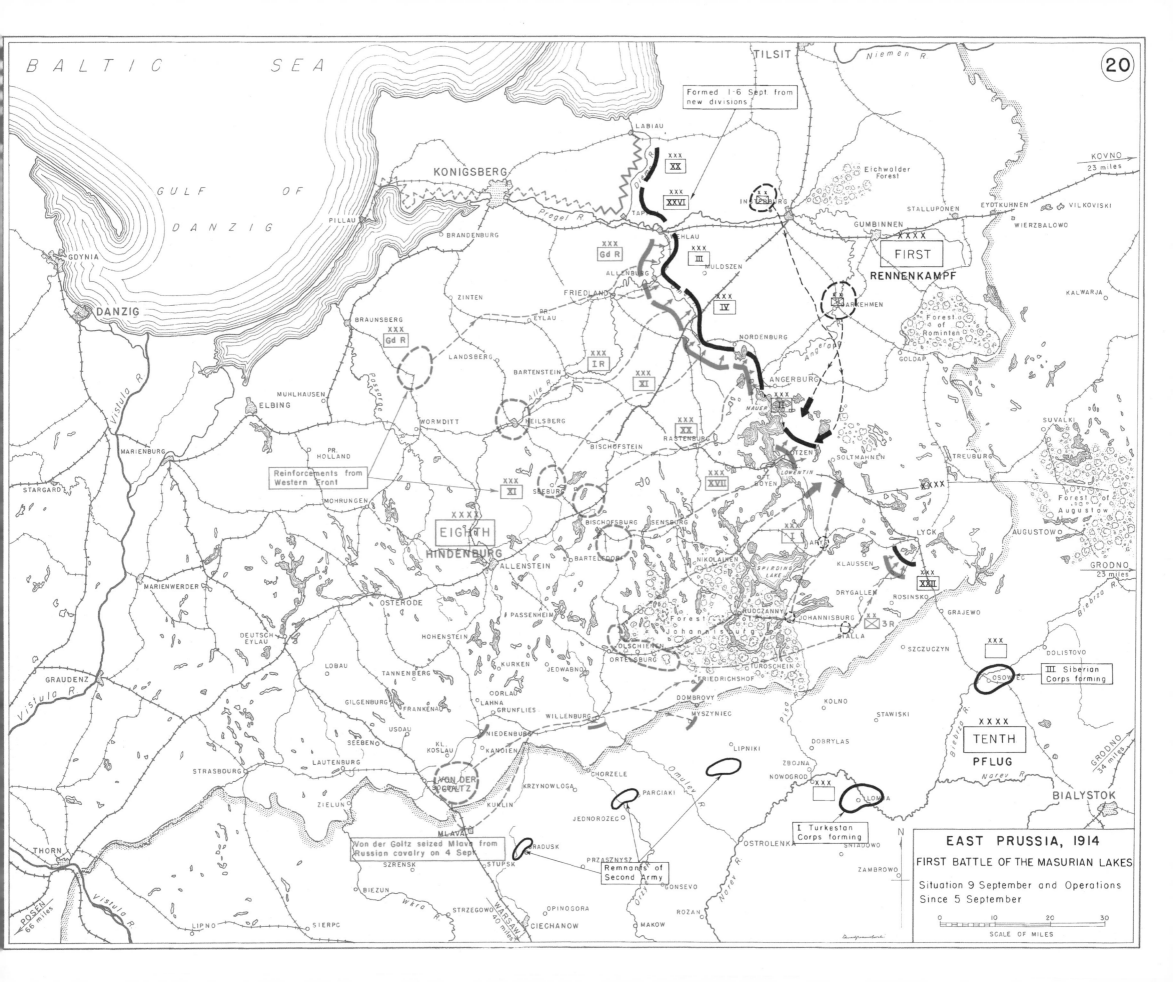

BALTIC SEA

GULF OF DANZIG

KOVNO
23 miles

TILSIT

Niemen R.

20

Formed 1-6 Sept. from
new divisions

LABIAU

KONIGSBERG

XXX
XX

XXX
XXVI

INSTERBURG

Eichwalder
Forest

STALLUPONEN

EYDTKUHNEN

VILKOVISKI

Pregel R.

TAPIAU

WEHLAU

GUMBINNEN

WIERZBALOWO

KALWARJA

PILLAU

BRANDENBURG

XXX
Gd R

XXX
III

MULDSZEN

FIRST

RENNENKAMPF

ZINTEN

ALLENBURG

FRIEDLAND

XXX
IV

XX
GARKEHMEN

Forest
of
Rominten

Angerapp

NORDENBURG

GOLDAP

DANZIG

BRAUNSBERG

PR.
EYLAU

XXX
Gd R

LANDSBERG

BARTENSTEIN

Alle R.

ANGERBURG

XXX
IR

XX
MAUER

GDYNIA

ELBING

MUHLHAUSEN

WORMDITT

HEILSBERG

XXX
XI

BISCHOFSTEIN

RASTENBURG

XXX
XX

LOTZEN
FT.
BOYEN

LOWENTIN

SOLTMAHNEN

TREUBURG

SUVALKI

MARIENBURG

PR.
HOLLAND

Passalge R.

Reinforcements from
Western Front

XXX
XI

SEEBURG

BISCHOFSBURG

XXX
XVII

ARTS

XXXX

GRODNO
23 miles

Forest of
Augustow

STARGARD

MOHRUNGEN

SENSBURG

XXX
I

LYCK

AUGUSTOWO

EIGHTH

HINDENBURG

BARTELSDORF

NIKOLAIKEN

*Spirding
Lake*

KLAUSSEN

XXX
XXII

MARIENWERDER

ALLENSTEIN

DRYGALLEN

ROSINSKO

GRAJEWO

GRODNO
23 miles

OSTERODE

PASSENHEIM

Forest
Johannisburg

RUDCZANNY

JOHANNISBURG

XX
3R

BIALLA

SZCZUCZYN

DOLISTOVO

DEUTSCH
EYLAU

HOHENSTEIN

OLSCHIENEN

ORTELSBURG

TUROSCHEIN

XXX

III Siberian
Corps forming

GRAUDENZ

TANNENBERG

KURKEN

JEDWABNO

FRIEDRICHSHOF

OSOWIEC

Biebza R.

LOBAU

GILGENBURG

FRANKENAU

OORLAU

DOMBROVY

KOLNO

STAWISKI

TENTH

GRUNFLIES

WILLENBURG

MYSZYNIEC

Piso R.

PFLUG

USDAU

NIEDENBURG

LIPNIKI

DOBRYLAS

Narev R.

GRODNO
34 miles

SEEBEN

KL.
KOSLAU

KANDIEN

ZBOJNA

NOWOGROD

XXX

I Turkestan
Corps forming

BIALYSTOK

STRASBOURG

LAUTENBURG

VON DER
GOLTZ

KRZYNOWLOGA

KUKLIN

CHORZELE

Omulev R.

PARCIAKI

JEDNOROZEC

LOMZA

N

EAST PRUSSIA, 1914

FIRST BATTLE OF THE MASURIAN LAKES

THORN

MLAVA

Von der Goltz seized Mlava from
Russian cavalry on 4 Sept.

GRADUSK

STUPSK

PRZASZNYSZ

SNIADOWO

OSTROLENKA

ZAMBROWO

Situation 9 September and Operations
Since 5 September

Wkro R.

POSEN
66 miles

Vistula R.

SZRENSK

ZIELUN

BIEZUN

LIPNO

SIERPC

STRZEGOWO

OPINOGORA

CIECHANOW

Orzy R.

GONSEVO

MAKOW

Narev R.

ROZAN

WARSAW
40 miles

Remnants of
Second Army

0   10   20   30

SCALE OF MILES

Rennenkampf's decision to withdraw his army reflected the desperation of his situation late on 9 September. His left-flank corps, battered and disorganized, was unable to stem the victorious march of the German I and XVII Corps. Francois' troops had covered seventy-seven miles in four days, deploying and fighting on two of them; but, driven and inspired by their fiery leader, they were still capable of exploiting their success. It was his acceptance of the certainty that Francois and Mackensen—marching upon Stallupönen (*upper right*)—could block his retreat and reenact another Tannenberg that caused Rennenkampf to react with a celerity not previously displayed. With the issuance of his orders late on the night of 9 September, the general withdrawal began. Desperately, the Russians moved to the east, divisions marching parallel on either side of a single road, which itself was clogged with the endless columns of transport. Onward they surged, marching all that night, the following day, and the next night; still, they were not out of danger, so eastward they wearily stumbled.

But not all the Russians moved east early on 10 September. Appreciating the necessity for a diversion to gain time, Rennenkampf had ordered a two-division counterattack for the 10th between Nordenburg and Angerburg. The German XX Corps, standing in the path of this attack, reeled backward with heavy losses; by the end of the day, it had been stunned into a state of apathy that persisted for forty-eight hours. Ludendorff became concerned over this German setback, and feared for the exposed right flank of the inexperienced XI Corps: the Russians at Tannenberg had not hesitated to attack, even when hopelessly surrounded; here, with a much better opportunity for success, they might well continue their counterattack. So, sacrificing the likely strategic gain to ensure a tactical success, Ludendorff limited the advance of the I and XVII Corps on 10 September; the following day, expecting a fight near Darkehmen (*upper*

right), he directed them to continue moving north, but by a route west of the Forest of Rominten. Thus, because a shallow envelopment had been substituted for the planned deeper one aimed at Vilkoviski (*upper right*), Rennenkampf was able to extricate much of his army from the trap. In spite of the supreme marching effort (in one fifty-hour period, his troops covered fifty-five miles across country and along roads jammed with traffic), it is doubtful that Rennenkampf could have escaped had Ludendorff not temporarily lost his nerve.

By late on 12 September, Ludendorff appreciated the true state of events, but the opportunity to block the Russian retreat had vanished. There was some rear-guard fighting as late as the 17th, but the German pursuit slackened on the 13th. The last fighting was at Vilkoviski, where Rennenkampf abandoned his rear guard to gain a few more precious hours.

The Russian First Army had escaped, but not without frightful casualties and tremendous loss of morale. In twenty-eight days in East Prussia, Rennenkampf had lost 145,000 men—all but 20,000 of them in this last battle. German losses have been estimated as low as 10,000.

In three weeks, the Hindenburg-Ludendorff team had cleared East Prussia of a superior enemy. With this brilliant triumph in the East, the competent duo had marked themselves for greater responsibilities. Eventually, they were to reach the top of the German command ladder.

Their less fortunate counterpart, Zhilinskii, had continued to issue orders to Rennenkampf as late as the 15th, but that general, having broken contact, never received them. The Germans did, but had no need for them. Zhilinskii poured forth his wrath over his subordinate's deficiencies in wires to supreme headquarters; the reply was notification that General Ruzski—who had been successful in the Galician theater—would take over Zhilinskii's command on the 17th.

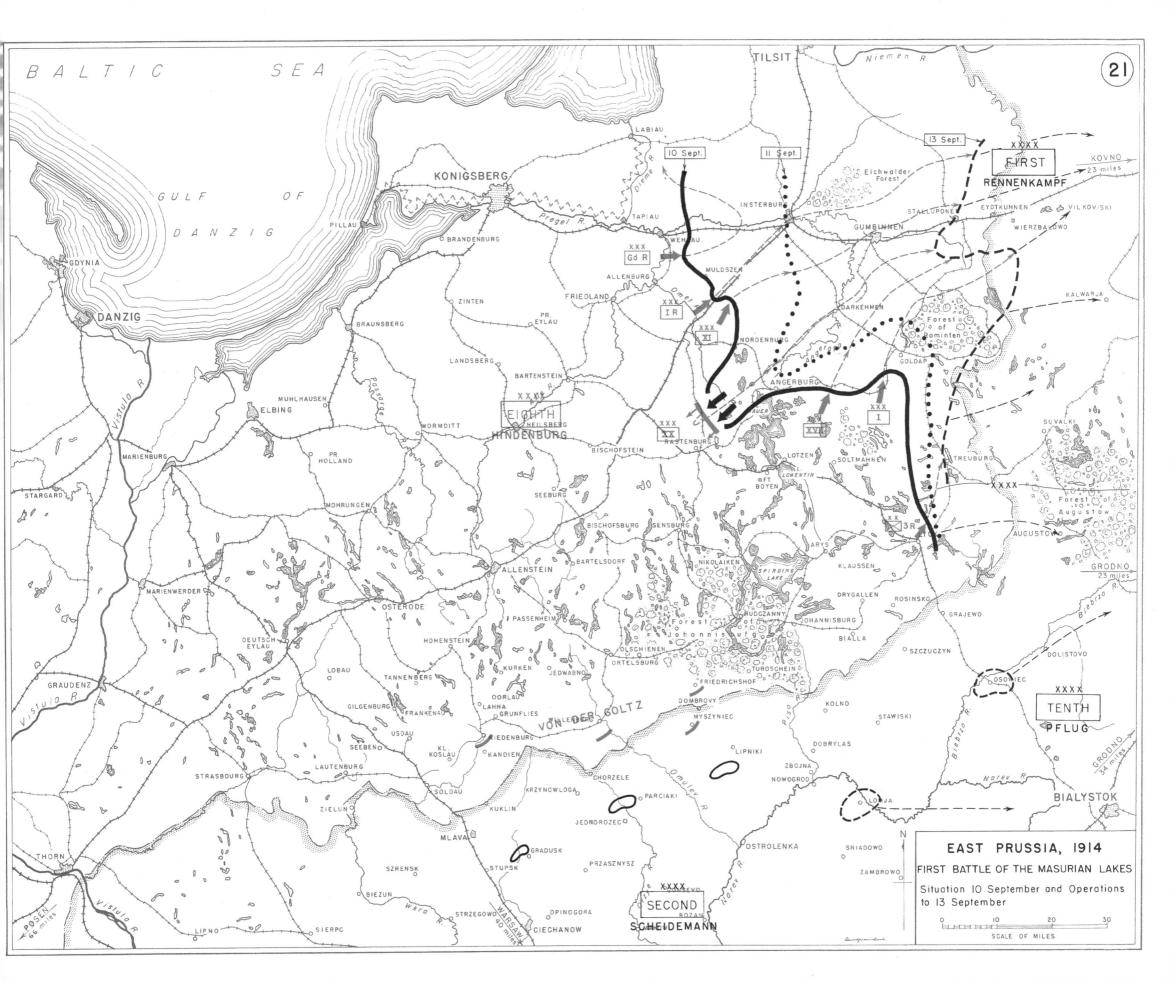

BALTIC SEA

GULF OF DANZIG

TILSIT

Niemen R.

21

KONIGSBERG

10 Sept.

11 Sept.

13 Sept.

XXXX
FIRST
RENNENKAMPF

KOVNO
23 miles

LABIAU

Dieme R.

Pregel R.

TAPIAU

WEHLAU

INSTERBURG

STALLUPONE

EYDTKUHNEN

VILKOVISKI

WIERZBALOWO

GUMBINNEN

Eichwalder Forest

PILLAU

BRANDENBURG

ALLENBURG

XXX
Gd R

FRIEDLAND

MULDSZEN

Omet R.

DARKEHMEN

KALWARJA

ZINTEN

XXX
I R

NORDENBURG

Angerapp R.

Forest of Rominten

GOLDAP

PR. EYLAU

XXX
XI

BRAUNSBERG

LANDSBERG

BARTENSTEIN

ANGERBURG

GRODNO

XXX
I

DANZIG

GDYNIA

Passarge R.

R.

XXXX
EIGHTH
HINDENBURG

HEILSBERG

BISCHOFSTEIN

XXX
XX

RASTENBURG

AUER

XVII

SOLTMAHNEN

TREUBURG

SUVALKI

MARIENBURG

MUHLHAUSEN

ELBING

PR. HOLLAND

WORMDITT

SEEBURG

LOTZEN

L. LOWENTIN

Forest of Augustow

STARGARD

Vistula R.

MOHRUNGEN

OFT BOYEN

XXXX

AUGUSTOW

GRODNO
23 miles

MARIENWERDER

BISCHOFSBURG

SENSBURG

NIKOLAIKEN

SPIRDING LAKE

KLAUSSEN

DRYGALLEN

ROSINSKO

ALLENSTEIN

BARTELSDORF

ARYS

OSTERODE

PASSENHEIM

DEUTSCH EYLAU

HOHENSTEIN

KURKEN

JEDWABNO

OLSCHIENEN

ORTELSBURG

Forest of Johannisburg

RUDCZANNY

TUROSCHEIN

JOHANNISBURG

BIALLA

SZCZUCZYN

DOLISTOVO

GRAUDENZ

Vistula R.

LOBAU

TANNENBERG

OORLAU

LAHNA

GRUNFLIES

FRIEDRICHSHOF

DOMBROVY

KOLNO

STAWISKI

OSOWIEC

GRAJEWO

Biebrza R.

XXXX
TENTH
PFLUG

FRANKENAU

USDAU

VON DER GOLTZ

MYSZYNIEC

DOBRYLAS

Pisa R.

GRODNO
34 miles

SEEBENO

KL. KOSLAU

KANDIEN

NIEDENBURG

LIPNIKI

ZBOJNA

NOWOGROD

Narev R.

BIALYSTOK

STRASBOURG

LAUTENBURG

SOLDAU

CHORZELE

KRZYNOWLOGA

PARCIAKI

Omulev R.

LOMJA

ZIELUN

KUKLIN

JEDNOROZEC

OSTROLENKA

SNIADOWO

MLAVA

GRADUSK

PRZASZNYSZ

N

POSEN
66 miles

Vistula R.

THORN

STUPSK

SZRENSK

BIEZUN

LIPNO

SIERPC

Wkra R.

STRZEGOWO

OPINOGORA

CIECHANOW

ZAMBROWO

ROZAN

Narev R.

XXXX
SECOND
SCHEIDEMANN

WARSAW
40 miles

XX
3R

EAST PRUSSIA, 1914
FIRST BATTLE OF THE MASURIAN LAKES

Situation 10 September and Operations
to 13 September

0   10   20   30
SCALE OF MILES

While Zhilinskii's armies were suffering disastrous defeat in East Prussia, the main Russian forces were engaged with the Austrians in a massive struggle along a 200-mile front in Galicia. (In this series of maps, the situation in East Prussia is repeated, so that the reader can view the Eastern Front as a whole.)

It will be recalled that Austria had two war plans (*see text, map 3*) which differed only in one respect: in Plan B the Second Army would operate against Serbia, whereas in Plan R it would operate against Russia. On 25 July, General Conrad von Hotzendorff, the Austrian chief of staff, placed Plan B into effect; a week later, when Russia declared war, he suddenly shifted to Plan R. The Second Army, moving south to Serbia under Plan B, had to complete the movement and then reverse its course. As a result, it entered the first Galician Battles too late to play a significant role—and then only in part—for unexpected events in Serbia had forced Conrad to leave half of the army on that front.

Conrad had been urged by the Germans into immediate offensive action against the Russians to keep them occupied until a German victory could be achieved in France. He was further spurred to this line of action because his Serbian venture (*see map 46*) had been a failure, the Germans in East Prussia were retreating (at that time), the Balkan states were restive, and Russia was building up strength. His plan was based on the incorrect assumption that the main Russian forces would concentrate in the Lublin-Kholm area (*this map; center, right*). His First and Fourth Armies would advance in that direction, while the Third would remain on the defensive from Lemberg (*lower right*) south. Meanwhile, Woyrsch's German detachment and the Austrian Kummer and Kovess Groups would protect the flanks.

Oddly enough, the Russian plan was based on a similar misconception. General Ivanov expected the Austrians to make their major drive eastward from the Lemberg area; he therefore directed his main attack (Third and Eighth Armies) against that front, while the Fourth and Fifth Armies were to come down from the north across the Austrian communications.

The Russian cavalry was used to fill the gaps between their armies; Conrad dissipated his in a futile reconnaissance of the entire frontier. Consequently, the meetings of the opposing forces were more in the nature of collisions than planned engagements. The first encounter occurred on 23 August, when the Austrian First and Russian Fourth Armies ran into each other at Krasnik After three days of fighting, the Russians—outnumbered three to two, and enveloped on their right flank—were forced back seven miles. Ivanov relieved General Salza for mismanaging the battle, and replaced him with General Ewarth. Still unaware that the Austrian main attack was in the north, Ivanov ordered the Ninth Army (then forming) to reinforce the Fourth with a corps, and directed his Fifth Army to wheel to the right and strike the Austrian First Army in flank.

On the 26th, two entirely new battles began. Conrad, elated over the success at Krasnik, urged his Fourth Army forward, reinforcing it with a corps from the Third. Then, completely unaware of the Russian main advance toward Lemberg, he authorized his Third Army to strike offensively to the east. The Third soon stumbled into the Russian main attack beyond the Gnila Lipa River (*lower right*). Outnumbered three to one, it was driven back in confusion. By 1 September, it had retreated to the line shown; the following day, the Lemberg fortress fell, and the Austrians were forced back another twenty miles. Meanwhile, the Austrian Fourth Army collided with the Russian Fifth at Komarov while the Fifth was executing its wheel. Four days of confused fighting ensued. The Austrians began to achieve success in enveloping both Russian flanks, while General Plehve persisted stolidly in his right turn. On the 30th, perceiving his danger, Plehve decided to withdraw. On the 31st, just as a stunning Austrian victory was in sight, the two enveloping Austrian corps halted—because of rumors of danger to their flanks—and the Russians escaped.

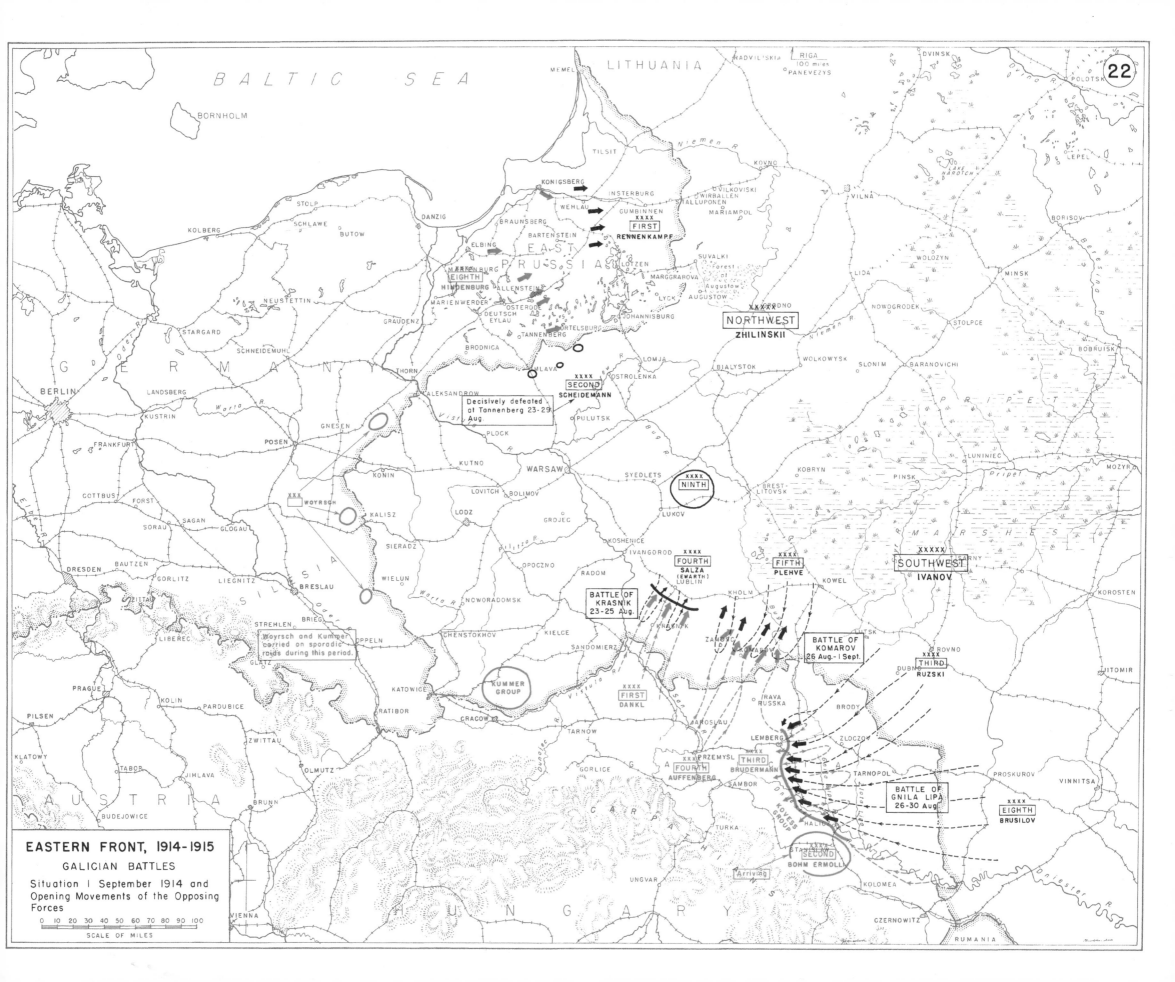

EASTERN FRONT, 1914-1915

GALICIAN BATTLES

Situation 1 September 1914 and
Opening Movements of the Opposing
Forces

0 10 20 30 40 50 60 70 80 90 100
SCALE OF MILES

BALTIC SEA

LITHUANIA

BORNHOLM

GERMANY

EAST PRUSSIA

Decisively defeated
at Tannenberg 23-29
Aug.

NORTHWEST
ZHILINSKII

XXXX
FIRST
RENNENKAMPF

XXXX
SECOND
SCHEIDEMANN

EIGHTH
HINDENBURG

XXX
WOYRSCH

XXXX
NINTH

Woyrsch and Kummer
carried on sporadic
raids during this period.

KUMMER
GROUP

XXXX
FIRST
DANKL

XXXX
FOURTH
SALZA
(EWARTH)
LUBLIN

XXXX
FIFTH
PLEHVE

SOUTHWEST
IVANOV

BATTLE OF
KRASNIK
23-25 Aug.

BATTLE OF
KOMAROV
26 Aug.- 1 Sept.

XXXX
THIRD
RUZSKI

XXX
FOURTH
AUFFENBERG

XXX PRZEMYSL

THIRD
BRUDERMANN

KOVESS
GROUP

BATTLE OF
GNILA LIPA
26-30 Aug.

XXXX
EIGHTH
BRUSILOV

XXXX
SECOND
BÖHM ERMOLL

Arriving

AUSTRIA

HUNGARY

RUMANIA

On 1 September, Conrad was confronted with a momentous decision. True, his armies in the north had defeated the Russian Fourth and Fifth Armies, but they had not destroyed either of them. In the south, his weak Third Army had been routed, and the strong Russian Third and Eighth Armies were even now beginning to veer to the northwest—actually, to support Plehve, but, in Conrad's mind, to cut off his First and Fourth Armies. In view of the troop dispositions and the Russian preponderance of force, a general withdrawal and consolidation were indicated; but Conrad boldly, if not desperately or rashly, decided to renew the offensive—this time, in the Lemberg area. Believing Plehve's Fifth Army to be disorganized and now an insignificant threat, he directed his Fourth Army to discontinue the pursuit, turn 180 degrees, and advance so as to strike the right flank of the Russian Third Army. His Second Army was to envelop the Russian Eighth Army's south flank.

The Russians, meanwhile, had revived the plan they had originally wanted to adopt—to advance from the north across the Austrian communications. Their Ninth Army had been advancing south along the Vistula and was coming abreast of the Fourth at Krasnik. The Fifth Army had escaped encirclement, but it seemed to need help. Accordingly, the westward drive of the Third and Eighth Armies had been turned northwest to aid Plehve. Thus, for the second time, the plans of the opposing forces tended to be similar, but now with the main efforts reversed.

The Austrian Fourth and Russian Third Armies collided on 3 September as they moved to execute their new plans. Both commanders were confused, but eventually the Austrian Fourth wheeled into line as shown. In so doing, it opened a forty-mile gap which offered Plehve clear passage to the Austrian rear. Meanwhile, the Austrian Second Army, tired and disorganized by many days of entraining and detraining, had made little progress in the attempted envelopment of the Russian south flank. Such was the situation on 8 September.

On the 9th, the forces in the Lemberg area were locked in bitter struggle. To the north, the Austrian First Army began to give ground before the combined strength of the Russian Ninth and Fourth. Plehve moved forward into the yawning gap, pushing before him the small Fourth Army rear guard. Conrad remained undaunted and ordered another attack on the 10th against the Russian Third and Eighth Armies; but Austrian strength had been sapped, and his orders were ignored. On the 11th, intercepted Russian radio messages announced Plehve's destination for that date to be a small town some twenty miles west of Rava Russka (*lower right*). Conrad now ordered a general withdrawal which soon got out of hand and continued for 100 miles (*dashed red line, dated 26 September*).

Thus, by 11 September, the Russians had gained a stupendous victory in Galicia. In East Prussia, however, they were in mass flight—and, significantly, by this same date the Germans had suffered defeat at the Marne. The Galician Battles cost the Austrians 350,000 casualties—over two-thirds of their Galician front forces. The number of Russian casualties is not accurately known, but they certainly were not light. Most important, however, the battle took a terrific toll of the Teutonic cadre, the backbone of the heterogeneous Austrian Army. Conrad would now need German troop support—a drain Germany could ill afford.

In view of the disastrous Austrian defeat and the consequent opening of a clear road to Silesia (*lower left*) for the Russians, Germany was compelled to rush troops to bolster the Austrian defenses. Falkenhayn refused to transfer troops from the West, so Hindenburg formed the Ninth Army from four of the six corps in East Prussia. This army, led by Hindenburg and Ludendorff, began its journey from East Prussia by rail on 17 September. After a remarkable eleven-day movement, involving 750 trains, it was concentrated in the area shown, ready to engage the southern Russian armies.

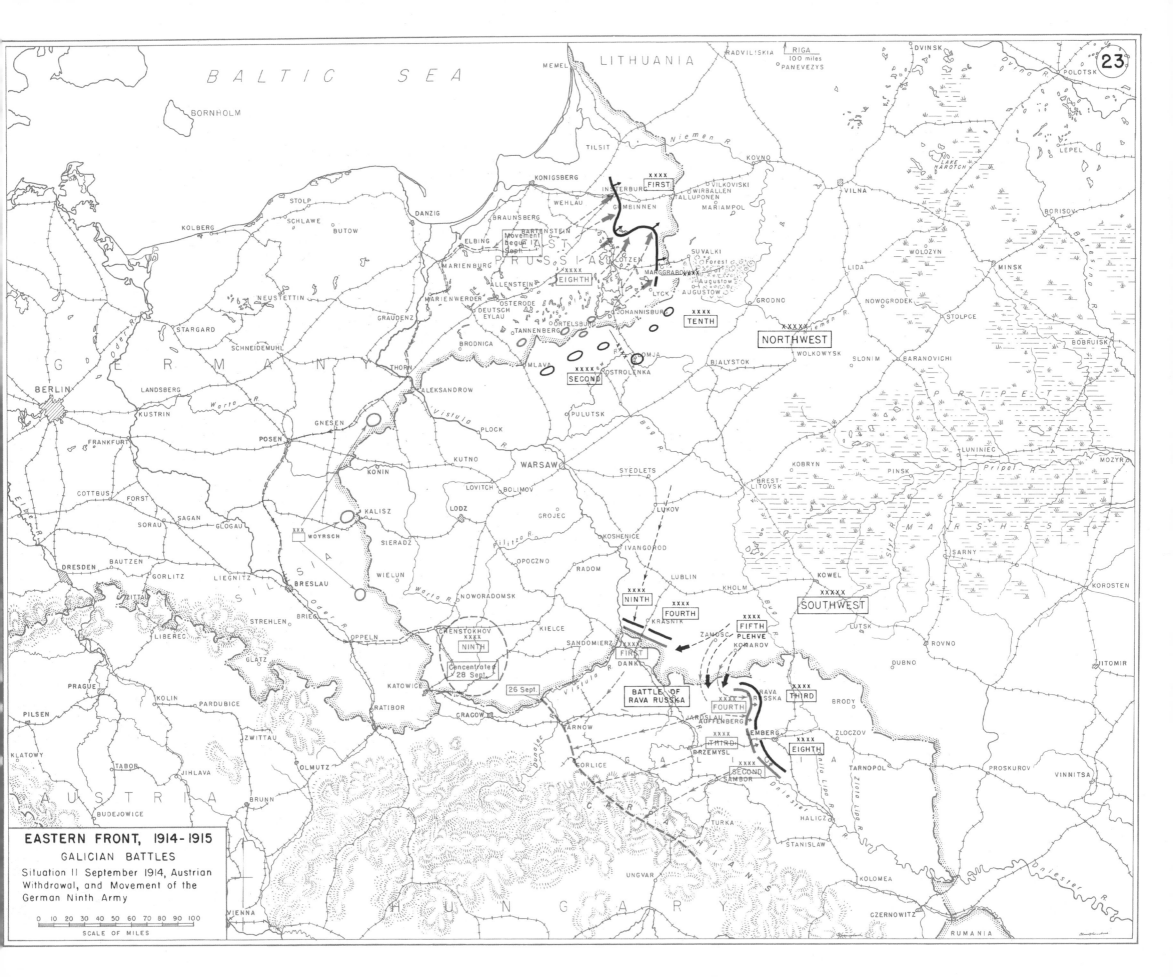

EASTERN FRONT, 1914-1915

GALICIAN BATTLES

Situation II September 1914, Austrian
Withdrawal, and Movement of the
German Ninth Army

0 10 20 30 40 50 60 70 80 90 100
SCALE OF MILES

By 28 September, Hindenburg had the newly formed Ninth Army in position on the Austrian north flank. The critical situation of the Austrians and the Russian threat to Cracow (*lower center*), one of the gateways to Silesia, dictated immediate offensive action. The German Ninth and Austrian First Armies were to close to the Vistula (*center*), seize crossings, and then advance on Warsaw. The three southern Austrian armies were to close to the San River (*center*) and raise the siege of Przemysl, which had not surrendered during the Russian advance. The weakened German Eighth Army was to defend the East Prussian border.

Meanwhile, in mid-September, the French again besought the Russians to invade Silesia via the Warsaw-Posen route. This entreaty—coupled with the worsening logistical situation in Galicia and Russian fear of a German advance from East Prussia against the ever-extending flank in Galicia—led the Stavka (Russian supreme headquarters) to order a regroupment of the Russian armies. The Fifth, Fourth, and Ninth Armies were to move north on 23 September to a line along the Vistula from Warsaw south to Sandomierz (*dashed blue line*). (On 23 September, the Russians were located just east of the dashed red line, dated 26 September, on map 23.) Thereafter, the Northwest Army Group (four armies—the Tenth, First, Second, and Fifth) would defend along the Vistula–Narew River line (*center*) to protect against invasion from East Prussia, while the Southwest Army Group moved into Silesia. This massive defense against invasion from East Prussia clearly indicates that the Russians were unaware of the southward movement of the German Ninth Army and of the actual weakness of the East Prussian defenses.

On 28 September—while the Russian Fifth, Fourth, and Ninth Armies were moving northward—Hindenburg struck. His advance was slow and deliberate; excellent communications were constructed, and key defiles prepared for demolition, in the event that a swift withdrawal became necessary. By the 30th, the Russians at last became aware of the presence of the German Ninth Army. Now, as they delayed the German-Austrian advance, the Russians prepared a trap.

The First and Second Armies were to concentrate at Warsaw, prepared to execute a massive envelopment of the German north flank once it reached the Vistula.

By 9 October, the Ninth Army had reached the Vistula. Here, a captured Russian order, added to information gained from the babbling Russian radio, gave Hindenburg a clear picture of his danger and of the great odds he faced. Nevertheless, the Germans pressed on and, by the 12th, were only twelve miles from Warsaw. But Russian pressure on the north flank became increasingly grave, while Austrian cooperation degenerated. On 17 October, Hindenburg began a general withdrawal from the line then held (*dashed red line*); by 1 November, the Germans and Austrians were back to their starting line (*solid red line*). The Russians promptly followed and—though delayed by German demolitions and other measures of an efficiently executed retrograde movement—reached the line shown by 1 November.

Now the Russians planned to drive straight west into Silesia with the Second, Fifth, Fourth, and Ninth Armies, while the First Army protected the north flank. Silesia's mineral resources and industrial facilities were vital to the German war effort. The Russian offensive must be stopped; the only large force available was the Ninth Army. With knowledge of Russian movements gained from intercepted radio dispatches, and being familiar with the characteristic slow rate of Russian advance, the Germans calculated that they could move the Ninth Army over the excellent rail net to the Posen-Thorn area (*inset sketch*) in time to attack the Russian First and Second Armies. Conrad would launch a secondary attack in the south.

On 4 November, the Ninth Army began its movement north in complete secrecy; by the 10th, it had filled the gap previously occupied only by border troops, and was in position to attack. Meanwhile, it had been reinforced with additional troops from East Prussia. Elements of the Austrian Second Army and fortress troops were moved into the void left by the Ninth Army's movement.

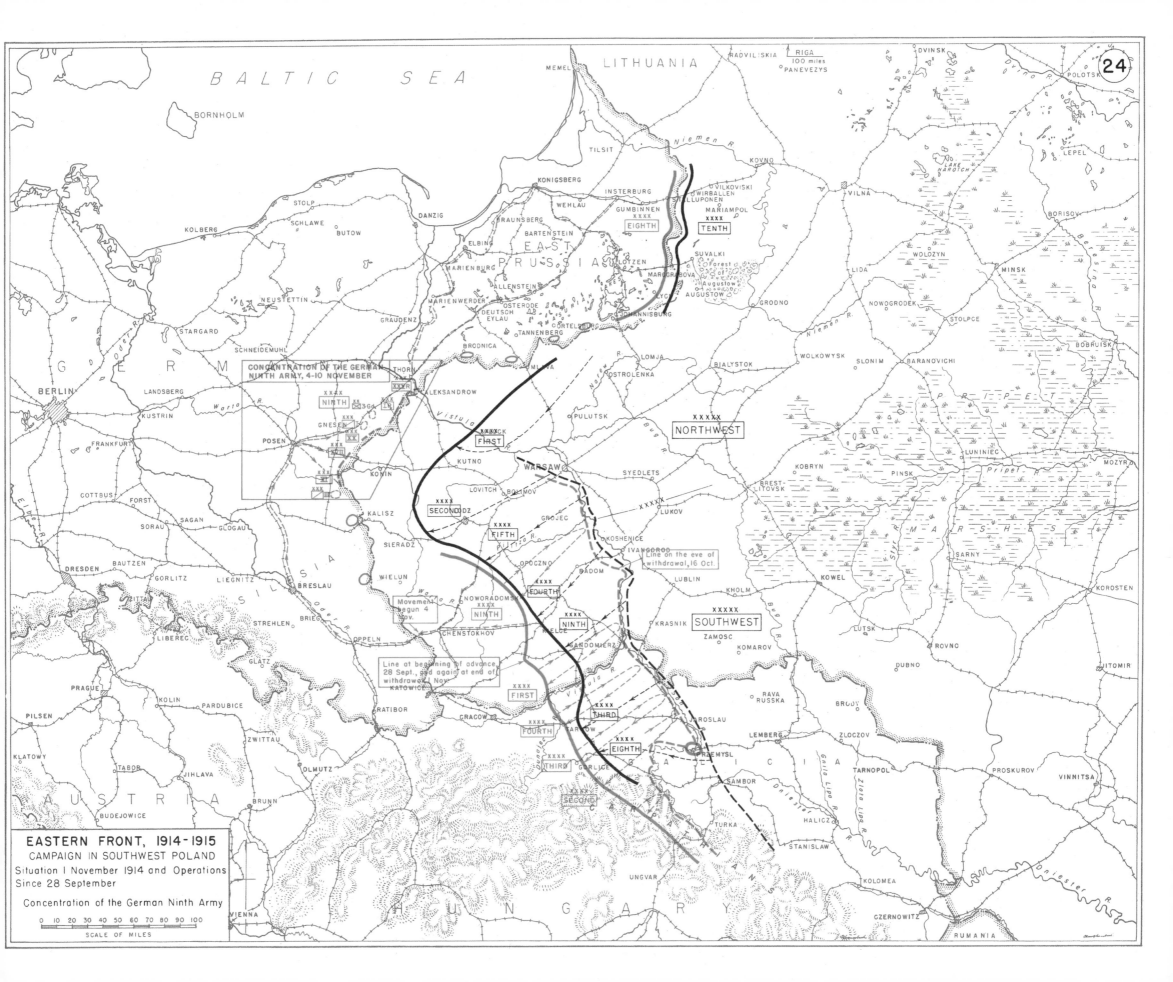

EASTERN FRONT, 1914-1915
CAMPAIGN IN SOUTHWEST POLAND
Situation 1 November 1914 and Operations
Since 28 September

Concentration of the German Ninth Army

0 10 20 30 40 50 60 70 80 90 100
SCALE OF MILES

CONCENTRATION OF THE GERMAN
NINTH ARMY, 4-10 NOVEMBER

NORTHWEST

SOUTHWEST

Line on the eve of
withdrawal, 16 Oct.

Line at beginning of advance,
28 Sept., and again at end of
withdrawal, 1 Nov.

Movement
begun 4 Nov.

RIGA
100 miles

On 10 November, the German Ninth Army—now under Mackensen, Hindenburg-Ludendorff having been elevated to the command of all German forces in the East—prepared to attack the next day. On the same day, Falkenhayn, anticipating early victory over the British at Ypres in the West, promised to send four corps to the East in about ten days. This posed a problem for Hindenburg: should the Ninth Army attack on the 11th, as planned, or should the attack be delayed until the four corps arrived? The temptation to postpone the offensive was great, but Hindenburg was convinced that the Russians would advance into Silesia by the 22d, and was fully cognizant of the uncertainties of war. He decided to attack on the 11th. His decision was correct, for the four promised corps arrived late and piecemeal.

The initial advance of the Ninth Army achieved great success (*sketch* a). Rennenkampf, still commanding the First Army and performing as lackadaisically as he had in East Prussia, had two corps widely dispersed between the Vistula and the Bzura (*center, dashed blue symbols*). The advanced V Siberian Corps (*map symbol:* V S) was defeated and forced back as shown on 12 November. The II Corps met a like fate two days later and withdrew to Kutno (*center*). In four days, the Germans had advanced fifty miles over poor roads. Mackensen maintained pressure on the II Corps and, by the 16th, had routed and sent it fleeing eastward. Meanwhile, the German XI Corps had overwhelmed the Russian XXIII Corps of the Second Army. The Russian II S and IV Corps moved north, but were turned back. By the night of the 16th, Mackensen had achieved his initial goal—a penetration between the First and Second Armies.

The Russian drive into Silesia had started on 14 November, as planned. It was not until the 16th that the plight of the two northern armies became clear to the Stavka. Then the Silesian offensive was halted, the Fifth Army ordered north to aid the Second, and a counterattack force ordered concentrated at Lovitch (*right center*) for movement southwest against the German flank.

Mackensen proceeded to exploit the penetration and encircle the Second Army. The XXV R Corps—with the 3d Guards Division attached—and the I Cavalry Corps were to move southeast to Lódz (*lower right*), then swing westward; simultaneously, the III Cavalry Corps and the Posen and Breslau "Corps" (three Landwehr brigades each) were to attack eastward. The XI, XVII, and XX Corps would continue their attacks to pin down Second Army units, while the I R Corps blocked any relief attempt by the First Army.

The German plan failed, for the Russian reaction was surprisingly quick (*sketch* b). The Russian Fifth Army moved north—two of its corps marching seventy miles in forty-eight hours—and stopped Mackensen's right on the 19th, actually pushing it back somewhat. General Scheffer's XXV R Corps got around the Russian right, but the V Corps assailed it from the south while the Lovitch Force, after forcing the XX Corps to pull back its flank, moved down on Scheffer's rear. The predicament of the XXV R Corps was indeed perilous, and the confident Russians had already ordered trains from Warsaw to carry prisoners. But the indomitable Scheffer—calm, fearless, and inspiring—kept his troops in hand and withdrew in the bitter cold to Karpin (*lower right*). Turning north, he collided with the crack 6th Siberian Division of the Lovitch Force along the Koluszki-Lódz railroad late on the 23d. That night, the heroic 3d Guards Division pushed through to Brzeziny, the corps' objective, and the next day the XXV R Corps attacked and practically destroyed the 6th Siberian Division. The Lovitch Force, threatened from two sides, withdrew; the XXV R Corps and the cavalry moved into position between the I R and XX Corps. Scheffer, in his remarkable exploit, had brought back 16,000 prisoners and 64 guns, and had suffered only 4,300 casualties.

The battle completely stopped the Russian invasion of Silesia. On 6 December, the Russians evacuated Lódz and rearranged their line south of Warsaw (*see map 26*). The Germans, now reinforced, closed up to the new line. Tactically, Hindenburg-Ludendorff had failed, but strategically, they had been highly successful.

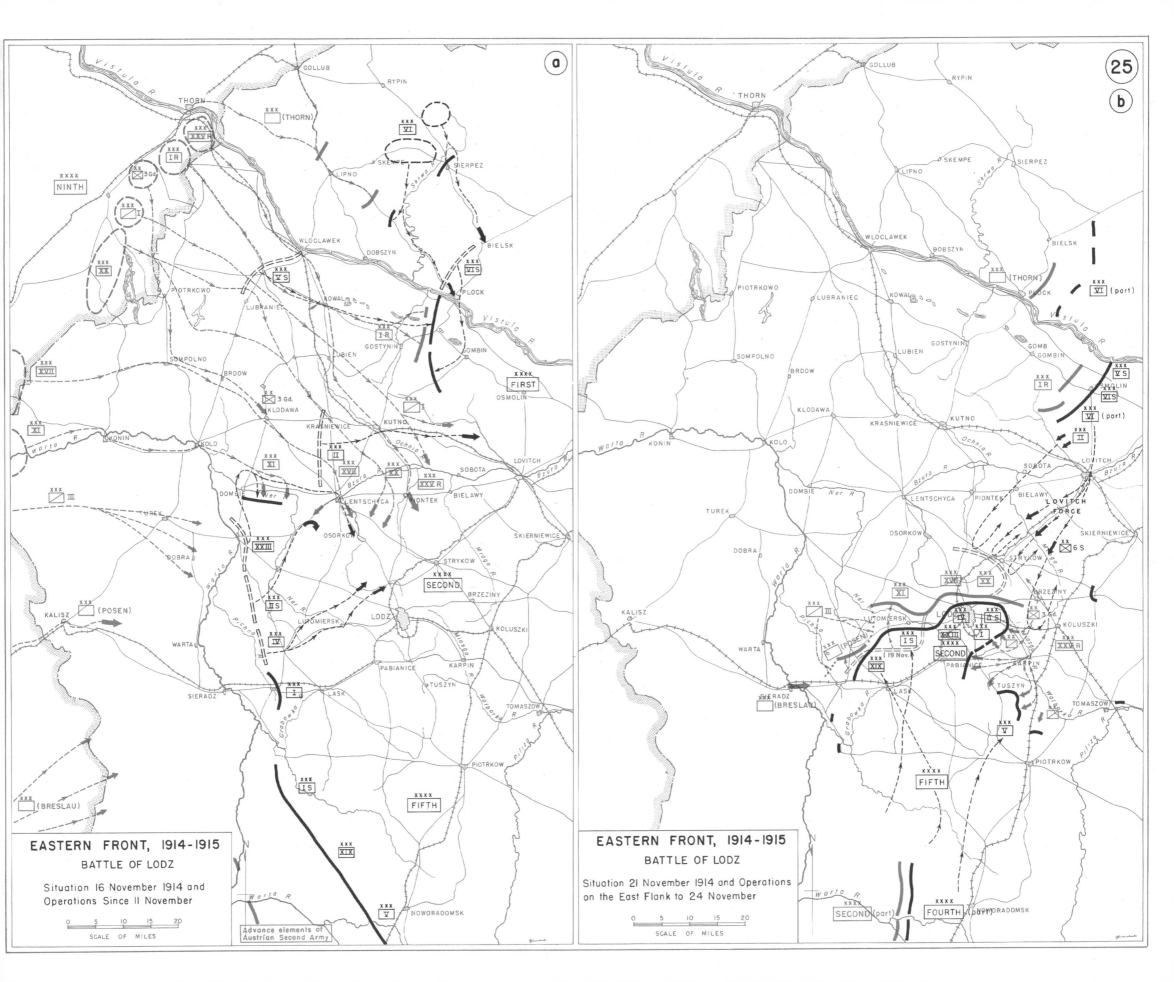

(a)

EASTERN FRONT, 1914-1915

BATTLE OF LODZ

Situation 16 November 1914 and
Operations Since 11 November

SCALE OF MILES
0   5   10   15   20

Advance elements of
Austrian Second Army

(b) 25

EASTERN FRONT, 1914-1915

BATTLE OF LODZ

Situation 21 November 1914 and Operations
on the East Flank to 24 November

SCALE OF MILES
0   5   10   15   20

Most of January, 1915, was spent by the German high command in evolving a new strategy. In the West, modern weapons, coupled with field fortifications, had given the defensive ascendancy over the offensive, and a stalemate had developed. In the East, Russian offensive designs had been frustrated, but—given time—another attack could be expected. Falkenhayn maintained that the war could not be won in the East, that Britain was the prime enemy, and that four new corps raised in Germany should go to France. Hindenburg-Ludendorff, supported by Conrad, professed an ability to cripple seriously, perhaps eliminate, Russia. Furthermore, they argued, some of the Balkan states—and Italy—might join the Allies unless a decisive success were gained in the East. Both Austria and Turkey (a recent addition to the Central Powers) were shaky and needed moral support. Thus the argument raged, with the Kaiser finally siding with Hindenburg-Ludendorff. On 8 January, he agreed to a Carpathian offensive by the Austrians, who were to be stiffened with German troops (*not shown*). Falkenhayn exacted a measure of revenge by sending Ludendorff to the Austrian front. But his victory was short-lived, for Hindenburg—indignant and exerting his great prestige—pressed for a concurrent East Prussian offensive and the restoration of Ludendorff as his chief of staff. By mid-January, he had won his points—and the four new corps as well. Falkenhayn, bitter over the Kaiser's second rebuff, sulked in Berlin, secure in his belief that the gigantic double envelopment—from the Carpathians and East Prussia—would be a failure.

The Russians were under no illusions as to their offensive capabilities. Many of their troops were without rifles, and there was a shortage of ammunition and artillery. The Stavka was content with plans for limited spring offensives on the flanks. The Twelfth Army was being formed to participate in a drive to sever East Prussia from Germany. It was hoped that a limited attack in the Carpathians would secure Rumania's allegiance and weaken Austria's position.

The Austrian offensive was a dismal failure. Even though stiffened with German troops, Conrad's forces—lacking inspiration and the desire to fight—achieved no success. In March, the starved-out Przemysl fortress surrendered. There, Conrad lost 100,000 men and 1,000 guns—and another Russian army was freed for active operations.

Hindenburg-Ludendorff, however, had expected that the decisive victory would have to be won in East Prussia. The enemy Tenth Army was their immediate objective, but severance of the Warsaw-Vilna line of communications (*center to upper right*) was the ultimate goal. The plan envisioned a double envelopment of the Russian Tenth Army by the Eighth Army and the newly formed German Tenth Army, with the last-named making the main attack. To protect the Eighth Army's flank, Mackensen moved the XX Corps to Mlava, and covered the movement with a diversionary attack at Bolimov (*center*) on 31 January—remarkable chiefly for the first (and unsuccessful) use of tear-gas shells in quantity (18,000). On 7 February, in a blinding snowstorm, the Eighth Army attacked. The Russians were unaware of the existence of the German Tenth Army; nor did they expect an attack in such miserable weather. The Eighth Army drive drew their attention southward. As a result, when the Tenth Army moved forward on 8 February, its attack was immediately successful. The map shows the progress of the offensive in which the Russians, fighting bitterly, were gradually forced back to the Forest of Augustow. Here, the heroic resistance of the Russian XX Corps enabled the other three Russian corps to escape encirclement. Exhausted and decimated, the XX Corps surrendered on 21 February.

In this battle, Russia suffered 200,000 casualties, half of them prisoners. German combat losses were light, but some units had 30 per cent of their personnel disabled by exposure. Again, the Germans had achieved a great tactical victory, but strategic gains were meager. Falkenhayn's prediction had come true.

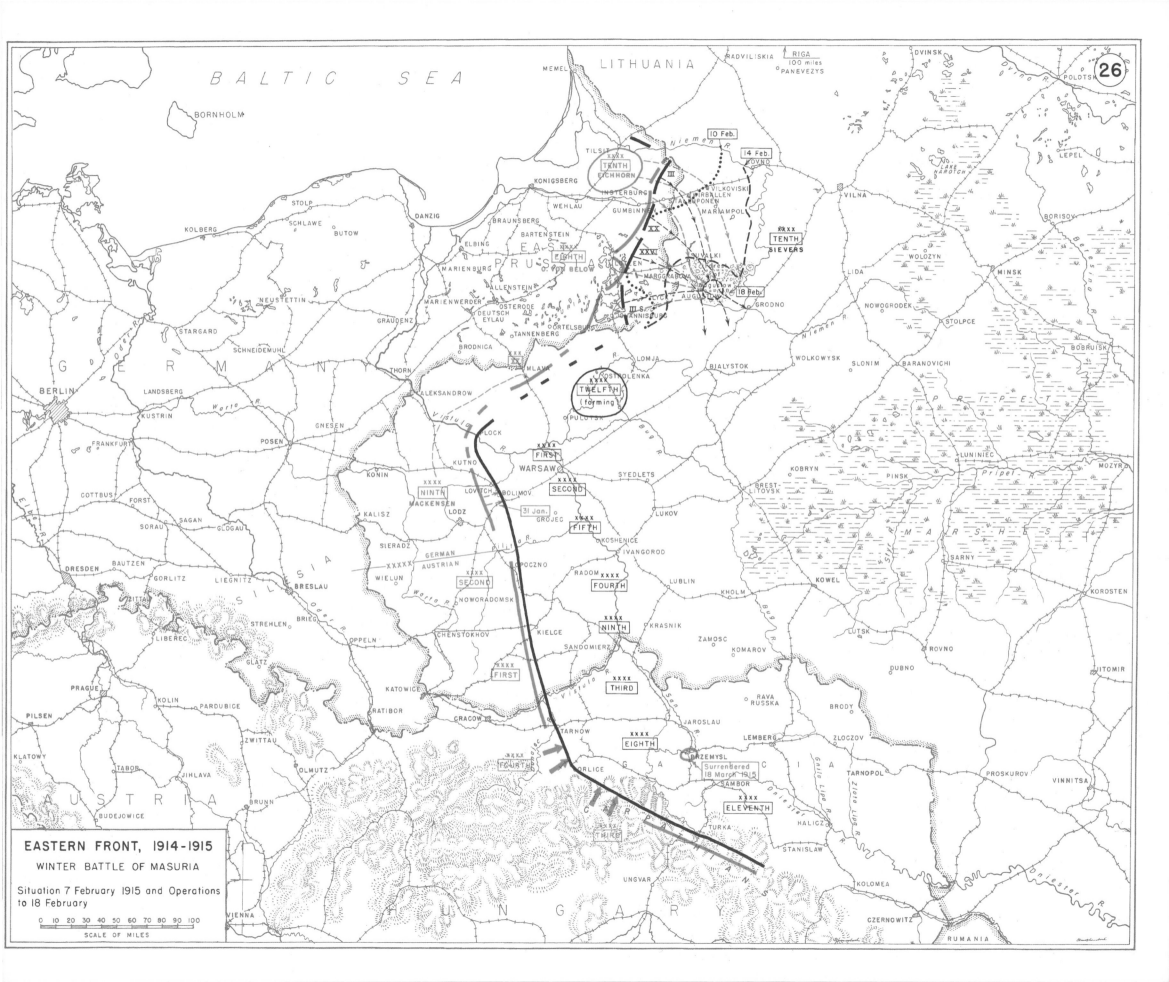

26

EASTERN FRONT, 1914-1915

WINTER BATTLE OF MASURIA

Situation 7 February 1915 and Operations
to 18 February

0 10 20 30 40 50 60 70 80 90 100

SCALE OF MILES

LITHUANIA

BALTIC SEA

RIGA
100 miles

TENTH
EICHHORN

EIGHTH
V. VON BELOW

TENTH
SIEVERS

TWELFTH
(forming)

FIRST

NINTH
MACKENSEN

SECOND

FIFTH

FOURTH

NINTH

FIRST

THIRD

EIGHTH

ELEVENTH

FOURTH

THIRD

SECOND

GERMAN
AUSTRIAN

PRZEMYSL
Surrendered
18 March 1915

GALICIA

CARPATHIAN

GERMANY

AUSTRIA

HUNGARY

RUMANIA

BERLIN

WARSAW

BRESLAU

DRESDEN

PRAGUE

VIENNA

10 Feb.

14 Feb.

18 Feb.

31 Jan.

By March, 1915, the equipment, training, and logistical support of the Russian armies had still not improved enough to allow a major offensive. The idea of an attack on East Prussia was given up, but preparations were made for a limited offensive in the Carpathians. In late March, the Eighth Army and part of the Third pushed forward (*action not shown*) in an attempt to reach the Hungarian plains. The fighting was severe, and gains were slight; on 18 April, the attack was stopped to await replacements and ammunition. It was never renewed, for on 2 May, Mackensen delivered a pulverizing blow at Gorlice-Tarnow (*lower center*).

Before tracing the course of the fighting in the next five months, the strategy of the Central Powers should be examined. In April, Germany had formed a new army (the Eleventh) by withdrawing infantry and artillery units from existing divisions on the Western Front. Falkenhayn proposed to use it in France, but he realized the precarious position of the Austrians (the Russians seemed capable of driving into Hungary in the summer), the need for subduing Serbia, and the importance of opening communications with Turkey. The decision, then, was to employ the army in the East—but where? Falkenhayn preferred Serbia; Hindenburg—commanding the front north of the Austrian First Army—advocated a penetration near Kovno (*upper center*) in the north, followed by an envelopment southward; Conrad—commanding the front to the south—wanted a penetration near Tarnow (*lower center*). Falkenhayn, who had little authority over the Austrians, eventually agreed with Conrad.

To divert Russian attention from the south, Hindenburg mounted a small attack (*not shown*) in Lithuania (*top center*) at the end of April, successfully luring considerable Russian strength north, but eventually using so many troops that they were later organized into the Niemen Army. To cover the transfer of the Eleventh Army to the East, Germany launched an attack at Ypres (*see map 32*) on 22 April. In the Gorlice-Tarnow sector (*this map*), every precaution was taken to maintain secrecy while the Germans built up a tremendous logistical base and massed 950 artillery pieces.

At 0600, 2 May, Mackensen struck behind a terrific artillery preparation. The Russian Third Army was completely surprised: there had been some reports of the Germans and Austrians concentrating, but these had been ignored. Russian troops, crazed and panic-stricken, fled blindly to the rear. The juggernaut of the German Eleventh and Austrian Fourth armies—well organized and controlled to perfection—rolled on, achieving a complete breakthrough by 4 May. The Russian Third Army had ceased to exist; Mackensen's advancing armies had captured 120,000 prisoners. The Russians now withdrew on the southern front. On 3 June, a strategy council was convened by Falkenhayn. Italy had entered the war on 24 May, and Conrad argued for the transfer of Austrian troops to that front; Falkenhayn, worried over Allied attacks in the West, considered sending some German troops there; Hindenburg wanted to execute a gigantic double envelopment of the entire Eastern Front. But the failure, so far, to cripple Russia seriously, and fear of Conrad's inability to stabilize the front if Germans were withdrawn, dictated a continuance of the current offensive.

Mackensen, reinforced with the newly created German Bug Army and the Austrian Third, continued his drive, taking Lemberg on 22 June. An inviting salient, with Warsaw in the center, now existed; Falkenhayn resolved to attack it concurrently from north and south. Mackensen turned north, aiming for Brest-Litovsk (*center, right*), and the German Twelfth Army attacked toward Warsaw on 13 July. To the credit of the Stavka, there were no large-scale encirclements of Russians as the retreat was accelerated. The salient was eliminated by 15 August, and two weeks later Mackensen took Brest Litovsk. By 30 September, the Russians had fallen back to the line shown. Most of the fighting during this month was on the flanks: Hindenburg tried unsuccessfully to take Riga and Dvinsk (*top right*), and Conrad failed to take Rovno (*lower right*).

The campaign cost Russia upward of 2,000,000 casualties, half of them prisoners. Grand Duke Nicholas, a fine soldier, was relieved, and the Tsar himself assumed command—a boon to the Germans.

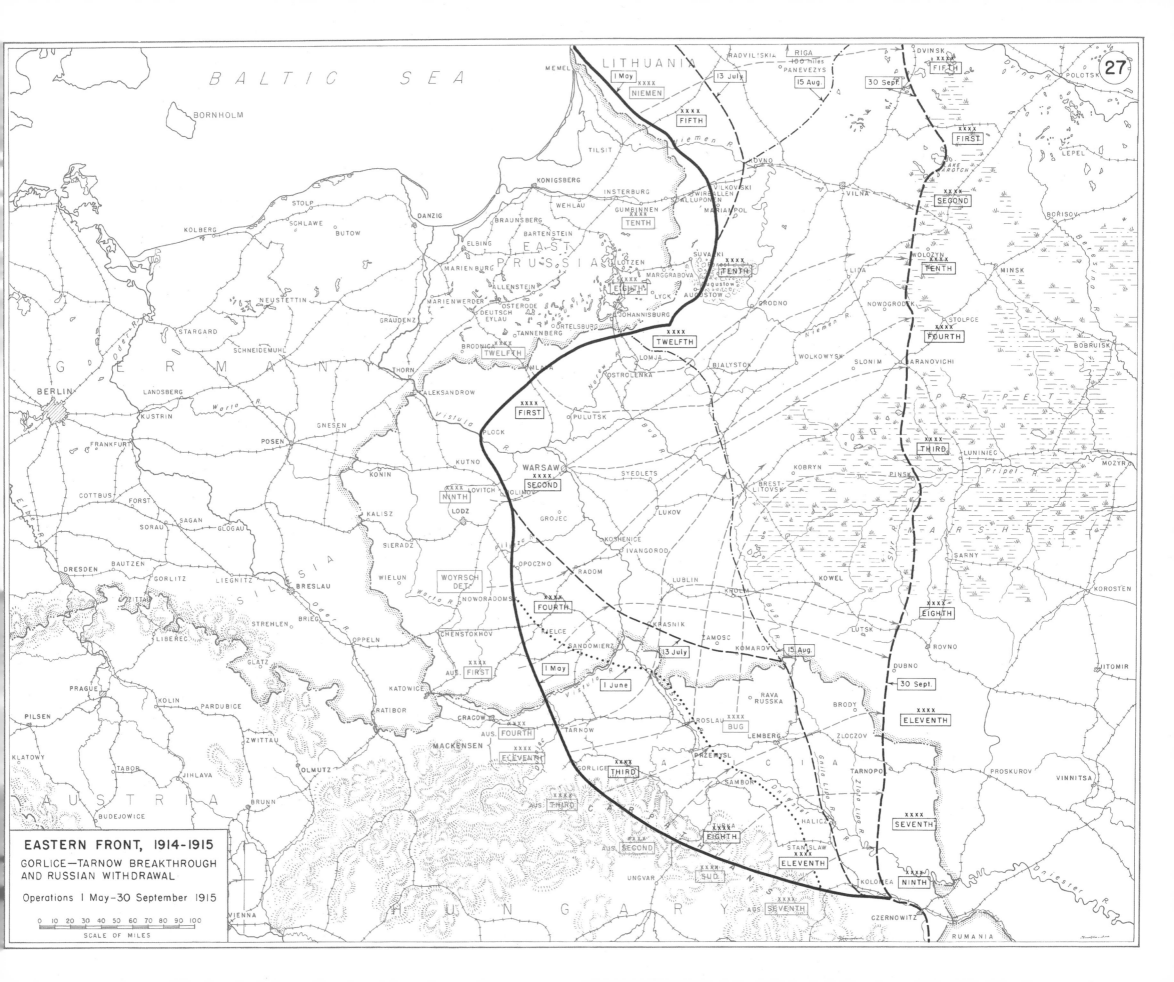

27

BALTIC SEA

LITHUANIA

1 May / NIEMEN

FIFTH

TENTH

EAST PRUSSIA

TWELFTH

TWELFTH

FIRST

WARSAW
SECOND

NINTH

WOYRSCH DET.

FOURTH

AUS. FIRST

1 May

1 June

AUS. FOURTH

MACKENSEN
ELEVENTH

THIRD

AUS. THIRD

EIGHTH

AUS. SECOND

SUD.

AUS. SEVENTH

G E R M A N Y

BERLIN

S I L E S I A

AUSTRIA

HUNGARY

13 July

15 Aug.

30 Sept.

FIFTH

FIRST

SECOND

TENTH

FOURTH

THIRD

EIGHTH

ELEVENTH

SEVENTH

NINTH

13 July

15 Aug.

BUG

30 Sept.

P R I P E T   M A R S H E S

G A L I C I A

C A R P A T H I A N

EASTERN FRONT, 1914-1915

GORLICE—TARNOW BREAKTHROUGH
AND RUSSIAN WITHDRAWAL

Operations 1 May–30 September 1915

0 10 20 30 40 50 60 70 80 90 100
SCALE OF MILES

RUMANIA

At the outbreak of war, Turkey, though clearly under German influence, remained neutral. For many years following the Crimean War she had leaned heavily upon England, but gradually—from 1905 onward—Germany had usurped Britain's place. The Balkan Wars (1912-13), which humbled Turkey and severely reduced her territory in Europe, served to solidify the control of the "Young Turk" regime. The British, lacking their usual political astuteness, had little confidence in the young revolutionary government and refused a proposal for an Anglo-Turkish alliance.

In December, 1913, General Liman von Sanders brought a German mission to Turkey to reorganize and train her army. Prussian efficiency soon impressed the Turks, who—though not appreciative of the arrogant attitude of some of the visitors— expected a German victory should war break out.

On 2 August, 1914, the Turks finally signed a secret pact with Germany, directed primarily at Russia. The next day, the British took over two battleships being built in England for Turkey, causing great resentment among the Turks and playing into the hands of German propagandists, who now offered Turkey two German ships. On 8 August, the German warships Goeben and Breslau, being hunted by the British, took refuge in the Dardanelles (lower center). Britain protested, but the Turks suavely replied that the two ships had been purchased to replace those seized by the British. Germans soon began reorganizing the Turkish Navy, and continued to man the two "Turkish" warships. Then, on 26 September, when the Royal Navy refused to allow a Turkish torpedo boat—manned by Germans—to leave the Dardanelles, the German officer commanding the Gallipoli fortifications closed the straits to all traffic. Repercussions were serious, for the move cut Russia's lifeline; but the Allies, gripped in life-and-death struggles on land with Germany, took no military action.

By October, the German defeat on the Marne and the Austrian reverses in Galicia had convinced Turkey that the Central Powers were not invincible. If they lost the war, Turkey would be menaced by her old enemy, Russia, more powerful than ever. On 30 October, a Turkish fleet, under German command, shelled Odessa, on the Black Sea. This overt act propelled Turkey into the war.

This map shows the situation on the various fronts as of 1 January, 1915. In the West, the Allies had suffered nearly 1,000,000 casualties since the outbreak of war; the front was stabilized, and one school of thought in Britain and France advocated enveloping this line—perhaps via Turkey and the Balkans. In the East, Hindenburg had temporarily stalled the Russians in the campaign that ended with the Lódz battle. Conrad had still been unable to make headway against recalcitrant Serbia. The Turks opposed the British at Suez (bottom center) and in Mesopotamia (lower right), where the British had landed a force from the Persian Gulf on 6 November to secure vital oil fields. On the Turko-Russian border, two armies watched each other.

Sanders had improved the Turkish Army immeasurably in a remarkably short time. It now had forty divisions (with an average rifle strength of about 9,000 each), grouped into four armies as shown. But Turkey's lack of roads and railroads hampered supply and troop movements. The lack of adequate munitions-manufacturing facilities meant dependence upon German supply; thus, the attitude of the Balkan states between Turkey and Germany was important.

The genesis of the Dardanelles campaign lay in a Russian request in early January for a British diversion against Turkey. On 4 January, the headstrong Enver Pasha, despite Sanders' advice to the contrary, launched the Turkish Third Army in an abortive attack in the Caucasus (right center). Only 10 per cent of the 90,000 Turks survived the battle, the cold, and starvation. But the Stavka had feared eventual collapse of the front when it made the plea for a British attack. The British—some of whom had, for months, been anxious to reopen the supply line to Russia—replied that an early effort would be made. The British War Council began to explore possibilities in an atmosphere tainted by an unrealistic appraisal of military capabilities.

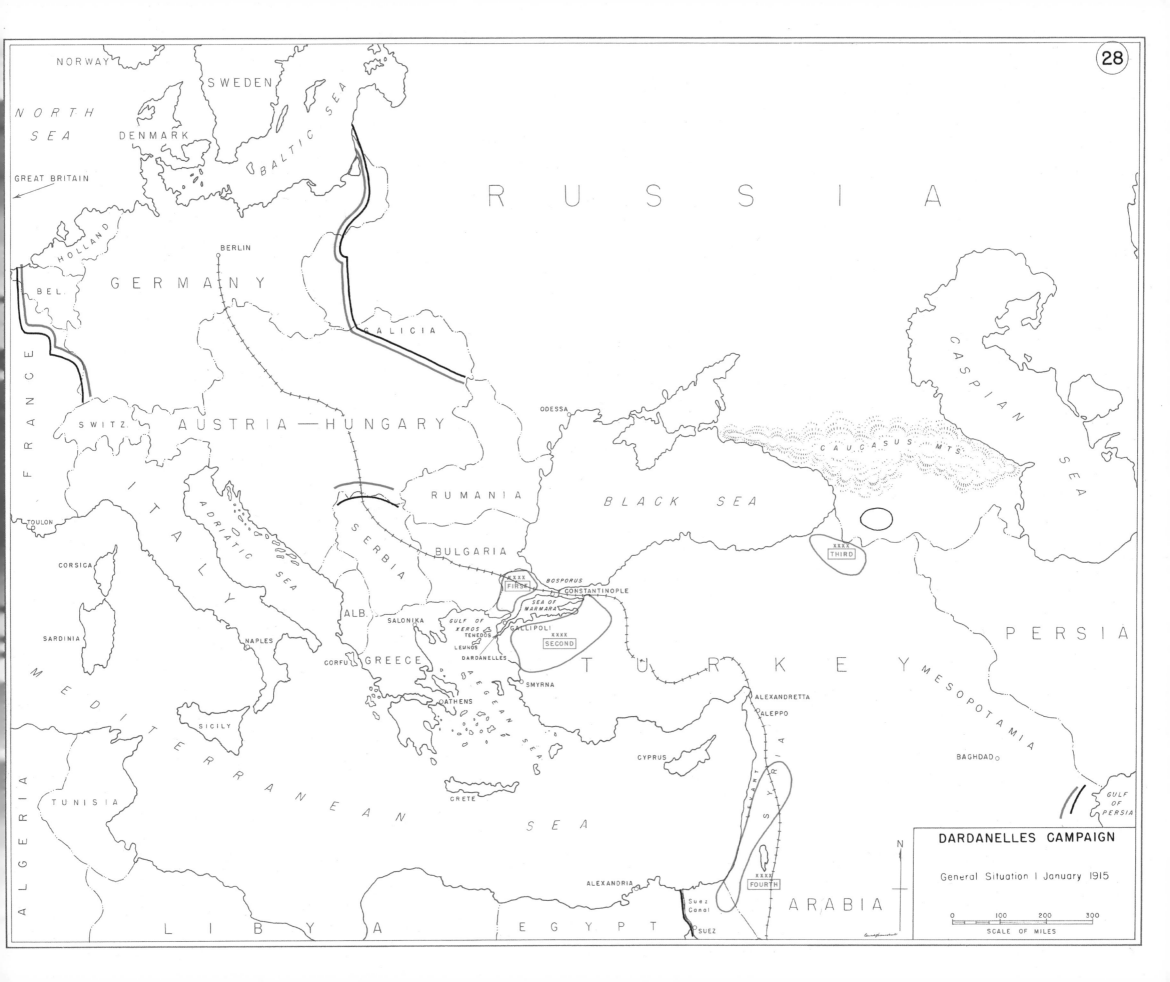

28

NORWAY

SWEDEN

NORTH
SEA

DENMARK

BALTIC SEA

R U S S I A

GREAT BRITAIN

HOLLAND

BERLIN

G E R M A N Y

BEL.

GALICIA

CASPIAN
SEA

FRANCE

SWITZ.

A U S T R I A — H U N G A R Y

ODESSA

CAUCASUS MTS

ITALY

ADRIATIC SEA

RUMANIA

B L A C K   S E A

XXXX
THIRD

SERBIA

BULGARIA

TOULON

CORSICA

ALB.

SALONIKA

GULF OF
XEROS

BOSPORUS

XXXX
FIRST

CONSTANTINOPLE

SEA OF
MARMARA

P E R S I A

SARDINIA

NAPLES

TENEDOS

GALLIPOLI

XXXX
SECOND

CORFU

GREECE

LEMNOS

DARDANELLES

T U R K E Y MESOPOTAMIA

M E D I T E R R A N E A N

SICILY

ATHENS

A E G E A N SEA

SMYRNA

ALEXANDRETTA

ALEPPO

S Y R I A

CYPRUS

BAGHDAD

S E A

CRETE

ALGERIA

TUNISIA

GULF
OF
PERSIA

DARDANELLES CAMPAIGN

ALEXANDRIA

XXXX
FOURTH

A R A B I A

N

Suez
Canal

L I B Y A

E G Y P T

SUEZ

General Situation 1 January 1915

0   100   200   300

SCALE OF MILES

Field Marshal Kitchener, Secretary of State for War and the dominant voice on the British War Council, insisted that all ground troops were needed on the Western Front and would not sanction their use in the Dardanelles. Mr. Winston Churchill, First Lord of the Admiralty, together with several of his subordinates, believed that the Royal Navy alone could force the straits. The magnetic and forceful Churchill pressed his point and won; the Admiralty was instructed "to bombard and take the Gallipoli peninsula with Constantinople as its objective." Vice Admiral Sackville Carden, commander of the Dardanelles Blockading Squadron and a supporter of Churchill's views, was reinforced and directed to attack as soon as possible. This he did on 19 February, 1915.

Earlier—in November, 1914—a short, useless British naval bombardment had revealed to the Turks the weaknesses of their Dardanelles defenses; by now, these had been substantially improved. The defenses of the Dardanelles (*sketch* a) consisted of the outer forts at Cape Helles and Kum Kale, an intermediate group of forts on both sides of the strait at Kephez Point, and the inner defenses—the strongest—at the Narrows. Ten belts of mines and an antisubmarine net blocked the channel.

Carden quickly reduced the outer forts. but the intermediate defenses proved more troublesome. Mine sweeping was difficult under the guns of the forts and mobile field artillery. On 8 March, Carden went into the straits to engage the forts; some were silenced, but the British were forced to withdraw. By 17 March, enough mines had been cleared to make Carden believe that a determined effort might succeed: while smaller ships attacked the intermediate forts and trawlers swept more mines, the forts at the Narrows would be taken under long-range bombardment, after which Carden's twelve dreadnaughts would close to the Narrows and destroy the forts there. At this point, however, Carden was invalided home; Admiral John M. De Robeck succeeded him. At 1000, 18 March, the attack began; by 1400, the dreadnaughts had closed to the Narrows. However,

in maneuvering for position, five ships struck mines (Belt No. 11) in an area that the British thought was clear. De Robeck, believing the Turks to be using floating mines, became unnerved and withdrew, having lost two ships to the mines.

The Turkish defenses had been badly battered. In retrospect, a determined naval assault would very likely have cleared the Narrows and enabled the fleet to enter the Sea of Marmara for an attack on Constantinople (*off map, east*). In view of the brave and stubborn resistance of the Turks throughout the war, however, it is unlikely that Constantinople would have capitulated because of naval bombardment alone.

Meanwhile, there was some apprehension over the lack of ground forces in the operations. Greece offered three divisions, but Russia—suspicious of Greece's territorial ambitions—vetoed the offer. Finally, Kitchener made available the 29th Division and also the Anzac (Australian–New Zealand) Corps, then in Egypt. The French provided a division, and the Royal Naval Division joined the force. General Ian Hamilton was placed in command on 12 March and preceded his troops to the area. He joined De Robeck in time to witness the 18 March naval failure, and reported to London that the navy alone could not do the job. De Robeck concurred. Churchill pressed for continuation of the naval attack, but to no avail.

The 29th Division, hastily loaded, left England in no condition to move directly into operations. Hamilton assembled all his troops at Alexandria, Egypt, and formulated plans for the assault. The parts to be played by his forces are shown in sketch b. The French division, after landing and making a feint at Kum Kale, was to follow the main landing.

Meanwhile, the Turks had put to good use the four weeks of grace following the naval attack. The Fifth Army, 60,000 troops under Sanders, was disposed in the Dardanelles area as shown. No attempt was made to garrison the widely separated beaches in strength; instead, most units were held in central positions from which they could move rapidly when and where needed.

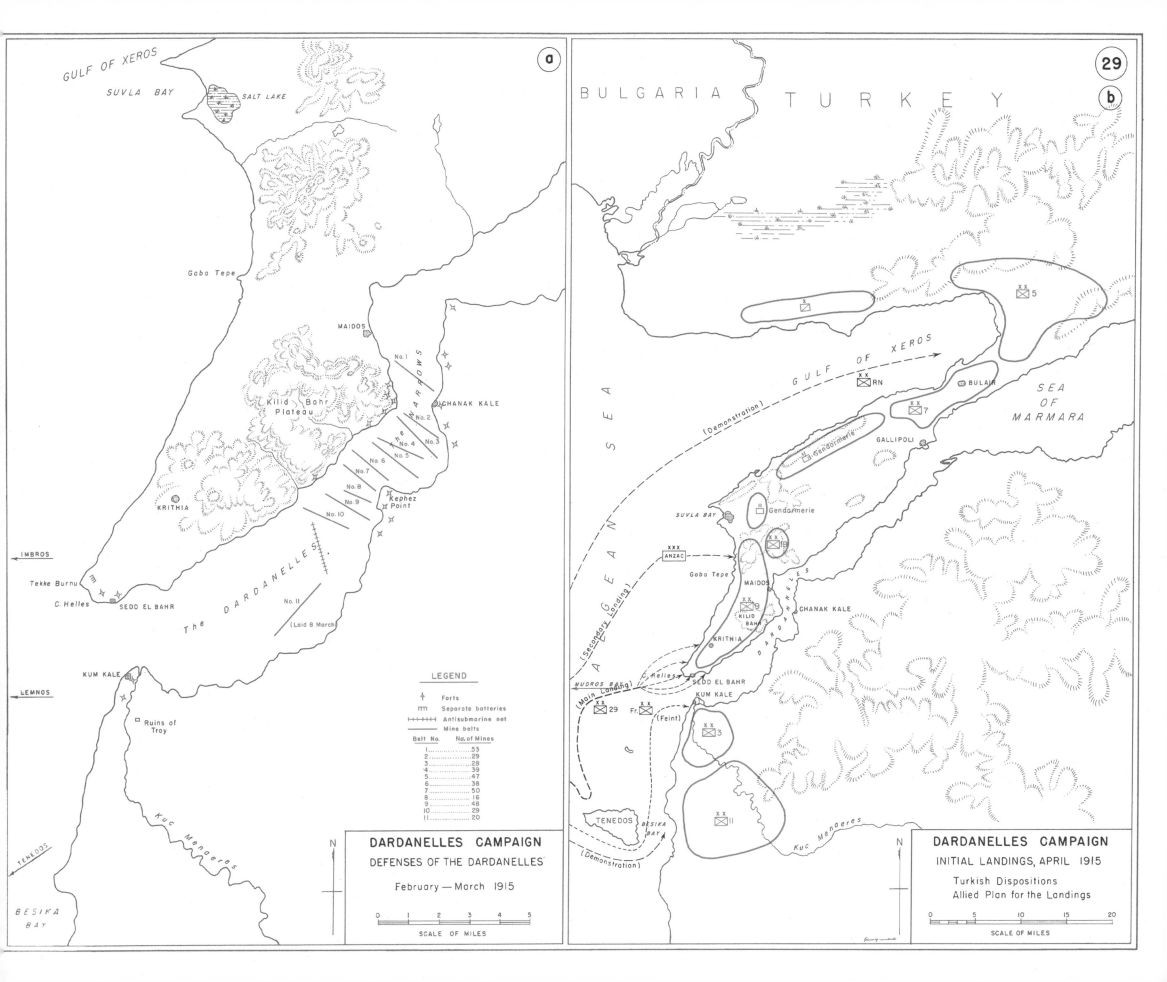

GULF OF XEROS

SUVLA BAY

SALT LAKE

Gaba Tepe

MAIDOS

No.1

CHANAK KALE

Kilid Bahr
Plateau

No.2

No.4   No.3

No.5

No.6

No.7

No.8

No.9   Kephez
Point

KRITHIA

No.10

IMBROS

Tekke Burnu

C. Helles

SEDD EL BAHR

The DARDANELLES

No.11

(Laid 8 March)

LEMNOS

KUM KALE

Ruins of
Troy

LEGEND

Forts

Separate batteries

Antisubmarine net

Mine belts

Belt No.	No. of Mines
1	53
2	29
3	28
4	39
5	47
6	38
7	50
8	16
9	48
10	29
11	20

KUC Menderes

N

DARDANELLES CAMPAIGN

DEFENSES OF THE DARDANELLES

February — March 1915

0 1 2 3 4 5

SCALE OF MILES

BESIKA
BAY

29

BULGARIA   TURKEY

SEA
OF
MARMARA

GULF OF XEROS

XX 5

A E G E A N   S E A

(Demonstration)

XX RN

BULAIR

XX 7

GALLIPOLI

Gendarmerie

(Secondary Landing)

SUVLA BAY

Gendarmerie

XXX
ANZAC

XX 19

Gaba Tepe

MAIDOS

(MUDROS BASE)

C. Helles

XX KILID
BAHR

CHANAK KALE

DARDANELLES

(Main Landing)

KRITHIA

C. Helles

SEDD EL BAHR

XX 29   Fr. XX   (Feint)

KUM KALE

XX 3

TENEDOS   BESIKA
BAY

XX 11

KUC Menderes

(Demonstration)

N

DARDANELLES CAMPAIGN

INITIAL LANDINGS, APRIL 1915

Turkish Dispositions
Allied Plan for the Landings

0 5 10 15 20

SCALE OF MILES

Considering the difficult conditions under which Hamilton and his staff labored, it is amazing that the British managed to land as early as 25 April. His logistician had no experience factors upon which to base his plans, intelligence concerning enemy positions was meager, weapons were in short supply, maps were practically nonexistent, there was a shortage of ships and landing craft, and joint planning with De Robeck was only introduced in the final stages. The entire period in Egypt was one of hectic improvisation. But, somehow, Hamilton managed to have his troops loaded and assembled in seventy-seven ships at Lemnos Island, fifty miles from the Dardanelles, by 21 April. There, final plans were made for the landings on the 25th.

The Royal Naval Division's demonstration near Bulair was highly successful (*see map 29*b). The division spent the entire day afloat there, covered by naval shelling of the beaches, and simulated preparations for landing. Sanders himself rode to the area and ordered the Turkish 7th Division to move up reinforcements. Similarly, the French feint at Kum Kale, where a regiment spent thirty hours ashore, was instrumental in holding Turkish troops in position.

The Anzac Corps landed at dawn but, because of an unexpected current, came ashore against negligible resistance, a mile north of the planned beach (*this map, sketch* a). There was considerable confusion, but, by 0930, General Sir William Birdwood had advance elements moving toward his objective—Sari Bahr Ridge (*upper right*). About this time, Turkey's most able soldier, Mustapha Kemal, arrived and hurried a regiment from his 19th Division forward to halt the advance. The fighting was fierce, but the Turks, though outnumbered three to one, halted Birdwood's troops. Birdwood became discouraged and asked Hamilton for authority to reembark his troops. The answer was "Dig yourselves in and stick it out," and Birdwood complied. The following day, Mustapha Kemal moved the rest of his division into line.

Meanwhile, the main landing was achieving no greater success. A covering force of seven and a half battalions, all under one commander. landed at the five beaches as shown (*sketch* b). The battalions of the main body, under another commander, were to follow when the beaches were secured. The troops landed in "tows," most consisting of four lifeboats drawn by a small motorboat, which cut them loose near the shore (*sketch* c). The troops at Y Beach (*sketch* b) met only slight resistance and had reached Krithia by nightfall; then counterattacks drove them back to the beach, and—due to a command mix-up—they evacuated the area next morning. The landings at S and X Beaches also met only sporadic opposition. By noon, Hill 114 at the latter beach had been seized, and the two reserve battalions of the main body landed. But Turkish resistance at Beaches W and V was better organized. The assault troops encountered wire, mines, and entrenchments relatively undamaged by naval gunfire. The Turks withheld their fire until the boats grounded, and then inflicted severe losses. Casualties were particularly heavy at V Beach, where the British, seeking to place maximum strength ashore quickly, attempted to beach the collier River Clyde. Caught under fire as they emerged from holes cut in the boat's sides, the troops were literally massacred. Late in the day, the rest of the main body, destined for V Beach, was rerouted to W.

All troops were now ashore, but, lacking vigorous leadership, they made no attempt to push forward. The covering-force commander had become a casualty, and none of the subordinate commanders displayed the initiative so vitally needed. Hamilton influenced the action only through occasional suggestions. Had the desirable flexibility of communications existed, and had the success at Y Beach been exploited vigorously with the main body, Achi Baba (*upper right*) might well have been captured.

The British inched forward the next few days, but Sanders, initially deceived by the Bulair demonstration, promptly moved in reserves and established a formidable line. By 8 May, stalemate had set in at both the Anzac and Helles beachheads. If the British were to open the Dardanelles, reinforcements and a new plan would be necessary.

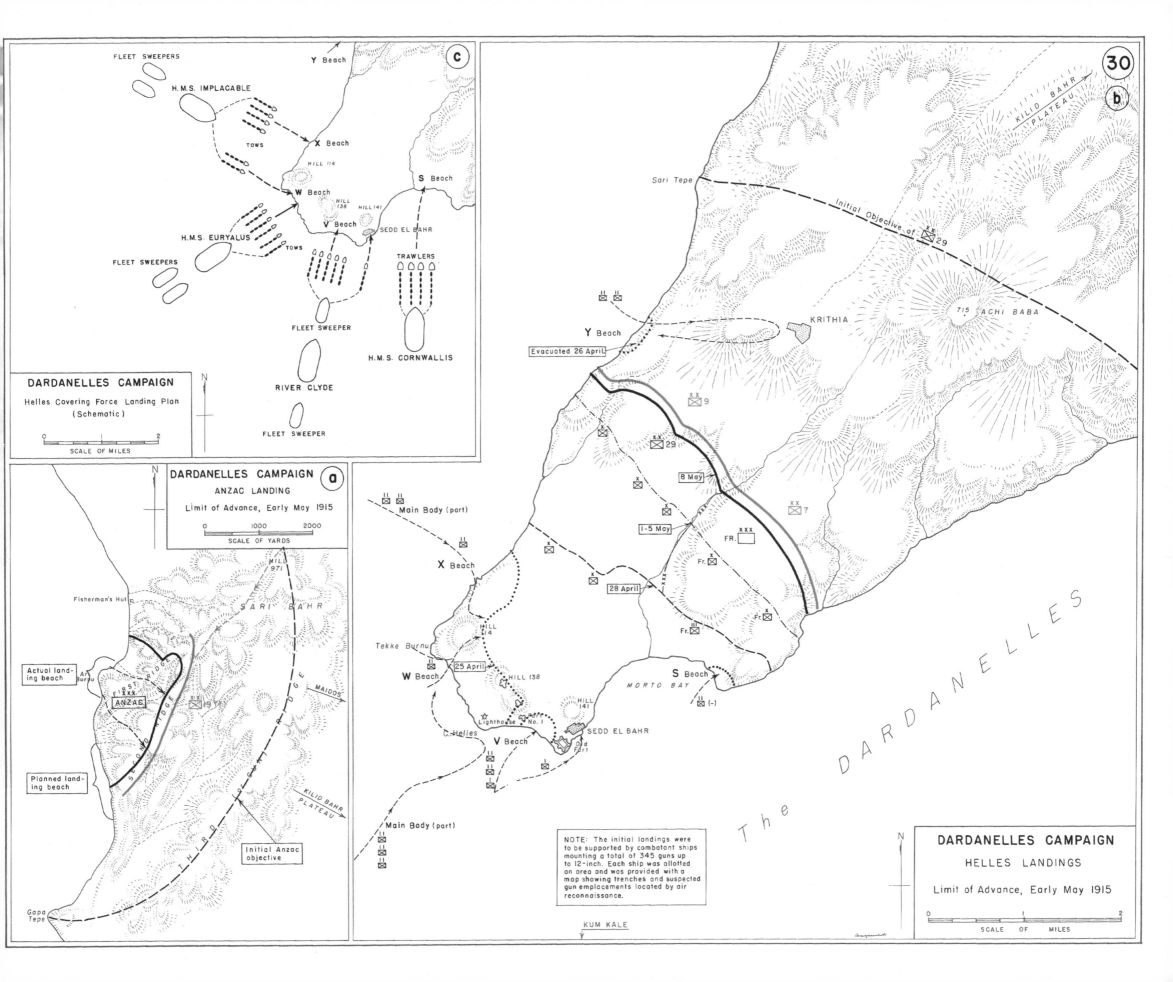

30

DARDANELLES CAMPAIGN

Helles Covering Force Landing Plan
(Schematic)

FLEET SWEEPERS

H.M.S. IMPLACABLE

Y Beach

X Beach

HILL 114

TOWS

S Beach

W Beach

HILL 138

HILL 141

V Beach

H.M.S. EURYALUS

SEDD EL BAHR

FLEET SWEEPERS

TOWS

TRAWLERS

FLEET SWEEPER

H.M.S. CORNWALLIS

RIVER CLYDE

FLEET SWEEPER

SCALE OF MILES

DARDANELLES CAMPAIGN

ANZAC LANDING

Limit of Advance, Early May 1915

SCALE OF YARDS

HILL 971

Fisherman's Hut

SARI BAHR

Actual landing beach

Ari Burnu

FIRST RIDGE

ANZAC

SECOND RIDGE

MAIDOS

THIRD RIDGE

KILID BAHR PLATEAU

Planned landing beach

Initial Anzac objective

Gaba Tepe

KILID BAHR PLATEAU

Initial Objective of 29

Sari Tepe

KRITHIA

715 ACHI BABA

Y Beach

Evacuated 26 April

9

29

8 May

1-5 May

7

FR.

Main Body (part)

X Beach

28 April

Fr.

HILL 114

Tekke Burnu

25 April

Fr.

W Beach

HILL 138

S Beach

MORTO BAY

Lighthouse No. 1

HILL 141

V Beach

C. Helles

SEDD EL BAHR

Old Fort

Main Body (part)

(-)

NOTE: The initial landings were to be supported by combatant ships mounting a total of 345 guns up to 12-inch. Each ship was allotted an area and was provided with a map showing trenches and suspected gun emplacements located by air reconnaissance.

KUM KALE

The DARDANELLES

DARDANELLES CAMPAIGN

HELLES LANDINGS

Limit of Advance, Early May 1915

SCALE OF MILES

After the failure of the May attacks at Helles, Hamilton lost hope of making progress without sizable reinforcements. That assault had gained little ground at great cost—by 8 May, his casualties had reached 20,000, a third of the Allied force engaged. At Anzac, conditions were no better. Though Mustapha Kemal finally accepted his inability to drive the Allies into the sea, the latter were not able to dislodge him from his commanding position. So, while the heat, unsuitable diet, flies, and crowded conditions bred disease and sickness—further crippling the British—Hamilton continued sporadic attacks through June. None were successful. Back in London, reactions to the dismal failure were serious.

April brought the slaughter at Ypres and the sensational disclosure of German use of poison gas. The Russian reverses brought no comfort either. Meanwhile, Hamilton's timid requests for reinforcements were largely ignored by Kitchener. In mid-May, a dispatch from De Robeck created a controversy. Desirous of aiding the despondent Hamilton, the navy had decided to try to force the straits again—provided that London approved. De Robeck's message completely upset the Admiralty, which was actually planning to reduce his fleet strength. Kitchener fumed, and there were political repercussions. Admiral Lord Fisher, First Sea Lord, resigned in a huff; the Asquith government tottered, but remained in power by accepting a coalition and jettisoning Churchill, upon whom the stigma of failure was placed. De Robeck's suggestion was flatly disapproved. But now, in June, Kitchener at last began to provide the supplies and men Hamilton so desperately needed. By the end of July, Hamilton had fourteen divisions; Sanders now had sixteen divisions.

Hamilton's plan for his second offensive is shown in sketch a. The Helles secondary attack was designed to hold and draw Turkish forces southward. The IX Corps, at Suvla Bay, was to seize quickly the dominating heights around the bay and then capture Anafarta Gap (*upper center*), which, in British hands,

would compromise the enemy position commanding the Anzac area. The main attack sought the capture of Sari Bahr Ridge.

The Helles attack, launched at 0530, 6 August, and continuing through the 8th, made only minor gains, but did hold the Turkish troops in position. The main attack involved a major effort against Hill 971 and Chunuk Bahr, and secondary attacks against Lone Pine Ridge and The Nek (*sketch* b). The Lone Pine operation (1530, 6 August) successfully attracted the local Turkish reserves, plus two regiments from Kilid Bahr. The main effort, however, hoping to achieve surprise, attempted a difficult night march over unfamiliar terrain. Men straggled, units became lost. Consequently, though its assault on the morning of the 7th surprised the thinly spread Turks, it was too feeble to break their line—especially after the two regiments from Kilid Bahr quickly reinforced it. The attack at The Nek was a complete fiasco. Thus, Hamilton's main attack ended in unqualified failure.

But at Suvla Bay, a great opportunity to retrieve the campaign arose. The IX Corps, commanded by Gen. Sir Frederick Stopford, landed against negligible resistance. But confusion reigned on the beaches, and there was a pitiful lack of leadership at corps and division level. Sanders at once ordered two divisions to move by forced march from Bulair. Stopford spent two days dawdling on the beach and unloading supplies. Finally, late on 8 August, Hamilton exercised some direction and ordered Stopford to seize the heights. By the time the attack was made on the 9th, it was too late, for Sanders had his reinforcements in position.

On this sorry note, the campaign virtually ended. Hamilton journeyed to the area and saw no reason to continue the operation. All Allied troops—but little equipment—were evacuated in January 1916 without the loss of a single life. This humiliating operation, performed to perfection, was the most laudatory part of the entire Allied campaign. In the nine months of fighting, casualties for each side totaled about 250,000.

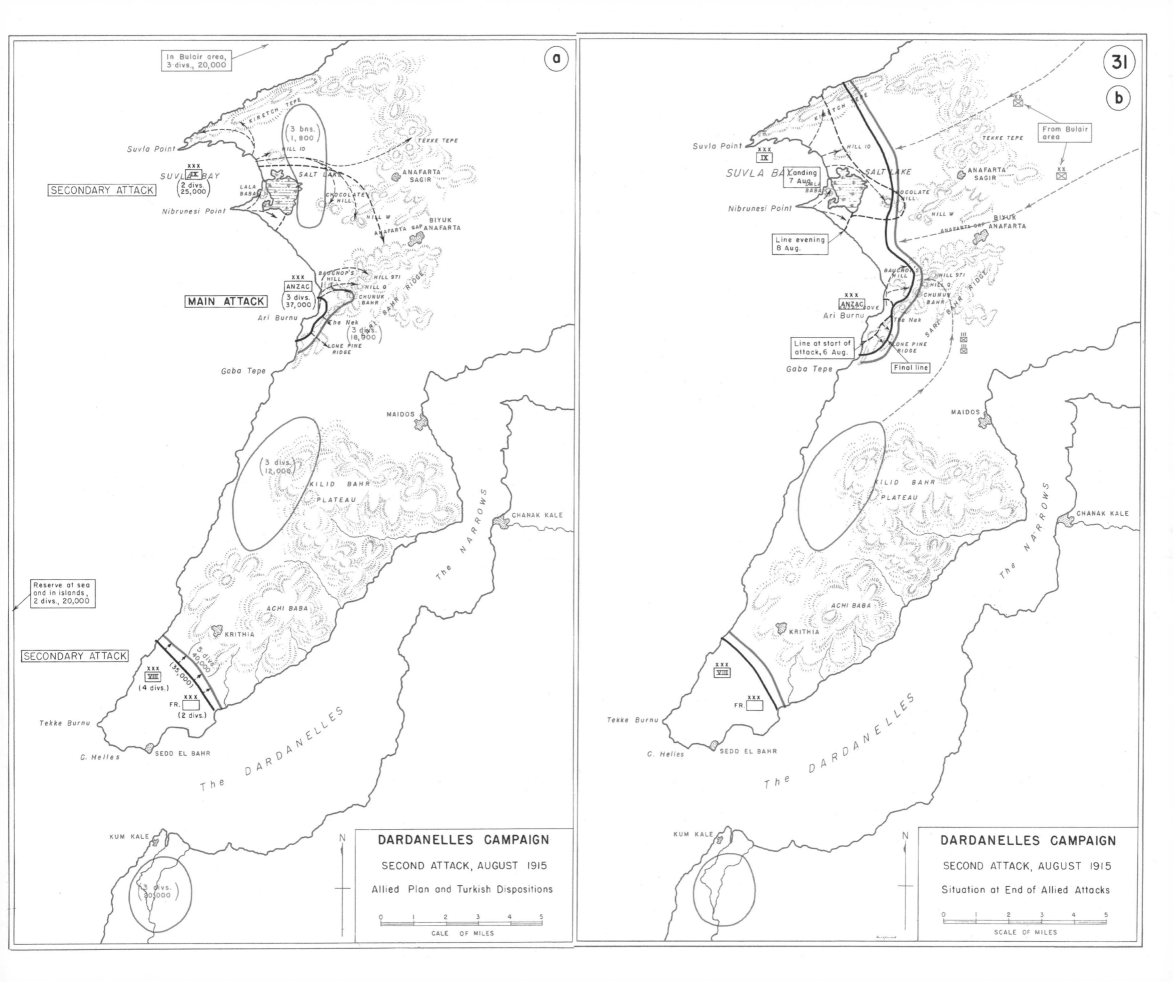

a

In Bulair area, 3 divs., 20,000

KIRETCH TEPE

TEKKE TEPE

Suvla Point

(3 bns. 1,800)

HILL 10

XXX
IX
2 divs. (25,000)

SUVLA BAY

SALT LAKE

ANAFARTA SAGIR

SECONDARY ATTACK

LALA BABA

CHOCOLATE HILL

Nibrunesi Point

HILL W

BIYUK ANAFARTA

ANAFARTA GAP

BAUCHOP'S HILL

HILL 971

XXX
ANZAC
3 divs. (37,000)

HILL Q

CHUNUK BAHR

SARI BAHR RIDGE

MAIN ATTACK

Ari Burnu

The Nek

3 divs. 18,900

LONE PINE RIDGE

Gaba Tepe

MAIDOS

(3 divs. 12,000)

KILID BAHR PLATEAU

CHANAK KALE

The NARROWS

Reserve at sea and in islands, 2 divs., 20,000

ACHI BABA

KRITHIA

SECONDARY ATTACK

5 divs. (40,000)

XXX
VIII
(4 divs.)

FR. XXX (2 divs.)

Tekke Burnu

The DARDANELLES

C. Helles

SEDD EL BAHR

KUM KALE

(3 divs. 20,000)

N

DARDANELLES CAMPAIGN

SECOND ATTACK, AUGUST 1915

Allied Plan and Turkish Dispositions

0 1 2 3 4 5

SCALE OF MILES

31

b

From Bulair area

XX

KIRETCH TEPE

Suvla Point

XXX
IX

HILL 10

TEKKE TEPE

XX

SUVLA BAY

Landing 7 Aug.

SALT LAKE

ANAFARTA SAGIR

LALA BABA

CHOCOLATE HILL

Nibrunesi Point

HILL W

BIYUK ANAFARTA

ANAFARTA GAP

Line evening 8 Aug.

BAUCHOP'S HILL

HILL 971

XXX
ANZAC

HILL Q

CHUNUK BAHR

SARI BAHR RIDGE

Ari Burnu

COVE

The Nek

Line at start of attack, 6 Aug.

LONE PINE RIDGE

XX

Gaba Tepe

Final line

MAIDOS

KILID BAHR PLATEAU

CHANAK KALE

The NARROWS

ACHI BABA

KRITHIA

XXX
VIII

FR. XXX

Tekke Burnu

The DARDANELLES

C. Helles

SEDD EL BAHR

KUM KALE

N

DARDANELLES CAMPAIGN

SECOND ATTACK, AUGUST 1915

Situation at End of Allied Attacks

0 1 2 3 4 5

SCALE OF MILES

Nineteen fifteen was a year of deadlock in the West. This was due to the simple fact—probably less apparent then than now—that contemporary weapons had given the defender a definite advantage over the attacker. Barbed wire, machine guns, entrenchments, and supporting artillery could form a barrier that massed bayonets and human courage could not breach. Maneuver was impossible in the West; the opponents' flanks rested on the sea and neutral Switzerland. Even on those rare occasions when the enemy's front was broken—usually through surprise—large exploiting forces could neither be moved rapidly enough nor supported adequately to take advantage of the momentary rupture.

Falkenhayn recognized this fact and based his strategy upon it. He believed that a decisive victory could be won only in the West, but a variety of reasons—Hindenburg's and Ludendorff's pleas for a strong offensive against the Russians, the dangerous situation on the Austrian front, and his own failure at Ypres—made him decide to go on the defensive in the West for the time being. Realizing that the war would be a long one, he expanded the German military rail net to permit rapid movement of reinforcements and supplies, stepped up German industrial mobilization, and trained his troops for trench warfare. Meanwhile, he increased the German forces on the Eastern Front.

Confronted with the German defensive system, French and British leaders considered the two obvious methods of dealing with it: to break through, or to go around it. The French, who provided most of the troops on the Western Front, instinctively favored the first method. British opinion was divided: most commanders, like Sir John French and Sir Douglas Haig, agreed with the French; others favored a strategic envelopment of the German position, to be carried out by exploiting the inherent mobility of British sea power for attacks against Germany's allies. No clear decision was ever reached. Usually, the British government attempted to carry out both strategies with insufficient forces. The strategic envelopment took the forms of the Dardanelles campaign, the Salonika front, and campaigns in Mesopotamia and Palestine. Finally, there were a few English

and French leaders who sought a technological solution to their problem: the development of a weapon that could penetrate barbed wire, trenches, and machine-gun fire. Eventually, this idea produced the tank.

During the winter of 1914-15, the Allies had launched several minor offensives with uniform lack of success. Their general scheme of maneuver involved offensives against both flanks of the great German-held salient in northern France, designed to break through and cut the German rail communications within the salient, thus forcing the Germans to withdraw or risk entrapment.

The 1915 French attacks in Champagne (*center*) were a continuation of the winter offensive in that area. Some 240,000 casualties brought minute gains. A small-scale British attack in March at Neuve Chapelle (*upper left*) was carefully rehearsed and obtained complete surprise. Communications failures, however, halted it after early successes. In April, the French suffered another bloody failure at St. Mihiel.

Shortly thereafter, the Germans made a limited attack in the Ypres area to straighten their line and to divert attention from troops moving to the Eastern Front. Apparently as an afterthought, they used poison gas experimentally. (Both sides had already used tear gas in various forms.) A panic among the French troops first engulfed by the gas cloud left a four-mile gap in the Allied line, but the Germans had no reserves available to exploit this success. Eventually, the Allies withdrew slightly. In May, the French and British failed in a joint attack at Souchez and Festubert. The final Allied offensive of 1915, beginning in September, consisted of a main attack by the French in Champagne and of French and British secondary attacks at Vimy Ridge and Loos, respectively. French preparations for their Champagne offensive were so massive that they could not be concealed. The Germans prepared a secondary defensive system, before which the offensive collapsed. Both Allied attacks in the north also failed.

The major operations in 1916—the Battles of Verdun and the Somme—are covered in the texts of maps 33 and 34.

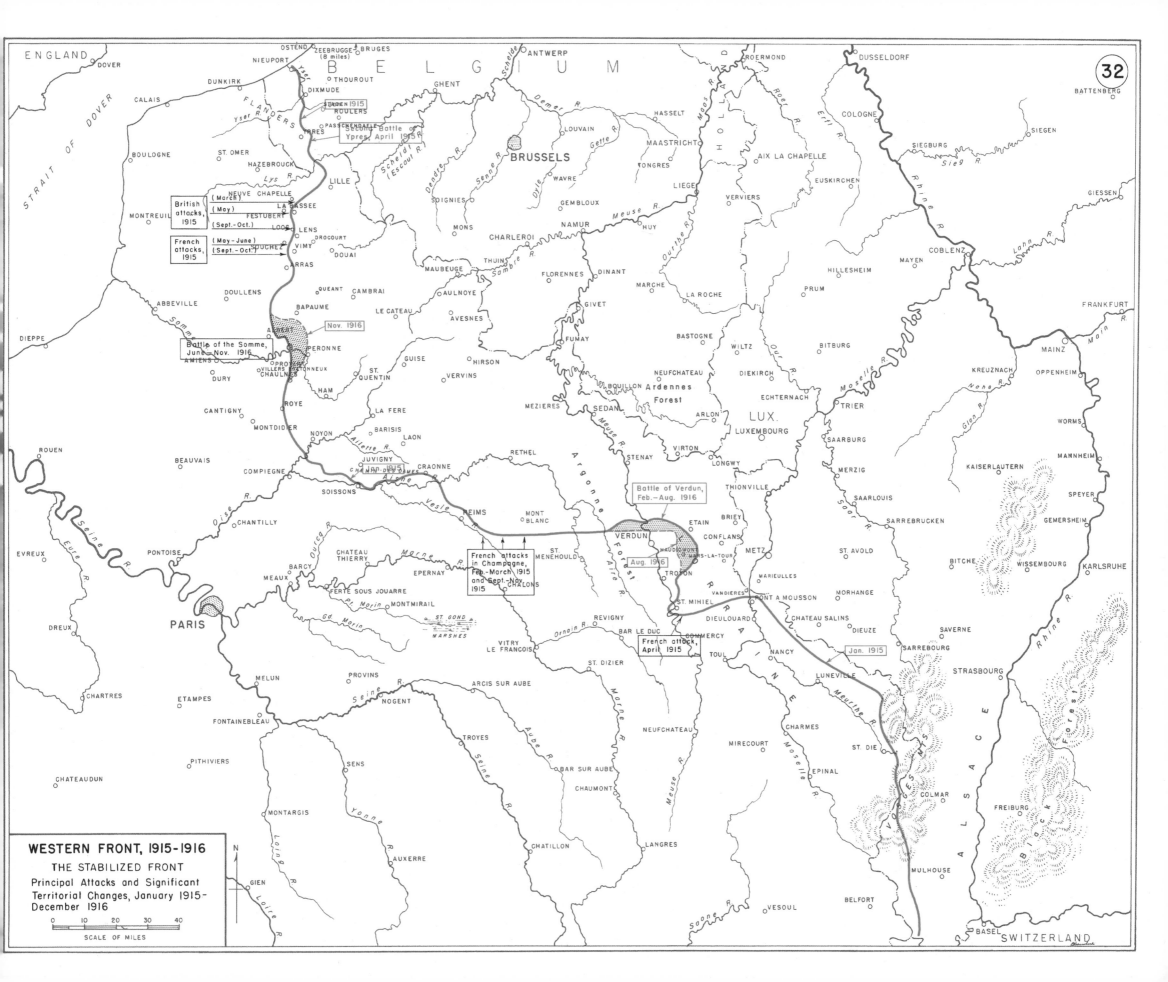

WESTERN FRONT, 1915-1916

THE STABILIZED FRONT

Principal Attacks and Significant
Territorial Changes, January 1915-
December 1916

After the failure of the autumn 1915 offensive in Champagne, Joffre decided that the war would have to be won by attrition. An Allied conference at Chantilly in December, 1915, planned a coordinated offensive against the Central Powers on the Western, Eastern, and Italian Fronts. The effort in the West was to be an attack astride the Somme River.

Falkenhayn anticipated the Allies. He felt that the best course of action would be an attack in Flanders, to drive the British into the sea and the French below the Somme. Unfortunately, this operation would require more troops than were available, and he consequently decided on an attack on a narrow front against either Verdun or Belfort. Signs of war-weariness, prompted by German propaganda, were appearing in France; the fall of either of these historic fortress cities would shake French morale and possibly force an early peace. Knowing this, Joffre would thrust every available French soldier into the battle, thus enabling the Germans—regardless of whether they took their objective—to bleed the French Army white. Verdun was finally chosen as the objective, largely because of its symbolic value to the French and its proximity to German railway communications.

At the beginning of the war, Verdun had been a powerful fortress. The fall of Liège and Maubeuge, however, had left Joffre dubious as to the value of permanent fortifications; the French Army's need for heavy artillery led him to strip the Verdun forts of most of their guns. Afterward, he neglected this vital sector.

In spite of precautions, the German build-up could not be concealed; on 8 February, a deserter warned the French of the impending attack. The Crown Prince (commanding the Fifth Army) was ready to attack on 12 February, but storms delayed him until the 21st. Meanwhile, French reinforcements arrived.

A twelve-hour bombardment opened the methodical German assault. French defenses were first wrecked by massed artillery fire, then occupied by infantry. German air support was aggressive. By 24 February, the two French trench lines north of Verdun had been breached, and French commanders prepared to withdraw to the west bank of the Meuse River. Imperturbable, Joffre offered to court-martial any general who retreated. General Philippe Pétain took command of the defense; the French improvised a new line around the dismantled forts on the dominating heights just east of the Meuse. On the 25th, the Germans seized Fort Douaumont (*center*), but French resistance stiffened; by the 29th, exhaustion halted the attack.

Meanwhile, French reinforcements poured in. Verdun's rail communications were limited (one standard-gauge and one narrow-gauge railroad), but this logistical problem was solved by operating an endless chain of trucks along the highway from Bar-le-Duc (*off map, bottom left*).

On 6 March, the Germans shifted their attack to the west bank of the Meuse. Pétain's strongpoints here were two commanding hills—Hill 304 and Le Mort Homme. German progress was slow. Renewed assaults east of the Meuse took Vaux (*center*) on 31 March, but a major assault on both sides of the river on 9 April failed. Falkenhayn now wished to halt the offensive, but the Crown Prince demanded that it be continued and expanded. Falkenhayn finally agreed to continue the operation, but refused to enlarge it.

The fighting west of the Meuse dwindled after 29 May. East of it, the Germans attacked on 1 June, clearing Fort Vaux and Thiaumount Farm on the 9th. On 23 June, they drove for the ridge line Fort Froide Terre–Fleury–Fort Souville, which commanded Verdun and the Meuse bridges. In one day they reached Fort Froide Terre. Pétain requested authority to withdraw; Joffre, knowing that the British were about to attack on the Somme, refused. The French hung on, though a final attack on 11 July almost broke their line.

Falkenhayn was relieved as chief of staff. Hindenburg-Ludendorff, who replaced him, suspended the Verdun offensive, since the Somme demanded priority. The French then launched a series of skillful counterattacks, regaining the area shown (*dashed red line*). Though estimates of casualties vary widely, losses at Verdun numbered approximately 377,000 French and 337,000 Germans.

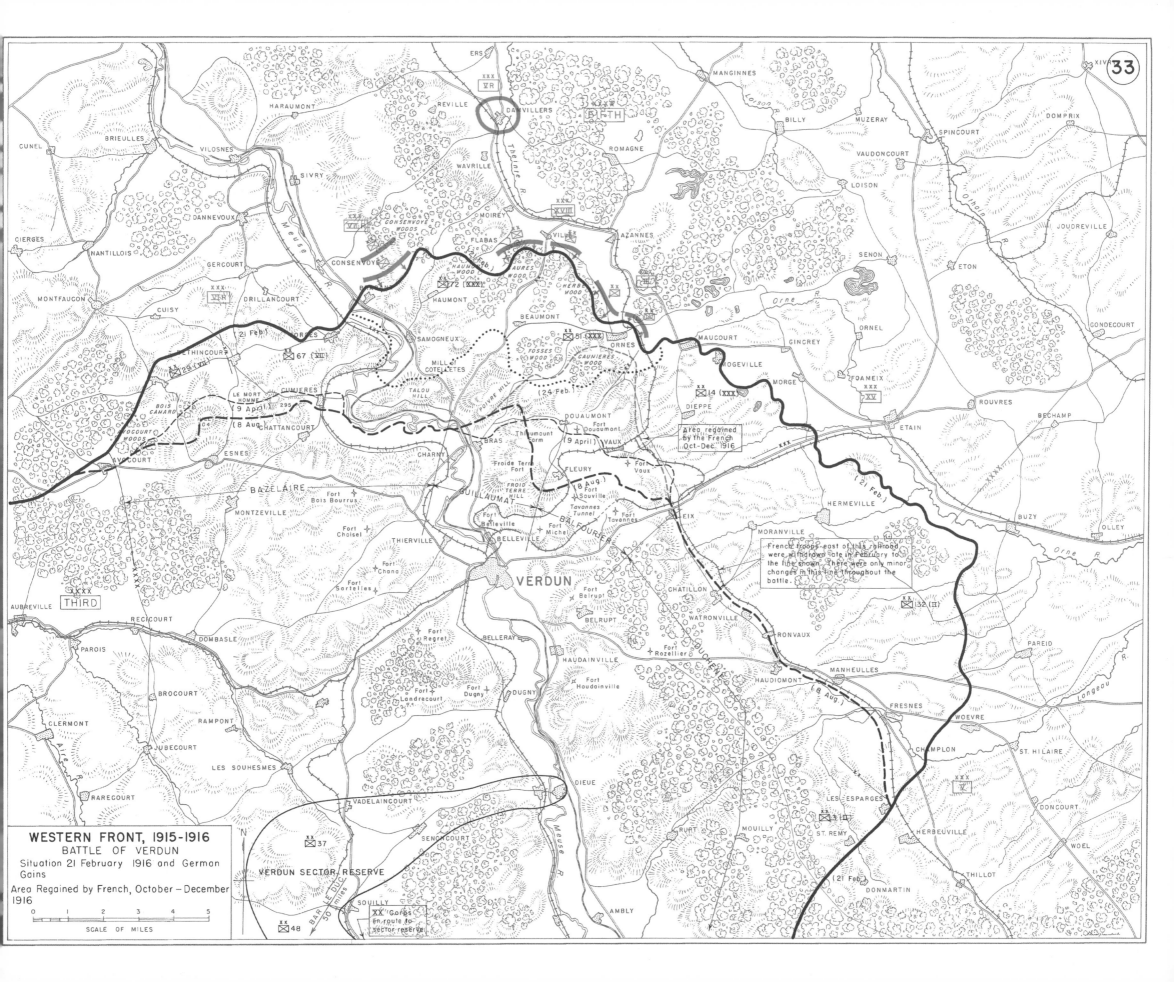

WESTERN FRONT, 1915-1916
BATTLE OF VERDUN
Situation 21 February 1916 and German Gains

Area Regained by French, October – December 1916

0 1 2 3 4 5
SCALE OF MILES

Joffre chose the Somme area for the 1916 offensive so he could launch a large combined offensive with the British. The Somme marked the boundary between the French and British, but the area had little strategic importance and had seen no fighting for two years, during which time the Germans had developed a defensive system of enormous depth and strength.

Originally, Joffre had planned to launch his main attack south of the Somme with forty French divisions, while the British made a secondary effort to the north. After Verdun used up so many French divisions, however, the roles were reversed, and the French made only a limited secondary attack.

According to the final plan, the French, with one corps north of the Somme, would attack generally east; the British Third Army would make a diversionary attack on the Gommecourt salient. The British Fourth Army, making the main effort, would penetrate the German lines between Maricourt and Fricourt, and seize the ridge from Montauban (*center*) to Serre (*upper left*). This gap would be widened by an advance to the high ground Ginchy (*center*)–Bapaume (*upper center*), along which a defensive line would be established. Its right flank thus protected, the British main attack would turn north, aided by a secondary attack between Fricourt and Thiepval. The final blow was to be an exploitation by the British Reserve Army—including all available cavalry—toward Douai (*off map, top right*) and Cambrai (*top right*).

The British established air superiority and massed 1,500 guns on an eighteen-mile front; the French had, proportionally, even heavier artillery support. Activity on this scale could not be hidden, but, by carrying out elaborate deceptive measures along the entire British front, Haig led Falkenhayn to believe that the Allied attack would be farther north. Falkenhayn also assumed that Verdun had so exhausted the French that they would not be able to attack on the Somme.

The artillery preparation began on 24 June. The assault was scheduled for the 29th, but bad weather delayed it until 1 July.

British infantry-artillery cooperation immediately proved to be insufficiently developed. The advance of the XIII Corps was covered by a creeping barrage, but the artillery of the other corps lifted directly from one German trench line to the next, giving the German machine-gunners time to emerge from their dugouts and get into action before British infantrymen could reach them. From Fricourt north, the British were stopped with shattering losses. The XIII Corps carried Montauban, while the French made deep gains from Hardecourt south.

Lacking forces to renew his attack on the whole front, Haig reinforced his successful right flank. Falkenhayn poured in reinforcements, ordering that, if a foot of ground were lost, "put in the last man to recover it." As at Verdun, these tactics hurt the defenders worse than the attackers. After twelve days of fighting, in which Fricourt was taken, a major assault at 0325 on 14 July cracked the German second line between Bazentin-le-Petit Wood and Delville Wood. For a moment, victory seemed at hand. Cavalry got through, High Wood was cleared, but reinforcements came forward too slowly. A German counterattack restored the line.

On 15 September, after two months of costly small actions, Haig delivered his third major attack—employing tanks for the first time—against the German position between Morval and Le Sars. The tanks were effective, but mechanically unreliable; considerable gains were made, but no breakthrough. The attack was renewed on the 25th, the French helping by attacking due north against Bouchavesnes. By the end of October, the Germans had been driven off the main ridge and were fighting from a last, improvised line. The weather had grown steadily worse, but Joffre insisted on continuing a battle of attrition. A short period of better weather on 13 November allowed a successful surprise attack at Beaumont-Hamel (*upper left*) and Beaucourt in the north before Haig halted the fighting. The French had lost 195,000 men; the British, 420,000. German losses remain uncertain, but they may have suffered as many as 500,000 casualties.

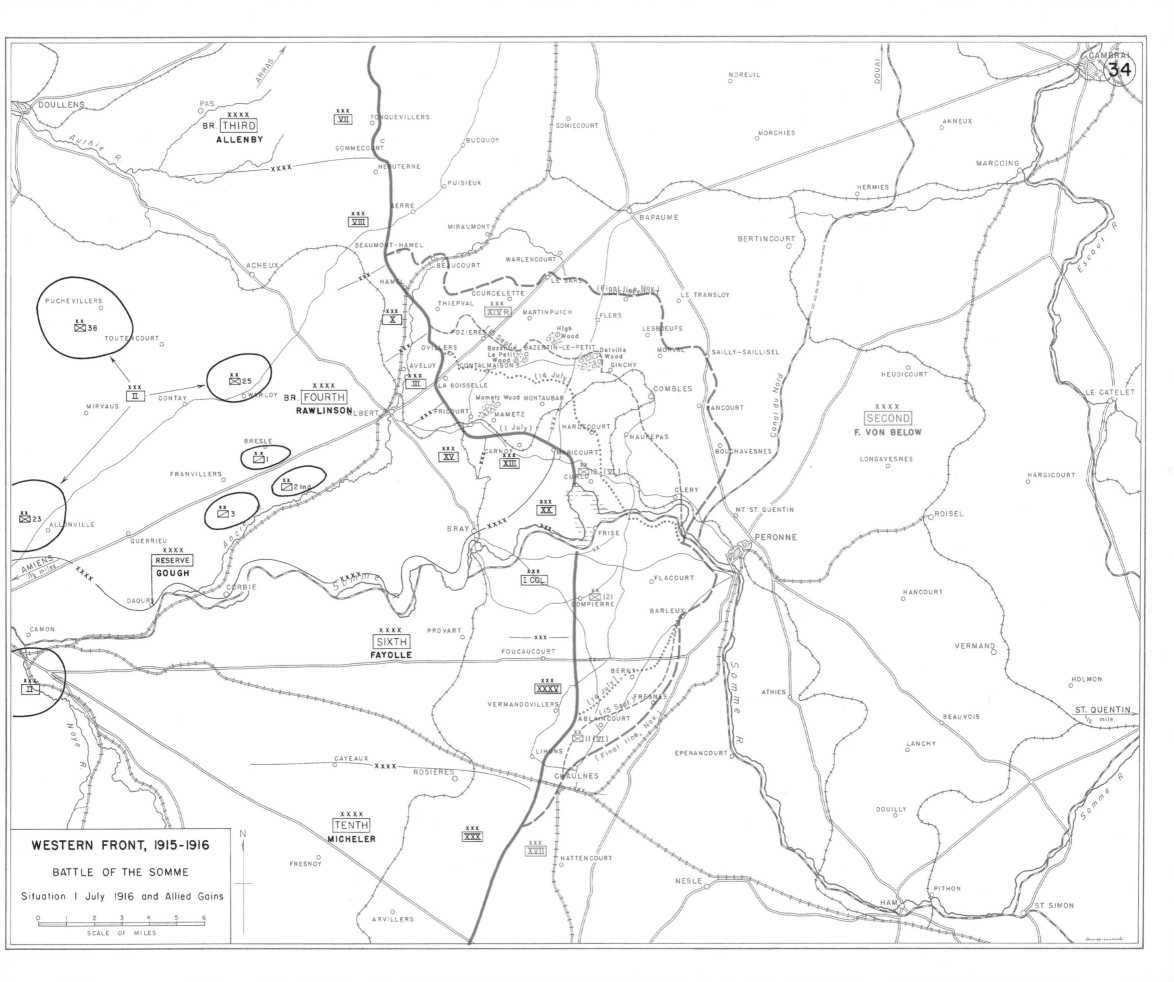

CAMBRAI
34

DOULLENS
PAS
ARRAS
NOREUIL
DOUAI
MORCHIES
ANNEUX
Authie R.
BR. THIRD
ALLENBY
XXXX
VII
FONQUEVILLERS
BUCQUOY
GOMIECOURT
MARCOING
GOMMECOURT
HEBUTERNE
PUISIEUX
HERMIES
BERTINCOURT
XXXX
XXX
VIII
SERRE
MIRAUMONT
BAPAUME
Escaut R.
BEAUMONT-HAMEL
WARLENCOURT
BEAUCOURT
LE SARS
(Final line Nov.)
LE TRANSLOY
PUCHEVILLERS
HAMEL
COURCELETTE
XXX
XIV R
THIEPVAL
MARTINPUICH
FLERS
LESBŒUFS
XX 38
TOUTENCOURT
XXX
X
POZIERES
(5 Sept.)
High Wood
Bazentin BAZENTIN-LE-PETIT
Le Petit Delville
Wood Wood
MORVAL
SAILLY-SAILLISEL
HEUDICOURT
OVILLERS
AVELUY
CONTALMAISON
GINCHY
XXX
II
CONTAY
XX 25
WARLOY
BR. FOURTH
RAWLINSON
XXX
III
LA BOISSELLE
(14 July)
COMBLES
LE CATELET
MIRVAUS
ALBERT
Mametz Wood MONTAUBAN
RANCOURT
BRESLE
FRICOURT
MAMETZ
HARDECOURT
MAUREPAS
BOUCHAVESNES
SECOND
F. VON BELOW
LONGAVESNES
HARGICOURT
XX 1
FRANVILLERS
(1 July)
XXX
XV
CARNOY
XXX
XIII
MARICOURT
XX 18 (VI)
CURLU
XX 2 Ind
CLERY
XX 23
ALLONVILLE
XX 3
QUERRIEU
BRAY
XXX
XX
FRISE
MT. ST. QUENTIN
ROISEL
AMIENS
1½ miles
Ancre
RESERVE
GOUGH
Somme R.
PERONNE
DAOURS
CORBIE
I COL
FLACOURT
HANCOURT
CAMON
XXX
IX
PROVART
FOUCAUCOURT
XX 121
DOMPIERRE
BARLEUX
Canal du Nord
VERMAND
SIXTH
FAYOLLE
BERNY
ST. QUENTIN
½ mile
CAYEAUX
ROSIERES
XXX
XXXV
VERMANDOVILLERS
(14 July)
(15 Sept.) FRESNES
ABLAINCOURT
(Final line, Nov.)
LIHONS
EPENANCOURT
BEAUVOIS
Noye R.
CHAULNES
LANCHY
Somme R.
TENTH
MICHELER
XXX
XXX
XXX
XVII
HATTENCOURT
DOUILLY
FRESNOY
ARVILLERS
NESLE
HAM
PITHON
ST SIMON

WESTERN FRONT, 1915-1916

BATTLE OF THE SOMME

Situation 1 July 1916 and Allied Gains

N

0 1 2 3 4 5 6
SCALE OF MILES

The British Grand Fleet (Admiral Sir John R. Jellicoe) had thirty-seven battleships and battle cruisers, eight armored cruisers, twenty-six light cruisers, and eighty destroyers. It was divided into the Battle Cruiser Fleet (Admiral Sir David Beatty)—which included four fast, new battleships (under Admiral Evan-Thomas)—and the Battle Fleet (under Jellicoe himself). The German High Sea Fleet (Admiral Reinhard von Scheer) had twenty-seven battleships and battle cruisers, eleven light cruisers, and sixty-three destroyers. It was divided into the Scouting Forces (Vice Admiral Franz von Hipper) and the Main Fleet (Scheer).

(In this map's schematic depiction, battle cruiser movements are indicated by dashed lines; battleship movements, by solid lines. Each arrow represents several such major ships. Light cruisers and destroyers are not shown. The numbers enclosed in circles match those used in this text to identify significant locations and actions; in sketches *b* and *c*, they also show the relative positions of the opposing forces at particular times.)

Sketch a. Admiral Scheer, commander of the German Fleet, was naturally aggressive; he was also under public pressure to break the throttling British blockade. He therefore launched a series of raids against the English east coast, seeking to force the dispersion of the British Grand Fleet to protect the various seaports. Apparently believing he had accomplished this, he planned a cruiser raid against Sunderland ①, to draw British warships in that vicinity toward his High Sea Fleet, which would be lurking south of Dogger Bank. Meanwhile, German submarines ② would cruise off the British coast and mine ports used by the British Navy.

Unfavorable weather having prevented air reconnaissance, and his submarines having begun to exhaust their supplies (none participated in the ensuing battle), Scheer abandoned his original plan. Instead, he sent Hipper ③ out on 31 May as a decoy, following with his Main Fleet. British intelligence, however, had discovered his intentions, and Jellicoe ④ and Beatty ⑤ had put to sea on 30 May. At 1400, 31 May, these four naval forces were at position ⑥.

Sketch b. ① 1531: Beatty (six battle cruisers) sighted Hipper (five battle cruisers), who had already sighted Beatty and was turning back toward Scheer. ② 1548: Both forces opened fire: Beatty attempted to get between Hipper and his base; Evan-Thomas was unable to catch up. ③ 1606: The British battle cruiser *Indefatigable* was sunk; Beatty shifted westward, increasing the range, but later closed it; Evan-Thomas opened fire at 1619; the British battle cruiser *Queen Mary* was sunk at 1626. ④ 1642: Beatty sighted Scheer's Main Fleet and turned north to lure it toward Jellicoe (*off map, upper left*). ⑤ 1647: Hipper had just turned north; Evan-Thomas now turned, heavily pounded by Hipper and Scheer. ⑥ 1730: The Germans pursued Beatty northward.

Sketch c. ⑦ 1740: Beatty turned east in search of Jellicoe; Hipper turned to close in on Scheer. ⑧ 1816: Jellicoe approached with his Battle Fleet in six columns, and began to form line of battle; Evan-Thomas took position behind him; the British battle cruiser *Invincible* was sunk at 1834, but Jellicoe's battleships were opening fire and the Germans were beginning to suffer. ⑨ 1835: Scheer turned west under cover of a heavy smoke screen and destroyer attacks; at 1850, Jellicoe turned south. ⑩ 1855: Scheer, possibly thinking that Jellicoe had divided the Grand Fleet, headed back toward Jellicoe, but found he was facing the massed fire of the British line of battle. ⑪ 1917: Scheer again turned west, covering his retreat by a smoke screen, destroyer torpedo attacks, and a "charge" by Hipper's battle cruisers; Jellicoe turned left to avoid the torpedoes; Hipper was badly battered, but got away. ⑫ 2020: Beatty had a last, brief clash with Scheer; at 2030, Jellicoe turned southwest. ⑬ 2100: Jellicoe turned south for the night. At 2106, Scheer closed up his formation; after dark, he cut behind the Grand Fleet (*action not shown*), fought his way through the British light craft covering its rear, and regained his bases. En route, he lost the old battleship *Pommern* and had to sink the crippled battle cruiser *Lützow*. In addition to the major ships already mentioned as sunk, the British lost three armored cruisers and eight destroyers; the Germans, four light cruisers and five destroyers.

The jubilant Germans immediately claimed a victory; the British were correspondingly discouraged. Jellicoe, with some reason, was condemned as overly cautious. The Germans, however, never sought another open battle.

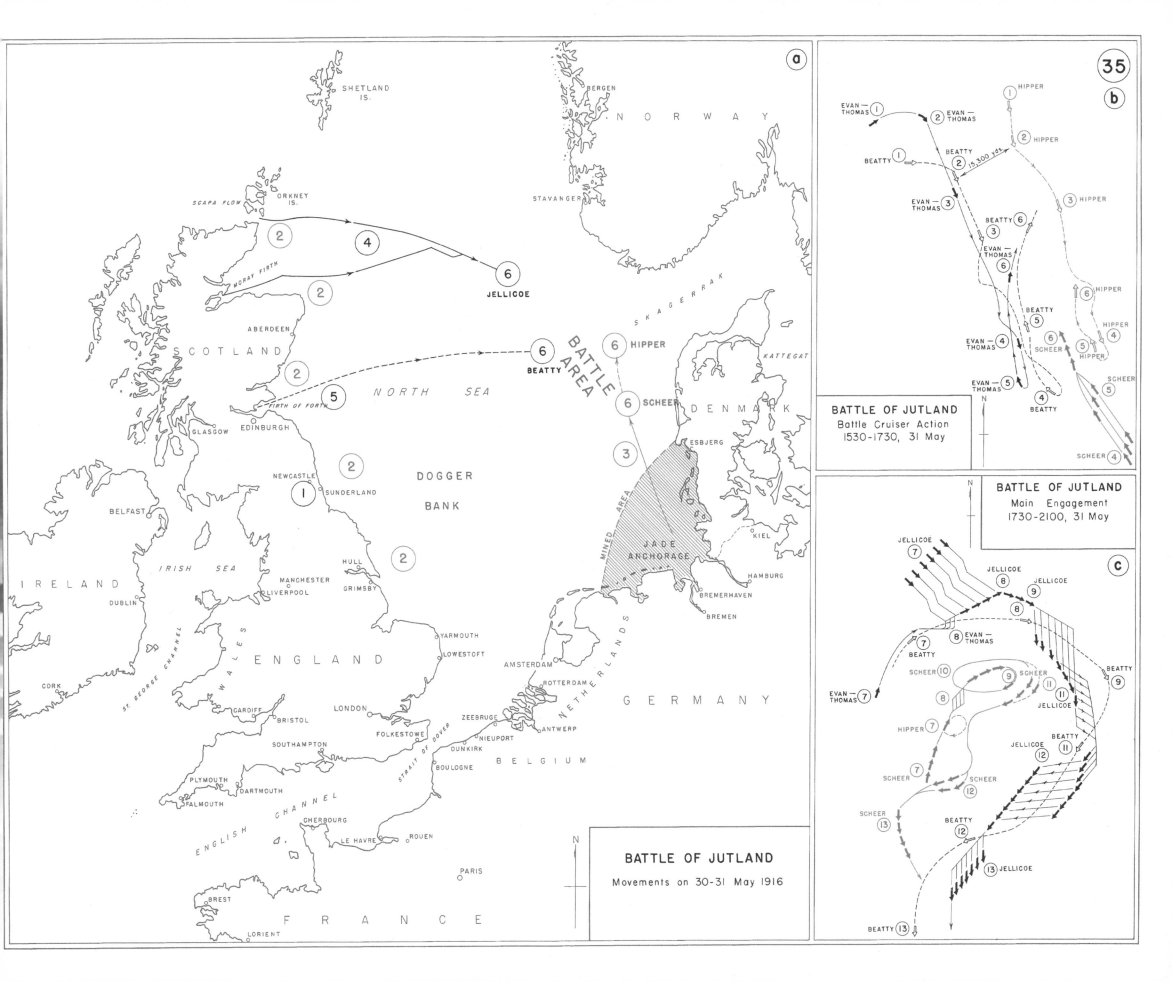

a

SHETLAND IS.

NORWAY

BERGEN

STAVANGER

SCAPA FLOW
ORKNEY IS.

② ④

⑥

② JELLICOE

MORAY FIRTH

SKAGERRAK

ABERDEEN

SCOTLAND

KATTEGAT

⑥ HIPPER

⑥ BEATTY

② ⑥ SCHEER

DENMARK

FIRTH OF FORTH ⑤

NORTH SEA

③

ESBJERG

GLASGOW
EDINBURGH

JADE ANCHORAGE

KIEL

② DOGGER

NEWCASTLE

① SUNDERLAND

BANK

HAMBURG

BELFAST

BREMERHAVEN

BREMEN

IRISH SEA

②

DUBLIN

MANCHESTER
LIVERPOOL

GRIMSBY

YARMOUTH

LOWESTOFT

IRELAND

AMSTERDAM

ROTTERDAM

NETHERLANDS

GERMANY

ST. GEORGE CHANNEL

WALES

ENGLAND

ANTWERP

CORK

CARDIFF

LONDON

BRISTOL

ZEEBRUGE

NIEUPORT

BELGIUM

SOUTHAMPTON

FOLKESTOWE

DUNKIRK

PLYMOUTH

DARTMOUTH

STRAIT OF DOVER

BOULOGNE

FALMOUTH

ENGLISH CHANNEL

CHERBOURG

LE HAVRE

ROUEN

N

BREST

PARIS

FRANCE

LORIENT

BATTLE OF JUTLAND

Movements on 30-31 May 1916

35

b

① HIPPER

EVAN — THOMAS ①

EVAN — THOMAS ②

② HIPPER

BEATTY ①

BEATTY ② 15,300 yds

③ HIPPER

EVAN — THOMAS ③

BEATTY ③ ⑥

BEATTY ⑥

EVAN — THOMAS ⑥

⑥ HIPPER

BEATTY ⑤

EVAN — THOMAS ④

⑥ SCHEER ⑤ HIPPER

④ HIPPER

SCHEER ⑤

EVAN — THOMAS ⑤

④ BEATTY

N

SCHEER ④

BATTLE OF JUTLAND

Battle Cruiser Action
1530-1730, 31 May

BATTLE OF JUTLAND

Main Engagement
1730-2100, 31 May

N

c

JELLICOE ⑦

JELLICOE ⑧

JELLICOE ⑨

⑧

⑦ ⑧ EVAN — THOMAS

BEATTY ⑨

BEATTY ⑦

SCHEER ⑩ ⑨ SCHEER ⑪

EVAN — THOMAS ⑦

⑧ ⑪ JELLICOE

HIPPER ⑦

BEATTY ⑪

JELLICOE ⑫

SCHEER ⑦

SCHEER ⑫

SCHEER ⑬

BEATTY ⑫

⑬ JELLICOE

BEATTY ⑬

As 1915 drew to a close, the battle fronts were everywhere stabilized (*sketch* a). The 1915 Allied and German offensives in the West (*see map 32*) had made insignificant gains and had cost both sides heavily. The Russians, driven 180 miles east of Warsaw in the Gorlice-Tarnow disaster (*see map 27*), had desperately sought to rebuild their armies for the coming summer. Falkenhayn, convinced that Russian power was broken for some time, had turned to the West and moved troops to the Verdun area for his heralded battle of attrition (*see map 33*). But first he had to rid the Balkans of a nuisance—Serbia. In a whirlwind campaign in late 1915 (*see map 48*), Serbia had been overrun, and the front advanced to the Greek border. The Allies tried to assist the Serbs by sending an expedition to Salonika, but the Serbs had to retreat into Albania. In Italy, the first four battles of the Isonzo had been fought (*see map 42*), and the Italians had little to show for 250,000 casualties. On the minor fronts (*none shown*), the tide of battle had turned against the Allies. The Dardanelles venture (*see map 31*) had been reluctantly abandoned; in Egypt, Turks and Britons watched each other across the Suez Canal; in Mesopotamia, General Sir Charles V. F. Townshend's force was under siege at Kut (*see map 52*); and in German East Africa, a British expeditionary force had been trounced.

At Chantilly in December, 1915, the Allies finally agreed on a combined offensive for the summer of 1916. We have seen that this plan was initially frustrated by Falkenhayn's Verdun offensive. When this began, the French appealed to the Russians for assistance. In quick response, the Russians launched a two-pronged drive (*this map, action not shown*) in the vicinity of Lake Narotch (*sketch* a, *right center*) on 18 March, 1916. During the winter, the Tsar's armies had recovered somewhat, but they were still no match for the efficient Germans. By the 26th, the costly offensive had bogged down in the seas of mud resulting from the spring thaw.

Quiet returned to the Eastern Front; Russia resumed planning for the July offensive which was to be spearheaded by the West Army Group, making the main effort toward Vilna (*right center*). Again, an enemy offensive disrupted plans—this time by Austria's attacking in Italy on 14 May, 1916 (*see map 42*). When Italy appealed to the Tsar for help, he promised a diversion. The intent was to move the July offensive up, but—except for General Alexei A. Brusilov—the army group commanders lacked enthusiasm. Hence, the courageous Brusilov volunteered to attack alone on 4 June. The Stavka expected the main attack to follow ten days later. Brusilov had studied German tactics and judged that concentration of combat power could be sacrificed if surprise were gained. Thus he planned to attack with all his armies (*this map, sketch* b) and forgo pronounced massing of troops. Every effort was made to preserve secrecy, enemy positions were studied in detail, artillery ammunition was accumulated, and divisions were thoroughly briefed. As a result, the attack was the greatest Russian success of the war. By 10 June, the Austrian line had been breached in two places. By late June, the important transportation center of Kowel (*upper left*) was in danger, and Germany again had to aid Austria. General Alexander von Linsingen was ordered to stop the critical northern drive. The battle seesawed, and Brusilov was slowed but not halted. Since West and North Army Groups produced no effective diversions, the Tsar elected to reinforce Brusilov and let him continue attacking. Thus it became a race between the excellent German-Austrian lateral communications and the inferior Russian railroads. The Germans won. Though Brusilov's attacks continued in desperation during August and September, they gained little and resulted in tremendous losses. By 20 September, the offensive collapsed of sheer exhaustion.

Brusilov's offensive, in conjunction with reverses in France, had far-reaching strategic consequences: Conrad's Italian and Falkenhayn's Verdun attacks were weakened; Falkenhayn's position as chief of staff was undermined; Rumania joined the Allies; and a battered Austria accepted German direction of the war. The Russians, however, had lost more than 1,000,000 men and were crippled and depressed. The stage was set for Lenin's return and the Revolution.

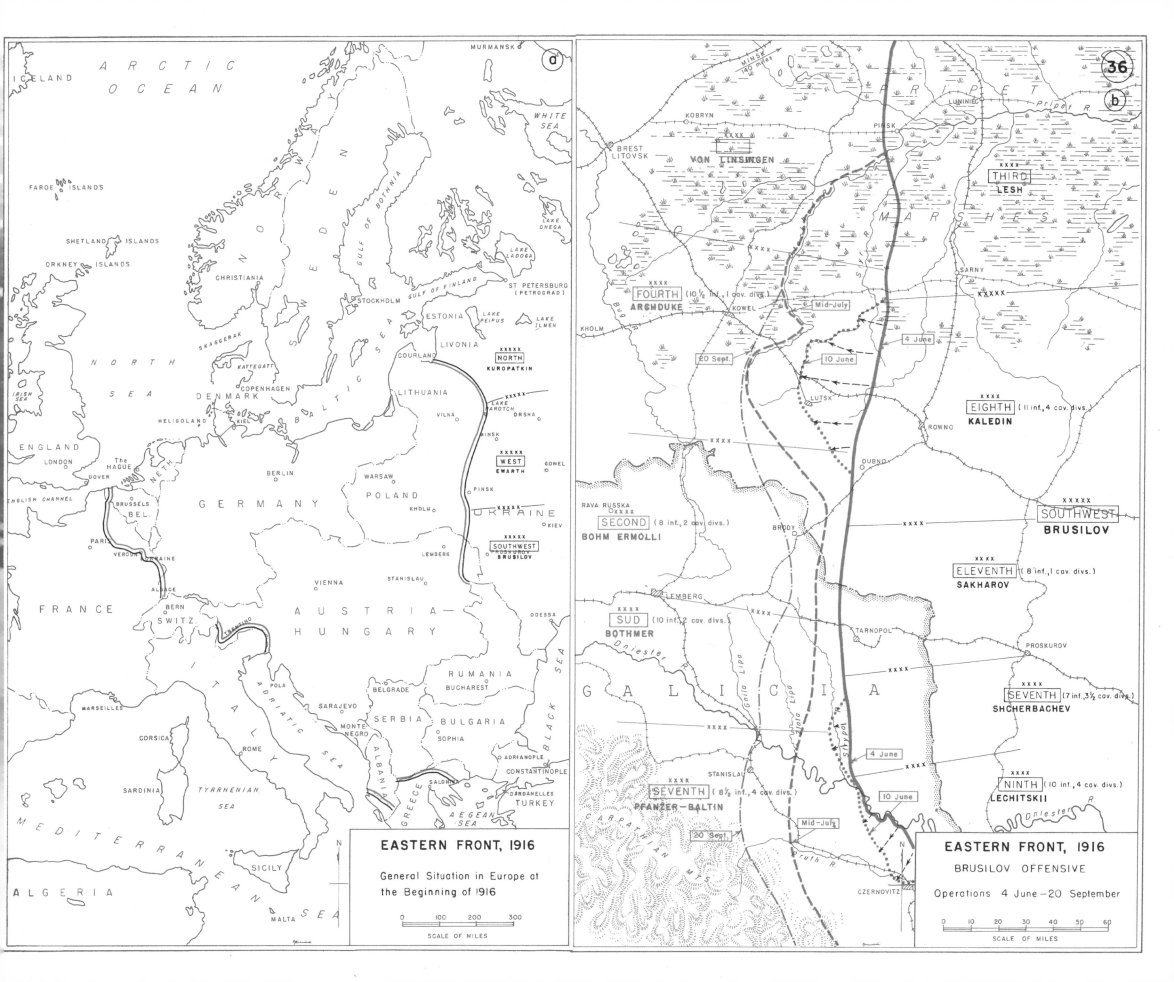

36

EASTERN FRONT, 1916

General Situation in Europe at
the Beginning of 1916

SCALE OF MILES
0   100   200   300

EASTERN FRONT, 1916

BRUSILOV OFFENSIVE

Operations 4 June—20 September

SCALE OF MILES
0   10   20   30   40   50   60

On 27 August, 1916, Rumania declared war on the Central Powers. For two years, she had watched the progress of the great struggle and contemplated joining the Allies. When the Central Powers closed the Dardanelles, she considered permitting the transport of supplies from Serbia to Russia across Rumanian railways, but fear of the Central Powers, surrounding her on three sides as they did, caused her grave concern. In 1915 Russian defeats after Gorlice-Tarnow increased her concerns and delayed her joining the Allies. Then, as the news in the East seemed to indicate an Austrian disaster—Brusilov's offensive being the cause—Rumania bargained with the Western Allies, establishing an imposing list of territorial demands as her price for driving the last nail into the Austrian coffin. France and Britain, disconsolate over events in the West, eagerly sought her aid and were quite willing to meet almost any demand. But Russia, suspicious of her neighbor because of her pre-1914 Austrian ties, and disdainful of her military capabilities, was not at all happy about developments. (The Russians well knew that Rumania coveted Bessarabia [upper right; territory between Pruth and Dniester Rivers]: in 1877, a Russo-Rumanian war with Turkey had wrested this province from Turkey, and Russia had claimed it, giving to her ally the barren Dobruja [lower right].) So, after almost two months of bickering, Rumania joined the Allies; in exchange for four military commitments, she had forfeited her most precious advantage—time. In June, while Brusilov hammered the Galician front, a Rumanian offensive might have succeeded; but by August the Russians had been contained, and German troops were now available to test Rumania's mettle. Furthermore, Falkenhayn, watching the fence-straddling act carefully, had foreseen Rumania's likely entry into the war and prepared accordingly. Consequently, Mackensen was in Bulgaria organizing the Danube Army, and offensive plans were prepared for implementation by 30 September, the earliest date anticipated for the Rumanian entry into the war.

The map illustrates Rumania's weak strategic position. The length of her borders was out of proportion to the country's depth—Bucharest was only thirty miles from Bulgaria. The rugged Transylvanian Alps served as a barrier against Austria, as did the Danube against Bulgaria in the south. There were several passes through the mountains, the most important being those traversed by the railroads shown. The only permanent Danube bridge was at Cernavoda on the railroad to the seaport of Constanza. This latter city was important to Rumania for it was the best link to outside help—the railroads leading into Moldavia had been purposely neglected by Russia before the war when Rumania and Austria were friendly. In contrast to the excellent railroad net in Transylvania, Rumania's system was poor and afforded little capability for rapid lateral movement. Using Austrian railroads, the distance between Predeal and Red Tower Passes (center) was 80 miles; via the Rumanian system, it was 270 miles.

Nor was the Rumanian Army very efficient. By 1916, it had twenty-three divisions, but was short of artillery, communications equipment, aircraft, rifles, and machine guns. Its senior leaders were inexperienced and none too well qualified; staff work and the state of training were notoriously poor. Lacking manufacturing facilities, the country had to rely upon Allied support.

Rumania's war plan was based upon Allied promises to: attack northward from Salonika (off map, bottom) to divert Bulgaria; attack Austria in the Bukovina (top center); send three Russian divisions to Dobruja; and supply munitions. She considered two plans: Plan A—to defend against Austria, while launching a major drive into Bulgaria to link up with the Salonika offensive; and Plan B—to launch the major attack into Transylvania, defending elsewhere. Swayed by political aims, and against Allied advice, Rumania chose Plan B. She disposed her troops as shown and prepared to attack, the initial objective being the line of the Maros River.

The plan of the Central Powers envisaged holding attacks by the First Army, while the Ninth Army, making the main effort, moved through the mountains on Bucharest. Meanwhile, Mackensen would subjugate Dobruja and eventually cross the Danube to support the Ninth Army. As chief of the general staff, Falkenhayn approved the plan, little suspecting that, upon his relief, it would be his lot to execute it.

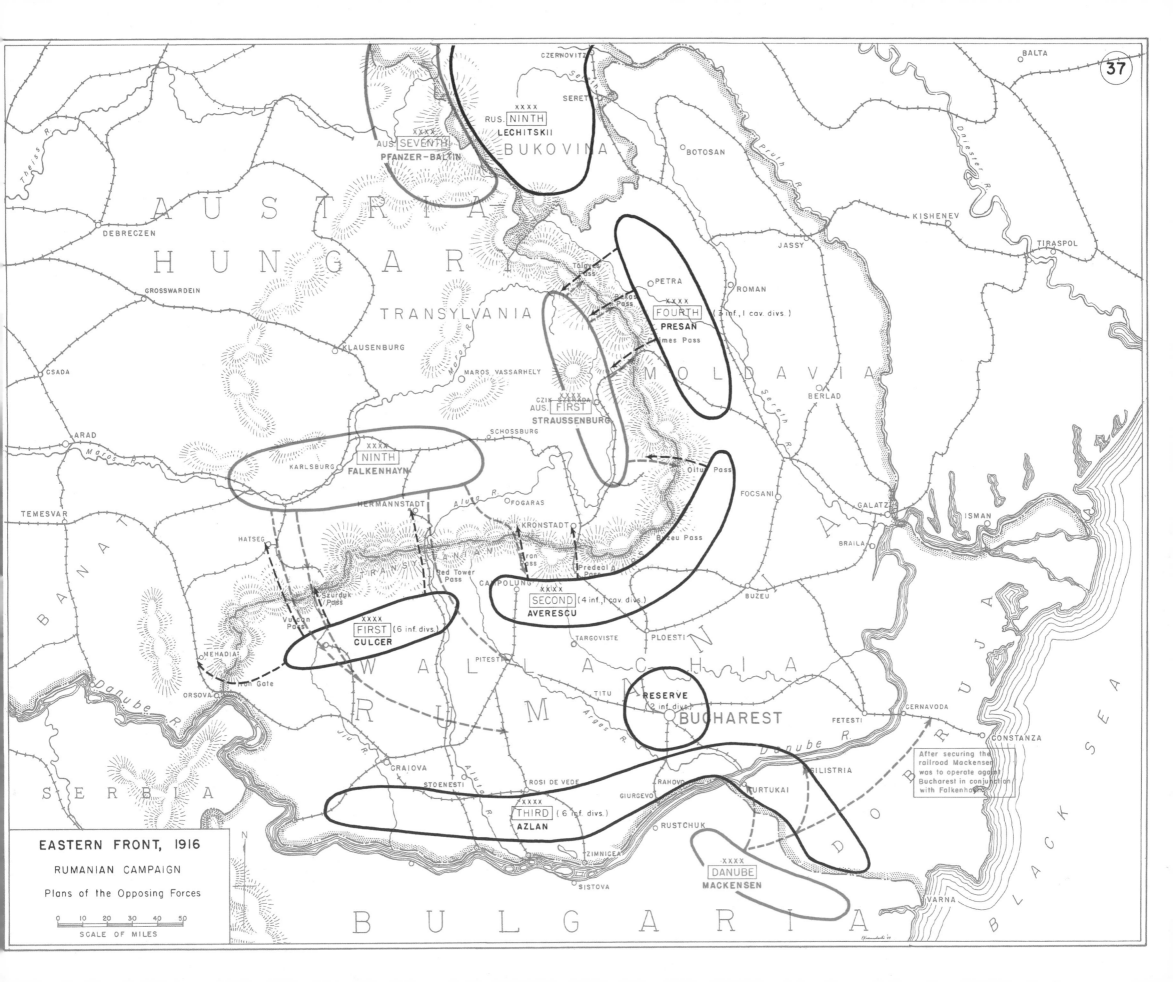

EASTERN FRONT, 1916

RUMANIAN CAMPAIGN

Plans of the Opposing Forces

0 10 20 30 40 50
SCALE OF MILES

After securing the
railroad Mackensen
was to operate against
Bucharest in conjunction
with Falkenhayn

On the night of 27-28 August, the First, Second, and Fourth Rumanian Armies began their advance into Transylvania. Ill-equipped and poorly trained for mountain warfare, hindered by lack of lateral communications, and obstructed by the dearth of roads, the Rumanians moved slowly. Austrian resistance was not spirited, their units being understrength and for the most part recuperating from the mauling administered by Brusilov. In two weeks, the Second Army had made gains of fifty miles, but, by 18 September, the Rumanian armies had been stopped on the line shown. Austrian resistance had stiffened as the defenders fell back to a shorter front, and as German troops continued to arrive to fill up the Ninth Army. To the Rumanians, now striving to improve their logistical situation, the outlook on the northern front seemed promising. Already through the worst of the mountains, they anticipated breaking out into the Hungarian plain very shortly.

But from Dobruja (*lower right*), ominous news was trickling in to Bucharest, and in the Hermannstadt-Hatseg area (*center, left*) Falkenhayn's Ninth Army was almost ready to launch a counterattack designed to isolate the northern Rumanian armies.

Outside Rumania, the Allies were belatedly carrying out their promised diversionary operations. Prior to the Rumanians advancing into Transylvania, the Bulgars struck the Salonika front. This attack delayed the Allied offensive from Salonika until 10 September. Though the Allied offensive continued until November, it made only meager gains and had little influence on the campaign in Rumania. Russia, the most reluctant ally, was exerting pressure—if only token—on the common enemy in Bukovina (*this map, top center*) and had dispatched the three promised divisions to Dobruja.

South of the Danube, Field Marshal von Mackensen had not tarried in implementing his part of the Austro-German plan. On 1 September, his conglomerate army—made up of Bulgars, Turks, and a few Germans—crossed the border into Dobruja. Two of his Bulgarian divisions brushed aside covering forces and reached Turtukai the next day. Meanwhile, his right columns advanced north, parallel to the sea, and heavy artillery moved up from Rustchuk. The fortified city of Turtukai (25,000 men and 100 guns) surrendered on the 6th, after four days of heavy fighting and the failure of a relief column from Silistria to break through Mackensen's lines. The Danube Army continued its advance, occupying Silistria on the 9th. On the 16th, however, it came up against the remnants of the Rumanian Third Army—reinforced by a Russian corps and a division of Serbian volunteers—in a strong defensive position (*dashed blue line*) just south of the Cernavoda-Constanza railroad. The Russian General Zaionchovsky commanded this mixed force of nine divisions. Mackensen, who had left minimum security forces along the Danube, had about the same number of troops as his foe, but his artillery was superior. Appreciating the vital importance of Constanza to Rumania, he decided to attack.

Meanwhile, consternation reigned in Bucharest. There, under unopposed air attack and unnerved by Mackensen's success, the Rumanian strategists became panicky. Three divisions were ordered to Dobruja from Transylvania, thus slowing the drive on the northern front.

Mackensen's attack made no progress in four days of violent fighting. The Allies had hoped that the Bulgars would be reluctant to attack the Russians (traditionally their protectors), but Zaionchovsky made the mistake of sending his Serbs (their blood enemies) against Mackensen's Bulgars. Zaionchovsky, now reinforced with the three divisions from Transylvania, launched a counterattack. In three days, Mackensen was driven back ten miles. Here, the line temporarily stabilized as both sides, in an exhausted state, looked to their logistical problems. Up to this date, Rumania had been receiving only thirty tons of ammunition per day—one-tenth of that promised by her allies. Supplies could reach Rumania only by way of Russia, and large backlogs had developed at all Russian ports.

In the northwest, Falkenhayn had opened his counteroffensive on the 18th; and in Bucharest, Rumanian high councils were brewing a new strategy.

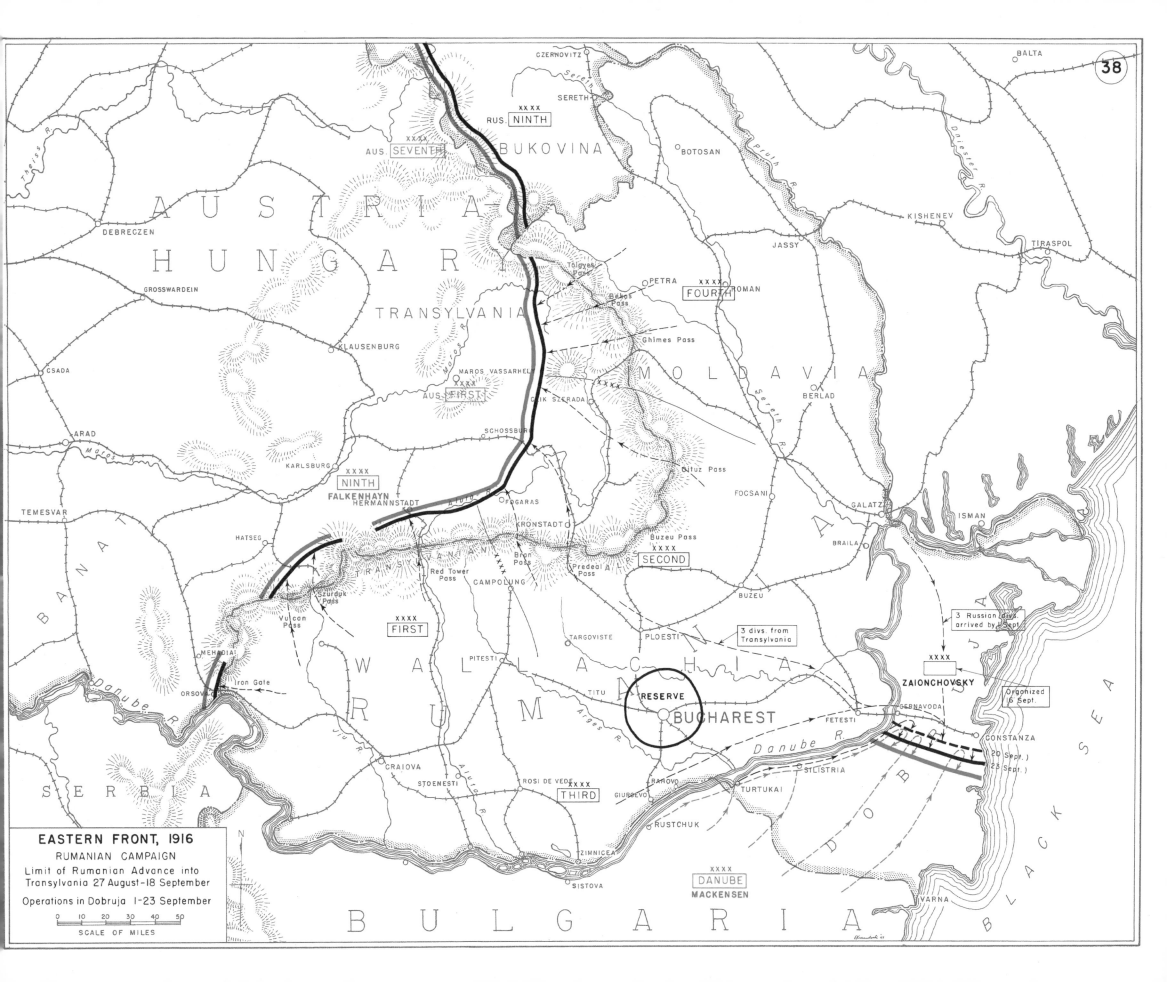

BALTA

CZERNOVITZ

SERETH

RUS. NINTH

BUKOVINA

BOTOSAN

KISHENEV

TIRASPOL

DEBRECZEN

AUSTRIA-

AUS. SEVENTH

JASSY

HUNGARY

GROSSWARDEIN

TRANSYLVANIA

Tölgyes Pass

Bekas Pass

PETRA

FOURTH

ROMAN

Ghimes Pass

MOLDAVIA

KLAUSENBURG

CSADA

MAROS VASSARHELY

AUS. FIRST

CIIK SZERADA

BERLAD

ARAD

SCHOSSBUR

Oituz Pass

KARLSBURG

NINTH

FALKENHAYN

HERMANNSTADT

FOGARAS

FOCSANI

GALATZ

ISMAN

TEMESVAR

HATSEG

KRONSTADT

Buzeu Pass

BRAILA

Bran Pass

SECOND

Predeal ALPS

TRANSYLVAN

Red Tower Pass

CAMPOLUNG

BUZEU

Szurduk Pass

Vulcan Pass

FIRST

3 Russian divs. arrived by Sept.

3 divs. from Transylvania

TARGOVISTE

PLOESTI

ZAIONCHOVSKY

MEHADIA

Iron Gate

Organized 16 Sept.

ORSOVO

TITU

RESERVE

BUCHAREST

FETESTI

CERNAVODA

CONSTANZA

W A L L A C H I A

R U M A N

Danube R.

20 Sept.

23 Sept.

Jiu R.

TARGOVISTE

PITESTI

Arges R.

SILISTRIA

BANAT

CRAIOVA

STOENESTI

Aluta R.

ROSI DE VEDE

THIRD

RAHOVO

GIURGEVO

TURTUKAI

D O B R U J A

SERBIA

Danube R.

RUSTCHUK

ZIMNICEA

DANUBE

MACKENSEN

VARNA

B L A C K   S E A

SISTOVA

B U L G A R I A

38

EASTERN FRONT, 1916

RUMANIAN CAMPAIGN

Limit of Rumanian Advance into
Transylvania 27 August-18 September

Operations in Dobruja 1-23 September

0 10 20 30 40 50
SCALE OF MILES

Falkenhayn arrived to assume command of the Ninth Army on 18 September. As previously noted, the Rumanian advance through the mountains had generally stalled by that date (*dashed blue line*). The German general's first concern was the Rumanian First Army's drive toward Hatseg (*lower left*) and the important railroad to the north. Here, on 18 September, he launched his first counterattack, seeking to force the Rumanians back through Vulcan Pass. The attack stopped the First Army advance but did not achieve its ultimate aim. On 26 September, Falkenhayn struck at the Rumanian column moving on Hermannstadt. Elite German Alpine troops enveloped both flanks of the column and barely missed cutting it off from its escape routes. The Rumanians were forced back across the border, and the Germans seized Red Tower Pass. Meanwhile, the Rumanian Second and Fourth Armies, in an attempt to remove pressure from the First Army, had advanced toward Schossburg and Maros Vassarhely by the 29th. On 4 October, the Germans attacked the left flank of the Second Army, forcing it to fall back on Kronstadt. By 10 October, the bulk of the Second Army, like the First Army, had been compelled to retreat within the Rumanian border. To the north, the Fourth Army—less from Austrian pressure than from fear of isolation when its southern neighbor withdrew—fell back on the eastern mountain passes. Now the Rumanians were on the defensive everywhere.

Meanwhile, what had been the decision of the Rumanian council of war sitting at Bucharest in late September? Concerned with Mackensen's unexpected thrust into Dobruja, but still primarily motivated by the desire to subjugate Transylvania, the high command had compromised. General Averescu's Third Army (*not shown, but then south of Bucharest*) was given the reserve divisions at Bucharest and ordered to strike Mackensen's rear by crossing the Danube at Rahovo while Zaionchovsky held him in place near Constanza with a secondary attack. At the same time, on the Transylvanian front, the Rumanian armies would continue the advance.

We have seen the repulse of the advance into Austria-Hungary. The same fate awaited Averescu's attack. About 1 October, the crossing (*action not shown*) was begun at Rahovo, but a sudden flood disrupted it; the few units which reached the south bank were eliminated by Danube Army detachments. By then, Falkenhayn's Hermannstadt attack had created the need for Rumanian reinforcements in Transylvania; most of Averescu's troops were promptly dispatched there.

On the Transylvanian front, Falkenhayn pushed his drive through the passes. Campolung (*center*) fell on 14 October. Predeal Pass was in German hands by 25 October, but winter snows and stiffening resistance combined to halt the advance. Meanwhile, to the west, Delmensingen's troops pushed south of Red Tower Pass. In the north, the Fourth Army gave ground slowly. By 25 October, the German advance had reached the position shown (*dotted blue line*). In early November, the Russians assumed responsibility for part of the Fourth Army front.

In Dobruja, Mackensen, reinforced with two Turkish divisions, renewed the offensive on 20 October. Three days later, Constanza fell, followed by Cernavoda on the 25th. Having eliminated the vital sea and rail link to Russia, Mackensen now moved part of his army to Sistova (*bottom center*) in preparation for an attack toward Bucharest.

Since the approaching winter would soon make the mountains almost impassable, Falkenhayn had to move quickly. Though he preferred a movement through the northern passes—thus isolating more Rumanian troops—he elected to attack in the Vulcan Pass area (*lower left*), where the defenses were weaker. Reinforced by four German divisions from the Western Front, this attack jumped off on 10 November and reached Craiova by the 21st. Only one Rumanian division was cut off, the rest of the First Army withdrawing east of the Aluta River. Meanwhile, Delmensingen and Morgen were pushing forward slowly, as the Rumanians, their defenses turned on their left, withdrew (*solid blue lines*). In the south, Mackensen crossed the Danube against feeble opposition on 23 November, and advanced in the next three days to the line shown.

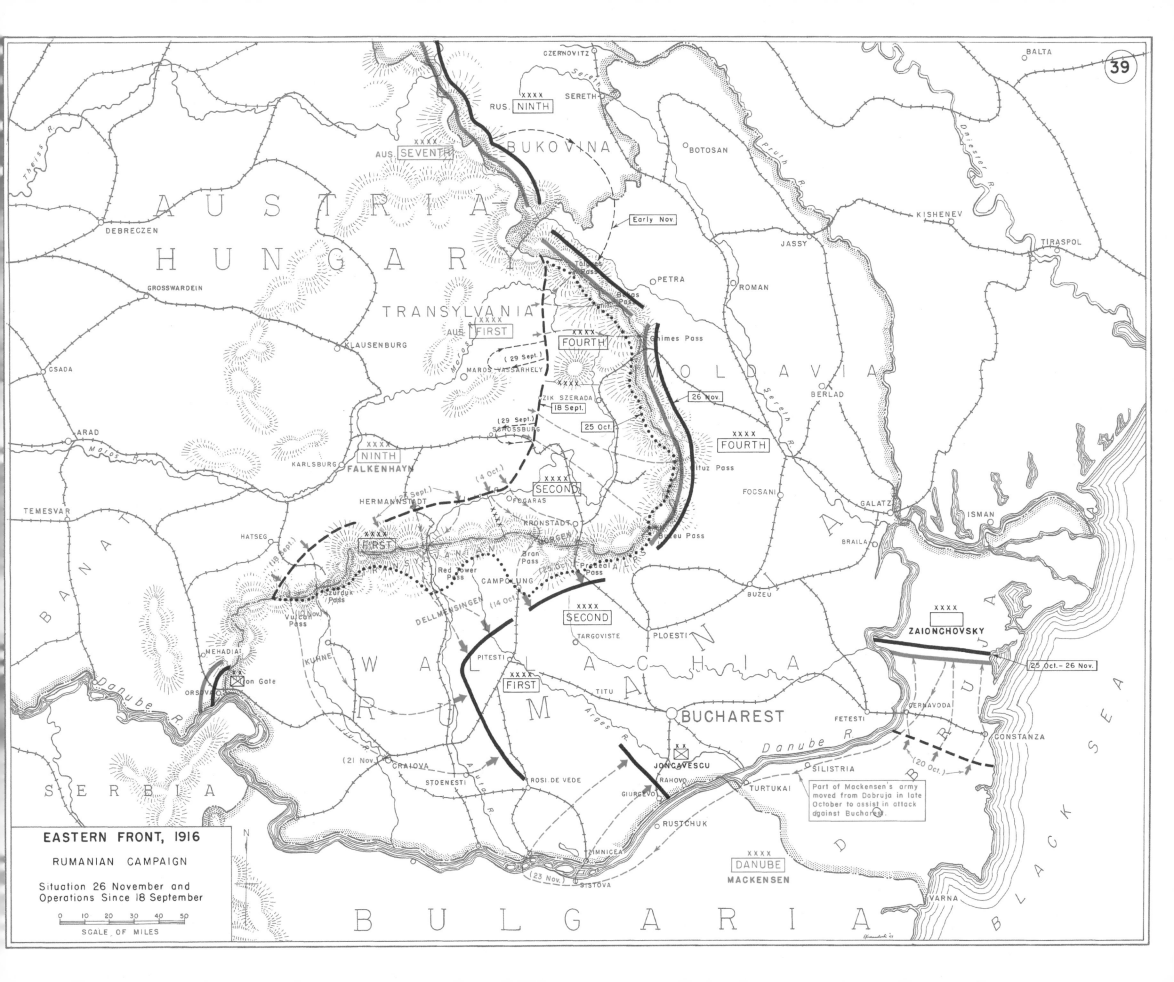

39

EASTERN FRONT, 1916

RUMANIAN CAMPAIGN

Situation 26 November and
Operations Since 18 September

0 10 20 30 40 50
SCALE OF MILES

Part of Mackensen's army
moved from Dobruja in late
October to assist in attack
against Bucharest.

On 26 November, the situation of the Rumanian Army (reduced to seventeen infantry and three cavalry divisions) was desperate. Its line bulged west of Bucharest in a huge salient which invited a converging attack on the capital. Under these conditions, Falkenhayn did not anticipate a determined Rumanian stand against his twenty divisions. But there was a gap between Mackensen's army and Falkenhayn's right which served to expose the former to attack before he could be supported by the Ninth Army. Averescu, now supreme Rumanian commander, agreed to the plan proposed by General Presan (commanding the forces concentrating at Bucharest), whereby Mackensen would be struck a blow while the First and Second Armies held off Falkenhayn. Under the circumstances, the Rumanians are to be admired for the boldness of their concept. Defeat was certainly not to be prevented by remaining passively on the defensive everywhere. There appeared to be little chance of success against the Ninth Army while Mackensen was on the Rumanian rear. But if Mackensen could be driven against the Danube, enough time might be gained to allow for the arrival of expected Russian reinforcements.

Presan's plan provided that three Rumanian infantry divisions—their right flank screened by two cavalry divisions which would push into the gap between Mackensen and Falkenhayn—would emerge from the Bucharest area and envelop Mackensen's left flank. Simultaneously, three Russian divisions would strike his right, while the force already in contact with him would fix him in position by frontal attacks. Two divisions were to be held in reserve.

The attack commenced on 1 December, but without the support of the Russians, who disagreed with the plan. It achieved initial success, cutting off part of Mackensen's force, but the reserve was committed too late to be of decisive value. The cavalry flank guard—its inferiority in strength was the weak link in the plan—was brushed aside by a superior force dispatched by Falkenhayn on 2 December. This force then attacked Presan's right and rear and drove the Rumanians back in panic. At the same time, Ninth Army elements applied pressure all along the line, particularly in Delmensingen's sector.

The dispirited Rumanian troops now fell back all along the line, abandoning Bucharest, which Falkenhayn's patrols entered on 6 December. The exhausted condition of the German troops, heavy rainfall, and the resultant poor roads slowed the pursuit. By 7 January, 1917, when the campaign ended, the opposing forces were on the line shown. The last days of campaigning had seen several battles between Germans and Russians, the latter having been reinforced heavily in fear of a German advance into southern Russia.

Thus, Germany solved another Balkan problem. The Rumanians did not formally capitulate, but the bulk of the country—including the grain- and oil-producing areas—was in German hands. The Rumanian Army was no longer a threat, having been reduced to a state of impotency. (In January, it was considered capable of defending only a twenty-mile front.) The campaign cost Germany about 60,000 combat casualties (and about the same number sick); estimates of Rumanian losses vary between 300,000 and 400,000.

In retrospect, the Rumanian government obviously committed a serious error by letting its concerns with postwar acquisitions delay its declaration of war. Militarily, Rumania's strategy could not have been worse. In choosing Transylvania as the initial objective, she ignored the threat to her rear. When the advance through the mountains failed, the high command refused to economize forces on that front to allow the creation of a mobile reserve, with which Falkenhayn's later thrust could be countered. Nowhere did the Rumanians properly mass their forces to achieve concentration of combat power. But, in the final analysis, the pronounced Austro-German superiority in leadership and training probably had the most decisive effect on the campaign.

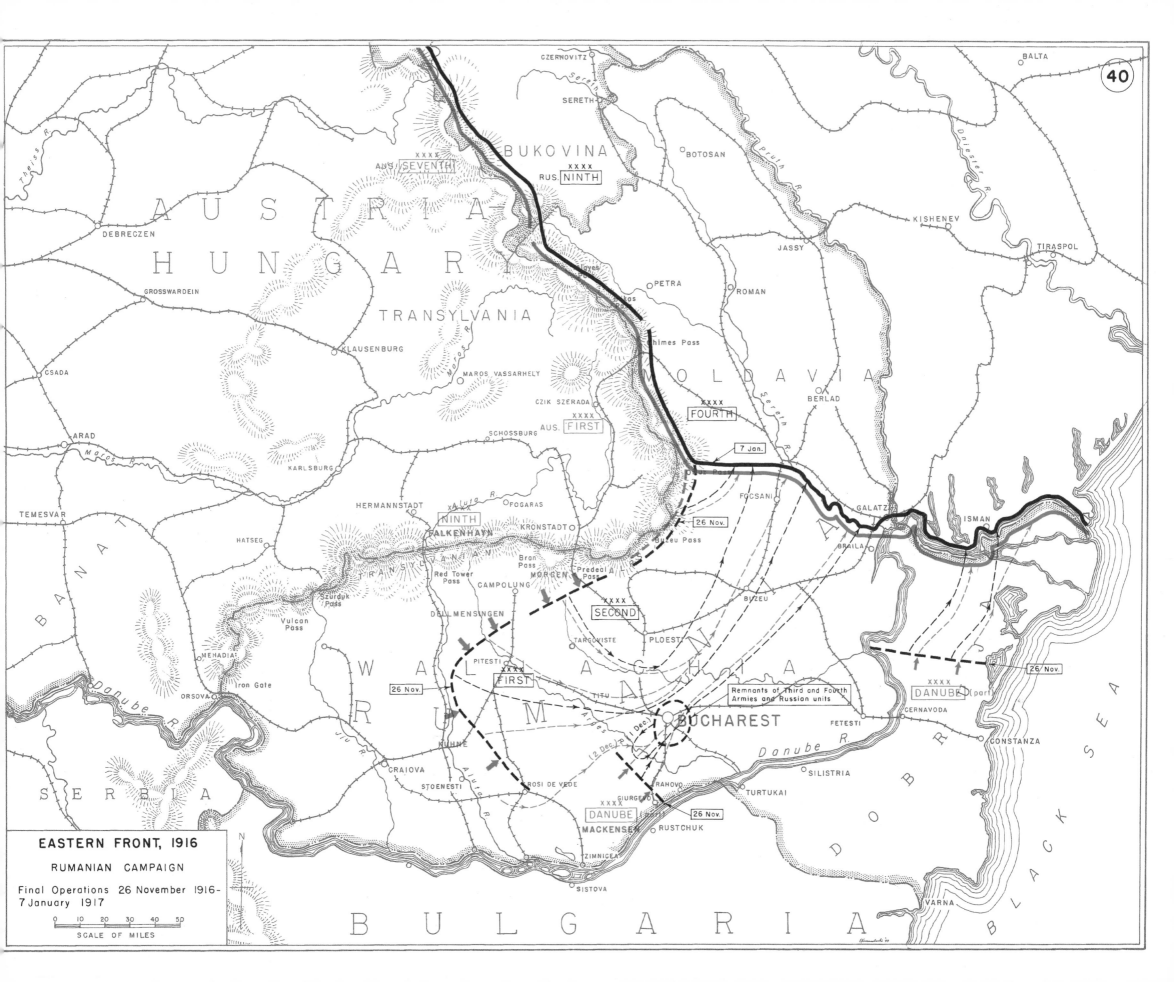

EASTERN FRONT, 1916

RUMANIAN CAMPAIGN

Final Operations 26 November 1916–
7 January 1917

0   10   20   30   40   50
SCALE OF MILES

Morale in the Russian armies had deteriorated rapidly since August, 1916. The callous disregard of the top-level leadership for loss of life among the troops was the principal cause. Nor had the Tsar, under Rasputin's sinister influence, yielded to demands for governmental reforms; instead, he became more autocratic and seemed bent on destroying the limited support he still enjoyed from the liberal middle class.

The Tsar, reacting to Rasputin's assassination in December with unexpected ruthlessness, governed more than ever through mysticism. By then, all elements of the army were ripe for change, and, when rebellion broke out in St. Petersburg on 12 March, Nicholas was without major support. Three days later, he abdicated, and a liberal provisional government swept into power. Its avowed leader was the socialist Kerensky, but an organization, "The Soviet of Workmen and Soldiers Representatives," controlled much of the capital. This "Soviet," one of whose prime aims was the destruction of discipline in the army, took to its bosom the exiled Bolshevik revolutionaries, Lenin and Trotsky, upon their return to the country. Meanwhile, the Kerensky government had issued its famous "Order No. 1," designed to create a more democratic army. The result was complete chaos, the breakdown of discipline, mass desertions by peasants eager to claim land of their own, the murder of many officers, and the eventual disintegration of the army.

The Germans were quick to appreciate that the growing demoralization in Russian ranks would spread with inaction. So, during the spring and summer, they suspended offensive operations. Perhaps they might have been wiser to attack while Russia was so disorganized, force a peace, and then concentrate maximum strength in the West months earlier than Ludendorff finally did.

The Allies eventually pressed the Kerensky government to resume offensive operations to prevent Germany from taking advantage of the disastrous consequences of the Nivelle offensive in the West. Kerensky and Brusilov (now chief of staff)

tried to whip up enthusiasm for an attack among the troops; but the seeds of Bolshevik propaganda, lack of discipline, and an earlier affirmation of a policy of peace were too strong. Nevertheless, the offensive was planned for 1 July.

Brusilov selected the most reliable formations (Finns, Siberians, and Poles) and launched the attack toward Lemberg (*sketch* a). Gains of thirty miles were made, but the troops soon became discouraged and rebellious. On the 19th, a well-prepared German counteroffensive—sparked by troops moved from the Western Front—struck the north flank of the Russian offensive and, by 3 August, had driven to the Galician border.

The Russian defeat was the signal for an unsuccessful attempt by Lenin to usurp control. Kerensky might have been able to retain his power, if Ludendorff had not decided to attack at Riga (*top center*) in order to force Russia into an armistice. This attack, on 1 September, was highly successful and was an early use of a new German assault technique, eventually to be known as "infiltration tactics." The Riga attack had the desired effect on the Kerensky government: it toppled on 8 October. Lenin, vaulting into power, immediately asked for an armistice. On 2 December, hostilities were suspended, and in January, 1918, delegates met at Brest Litovsk to agree on terms. For two months Trotsky haggled and propagandized, until Hoffman—introducing him to the cold realities of the situation—arranged for a German advance along the Gulf of Finland toward St. Petersburg. Russia, powerless to interfere, finally signed the treaty on 3 March. Germany occupied the territory shown (*sketch* b), thereby ensuring additional food supplies for a needy homeland but not enough to overcome the strangling effects of the Allied blockade.

The war on the Eastern Front was over. The Bolsheviks were free to carry on their first-priority task—subjugation of Russia—and Ludendorff had extra strength for the Western Front. But it had lasted long enough to prevent Germany from ever massing her total strength in the West to achieve a decisive victory.

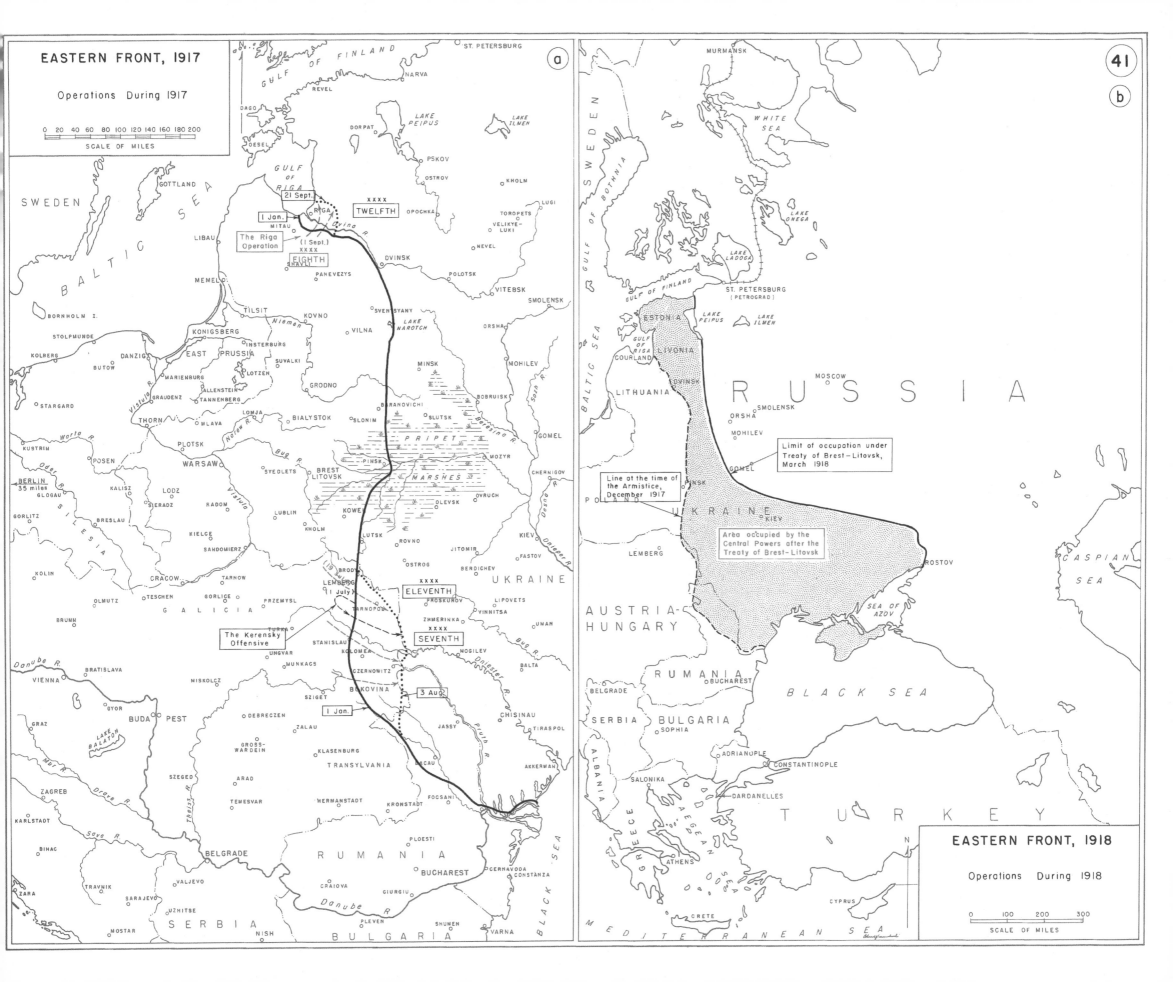

EASTERN FRONT, 1917

Operations During 1917

0 20 40 60 80 100 120 140 160 180 200
SCALE OF MILES

41
a
b

21 Sept.
1 Jan.
The Riga Operation
(1 Sept.)
XXXX
TWELFTH
XXXX
EIGHTH
SHAVLI

ELEVENTH
(1 July)
XXXX
The Kerensky Offensive
XXXX
SEVENTH
3 Aug.
1 Jan.

SWEDEN

BALTIC SEA

GULF OF FINLAND
ST. PETERSBURG
NARVA
REVEL
DAGO
LAKE PEIPUS
LAKE ILMEN
PSKOV
OSTROV
KHOLM
GULF OF RIGA
OESEL
RIGA
MITAU
Dvina R.
LUGI
TOROPETS
VELIKYE-LUKI
DVINSK
NEVEL
POLOTSK
VITEBSK
SMOLENSK
GOTTLAND
LIBAU
MEMEL
TILSIT
KOVNO
SVEN SYANY
VILNA
LAKE NAROTCH
ORSHA
MOHILEV
PANEVEZYS
Niemen R.
BORNHOLM I.
STOLPMUNDE
KONIGSBERG
INSTERBURG
SUVALKI
GRODNO
MINSK
BOBRUISK
Soin R.
KOLBERG
DANZIG
EAST PRUSSIA
LOTZEN
BARANOVICHI
SLUTSK
Beresino R.
GOMEL
BUTOW
MARIENBURG
ALLENSTEIN
TANNENBERG
GRAUDENZ
MLAWA
Narew R.
BIALYSTOK
SLONIM
PRIPET
PINSK
MARSHES
MOZYR
CHERNIGOV
STARGARD
THORN
Vistula R.
Bug R.
BREST LITOVSK
OVRUCH
Desna R.
KUSTRIN
Warta R.
PLOTSK
WARSAW
SYEDLETS
KOWEL
OLEVSK
POSEN
LODZ
SIERADZ
RADOM
LUBLIN
LUTSK
ROVNO
JITOMIR
KIEV
FASTOV
Dnieper R.
BERLIN 35 miles
GLOGAU
SILESIA
KALISZ
KHOLM
OSTROG
BERDICHEV
GORLITZ
BRESLAU
KIELCE
SANDOMIERZ
UKRAINE
BRODY
PROSKUROV
LIPOVETS
VINNITSA
UMAN
KOLIN
CRACOW
TARNOW
PRZEMYSL
LEMBERG
TARNOPOL
ZHMERINKA
OLMUTZ
TESCHEN
GORLICE
GALICIA
TURKA
STANISLAU
KOLOMEA
NOGILEV
BALTA
BRUNN
UNGVAR
MUNKACS
CZERNOWITZ
BUKOVINA
Dniester R.
Bug R.
CHISINAU
Pruth R.
BRATISLAVA
MISKOLCZ
SZIGET
JASSY
TIRASPOL
VIENNA
AKKERMAN
GYOR
BUDA PEST
DEBRECZEN
ZALAU
BAKAU
FOCSANI
GRAZ
LAKE BALATON
GROSS-WARDEIN
KLASENBURG
TRANSYLVANIA
HERMANSTADT
KRONSTADT
ZAGREB
Drave R.
SZEGED
ARAD
TEMESVAR
KARLSTADT
Save R.
Mur R.
Theiss R.
RUMANIA
PLOESTI
BIHAC
BELGRADE
BUCHAREST
CRAIOVA
GIURGIU
TRAVNIK
Danube R.
ZARA
SARAJEVO
UZHITSE
SERBIA
BULGARIA
PLEVEN
SHUMEN
VARNA
MOSTAR
NISH
Danube R.
BLACK SEA

EASTERN FRONT, 1918

Operations During 1918

0 100 200 300
SCALE OF MILES

Limit of occupation under Treaty of Brest-Litovsk, March 1918
Line at the time of the Armistice, December 1917
Area occupied by the Central Powers after the Treaty of Brest-Litovsk

SWEDEN
MURMANSK
WHITE SEA
GULF OF BOTHNIA
LAKE ONEGA
LAKE LADOGA
GULF OF FINLAND
ST. PETERSBURG (PETROGRAD)
ESTONIA
LAKE PEIPUS
LAKE ILMEN
GULF OF RIGA
LIVONIA
COURLAND
MOSCOW
RUSSIA
LITHUANIA
DVINSK
SMOLENSK
ORSHA
MOHILEV
BALTIC SEA
POLAND
GOMEL
PINSK
UKRAINE
KIEV
LEMBERG
ROSTOV
CASPIAN SEA
AUSTRIA-HUNGARY
SEA OF AZOV
RUMANIA
BUCHAREST
BLACK SEA
BELGRADE
SERBIA
BULGARIA
SOPHIA
ALBANIA
ADRIANOPLE
CONSTANTINOPLE
TURKEY
SALONIKA
DARDANELLES
GREECE
ATHENS
AEGEAN SEA
CRETE
CYPRUS
MEDITERRANEAN SEA

Although a member of the Triple Alliance, Italy had remained neutral in 1914, on the grounds that the terms of the alliance required her to take action only if her partners were attacked. Actually, Italy had regarded that alliance merely as a means of ensuring German protection against Austria, her traditional enemy. She had long laid claim to Trieste (*lower right*), Istria, and Trentino (*left center*); now she insisted that Austria surrender them as the price of continued Italian neutrality. Austria refused; the Allies gladly promised Italy large sections of Austrian territory if she would join them against the Central Powers. On 23 May, 1915, therefore, Italy went to war.

By her geographical position, Italy flanked the Central Powers, but she suffered definite strategic and tactical handicaps. Except for a narrow, extremely rugged strip along the Isonzo River (*right center;* hereafter termed "the Isonzo") at the northeastern end of the Adriatic Sea, Italy's frontiers followed the southern slopes of the Alps, below the Austrian-held heights. Only two good passes led into Austria—one through the Isonzo, the other through Trentino. Both were fortified and had only limited road and rail facilities. Finally, northeastern Italy was largely flanked by Austrian territory; a successful Austrian attack from the Trentino could cut off Italian troops on the Isonzo front. Italy's one major advantage was her ability to shift troops between the Isonzo and Trentino more rapidly than the Austrians could over their circuitous railroads.

The Italian commander, General Count Luigi Cadorna, planned to make his main attack on the Isonzo front, attacking toward Trieste, meanwhile carrying out minor diversionary operations at various points along the front. His initial advance (*shaded blue areas*) was opposed largely by second-line Austrian troops, who withdrew slowly to their frontier defenses. There, Austrian resistance hardened. During the rest of 1915, Cadorna fought the first four battles of the Isonzo. Handicapped by lack of heavy artillery, he paid almost 250,000 casualties for imperceptible gains.

In March, 1916, as part of the coordinated Allied offensive planned for that year, the Italians fought their Fifth Battle of the Isonzo—again unsuccessfully. Conrad, in the meantime, had requested German help for an Austrian offensive from Trentino against Padua (*lower center*). Falkenhayn—then busy with the planning that led to his Verdun offensive—refused, stating that such an offensive would require more troops than the Trentino railroad system could supply; but Conrad stubbornly concentrated fifteen divisions and heavy artillery by stripping his Isonzo and Eastern fronts. Surprise was impossible because of the time required to assemble these troops, but the overconfident Italian First Army disobeyed Cadorna's orders to prepare defenses in depth. Consequently, Conrad's attack on 14 May (the so-called "Asiago offensive") threw it back; but supply problems, rugged terrain, and Italian reinforcements finally slowed the Austrian advance. On 4 June, however, the Russians answered an Italian appeal for help by launching the "Brusilov offensive" (*see map 36*b). Brusilov's success—made possible, in part, by Conrad's withdrawal of troops and artillery from the Eastern Front—forced Conrad to fall back to a strong defensive line (*this map, dashed red line*) on the Trentino front in order to return men and guns to the East. Cadorna, meanwhile, had organized the Italian Fifth Army for a counterattack. It advanced on 25 June (*action not shown*), but found the Austrians strongly entrenched.

Cadorna now rushed all available forces back to the Isonzo front, attacking before the Austrians could shift troops from the Trentino. In the Sixth Battle of the Isonzo, he won his first significant success, taking Gorizia, but three subsequent attacks during the autumn failed. He tried again in April, 1917, using heavy artillery supplied by his allies, but made only small gains in the Carso area. In August and September, 1917, a massive eleventh attack finally drove the Austrians out of their last defenses on the Bainsizza Plateau. The Italians, however, had outrun their artillery and supplies and were too exhausted to pursue.

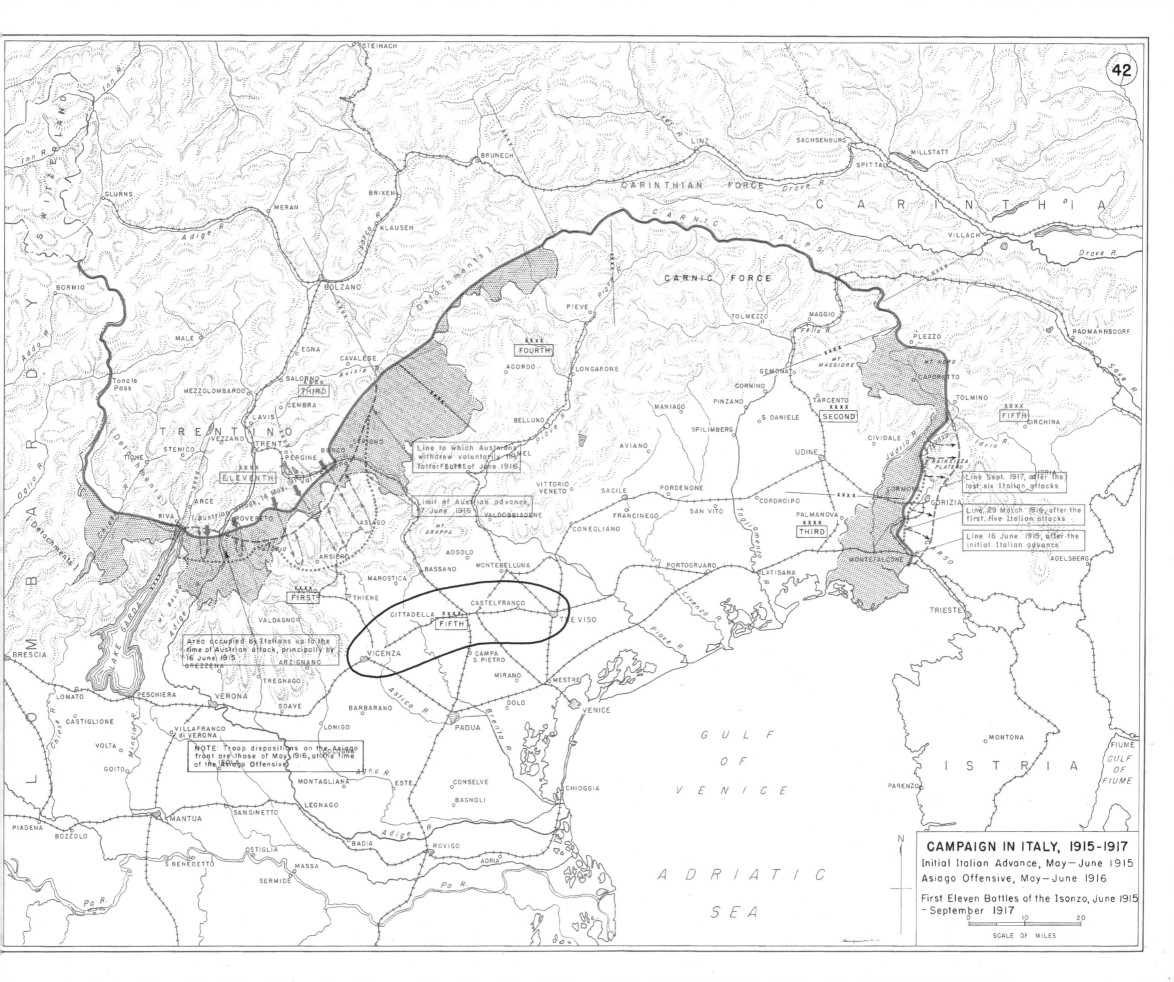

42

CARINTHIAN FORCE

CARINTHIA

CARNIC FORCE

XXXX
FOURTH

XXXX
MT.
MAGGIORE

XXXX
FIFTH

TRENTINO

XXXX
SECOND

XXXX
THIRD

XXXX
ELEVENTH

Line to which Austrians
withdrew voluntarily the
latter part of June 1916

Limit of Austrian advance
17 June 1916

Line Sept. 1917, after the
last six Italian attacks

Line 29 March 1916, after the
first five Italian attacks

Line 16 June 1915, after the
initial Italian advance

XXXX
FIRST

Area occupied by Italians up to the
time of Austrian attack, principally by
16 June 1915

XXXX
FIFTH

NOTE: Troop dispositions on the Asiago
front are those of May 1916, at the time
of the Asiago Offensive

GULF

OF

VENICE

ISTRIA

GULF
OF
FIUME

ADRIATIC

SEA

N

CAMPAIGN IN ITALY, 1915-1917

Initial Italian Advance, May—June 1915

Asiago Offensive, May—June 1916

First Eleven Battles of the Isonzo, June 1915
—September 1917

0   10   20

SCALE OF MILES

Repeated defeats on the Eastern Front had left the Austrians too weak to deal with the crisis resulting from the loss of the Bainsizza Plateau. German help was requested late in August; Hindenburg's available forces were then engaged in the Third Battle of Ypres (*see map 61*a), the Riga operation (*see map 41*a), and mopping-up operations in Rumania (*see map 40*), but he promised reinforcements as soon as possible, and meanwhile initiated the necessary reconnaissance and planning.

The Tolmino-Caporetto-Plezzo zone (*this map, right center*) was selected for the main Austro-German attack, to be delivered by the newly organized Fourteenth Army (which included seven German divisions) under General Otto von Below. The Austrian Fifth and Tenth Armies were to deliver secondary attacks on either flank of the main effort. The Fourteenth Army was held well behind the front until just before the offensive opened.

Cadorna, struggling to reorganize his forces for a renewed offensive in the Isonzo area, was soon aware of unusual enemy activity. Though larger and better armed and equipped than ever before, his forces were deeply discouraged. Most of their veteran officers and noncommissioned officers were dead or disabled; Communist and pacifist propaganda had eroded the discipline of some units; also, the army reflected the considerable discontent and war-weariness among the civilian population. Cadorna—a rigid, devoted soldier with no sympathy for human weaknesses—accepted continual danger and hardship as a soldier's natural lot, without concerning himself particularly over methods of keeping up his men's morale. Consequently, it was low. In this situation, Cadorna decided to go on the defensive, ordering his army commanders to prepare defenses in depth all along the front. This the aggressive-minded commander of the Italian Second Army deliberately did not do. Cadorna himself misjudged the probable location of the coming attack; considering the Caporetto area too rugged for a large-scale offensive, he placed most of his reserves behind the Italian Third Army. Just before the attack, deserters brought the Italians detailed information on the enemy's plans, but it was then too late to do much more than warn the endangered Italian units.

At 0200, 24 October, 1917, massed Austro-German artillery opened a sudden surprise bombardment, using large quantities of gas and smoke shell mixed with high explosive. This quickly wrecked Italian signal communications, and demoralized many units. (Italian gas masks seem to have been relatively ineffective.) Six hours later, half-hidden by heavy rain and mist, the Fourteenth Army advanced, and the Italian front rapidly went to pieces.

The Germans were using infiltration tactics, which they had carefully developed and now gave a major test. These featured short, violent artillery preparations, like the one described above, to blind the defenders. Thereafter, the leading units advanced rapidly, bypassing centers of resistance, which were reduced by reserve units. These tactics worked perfectly. The Italian Second Army was shattered, and much of the Carnic Force trapped. The Third and Fourth Armies withdrew in relatively good order. Cadorna had meant to make a stand behind the flooded Tagliamento River, and Below had not intended to pursue farther, but, during the night of 2-3 November, driving Austro-German advance guards forced a crossing upstream near Cornino. Late on 4 November, Cadorna ordered a retreat to the Piave River. Below then continued the pursuit. Had he possessed a force of cavalry and armored cars, Italian losses might have been crippling. Though the Piave was high from recent rains, the Austro-Germans seized several bridgeheads on the far bank, but here the attack had to pause. The attackers had outrun their supplies, were short of transportation, and found themselves encumbered with more than 275,000 Italian prisoners. Minor fighting continued along the Piave and in the mountains for several weeks more. (Among the German officers who especially distinguished themselves in this campaign was a first lieutenant of mountain troops named Erwin Rommel.)

Fearing the collapse of Italy, her allies managed to scrape together six French and five British divisions, the last of which reached Italy in mid-December.

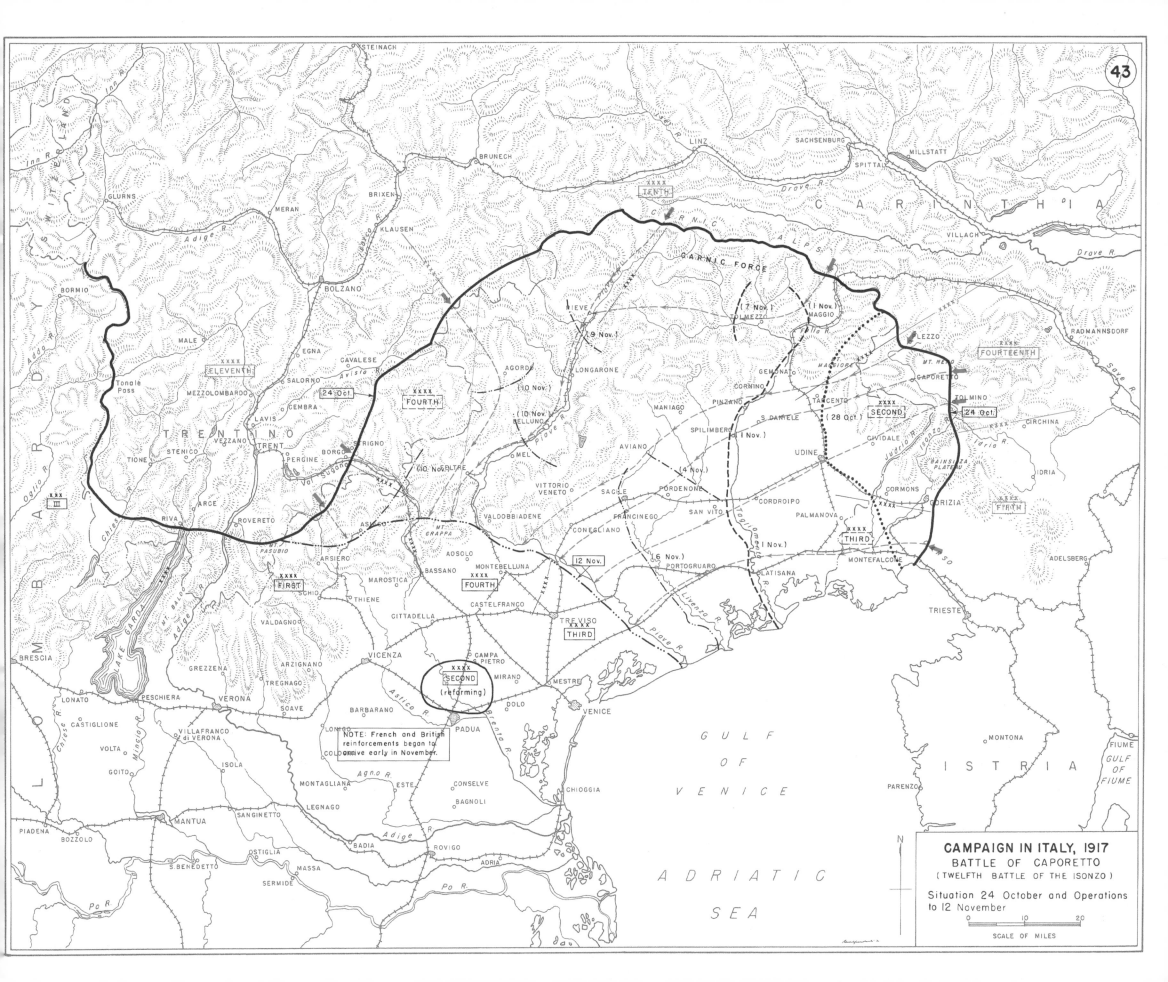

43

CAMPAIGN IN ITALY, 1917
BATTLE OF CAPORETTO
(TWELFTH BATTLE OF THE ISONZO)

Situation 24 October and Operations
to 12 November

SCALE OF MILES
0   10   20

NOTE: French and British
reinforcements began to
arrive early in November.

Though a costly and unpleasant defeat, the Caporetto disaster came to Italy as somewhat of a blessing in disguise. National pride was stirred to reassert itself; the army was reorganized, General Armando Diaz replacing General Cadorna. Foch, who had come to Italy with the French and British contingents, discreetly nursed this revival. Once it was apparent that the Austro-German offensive had exhausted itself at the Piave River, he refrained from putting his troops into the line there, allowing the Italians to reestablish themselves in order to demonstrate that, though defeated, they were not yet beaten. Late in November, some Allied divisions did take over positions along the foothills farther inland, where they shared in the last skirmishing of the campaign.

An important by-product of the Battle of Caporetto was the Allies' creation of a Supreme War Council at Versailles. This body was intended as the final authority on military policy, including the assignment of Allied forces to the various fronts. In practice, it proved somewhat ineffective, but it did represent a necessary initial move toward greater unity of command.

During the first part of 1918, the Germans completed the withdrawal of their troops from Italy, in preparation for their forthcoming major offensive on the Western Front. Two British and four French divisions were likewise withdrawn, their remaining units being stationed in the Asiago area. Late in April, as a complementary gesture, two Italian divisions were transferred to France.

With Russia out of the war after 3 March, 1918, the Germans felt that the Austrians alone should be capable of defeating Italy. They urged that this be accomplished as rapidly as possible, so that Austrian troops would be free to take over quiet sectors on the Western Front. The shaky Austrian government agreed, but its planning went awry in the tangle of palace politics which, throughout Austria's history as a nation, had snarled her military efforts. Conrad (recently relieved as chief of the Austrian General Staff) now commanded in the Trentino; General von Boroevic, on the Piave. Both insisted on the right to direct the decisive attack. A compromise solution allowed both of them to attack as shown, and divided the available forces almost equally between them, so that neither was strong enough to accomplish anything. In addition, there was to be a diversionary attack against Tonale Pass (*left center*). As usual, numerous deserters betrayed this plan to the Italians.

The Tonale Pass attack began on 13 June, 1918. On 15 June, both Boroevic and Conrad advanced. The latter struck the French and British contingents, but made slight gains during the first few hours. Counterattacks, however, drove him out again on the 16th—so roughly handled that he took little further part in the offensive. On the lower Piave, Boroevic forced a wide crossing, making gains of as much as three miles on the south bank. A combination of unexpected high water and aerial bombing attacks, however, played havoc with his bridges, and complicated the resupply of his bridgehead. Because of the lack of lateral communications, it was impossible to draw reinforcements from Conrad's army to maintain the momentum of the attack. Diaz rushed reinforcements into the area by truck. Boroevic therefore withdrew during the night of 22-23 June.

The collapse of this offensive cost Austria some 150,000 casualties and hurt Austrian morale badly. Foch—now charged with the coordination of all Allied armies—urged Diaz to attack immediately to exploit his success. Diaz refused, claiming he could expect no more success in an attack across the Piave than the Austrians had just experienced.

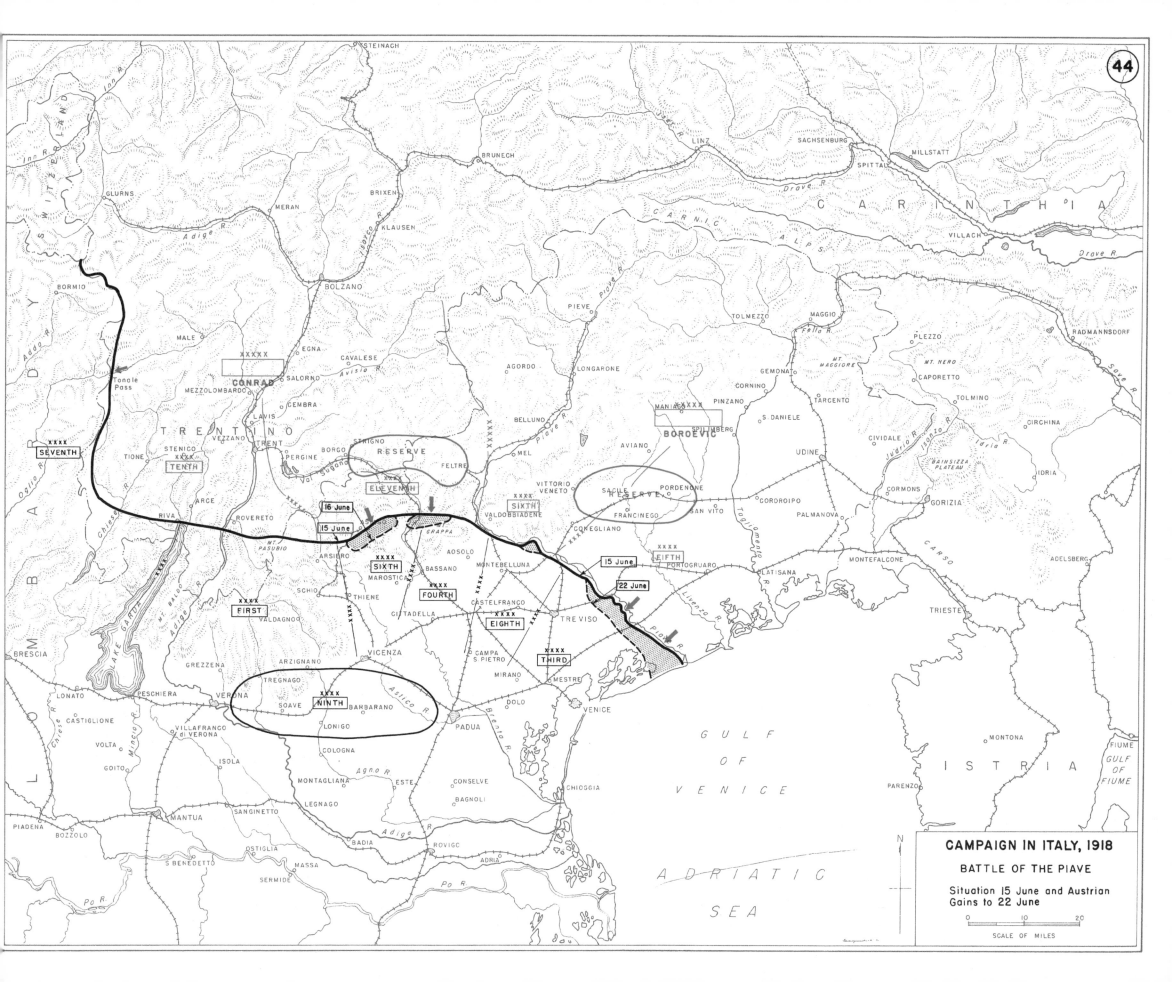

CAMPAIGN IN ITALY, 1918

BATTLE OF THE PIAVE

Situation 15 June and Austrian
Gains to 22 June

0   10   20
SCALE OF MILES

As the war turned definitely against the Central Powers during the latter half of 1918, Austria began to break up. Only along her frontiers—where her armies, though ragged and even hungry, kept their posts—was there any cohesion.

Nevertheless, Diaz was slow to act until Allied successes on the Western Front made it evident that Italy must move soon, if she hoped to profit at the eventual peace conference. Late in September, he began his preparations. Two new armies were activated and shifted to the Piave front. These were the Tenth (two British and two Italian divisions) under General Lord Cavan, commander of the British contingent, and the Twelfth (one French and three Italian divisions) under General Graziani of the French Army. One British and one French division were left in the Asiago sector to conceal the transfer of the rest of their contingents. A United States unit, the 332d Infantry Regiment of the 83d Division—sent to Italy as evidence of American participation in the war—originally formed part of the reserve. In view of the number of rivers in the objective area, large amounts of bridging equipment were provided.

Diaz's plan involved a double offensive. The Italian Fourth Army was to attack toward Feltre (*center*) to separate the Austrian army groups; the Eighth Army, supported on either flank by the Twelfth and Tenth Armies, was to attack across the Piave against Vittorio Veneto. After taking that town, part of its forces would advance westward to link up with the advancing Fourth Army, thus pocketing the Austrian Sixth Army. Such a dispersion of effort would have been foolhardy against this same Austrian Army a year earlier; now, Diaz apparently considered that he had sufficient combat superiority to risk it.

The offensive was scheduled for 0645, 24 October. Actual fighting began during the night of 23-24 October, when British troops of the Tenth Army, crossing a branch of the flooded Piave River in small boats handled by Italian rivermen, seized an important island. Thereafter, everything went otherwise than according to plan. The Austrian Imperial and Royal Army—short of ammunition, riddled by sickness—stood up to its last battle with a courage worthy of its greatest days. In the Mount Grappa area (*center, left; overprinted by blue arrow*), the Italian Fourth Army was beaten off with heavy losses. On the Piave front, high water aided the defenders in halting the Eighth Army. Eventually, during the night of 26-27 October, the Twelfth Army's French division won a small footing on the far bank. Some of its Italian units crossed on the 27th, while farther downstream Lord Cavan's English shattered the Austrian line, seizing a big bridgehead. Attacks out of this last position now linked up the different bridgeheads and cleared the fronts of the Eighth and Third Armies. The Austrian defense was further weakened by events at home; Austria-Hungary had been officially transformed from an empire into a group of separate states. Their former ties of allegiance thus canceled, Hungarian units mutinied and refused to fight; other nationalities deserted in mass. Even so, on 30 October, the Allied advance was checked at the Livenza River, but on 1 November, the Tenth Army (which now included the 332d Infantry Regiment) forced a crossing at Sacile. Austrian resistance crumbled. On the Sixth Army front, the remaining French division opened a gap on 1 November through which its British partner passed to capture Trent (*action not shown*) on 3 November, just before Italian armored cars arrived from the south. In the Fourth Army sector, the Austrians withdrew in time, but in the more open terrain to the east, Italian cavalry and armored cars and British and Italian aircraft hunted down their fleeing remnants.

The Austrians had been seeking an armistice since early October, but—incompetent to the last—their high command bungled the proceedings. As a result, it was not signed until late on 3 November, to take effect the next day. This delay gave the Italians time to send a naval expedition to force the surrender of Trieste.

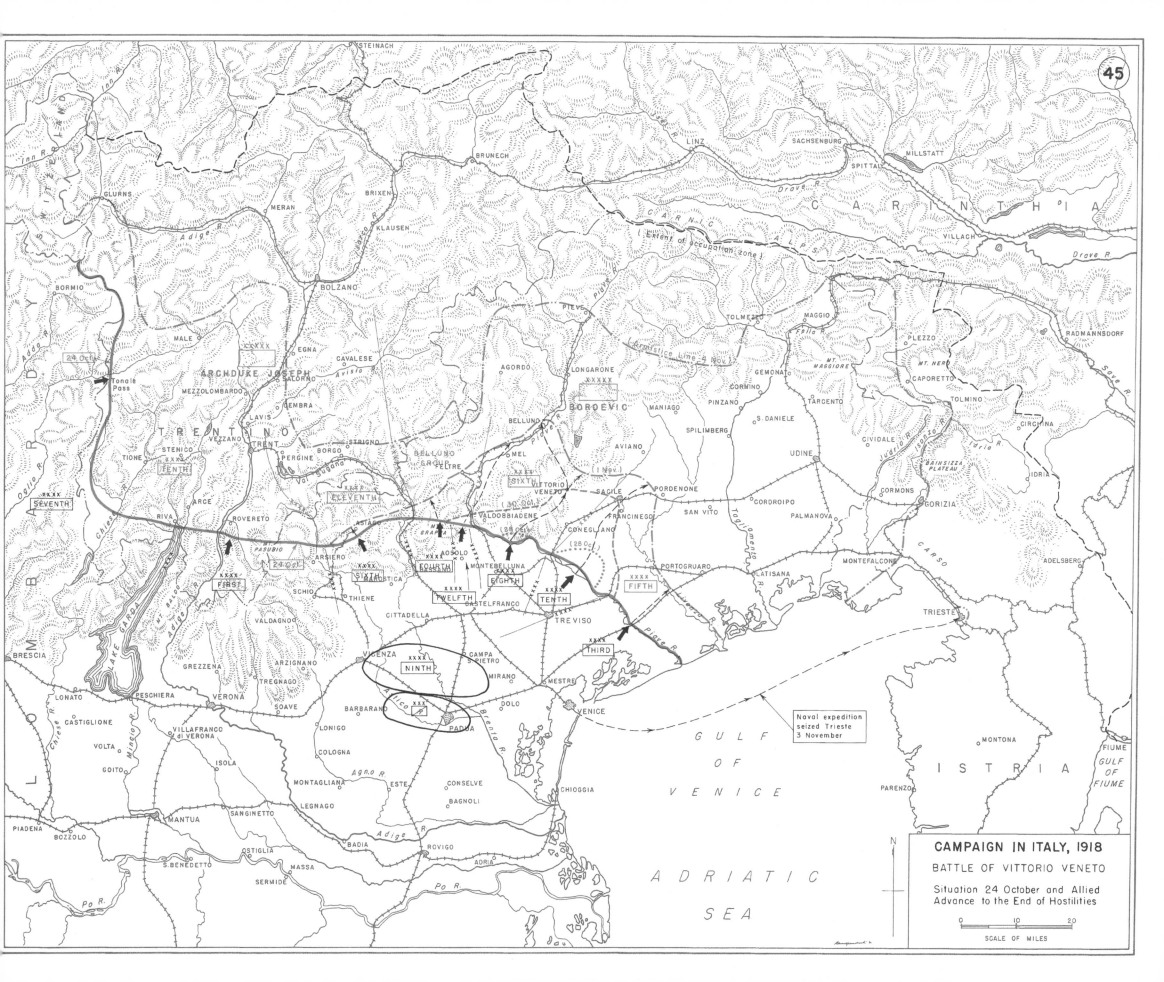

CAMPAIGN IN ITALY, 1918

BATTLE OF VITTORIO VENETO

Situation 24 October and Allied
Advance to the End of Hostilities

SCALE OF MILES

0   10   20

Naval expedition
seized Trieste
3 November

Since the immediate cause of the war—the murder of the Austrian Archduke Ferdinand—was the result of conflicting Serbian-Austrian ambitions, the Serbians knew that they could soon expect an Austrian invasion. Also, there would be more profound reasons behind the Austrian advance than simply a desire for vengeance. For one, the only feasible line of communications between the Central Powers and Turkey (their secret ally since 2 August) was by the Berlin-Belgrade-Nish-Adrianople-Constantinople railroad; Turkey would remain dangerously isolated until the portion of this line passing through Serbian territory could be cleared.

The Serbian Army was small (approximately 200,000 men) and lacked sufficient artillery and machine guns. Most of its supply trains were ox-drawn; it was dependent upon its allies for munitions and even food, which would have to be brought up the long haul from Salonika (*bottom center*). It was, however, a tough army of veterans from the two Balkan wars of 1913—men fired with a rough patriotism, accustomed to hardship. Their commander, Field Marshal Radomir Putnik, was a formidable semi-invalid who had a perfect knowledge of Balkan topography. The Montenegrin Army (Montenegro allied herself to Serbia at the beginning of the war) was a tiny, more primitive version of the Serbian Army.

The disparity of forces between the two opponents naturally forced the Serbs to wage a defensive war. In this, they had a strong ally in their rugged country. Any Austrian advance must cross either the Drina (*upper left*), the Save, or the Danube—all of them unfordable. Once beyond the river valleys, Serbia was a jumble of mountain ranges, where an invader's logistical problems multiplied with each mile he advanced, and his superior numbers were often more of an embarrassment than an asset. Putnik therefore left only an outpost line along the frontier, with the missions of determining the direction of the Austrian advance and of delaying it as long as possible. The main body of his army he held in a central position, ready to counterattack once the Austrians had committed themselves.

As described in the text of map 3, the Austrian plan for a war with Serbia alone (Plan B) specified that the Austrian Fifth and Sixth Armies would invade Serbia from the west, while the Second Army attacked from the north; whereas, the plan for war with both Serbia and Russia (Plan R) specified that the Second Army would be employed against the Russians. Blindly optimistic, the Austrians had mobilized according to Plan B on 25 July, 1914 only to discover that they had made the wrong choice.

Meanwhile, General Oskar Potiorek launched his Austrians across Serbia's northern frontier on 12 August. Only the Fifth Army, however, made noticeable progress. The Sixth Army, baffled by a screen of Serbian and Montenegrin frontier detachments, failed to push its attack. The Second Army had been warned that it would be transferred to the Galician front as soon as its rail transportation could be arranged; meanwhile, it was not to get "too deeply involved."

Putnik promptly identified the Austrian Fifth Army as the major threat, and moved the Serbian Second and Third Armies against it on 16 August (Battle of the Jadar). Initially, the Austrian XIII Corps drove the Serbian Third Army back, but the left-flank division of the VIII Corps was overwhelmed, and a demonstration by the IV Corps of the Austrian Second Army (its IX Corps had already moved north) ended in heavy losses. The IV Corps should then have followed the IX, but Potiorek begged for its retention on the Serbian front, and Conrad assented. The IV Corps managed to push the Serbians on its front back of the Dobrava River, but Putnik—reinforcing the Serbian Second Army with part of the Serbian First Army—completed the defeat of the Austrian VIII Corps. Meanwhile, the Serbian Third Army succeeded in checking the Austrian XIII Corps. Potiorek, his supplies exhausted by a week of heavy fighting, thereupon withdrew.

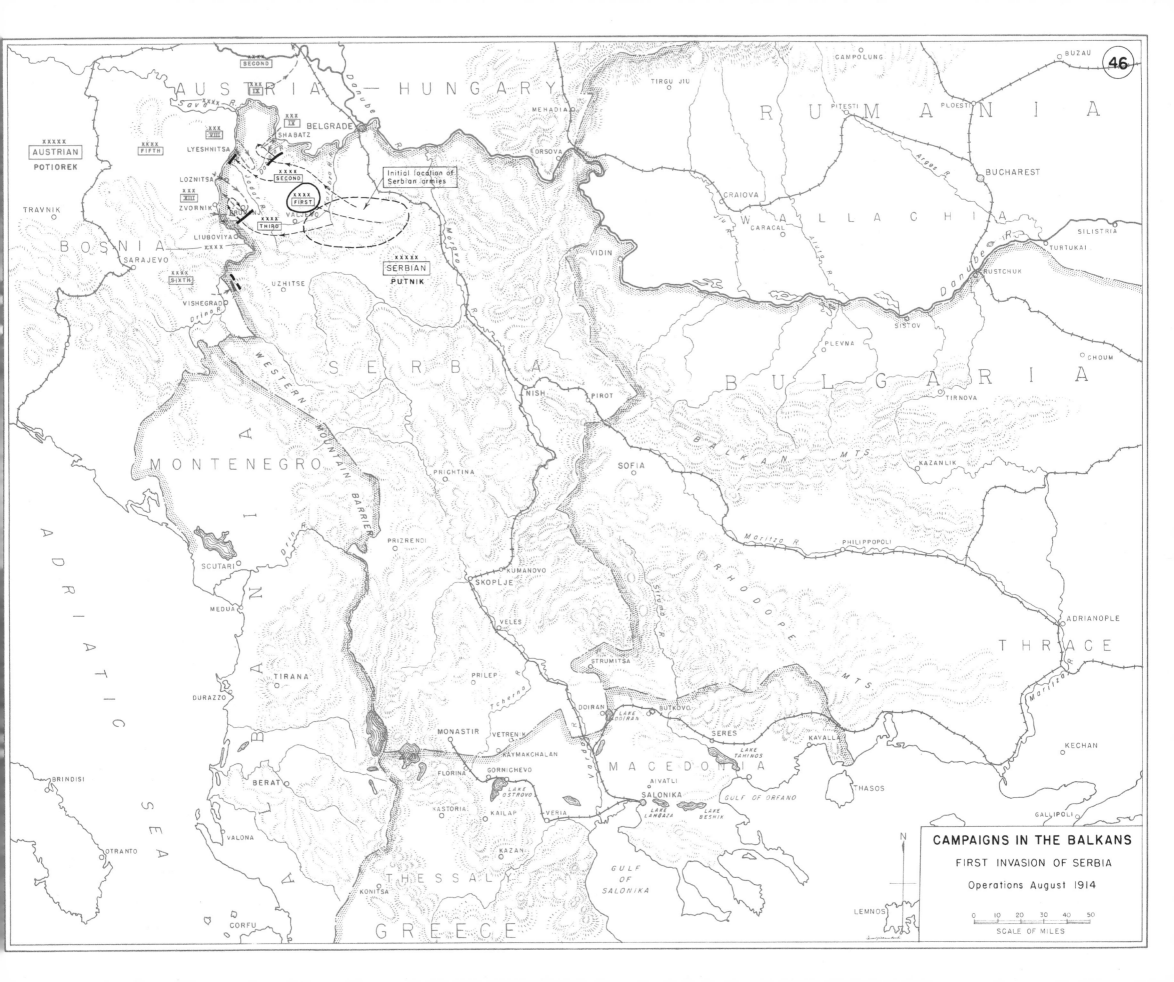

46

AUSTRIA — HUNGARY

RUMANIA

CAMPOLUNG

BUZAU

xxxx
SECOND

xxx
IX

Danube R.

TIRGU JIU

PITESTI

PLOESTI

Sav R.

xxxx

xxx
IV

BELGRADE

MEHADIA

ORSOVA

CRAIOVA

WALLACHIA

BUCHAREST

xxxxx
AUSTRIAN

POTIOREK

xxx
XVIII

SHABATZ

xxxx
FIFTH

LYESHNITSA

CARACAL

Argos R.

SILISTRIA

LOZNITSA

xxxx
SECOND

Initial location of
Serbian armies

Aluta R.

Danube R.

TURTUKAI

xxx
XIII

ZVORNIK

xxxx
FIRST

VALUEVO

RUSTCHUK

Drina R.

xxxx
THIRD

VIDIN

TRAVNIK

LIUBOVIYA

xxxx

BOSNIA

SARAJEVO

xxxx
SIXTH

SERBIAN

PUTNIK

Morava R.

SISTOV

PLEVNA

CHOUM

UZHITSE

VISHEGRADO

S   E   R   B   I   A

BULGARIA

WESTERN   MOUNTAIN   BARRIER

NISH

PIROT

BALKAN   MTS

TIRNOVA

KAZANLIK

MONTENEGRO

SOFIA

PRICHTINA

A

PRIZRENDI

Drin R.

Maritza R.

PHILIPPOPOLI

RHODOPE   MTS

SCUTARI

KUMANOVO

Struma R.

MEDUA

SKOPLJE

ADRIANOPLE

VELES

THRACE

B   A   N   I   A

TIRANA

PRILEP

Tcherna R.

STRUMITSA

Maritza R.

DURAZZO

Vardar R.

DOIRAN

BUTKOVO

MONASTIR

VETREN

LAKE
DOIRAN

KECHAN

A   D   R   I   A   T   I   C   S   E   A

KAYMAKCHALAN

SERES

KAVALLA

BRINDISI

FLORINA

GORNICHEVO

LAKE
OSTROVO

LAKE
TAHINOS

GULF OF ORFANO

THASOS

BERAT

AIVATLI

MACEDONIA

CAMPAIGNS IN THE BALKANS

KASTORIA

KAILAP

VERIA

SALONIKA

LAKE
LANGAZA

LAKE
BESHIK

GALLIPOLI

VALONA

KAZAN

FIRST INVASION OF SERBIA

Operations August 1914

OTRANTO

KONITSA

GULF
OF
SALONIKA

LEMNOS

N

CORFU

GREECE

0   10   20   30   40   50

SCALE OF MILES

Putnik had completely outgeneraled his opponent. With a smaller army, he had still managed to concentrate superior forces against the Austrian Fifth Army at the decisive point. Not only had he driven the Austrians from Serbian territory, but—by frightening Potiorek into retaining the IV Corps of the Austrian Second Army until 20 August—he had also forced them to fight their opening battles against the Russians in Galicia with insufficient forces. Then, on 6 September, the Serbs added insult to injury. Putnik sent his First Army north (*action not shown*) across the Save River into Austrian territory, hoping to inspire a revolt among the Slavic population of Bosnia.

Potiorek, who had shifted the Austrian Fifth Army north of the Save, countered this piece of impudence with a second invasion of Serbia during the night of 7-8 September. Putnik recalled his First Army, and again employed his defensive-offensive combination of delaying actions and heavy counterattacks. His success this time, however, was not so complete. Though he halted the Austrian advance, the invaders managed to hold bridgeheads (*dashed red line*) on Serbian territory.

Putnik immediately recognized the weakness of the new Serbian position (*dashed blue line*). Most of his army was concentrated in an exposed salient, dangerously vulnerable to any sudden Austrian attack through the Belgrade area. Also, the Serbian munitions expenditures during the first two invasions had not yet been made good by the Allies, and it would therefore be doubly hazardous to risk a major engagement in the near future. Consequently, Putnik ordered a withdrawal to more defensible terrain (*dotted blue line*).

Potiorek began his third advance on 5 November. The Serbs withdrew doggedly, through constant heavy rains that ruined the primitive roads and flooded the streams. Potiorek may have had some vague plan of enveloping the Serbian right flank; if

so, he failed to execute it with sufficient force and energy. But the Serbian retreat went on. Valjevo fell, and the Austrian advance pushed on across the Kolubra River. The rain had changed to snow in the higher passes, and Austrian supply problems were increasing. Then, as the situation grew tenser, Potiorek diverted troops to seize Belgrade, the Serbian capital (according to contemporary opinion, he felt it would make an acceptable birthday gift for Emperor Francis Joseph of Austria). Putnik, valuing the safety of his army above the temporary possession of his nation's capital, ordered the city evacuated and pulled back his right flank. About 30 November, having drawn the Austrians far enough into the interior, he halted on a good defensive position (*solid blue line*). His retreat had brought his army near their bases of supply; behind the Austrians, the Kolubra River was now in full flood. On 2 December, the Austrians occupied Belgrade. That same day, Putnik issued his orders for a counterattack on 3 December.

There was little finesse to Putnik's plan. The three Serbian armies attacked abreast—the Belgrade Detachment covering their right flank, and the Uzhitse Detachment their left. Their naturally pugnacious patriotism inflamed by the example and exhortations of their King Peter and the sufferings of their noncombatant refugees, the Serbs went forward furiously. The First Army broke into the Austrian front in the direction of Valjevo. On 9 December, Potiorek again ordered a withdrawal. The Austrian Sixth Army fell back through Shabatz, the Fifth through Belgrade. The Serbians reoccupied their capital on the morning of 15 December.

An unpleasant aftermath of this masterful campaign was a great typhus epidemic which ravaged Serbia through the winter, until checked by medical missions from Serbia's allies.

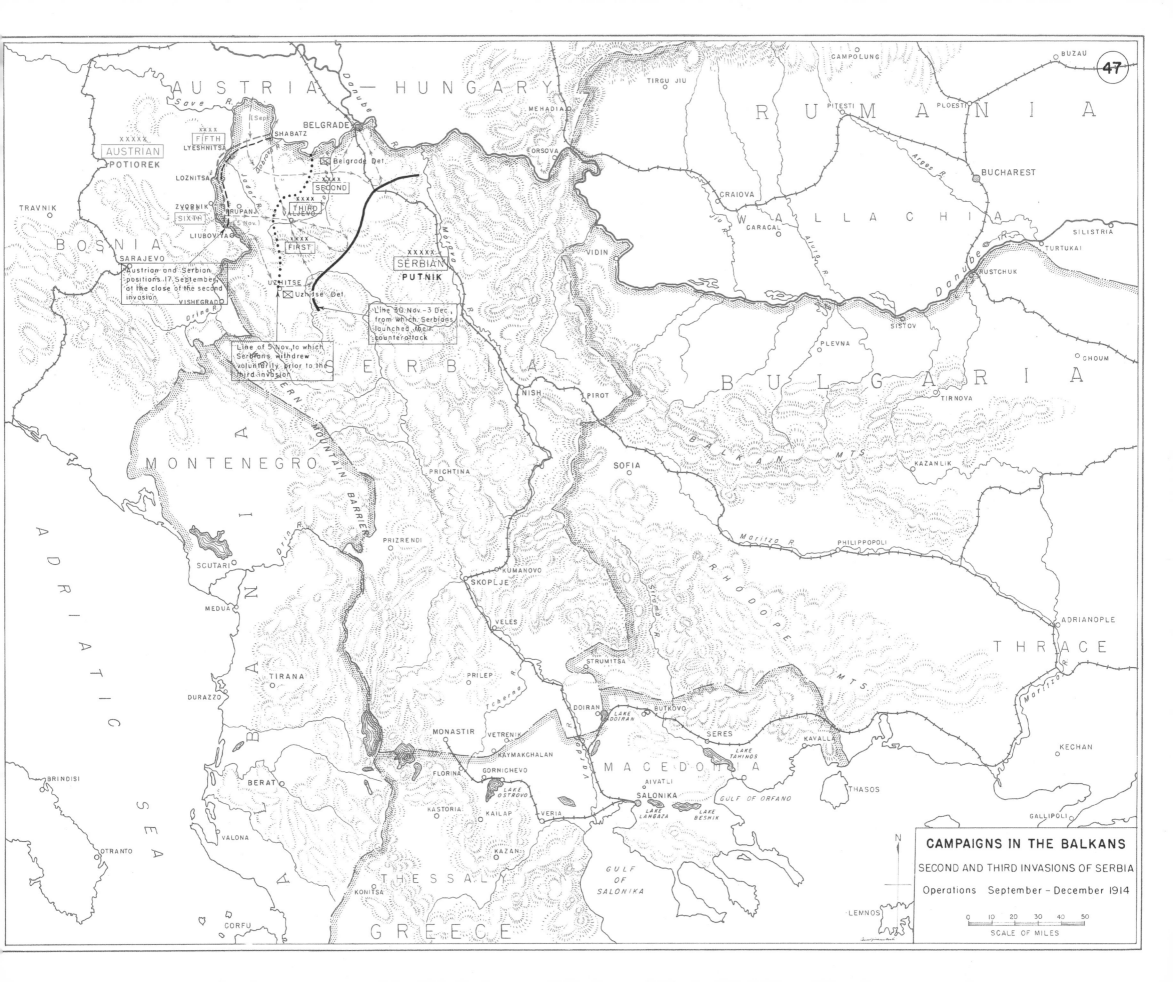

AUSTRIA — HUNGARY

RUMANIA

CAMPOLUNG
BUZAU

47

Save R.

Danube R.

TIRGU JIU
PITESTI
PLOESTI

(1 Sep.)
BELGRADE
SHABATZ
MEHADIA
ORSOVA

XXXXX
AUSTRIAN
POTIOREK

XXXX
FIFTH
LYESHNITSA

Belgrade Det.

XXXX
SECOND

CRAIOVA

W A L L A C H I A

ARGES R.

BUCHAREST

LOZNITSA

Dobrava R.

CARACAL

Aluta R.

SILISTRIA

TRAVNIK

ZVORNIK
RUPANJ
XXXX
SIXTH

XXXX
THIRD
VLJEVO

Jadar R.

Morava R.

VIDIN

Danube R.

TURTUKAI
RUSTCHUK

B O S N I A

LIUBOVIJA

XXXX
FIRST

SARAJEVO

Austrian and Serbian
positions 17 September,
at the close of the second
invasion

UZHITSE

XXXXX
SERBIAN
PUTNIK

SISTOV

B U L G A R I A

PLEVNA

CHOUM

VISHEGRAD

Drina R.

Uzhitse Det.

Line 30 Nov.-3 Dec.,
from which Serbians
launched their
counterattack

NISH

PIROT

Line of 5 Nov., to which
Serbians withdrew
voluntarily prior to the
third invasion

S E R B I A

TIRNOVA

KAZANLIK

B A L K A N   M T S

M O N T E N E G R O

SOFIA

Maritza R.

PHILIPPOPOLI

SCUTARI

Drina R.

PRIZRENDI

PRICHTINA

A L B A N I A

Drin R.

MEDUA

KUMANOVO

SKOPLJE

VELES

Struma R.

R H O D O P E   M T S

ADRIANOPLE

T H R A C E

Maritza R.

TIRANA

PRILEP

Tcherna R.

STRUMITSA

BUTKOVO

DURAZZO

Vardar R.

DOIRAN
LAKE
DOIRAN

SERES

KAVALLA

KECHAN

BERAT

MONASTIR

VETRENIK

KAYMAKCHALAN

LAKE
TAHINOS

M A C E D O N I A

THASOS

A D R I A T I C   S E A

FLORINA

GORNICHEVO

LAKE
OSTROVO

AIVATLI

GULF OF ORFANO

BRINDISI

VALONA

KASTORIA

KAILAP

VERIA

SALONIKA

LAKE
LANGAZA

LAKE
BESHIK

GALLIPOLI

OTRANTO

KAZAN

KONITSA

*GULF
OF
SALONIKA*

LEMNOS

CORFU

T H E S S A L Y

G R E E C E

N

CAMPAIGNS IN THE BALKANS

SECOND AND THIRD INVASIONS OF SERBIA

Operations September – December 1914

0   10   20   30   40   50
SCALE OF MILES

In early 1915, Falkenhayn urged Conrad to consider a combined German-Austrian-Bulgarian attack to crush Serbia and restore direct rail communications with Turkey. Conrad being more concerned with the Isonzo front (*see map 42*), Falkenhayn turned his attention to mounting the Gorlice-Tarnow offensive (*see map 27*), but—as a precaution—sent a party of staff officers to reconnoiter the Austrian-Serbian frontier.

As the situation in the Dardanelles became more threatening for Turkey, the Germans increased their efforts to enlist Bulgaria as an ally. France and Britain, at the same time, exerted diplomatic pressure to persuade her to remain neutral. King Ferdinand of Bulgaria, an ambitious and crafty intriguer, would not commit himself—until it was evident that Russia had taken a shattering defeat at Gorlice-Tarnow and the Allies had failed at Gallipoli. Then he signed a treaty of alliance with Germany and Austria and began mobilizing on 23 September.

During this period, France and Britain had also engaged in tortuous negotiations with other Balkan states in the hope of gaining their support, and had discussed sending an expeditionary force to aid the Serbs. No definite action had been taken when news came of the Bulgarian mobilization. Then one French and one British division were rushed from the Dardanelles, reaching Salonika (*this map, bottom center*) on 3 October.

Field Marshal Mackensen led the fourth invasion of Serbia. The forces under his direct command consisted of the Austrian Third Army (which included three German divisions), the German Eleventh Army, and the Bulgarian First Army. The Bulgarian General Staff controlled the Bulgarian Second Army, which was to operate independently against the Salonika-Belgrade railroad, thus isolating Serbia. These four armies totaled more than 300,000 men.

During the quiet spring and summer, Putnik had worked to strengthen his forces. Two new armies, the Timok and the Macedonian, were organized, but the over-all Serbian strength remained between 200,000 and 250,000. Weapons and munitions of all types were lacking. Nevertheless, both Italy and Russia demanded that the Serbs launch offensives to relieve enemy pressure on the Isonzo and Galician fronts. This the Serbs refused to do. With Bulgaria ready to join the Central Powers, Putnik faced the problem of defending both his northern and eastern frontiers. The Bulgars—between whom and the Serbs there was an ancient, treasured feud—were tough mountain fighters. Eventually, Putnik adopted the cordon defense shown here, hoping to fight a delaying action until Allied help reached him from Salonika. It lacked depth and provided no reserves for a counteroffensive, but probably was the best solution available.

At 2030, 7 October, after a heavy artillery preparation, Mackensen's Austrian and German armies began successful assault crossings of the Save and Danube, surprising Serbian outposts on the south banks. Demonstrations at Vishegrad (upper left) and Orsova (*top center*) helped to confuse the defense. Belgrade was cleared on the 9th. As previously arranged, the Bulgarians attacked on the 11th; their Second Army cut the railroad at Kumanovo on 23 October. Thus cut off from Salonika, and forced back into the snow-covered mountains by Mackensen's relentless pressure, the Serbs chose to attempt a retreat through the mountains of neutral Albania, rather than surrender. Accompanied by thousands of civilian refugees, the Serbian Army struggled through the winter wilderness in an epic retreat; between 100,000 and 150,000 soldiers finally reached the Albanian coast. Here, the French Navy retrieved them. Mackensen's pursuit halted at the Albanian frontier on 4 December.

In the meantime, a French column had pushed northward from Salonika, but it was too weak and too late to save the railroad. Allied reinforcements then established a strong position in the Doiran area (*lower center*). This was held until 3 December, when growing Bulgarian pressure and the increasingly enigmatic attitude of the Greek government made a withdrawal to Salonika necessary.

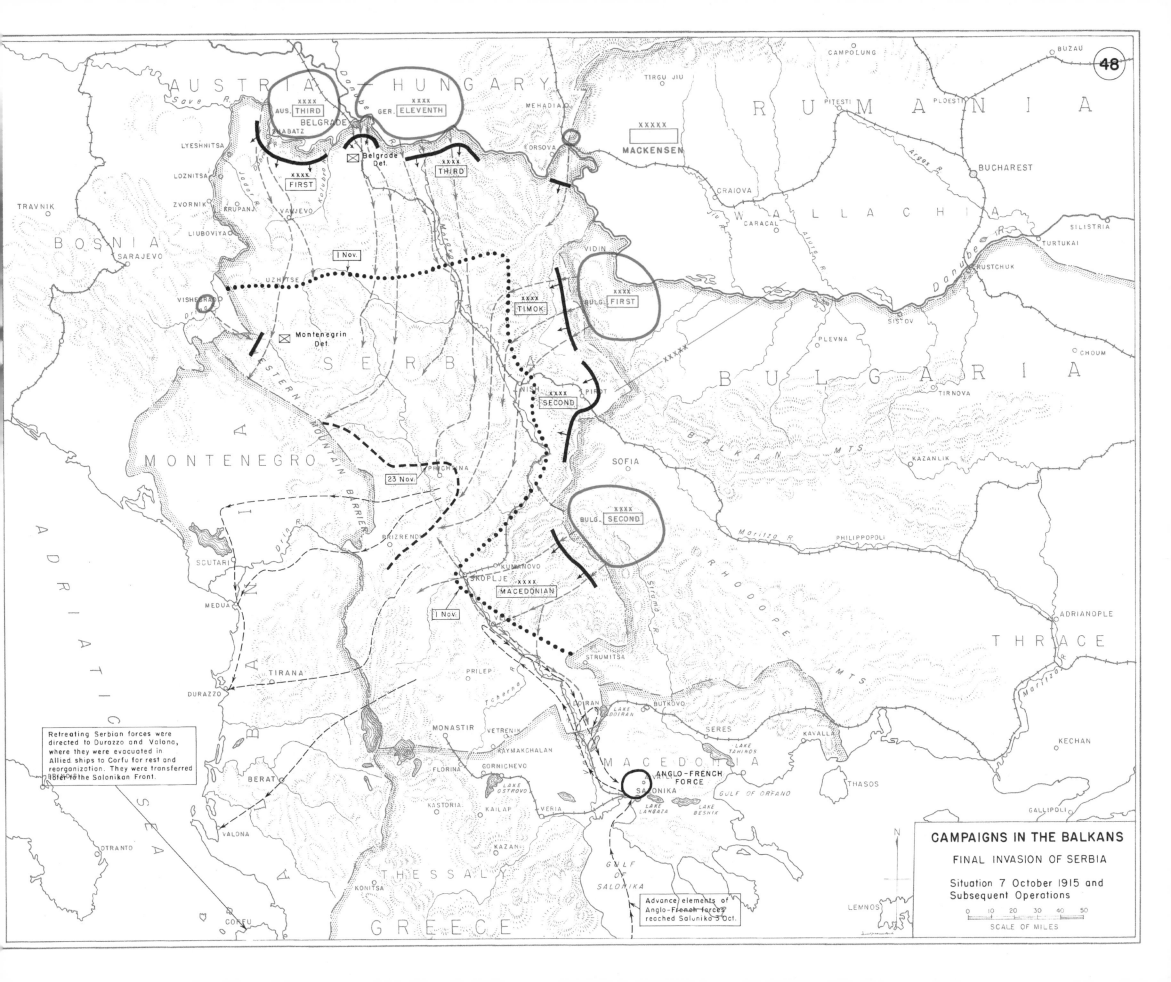

48

Retreating Serbian forces were
directed to Durazzo and Valona,
where they were evacuated in
Allied ships to Corfu for rest and
reorganization. They were transferred
later to the Salonikan Front.

Advance elements of
Anglo-French forces
reached Salonika 5 Oct.

CAMPAIGNS IN THE BALKANS

FINAL INVASION OF SERBIA

Situation 7 October 1915 and
Subsequent Operations

0 10 20 30 40 50

SCALE OF MILES

Following their retreat from the Doiran area, the French and British occupied a strong position, known ironically as "the Bird Cage," around the port of Salonika (*solid blue line*). The British, who had regarded the operation as unwise from the start, now insisted on withdrawing. The French government, however, argued for keeping Allied forces around Salonika to prevent the Central Powers from dominating the region and Greece and Rumania from joining the enemy camp. France and Britain eventually decided that Allied forces would remain.

On the side of the Central Powers, the Austrians and Bulgarians favored an all-out attack to drive the Allies into the sea, but Falkenhayn vetoed the idea. He feared that the presence of the Bulgarian troops in Greece would throw that country into the Allied camp. Also, the railroad from Nish to Salonika was single-tracked and could support only a limited body of troops. He therefore contented himself with holding the Greek frontier. The Austrians overran Montenegro and pushed southward through Albania (*action not shown*).

The political situation in Greece further complicated matters. The Allies had come into Salonika originally on the invitation of Eleutherios Venizelos, the Greek prime minister. King Constantine of Greece, however, was strongly pro-German. He succeeded in forcing Venizelos' resignation and began to talk of interning the Allied troops. The presence of strong Allied naval units off Athens forced him to decide otherwise, but he still kept the Central Powers fully advised as to Allied strength and activities.

Initially, the situation of the Allied forces was pure chaos. Theoretically, General Maurice P. E. Sarrail (a politically potent French officer whom Joffre had just removed from command of the French Third Army) was in full command. Actually, each contingent took its orders from its home government. Sarrail himself lacked the tact necessary to command a force of several nationalities. Logistics was another major problem: Salonika was a minor port; its hinterland had a limited road and rail net; in addition, it was necessary to construct all types of supply installations. The climate was vile, and a particularly virulent form of malaria was endemic. (The British alone reported 481,262 cases of sickness, as compared to 18,187 wounded during the campaign.)

During the late spring and summer of 1916, Sarrail, under pressure from Joffre to do something that would draw German troops away from Verdun, began moving forward (*dotted blue line*), nearer the Greek frontier. He now had approximately 250,000 men—French, British, Serbs (transferred from Corfu), Russians, and Italians. Rumania was expected to join the Allies in the near future, and Sarrail accordingly planned an attack up the Vardar Valley (*bottom center*) on 1 August. He hoped to link up with a possible Rumanian southward advance; but the Rumanians preferred to move northward into Hungary (*see map 37*). Supply difficulties forced a postponement until 20 August. On the 17th, the Bulgarians suddenly attacked. On the Allied right, a French cavalry screen (*not shown*) was driven in, but the British held the line of the Struma River (*this map, dotted blue line*). On the left flank, the Serbs were surprised and forced back to Lake Ostrovo, where the front stabilized on the 27th. That same day, Rumania entered the war.

Sarrail converted his planned offensive into a counteroffensive, attempting to pin down as many Bulgars as possible while the Rumanians opened their campaign; he now had about 350,000 men. Following a demonstration by the British toward Doiran on 10 September, the Serbs attacked northward on the 12th, while the French (with an attached Russian brigade) attempted to envelop the Bulgarian right flank. Rugged, wooded terrain slowed the Allied advance, but on 14 September the Serbians won a success at Gornichevo, and by 19 November the French enveloping movement had forced the Bulgars to retire behind Monastir. By this time, though, Rumania was obviously defeated, and Sarrail—furious because he had won no great victory—turned to quarreling with his subordinates. Operations dwindled away as the winter grew worse.

Meanwhile, the Italians carried out an independent operation in Albania in furtherance of their territorial ambitions in that area.

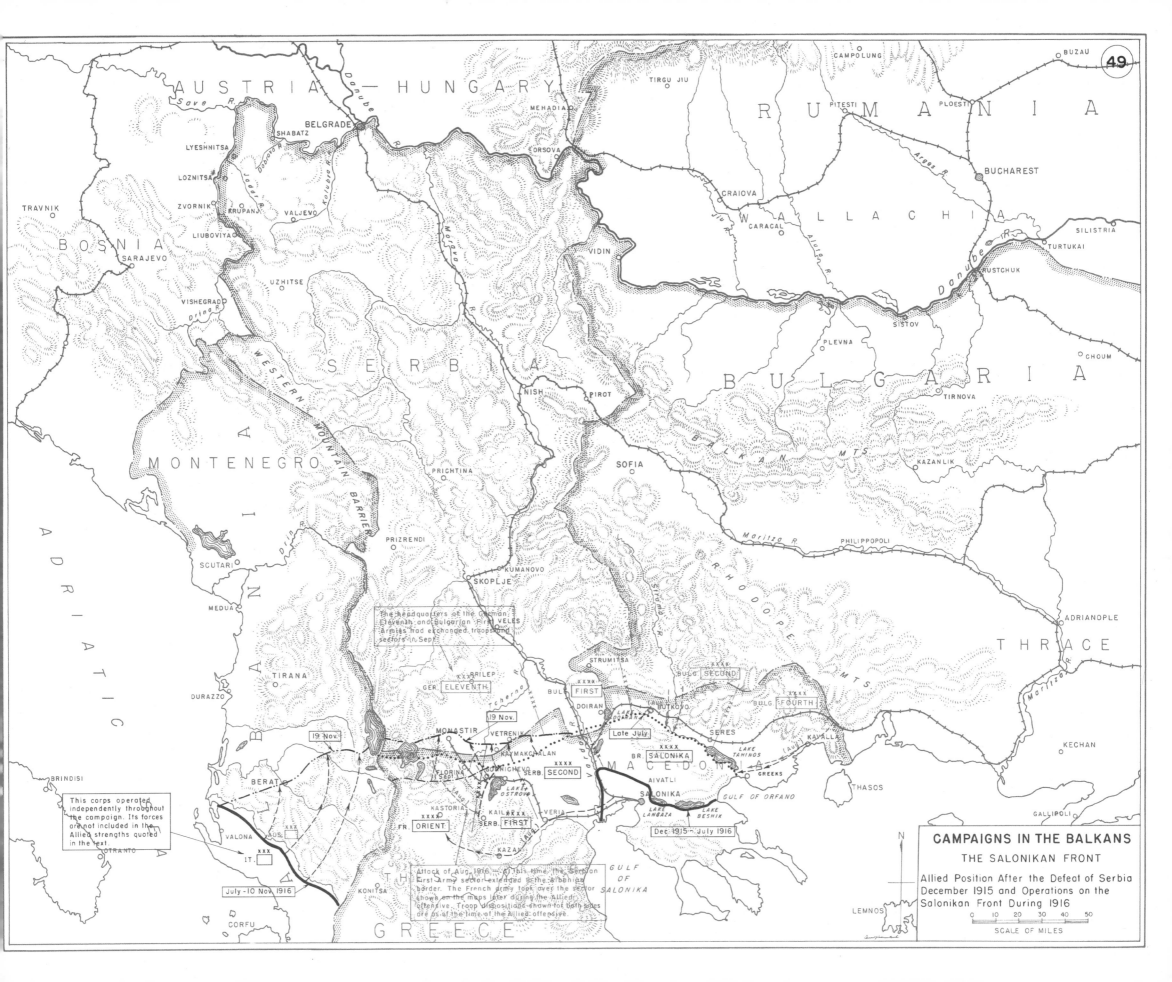

CAMPAIGNS IN THE BALKANS

THE SALONIKAN FRONT

Allied Position After the Defeat of Serbia December 1915 and Operations on the Salonikan Front During 1916

During the advance to Monastir in late 1916, Allied-Greek relations reached a crisis. Greek troops around Kavalla (*lower right*) surrendered to the Germans. This led to an Allied naval blockade of Greek ports, which forced the Greek government to agree—on 14 December, 1916—to expel the diplomatic representatives of the Central Powers, surrender the Greek Navy, demobilize its forces, and withdraw its regular troops southward from Thessaly (*bottom center*). Meanwhile, Venizelos set up a government in exile at Salonika and began raising Greek troops to serve with the Allied forces.

Reinforcements continued to flow into the Salonika area; shortly afterward, the hospitals began to fill. In early 1917, Sarrail had over 600,000 men (in addition to Venizelos' units), but only some 100,000 were available for duty. He attempted another offensive on 26 April, and mismanaged it thoroughly. The British made a costly diversionary attack on their front on the night of 24-25 April—according to orders—only to find that the main attack had been postponed because of bad weather. When launched, the main attack broke down on 23 May because of the poor behavior of the Serbs, who felt that they had not been properly supported during the Monastir operation, and consequently suspected that they were to be sacrificed. For the rest of 1917, there was little fighting; the British transferred two divisions to Palestine.

Affairs behind the lines were somewhat livelier. King Constantine was discovered to be secretly mobilizing his army in Thessaly. The result was his enforced abdication and exile on 11 June. Venizelos again became prime minister of Greece, and the Greek Army was reorganized to take over part of the Salonika front. However, the most encouraging development of 1917 was the recall of Sarrail on 10 December.

Sarrail's successor, the capable General Guillaumat, made careful preparations for a major offensive—which, however, the Supreme War Council forbade him to launch because of the uncertain situation on the Western Front. During July, 1918, he

was summoned back to France to take command of the garrison of Paris, again threatened by a German drive. His successor, General Franchet d'Esperey, adopted his plan. By September, with the Allies gaining ground everywhere, Franchet d'Esperey was allowed to attack. He had a total strength of 574,000 men—French, British, Serbs, Czechs, and Italians (not counting the Italian corps in Albania)—of whom approximately a third were available for duty. Opposing him, the Bulgarians had a total strength of about 400,000—many of them sick, all short of rations and ammunition, all with low morale. Practically all the German units that had formed the backbone of the Bulgarian Army had been withdrawn; in the German Eleventh Army, only the staffs were still German.

The Allied plan was for a French-Serbian force with heavy artillery support to penetrate the Bulgarian lines between the Vardar and the Tcherna (*lower center*), while the British made a secondary attack toward Doiran to prevent the Bulgarians from shifting troops westward against the flank of the breakthrough. The main attack was to be on 15 September; the secondary attack, on the 18th. One British division would feint an advance up the Vardar Valley on 1 September. Hard going was expected, because of the ruggedness of the terrain.

Almost from the first, Bulgarian resistance collapsed. By the 25th, the main attack had reached the Vardar River and split the Bulgarian front. The British entered Bulgaria, capturing Strumitsa; on the 26th, French cavalry passed through the infantry to exploit this success, taking Skoplje on the 29th. That same day, Bulgaria signed an armistice. Allied units, however, despite supply problems, kept up their advance until 11 November.

Since the campaign first began, many have criticized it as a glaring example of unnecessary diversion of effort. For three years, half the Bulgarian Army successfully pinned down from 300,000 to 600,000 Allied troops—troops that were urgently needed on the Western Front.

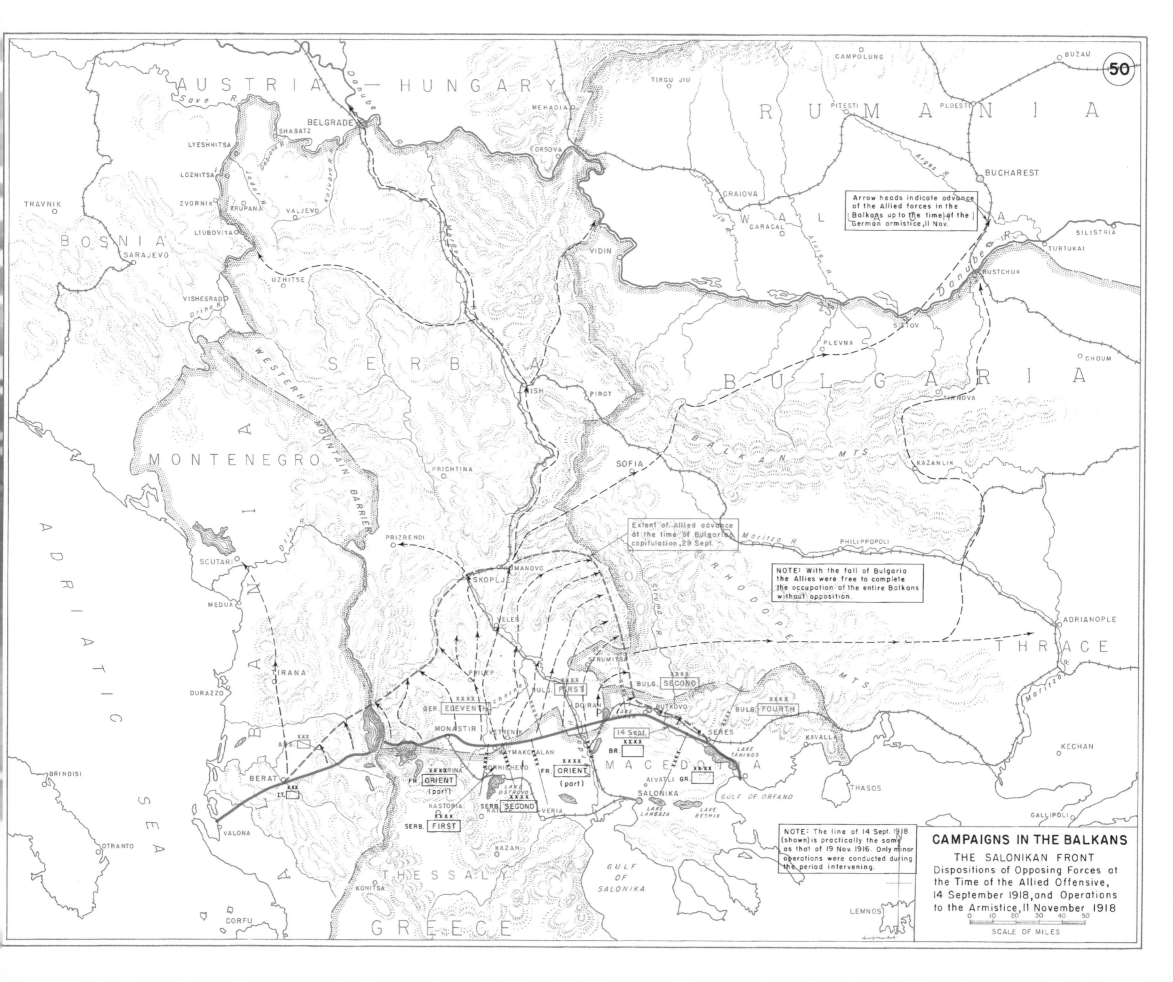

50

AUSTRIA – HUNGARY

RUMANIA

CAMPOLUNG

BUZAU

TIRGU JIU

PITESTI

PLOESTI

Danube

Save R.

BELGRADE

SHABATZ

ORSOVA

MEHADIA

CRAIOVA

CARACAL

BUCHAREST

LYESHNITSA

Drina R.

Kolubra R.

VIDIN

SILISTRIA

Danube R.

LOZNITSA

Jadar R.

VALJEVO

TURTUKAI

ZVORNIK

KRUPANJ

BOSNIA

TRAVNIK

LIUBOVIYA

RUSTCHUK

VISHEGRADO

UZHITSE

Drina R.

Arrow heads indicate advance of the Allied forces in the Balkans up to the time of the German armistice, 11 Nov.

SARAJEVO

SERBIA

WESTERN MOUNTAIN BARRIER

NISH

PIROT

PLEVNA

SISTOV

BULGARIA

GHOUM

SCUTARI

MONTENEGRO

PRICHTINA

SOFIA

BALKAN MTS.

KAZANLIK

Drin R.

MEDUA

PRIZRENDI

Extent of Allied advance at the time of Bulgarian capitulation, 29 Sept.

Maritza R.

PHILIPPOPOLI

ADRIANOPLE

KOMANOVO

SKOPLJE

RHODOPE

NOTE: With the fall of Bulgaria the Allies were free to complete the occupation of the entire Balkans without opposition.

VELES

THRACE

Struma R.

A

ADRIATIC SEA

TIRANA

PRILEP

STRUMITSA

Maritza R.

XXXX
BULG. FIRST

XXXX
BULG. SECOND

XXXX
ALB

Charna R.

XXXX
GER. ELEVENTH

VETRENIK

DOIRAN

BUTKOVO

XXXX
BULG. FOURTH

DURAZZO

MONASTIR

P.

MTS.

KAVALLA

XXX
ALB.

KORINA

FR. ORIENT (part)

SORNICHEVO

KAYMAKCHALAN

FR. ORIENT (part)

SERES

14 Sept

XXXX
BR.

Lake TAHINOS

KECHAN

BERAT

IT.

KASTORIA

Lake OSTROVO

SERB. SECOND

VERIA

AIVATLI

XXXX
GR.

MACEDONIA

GULF OF ORFANO

THASOS

VALONA

SERB. FIRST

NOTE: The line of 14 Sept. 1918 (shown) is practically the same as that of 19 Nov. 1916. Only minor operations were conducted during the period intervening.

SALONIKA

Lake LANGAZA

Lake BESHIK

GALLIPOLI

BRINDISI

OTRANTO

KAZAN

Lake

CAMPAIGNS IN THE BALKANS

THE SALONIKAN FRONT
Dispositions of Opposing Forces at the Time of the Allied Offensive, 14 September 1918, and Operations to the Armistice, 11 November 1918

CORFU

KONITSA

THESSALY

GULF OF SALONIKA

GREECE

LEMNOS

0 10 20 30 40 50

SCALE OF MILES

That part of the Near East shown on the map encompasses two widely separated areas in which troops of the British Empire fought campaigns against Turkey. These campaigns occurred despite criticisms from the French who felt the British were diverting resources from the Western Front and paying too much attention to defending their economic and imperial interests. In the overall pattern of strategy, the campaigns in the Near East were secondary, though each had grown into a sizable and expensive affair by 1918, and at least one of them bid fair to become a major operation. The two areas are Mesopotamia (*center*)—now Iraq—and Palestine, on the Mediterranean opposite Cyprus, extending from Gaza northward.

The area known in 1914 as Mesopotamia was generally that drained by the Tigris and Euphrates Rivers. It was inhabited by Arab tribes, under local rulers who paid more or less allegiance to Turkey. From the Persian border to the eastern edge of the Syrian Desert is about 150 miles; the distance from the Persian Gulf to Mosul (*upper center*) is approximately 500 miles. These limits defined, in general, the extent of Mesopotamia. The area was practically barren of trees. There were very few roads and even fewer bridges; consequently, during the rainy season, traffic was largely confined to the rivers. The Tigris and Euphrates join at Basra (*center*) to form the Shatt-al-Arab (Shatt means river bank.) From the Persian Gulf to Basra, the river was navigable to ships of less than seventeen feet draft; above that point, the Tigris was navigable as far as Baghdad to small craft drawing less than three and a half feet. The Shatt-al-Hai (*center*), extending between Kut-al-Amara and Nasiriya, is a sizable stream during the rainy season. During the rest of the year, it gradually dries up. In the wet season (January-May), the rivers overflow their banks—unless well diked—and inundate the surrounding countryside. (The river banks are actually higher than the inland areas.) The climate fluctuates drastically between recorded extremes of 19° and 123° F. August is the hottest month, and January the coolest, respective mean temperatures being 92.5° and 48.8° F. This was not a healthful area in 1914, such diseases as cholera, plague, malaria, and dysentery being endemic.

In September, 1914, when it became obvious that relations with Turkey had seriously deteriorated, the British Foreign Office in India recommended the dispatch of a small force to the head of the Persian Gulf to counter Turkish designs. This force, it was hoped, would encourage the Arabs to throw off the yoke of Turkish oppression (Arab-Turkish relations were none too warm) and would safeguard the interests of the two local pro-British sultans. More important, it would protect the vital oil pipeline from Persia to Abadan Island (*center, opposite Fao; shown more clearly on map 52*a). The Indian government concurred, and dispatched the reinforced 16th Brigade (5,000 men) to Fao on 16 October. It might be noted here that the Indian Army (seven divisions plus supporting troops—deficient in artillery and lacking its full complement of British officers) was the only troop source in 1914 for this campaign. Further, it had to expect calls for troops elsewhere and still maintain order in India. On 23 October, the 16th Brigade arrived at the head of the gulf, where it remained on ships for two weeks until Britain declared war on Turkey. Then the brigade landed against negligible opposition (*action not shown*). Within a few days, the remaining troops of the 6th Indian Division arrived, and the Turks, who had made an ineffectual counterattack earlier, fell back to Basra.

From the Turkish viewpoint, Mesopotamia was a relatively unimportant area in 1914. The Dardanelles, the Caucasus, and Egypt received higher priorities. Thus, there were only two divisions in the area south of Baghdad. One of these, with a rifle strength of 5,000, was in the Basra area and opposed the initial British operations.

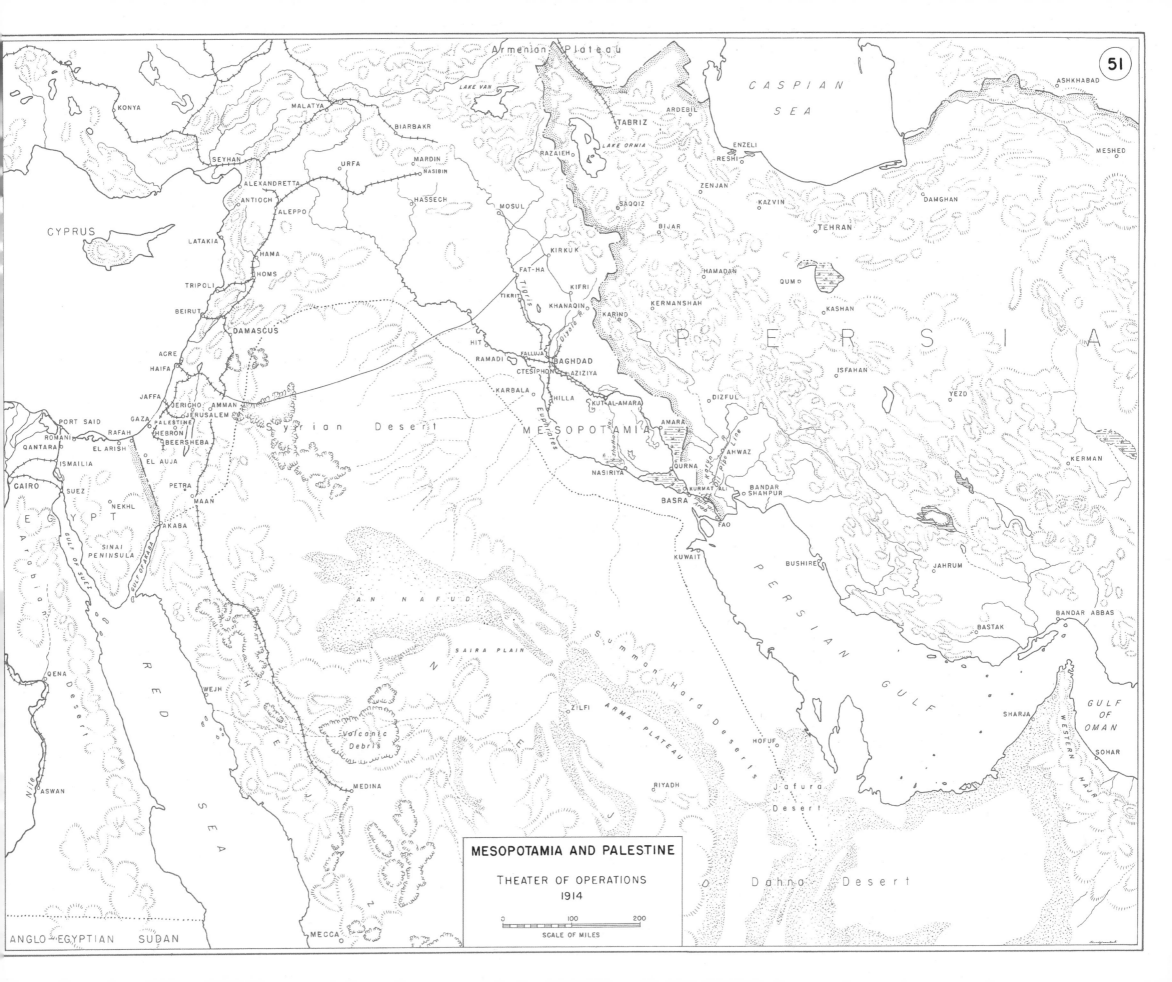

51

CASPIAN SEA

Armenian Plateau

LAKE VAN

ASHKHABAD

KONYA

MALATYA

BIARBAKR

TABRIZ

ARDEBIL

MESHED

RAZAIEH

ENZELI

LAKE ORMIA

RESHI

SEYHAN

URFA

MARDIN

NASIBIN

ZENJAN

DAMGHAN

ALEXANDRETTA

KAZVIN

ANTIOCH

HASSECH

MOSUL

SAQQIZ

ALEPPO

BIJAR

TEHRAN

CYPRUS

LATAKIA

KIRKUK

HAMADAN

QUM

HAMA

FAT-HA

P E R S I A

HOMS

TIKRIT

KIFRI

KERMANSHAH

KASHAN

TRIPOLI

KHANAQIN

BEIRUT

Diyala R.

KARIND

ISFAHAN

DAMASCUS

HIT

YEZD

ACRE

RAMADI

FALLUJA

BAGHDAD

DIZFUL

HAIFA

CTESIPHON

AZIZIYA

JAFFA

KARBALA

HILLA

KUT-AL-AMARA

S y r i a n   D e s e r t

JERICHO

AMMAN

AMARA

PORT SAID

GAZA

PALESTINE

JERUSALEM

M E S O P O T A M I A

Euphrates

shatt

ROMANI

RAFAH

HEBRON

AHWAZ

KERMAN

QANTARA

BEERSHEBA

NASIRIYA

QURNA

Karun R.

BANDAR SHAHPUR

CAIRO

SUEZ

EL ARISH

EL AUJA

Pipe Line

ISMAILIA

PETRA

KURMAT AL

E G Y P T

MAAN

BASRA

NEKHL

FAO

GULF OF SUEZ

GULF OF AKABA

AKABA

KUWAIT

BUSHIRE

JAHRUM

SINAI PENINSULA

A n   N a f u d

P E R S I A N   G U L F

BANDAR ABBAS

QENA

BASTAK

SAIRA PLAIN

Summon Hard Desert

ASWAN

RED SEA

WEJH

Volcanic Debris

ZILFI

ARMA PLATEAU

SHARJA

GULF OF OMAN

HOFUF

WESTERN HAJR

SOHAR

Nile

MEDINA

RIYADH

Jafura Desert

MESOPOTAMIA AND PALESTINE

THEATER OF OPERATIONS
1914

Dahna Desert

ANGLO-EGYPTIAN SUDAN

MECCA

0   100   200

SCALE OF MILES

Brushing aside the weak Fao defenses upon landing, the 16th Brigade moved to secure Abadan Island (*sketch* a, *bottom right*). By 15 November, the rest of the 6th Division had arrived, and the British pushed upstream. A spirited fight occurred east of Khora on the 17th. Basra was occupied four days later, and a detachment moved forward to Qurna. Now, for several months, both sides built up strength. The Turks moved the 37 R Division to Baghdad (*top left*) and concentrated troops at Nasiriya (*lower center*), while the Indian government scraped together another division and a cavalry brigade. These, together with the 6th Division, formed a corps under General Sir John E. Nixon. A Turkish strike at Ahwaz (*right center*) in February, 1915, drove the two battalions there into their defenses. Nixon, fearful of this Turkish threat to the oil line, sent a strong detachment up the Karun River in May which forced an enemy retreat. In April, the Turks—reinforced by Arabs who resented the presence of the British—fiercely attacked Shaiba (*bottom center*), but were decisively beaten. In June and July, Nixon captured Amara and Nasiriya against considerable opposition, thus accomplishing the original mission of the expedition.

By now, the climate, disease, combat, and logistical deficiencies had made themselves felt, but Nixon, a cheerful optimist, argued convincingly that the seizure of Kut-al-Amara (*upper left*) was desirable and feasible. The Indian government reluctantly consented, and Townshend's reinforced 6th Division was given the assignment. The Turks had concentrated at Kut and entrenched a formidable position (*sketch* b). But there was a weakness: the position lay astride the river, and the nearest bridge for lateral communications was five miles to the rear. The British, benefiting from aerial reconnaissance, planned to turn the Turkish north flank. But, to entice Nur-ud-Din into positioning his reserve near the river, Townshend conducted demonstrations as shown. The attack on the 28th was entirely successful, the Turkish reserve arriving too late to stop the envelopment. But Townshend's troops were tired, the cavalry lacked water, and a mirage played tricks; thus, the majority of

the Turks escaped northwest to Ctesiphon (*sketch* c, *top left*). Townshend pursued with his few boats and the cavalry, halting at Aziziya on 5 October to reorganize.

Political considerations now exerted their influence. Nixon was authorized to advance to Baghdad if he felt his force was sufficient for the task. The British government favored this advance: Persia was wavering, the Dardanelles venture had failed, and Baghdad appeared to be a fine political objective. Townshend dissented, pleading for more troops and a reliable line of communications; Nixon disagreed and ordered the advance. It got under way on 19 November. On the 22d, the well-entrenched Turks repulsed the vigorous British blow at Ctesiphon. Townshend—outnumbered and with no tactical advantage—withdrew to Kut, where he elected to accept investment. For five months, he stood off his enemy while hunger and disease decimated his force. Meanwhile, Nixon had sent a large force to relieve Townshend. All its efforts failed against floods and stubborn Turkish defenses; on 29 April, 1916, Townshend surrendered. The campaign to date had cost Britain 40,000 men.

In August, the competent General Sir Stanley Maude assumed over-all command in Mesopotamia and began improving the logistical arrangements. Reinforcements poured in, and by December he was ready to move on Kut. Maude spent two months clearing the Turks from the south bank of the river and then executed his well-conceived plan (*sketch* d). On 17 February, 1917, he attacked at Sannaiyat (top right), achieving few gains, but drawing some Turks north. Another attack was launched at Sannaiyat on the 22d, and that night a feint was made at Maqasis (*center*) and a demonstration at Kut. The next morning, the main crossing was successfully made at the lightly defended Shumran Peninsula (*left center*), compromising the Turkish position. On the 24th, the attacks at Dahra Ridge and Sannaiyat continued as the Turks withdrew. The pursuit encountered a skillfully employed Turkish rear guard and accomplished little. The Turks fell back to Diyala (*sketch* a, *top left*); Maude followed to Aziziya, where logistical problems forced a halt.

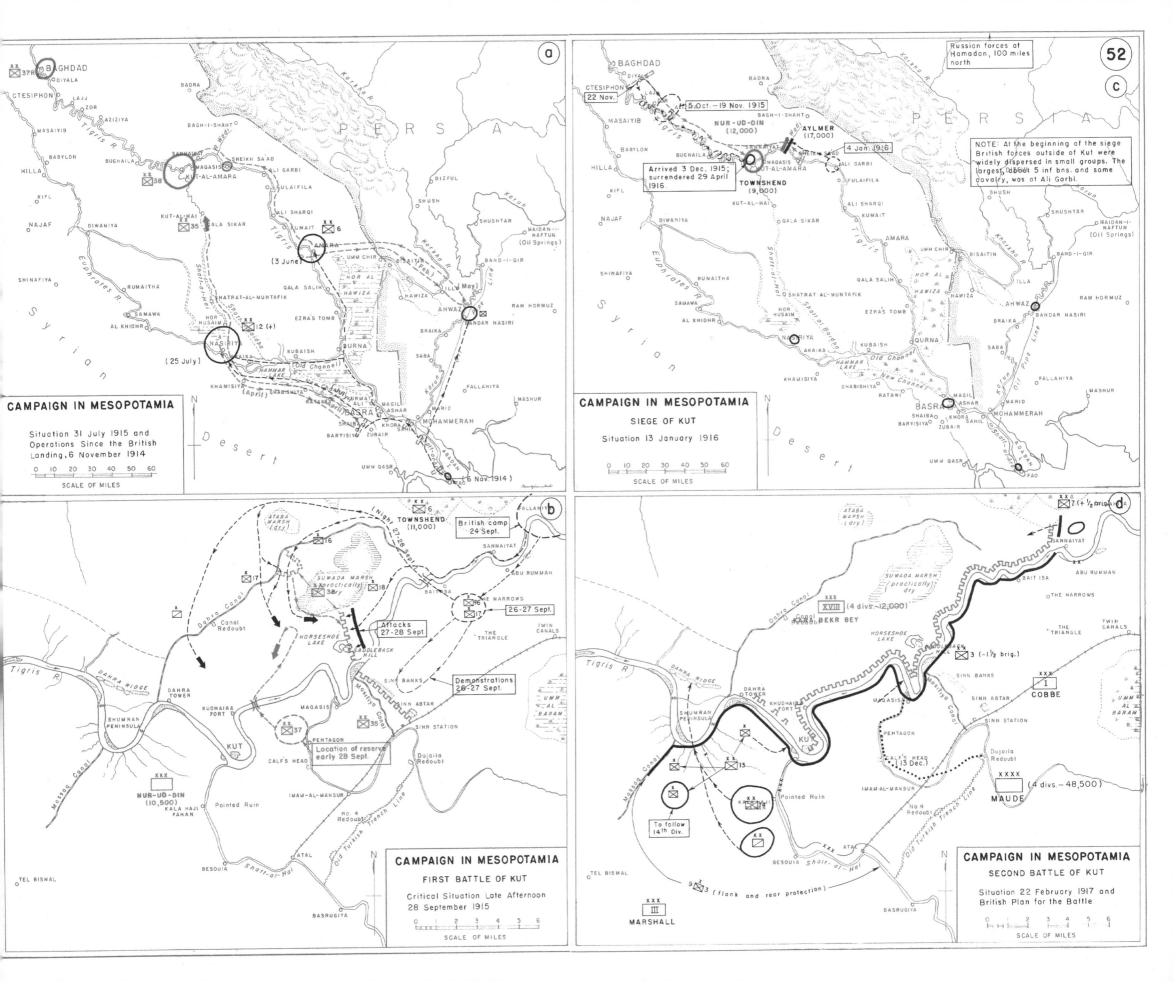

Map a:

CAMPAIGN IN MESOPOTAMIA

Situation 31 July 1915 and
Operations Since the British
Landing, 6 November 1914

0 10 20 30 40 50 60
SCALE OF MILES

Map b:

CAMPAIGN IN MESOPOTAMIA

FIRST BATTLE OF KUT

Critical Situation Late Afternoon
28 September 1915

0 1 2 3 4 5 6
SCALE OF MILES

Map c:

52

CAMPAIGN IN MESOPOTAMIA

SIEGE OF KUT

Situation 13 January 1916

0 10 20 30 40 50 60
SCALE OF MILES

Russian forces at Hamadan, 100 miles north

NOTE: At the beginning of the siege British forces outside of Kut were widely dispersed in small groups. The largest, about 5 inf bns. and some cavalry, was at Ali Garbi.

Arrived 3 Dec. 1915; surrendered 29 April 1916.

Map d:

CAMPAIGN IN MESOPOTAMIA

SECOND BATTLE OF KUT

Situation 22 February 1917 and
British Plan for the Battle

0 1 2 3 4 5 6
SCALE OF MILES

On 4 March, 1917, the British renewed the advance toward Baghdad (*center*). After three days of difficult fighting at the Diyala River, they entered Baghdad on the 11th. The long-sought prize held no enchantment for Maude, however, and he quickly moved north to consolidate his conquest. Detachments moved up the Tigris, Diyala, and Euphrates Rivers; by May, Maude's hold on Baghdad was secure, and he now rested during the burning summer.

Turkish troop dispositions on 11 March show the high priority given the Caucasus (where the Turks were massing in anticipation of a Russian collapse) and Palestine. The relative weakness of the forces assigned to Mesopotamia, however, was in large part due to the logistical problems involved in supporting that theater. The Baghdad-Constantinople trip (1,255 miles) required twenty-two days, for the railroad was not yet completed between Biarbakr and Tikrit (300 miles). Nevertheless, in the summer, Turkey concentrated available reserves (*not shown*) near Alexandretta at Aleppo (*upper left*) with a view toward recapturing Baghdad. However, the destruction of many of the supplies for this force (in an explosion near Constantinople), coupled with British successes in Palestine, thwarted the scheme.

On 18 November, General Maude died of cholera and was succeeded by General Sir William R. Marshall. In February and March, 1918, Marshall executed Maude's plan for a move on Mosul (*upper center*). He captured Kifri and Hit and then suspended operations for the summer.

Russia had moved about 20,000 troops into Persia in 1915, for political as well as military reasons. The next year, after Townshend surrendered at Kut, the Russians attempted a move down the Diyala River, but, when rebuffed by the Turkish XIII Corps, fell back to the positions shown. When Russia capitulated, this force disintegrated. As Turkey and Germany raced for the Caucasian oil fields, Britain became worried. She feared Bolshevik collaboration with Germany to invade Persia, Afghanistan, and then India; nor did she want Baku (*off map, top center; on western shore of Caspian Sea*) oil in German hands. Hence, General L. C. Dunsterville moved into Persia, logistically supported by Marshall, to rally the White Russian remnants and secure Baku. The tiny force, relying on British prestige rather than power, had little success; however, the fears of the British were never realized.

In October, 1918, Marshall's final campaign began. Though Turkish resistance was strong in places, the British eventually routed them at Fat-Ha (*upper center*) on the 24th and accepted the surrender of most of the Sixth Army on the 30th. The next day, Turkey signed an armistice—more because of her defeats in Palestine than her reverses in Mesopotamia. Marshall occupied Mosul on 14 November.

Thus ended the "sideshow" which cost the British Empire 92,501 men. Turkish casualties are not known, but 45,500 Turks became prisoners. When the war ended, the British had 414,000 men in the area, of whom only 112,000 were combat troops. The price for defending the oil line had indeed been high.

Concurrently with the Mesopotamian campaign, the British and Turks fought in Egypt and Palestine. The primary British concern here was the protection of the Suez Canal. When Turkey entered the war, Egypt became a British protectorate—somewhat against her will. By January, 1915, there were 70,000 British troops in the area, most of them Indians and Anzacs.

In 1915, a Turkish force of 20,000 crossed the waterless desert in an attempt to seize the canal; the Turks were handily repulsed and forced to withdraw. The British, now realizing that the Suez could not be defended from the west bank, made plans to move to the El Arish area where any Turkish advance could be directly opposed or taken in flank. By early 1916, there were 400,000 British troops in Egypt (many had just returned from Gallipoli for temporary billeting) and construction of the necessary rail and water lines leading east had started. Gradually, these logistical tools moved forward, governing the advance of the troops who fought an occasional engagement with the Turks. By 20 December, 1916, the British were established around El Arish as shown.

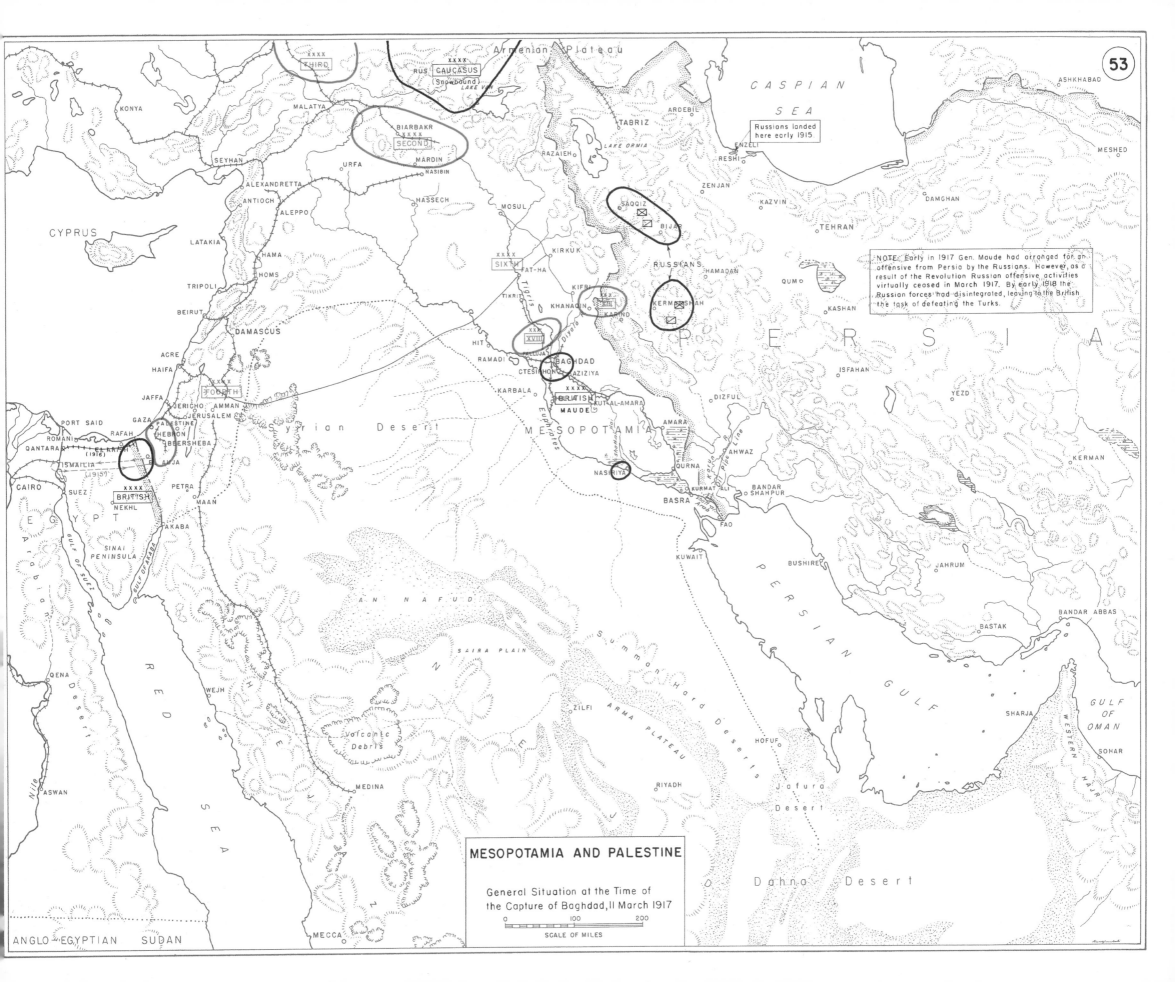

53

CASPIAN SEA

Russians landed here early 1915.

NOTE: Early in 1917 Gen. Maude had arranged for an offensive from Persia by the Russians. However, as a result of the Revolution Russian offensive activities virtually ceased in March 1917. By early 1918 the Russian forces had disintegrated, leaving to the British the task of defeating the Turks.

Armenian Plateau

XXXX
THIRD

XXXX
RUS. CAUCASUS
(Snowbound)
LAKE VAN

BIARBAKR
XXXX
SECOND

XXXX
SIXTH

RUSSIANS

XXXX
BRITISH
MAUDE

XXXX
FOURTH

XXXX
BRITISH

MESOPOTAMIA

Syrian Desert

PERSIA

PERSIAN GULF

EGYPT

RED SEA

AN NAFUD

Summan Hard Deserts

ARMA PLATEAU

Dahna Desert

Jafura Desert

GULF OF OMAN

ANGLO-EGYPTIAN SUDAN

MESOPOTAMIA AND PALESTINE

General Situation at the Time of
the Capture of Baghdad, 11 March 1917

0   100   200
SCALE OF MILES

With the capture of El Arish (*off map, bottom left*), the British had attained their original objective of securing the Suez Canal against attack. General Sir Archibald Murray had sufficient troops to stop effectively any Turkish attempts to drive across the Sinai Peninsula, but he was not strong enough to mount a major offensive into Palestine. Nevertheless, this was to be his mission. (Murray maintained a lavish headquarters at Cairo, but moved to a more advanced, austere site at El Arish for the coming operations.)

In December, 1916, following the collapse of Rumania and the British-French failure to achieve any great gains in the Somme offensive, David Lloyd George—a man of vast energy, guile, and self-confidence—had come to power in England. The British prime minister was prone to think in terms of political objectives, and he had reservations about battles of attrition like the Somme. He had been exploring the possibilities of peripheral war, and now urged an advance into Palestine. A victory here would add fuel to the flaming Arab revolt against the Turks—Lawrence ("of Arabia") was advising Hussein (the Sherif of Mecca) in this venture—and perhaps Jerusalem, an impressive objective, could be captured. Murray cautiously advised that he needed reinforcements to attempt a major advance. But none were forthcoming, for the Allies were scraping together all possible troops in preparation for the heralded Nivelle offensive (*see map 60*). So plans were prepared for an overland movement toward Gaza (*this map; center, left*). Paradoxically, the greatest sea power on earth was unable to exploit fully the strategic mobility conferred by its fleet; global commitments precluded it.

The advance to the border began in January, 1917; Rafah was seized by the British on the 9th. The railroad and pipeline were pushed forward, the railroad reaching the border in March. The Turks (whose forces in this area the British usually overestimated) gave up their forward positions and occupied the positions shown with about 16,000 men. Murray's army—only slightly superior to the Turks in total strength, but extremely dominant in cavalry—closed to the Wadi Ghazze (a sizable ravine, dry much of the time) and prepared to attack Gaza, the key to the enemy position.

The British field commander was General Sir Charles M. Dobell. He planned to move his two cavalry divisions around to the east and north of Gaza to prevent Turkish reinforcement of that locality; meanwhile, the 53d Division would seize the dominant Ali Muntar ridge and then rush the town. The 52d Division was to remain in reserve, and the 54th Division would protect the right flank.

The attack was launched on 26 March and, though initially delayed by a heavy fog, proceeded as planned. By 1830, the 53d Division had seized the ridge after a hard fight and was on the edge of the town; at the same time, one of the cavalry divisions was in the northern suburbs. But now confusion and misunderstanding, so frequent in war, set in to ruin British chances for what appeared to be a certain victory on the 27th. Through poor staff work and an inexplicable breakdown in communications, the commander of the cavalry was not aware of the success achieved by the 53d Division. Fearful that the Turks would attack his divisions from two sides—and also concerned over lack of water for his horses—he ordered the cavalry to withdraw that night. The 53d Division's flank was thus exposed, and it, too, withdrew to Wadi Ghazze. The next morning, attempts were made to retake Ali Muntar, but the reinforced Turks were too strong.

London, receiving an optimistic report on the outcome of the battle, now directed Murray to renew the offensive to capture Jerusalem. That commander had reported Turkish losses as 8,000 and his own as 3,500; actually, they were 2,447 and 3,967, respectively. The British had *not* won a great victory and were in no condition to plunge recklessly toward Jerusalem.

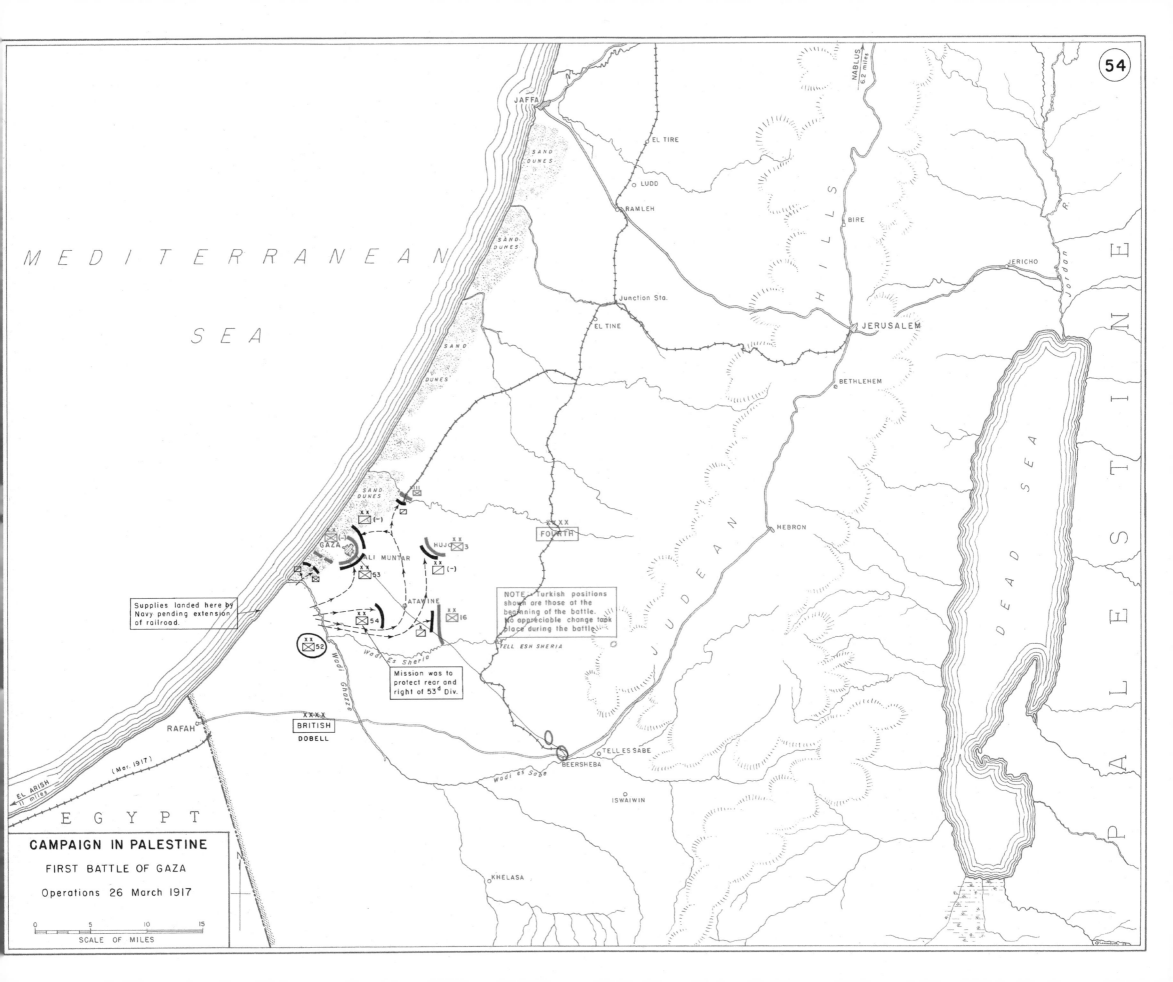

54

MEDITERRANEAN

SEA

JAFFA

NABLUS 6.2 miles

EL TIRE

SAND DUNES

LUDD

RAMLEH

BIRE

SAND DUNES

JERICHO

Jordan R.

Junction Sta.

JERUSALEM

EL TINE

BETHLEHEM

SAND DUNES

SAND DUNES

DEAD SEA

XII

XX (-)

XX (-)

GAZA

FOURTH

XX 3

HUJC

ALI MUNTAR

XX 53

XX (-)

HEBRON

P A L E S T I N E

Supplies landed here by
Navy pending extension
of railroad.

ATAWINE

NOTE: Turkish positions
shown are those at the
beginning of the battle.
No appreciable change took
place during the battle.

JUDEAN

XX 54

XX 16

XX 52

Wadi Es Sheria

TELL ESH SHERIA

Mission was to
protect rear and
right of 53d Div.

HILLS

XXXX

BRITISH

DOBELL

Wadi Ghazze

TELL ES SABE

RAFAH

BEERSHEBA

Wadi es Sabe

(Mar. 1917)

EL ARISH
11 miles

ISWAIWIN

E G Y P T

KHELASA

CAMPAIGN IN PALESTINE

FIRST BATTLE OF GAZA

Operations 26 March 1917

N

0   5   10   15

SCALE OF MILES

General Murray had not appreciated what extreme optimism his exaggerated report of success in the First Battle of Gaza would arouse in London. Consequently, he was somewhat surprised when immediately ordered to capture Jerusalem. He again asked for reinforcements, stressing the need for two more infantry divisions and additional artillery if such an ambitious task were to be accomplished. London replied that prompt action on his part was important and that the 74th Division would be made available. The implication of the necessity for a success to boost public morale was clear to Murray.

The task facing the British now was immeasurably more difficult than it had been previously. The Turks, soundly advised by Germans, had established a strong defensive position from Gaza to Beersheba (*lower center*), with the bulk of their troops in strong points at and southeast of Gaza. They also had adequate artillery and air support, the latter making it extremely difficult for Dobell to achieve secrecy in preparation for the attack.

Dobell learned that Beersheba was lightly held, but the problem of supplying a large force on that flank—particularly with water—precluded an envelopment there. Nor would the mounting pressure from Murray and London allow a delay to build up supplies to support such a move. Thus, the British resorted to a frontal attack on the well-prepared Turkish position—it was to be a battle of brute force. Dobell's plan called for an attack in two phases; in the first phase, he hoped to obtain an advantageous position from which the decisive assault (second phase) could be launched. The 53d Division, along the coast, was to be supported by naval gunfire; the 74th would be in reserve; the cavalry divisions would protect the right flank; and the other two infantry divisions, making the main effort, would attack Ali Muntar.

On 17 April, Dobell launched his offensive. The first phase went well, but in the decisive second phase the British failed everywhere. The three assaulting infantry divisions took little ground and suffered heavy casualties; the few tanks employed were of little assistance, either being picked off by Turkish artillery or stalled in the sand. At 1700, 19 April, Dobell broke off the attack and withdrew. He had lost 6,444 men, while Turkish casualties were about 2,000. Once more, the British had been given a convincing display of the Turk's ability to defend tenaciously a piece of terrain: Gallipoli and Mesopotamia had been earlier demonstrations whose lessons had not been heeded.

One of Murray's first acts after this Second Battle of Gaza was to relieve Dobell. But his own failure could not be condoned in a London which now looked upon the Palestinian campaign as the means of driving Turkey from the war. In June he, too, was recalled, being replaced by General Sir Edmund Allenby, a cavalryman who had recently achieved some prominence in the Battle of Arras. Before departing for Cairo, Allenby was given the mission "Jerusalem before Christmas" by Lloyd George.

The new commander was a forceful and energetic individual. He lived in the field with the troops, began overhauling the logistical establishment, and revitalized the command. After surveying the Gaza area, he concluded that the key to the position was Beersheba, the capture of which would enable him to turn the Turkish position. Allenby now asked for three more divisions, aircraft, artillery, and service units; this time, the government met the request of its field commander. Preparations began for the Third Battle of Gaza.

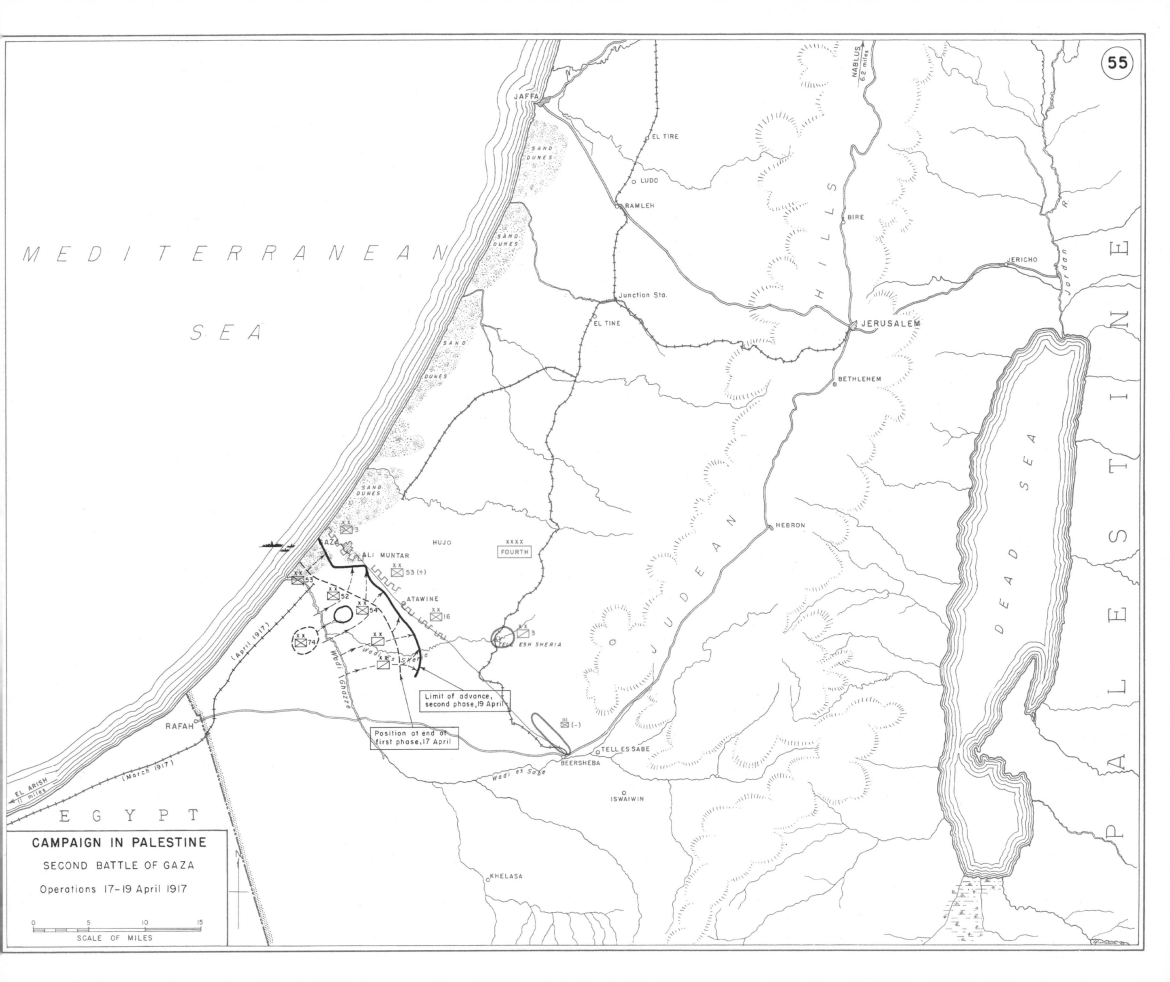

55

MEDITERRANEAN SEA

EGYPT

JAFFA

EL TIRE

LUDD

RAMLEH

Junction Sta.

EL TINE

SAND DUNES

SAND DUNES

SAND

DUNES

SAND DUNES

SAND DUNES

GAZA

ALI MUNTAR

HUJO

⊠ 3

XXXX
FOURTH

XX
⊠ 53 (+)

XX
⊠ 53

XX
⊠ 52

XX
⊠ 54

ATAWINE

XX
⊠ 16

XX
⊠ 74

(April 1917)

Wadi Ghazze

Wadi es Sheria

XX
⊠

XX
⊠ 3

TELL ESH SHERIA

JUDEAN HILLS

NABLUS
62 miles

BIRE

JERICHO

Jordan R.

JERUSALEM

BETHLEHEM

HEBRON

DEAD SEA

P A L E S T I N E

Limit of advance,
second phase, 19 April

Position at end of
first phase, 17 April

RAFAH

(March 1917)

EL ARISH
11 miles

BEERSHEBA

Wadi es Sabe

ISWAIWIN

TELL ES SABE

⊠ (-)

KHELASA

CAMPAIGN IN PALESTINE

SECOND BATTLE OF GAZA

Operations 17-19 April 1917

0   5   10   15
SCALE OF MILES

N

In early 1917, Turkey's fortunes were declining. The rigors of the previous winter had taken a heavy toll of her troops in the Caucasus; in Mesopotamia, General Maude advanced relentlessly; Arab uprisings, sparked by Lawrence, were proving troublesome; and the Rumanian campaign had drained off some of her better troops. But, with the defeat of Rumania and the impending collapse of Russia, it became possible to reinforce the Palestine front. By September, 1917, 35,000 Turkish troops were in the Gaza area. These troops were disposed in three general fortified areas (Gaza, Tell Esh Sheria, and Beersheba) connected by outposts. They were organized into two armies whose actions were to be coordinated by Falkenhayn. (After his Rumanian triumph, the German had been dispatched to Turkey, and eventually went on to Jerusalem, arriving there on 1 November.) As mentioned earlier, Turkey had concentrated a force at Aleppo (*off map, north*) in March to be used to recapture Baghdad; but Allenby's preparations convinced Falkenhayn that the force should be used in Palestine. This force (called "Yilderim") was thus routed southward to form the nucleus of the Seventh Army, though not all of it had arrived by the time Allenby struck.

On 31 October, the British force numbered 88,000 and was well supplied and competently commanded. The key to Allenby's plan—to seize Beersheba and then drive northwest to the coast—was surprise founded on deception. Every means of misleading the Turks to expect the main attack on Gaza was employed—including a faked attack order which was allowed to fall into enemy hands—while the XX Corps (four divisions) and two cavalry divisions were moved secretly to the Beersheba area at the last moment. To support his sizable army, Allenby also built additional railroads and extended the pipeline. Aerial reconnaissance provided the Turks with information of the movement toward Beersheba, but they greatly underestimated its strength. When Allenby attacked at dawn on the 31st, the Turks were taken completely by surprise.

The XX Corps succeeded in seizing the outer position at Beersheba, with the 74th Division encountering the most difficulty. By nightfall, the 74th and 60th Divisions had almost reached Beersheba (*dashed blue line*), while the 53d Division continued to guard their left flank. Meanwhile, late in the afternoon, the Australian Cavalry Division had made a mounted charge which captured Beersheba and its vital water supplies; the Turks, who had fairly well contained the attack of the Anzac Cavalry Division, then withdrew to the position west of Tell Esh Sheria.

From 1 to 4 November, the British assaulted the Gaza position, making only minor gains, while the Turks reinforced the Sheria position to the east. As the 53d Division applied more pressure, more enemy troops were moved from the center of the line to oppose it, thus inviting attack by the divisions of Allenby's XX Corps (*small division symbols*) at Sheria. This attack came at 0400, 6 November; by 0600, Allenby had achieved such success that he ordered the cavalry to move through to the coast.

The Gaza defenders, in danger of being cut off, withdrew toward Junction Station (*upper center*). They arrived there by 11 November, despite pressure maintained by the British cavalry, hampered as it was by water shortages. To the east, the Seventh Army also withdrew.

Allenby gave his foe no respite, attacking Junction Station on the 13th and capturing it the following day. The Eighth Army fell back northward, and Allenby turned his attention toward Jerusalem. After one unsuccessful attack (*action not shown*), it became obvious that the XXI and the Cavalry Corps could not effect the capture alone. Hence, Allenby paused, regrouped, and prepared for a major attack. On 8 December, he pushed forward all along the line; the next day, the long-sought political prize—Jerusalem—was in British hands. Allenby, shrewdly and humbly, made his official entry into the city on foot.

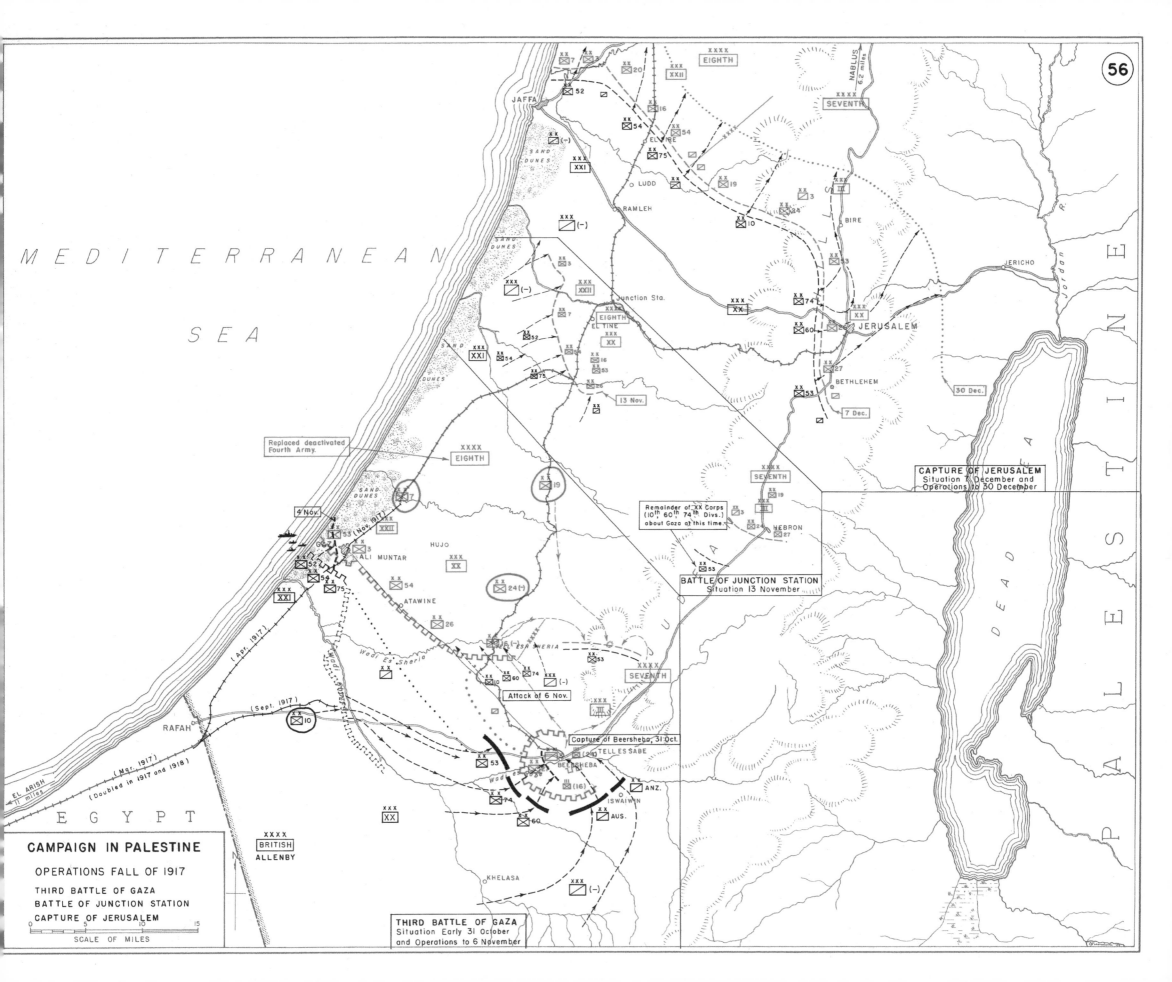

56

MEDITERRANEAN SEA

EGYPT

PALESTINE

DEAD SEA

JAFFA

LUDD

RAMLEH

Junction Sta.

EL TINE

JERUSALEM

BETHLEHEM

HEBRON

NABLUS
6.2 miles

JERICHO

Jordan R.

EIGHTH

SEVENTH

BIRE

ELTIRE

Replaced deactivated
Fourth Army.

EIGHTH

Remainder of XX Corps
(10th, 60th, 74th Divs.)
about Gaza at this time.

CAPTURE OF JERUSALEM
Situation 7 December and
Operations to 30 December

30 Dec.

7 Dec.

13 Nov.

BATTLE OF JUNCTION STATION
Situation 13 November

SEVENTH

4 Nov.

(1 Nov. 1917)

ALI MUNTAR

HUJO

ATAWINE

Wadi Es Sheria

ESA SHERIA

Attack of 6 Nov.

Capture of Beersheba, 31 Oct.

BEERSHEBA

TELL ES SABE

ISWAIWIN

ANZ.

AUS.

RAFAH

(1 Apr. 1917)

(Sept. 1917)

(Mar. 1917)
(Doubled in 1917 and 1918)

EL ARISH
11 miles

KHELASA

CAMPAIGN IN PALESTINE

OPERATIONS FALL OF 1917

THIRD BATTLE OF GAZA
BATTLE OF JUNCTION STATION
CAPTURE OF JERUSALEM

0   5   10   15
SCALE OF MILES

BRITISH
ALLENBY

THIRD BATTLE OF GAZA
Situation Early 31 October
and Operations to 6 November

SAND DUNES

The capture of Jerusalem and Maude's success in Mesopotamia provided the only bright spots in Allied operations in 1917. As such, they added fuel to Lloyd George's demands that Allenby be reinforced in order to eliminate Turkey from the war. This, he thought, would be the best means of applying pressure on Germany. He apparently chose to ignore the fact that the Germans, with their interior lines, could move troops between fronts more easily and quickly than the British. Nivelle's failure and the great losses in the Flanders battles preyed heavily on the prime minister's mind. Thus, against the advice of the Imperial General Staff, Allenby received two more divisions from Mesopotamia and was directed to undertake the offensive.

But Ludendorff's offensive on the Western Front (*see map 63*a), striking the weakened British line on 21 March, 1918, completely disrupted Allenby's plans. The British were forced to withdraw two divisions and supporting troops equivalent to three more from Palestine. Allenby postponed his attack and, during the spring and summer, resorted to training the green replacements received from India. He also conducted minor operations (*not shown*) east of the Jordan River—partly to secure bridgeheads, but primarily to deceive the Turks as to his eventual intentions: already, Allenby had decided to launch his main blow along the coast north of Jaffa (*this map, lower left*). Though these minor operations were tactically unsuccessful, they did direct Turkey's attention toward the vulnerability of the Amman-Dera railroad (*lower center*)—exactly as Allenby desired. Lawrence's Arabs added to the deception by increased forays on the railroad. British air power, by now, was so superior that the Turks were unable to conduct effective reconnaissance. Thus, by September, when the British were ready to attack, the Turks had one-third of their forces east of the Jordan and were poorly prepared for Allenby's devastating blow.

In March, Sanders had replaced Falkenhayn and had at once set about reorganizing the Turkish defenses to take full advantage of the Turkish forte for defense of prepared positions.

Thus, most of his troops were moved into line, and reserves were held to a minimum. But Turkish morale was low (except in the German Asia Corps), desertion reached high proportions, and the government withdrew troops to pursue political aims in Persia and the Caucasus.

Allenby launched his attack—the famous Battle of Megiddo—at 0430, 19 September. The XXI Corps (five divisions) made the main attack without the customary preparatory bombardment. By 0730, the enemy line had been rent asunder, and the Cavalry Corps burst through in the exploitation to seize the Megiddo (*center*)–El Affule–Beisan area and block the northern exits from the Judean Hills (*lower center*). That evening, the XX Corps took up the attack, and Chaytor Force pushed across the Jordan. By nightfall on 21 September, the cavalry had blocked the retreat of the Seventh and Eighth Armies, 25,000 prisoners had been taken, and Turkish resistance west of the Jordan had been broken. British aircraft were particularly effective in strafing and bombing the defiles through which the Turks struggled to escape—a portent of the coming influence of tactical air power. During the period 22-30 September, the Turkish Fourth Army, harried by cavalry and Arabs, disintegrated on its way to Damascus, its survivors surrendering near that city.

Damascus fell to Allenby on 2 October, and Aleppo on the 28th. The Battle of Megiddo cost the British 5,666 casualties; total Turkish casualties are unknown, but the British captured 76,000 men. The Turks, routed also in Macedonia (*see map 50*) and Mesopotamia (*see map 53*), asked for an armistice on the 28th and signed the surrender papers on the 30th.

Thus ended the campaign in Palestine, concluded brilliantly by Allenby, but at great over-all expense. Total British casualties from 1 January, 1915, were 554,828—90 per cent of them nonbattle. The question of whether the resources used in the Salonika, Mesopotamia, and Palestine campaigns could have been put to better use on the more decisive Western Front remained controversial.

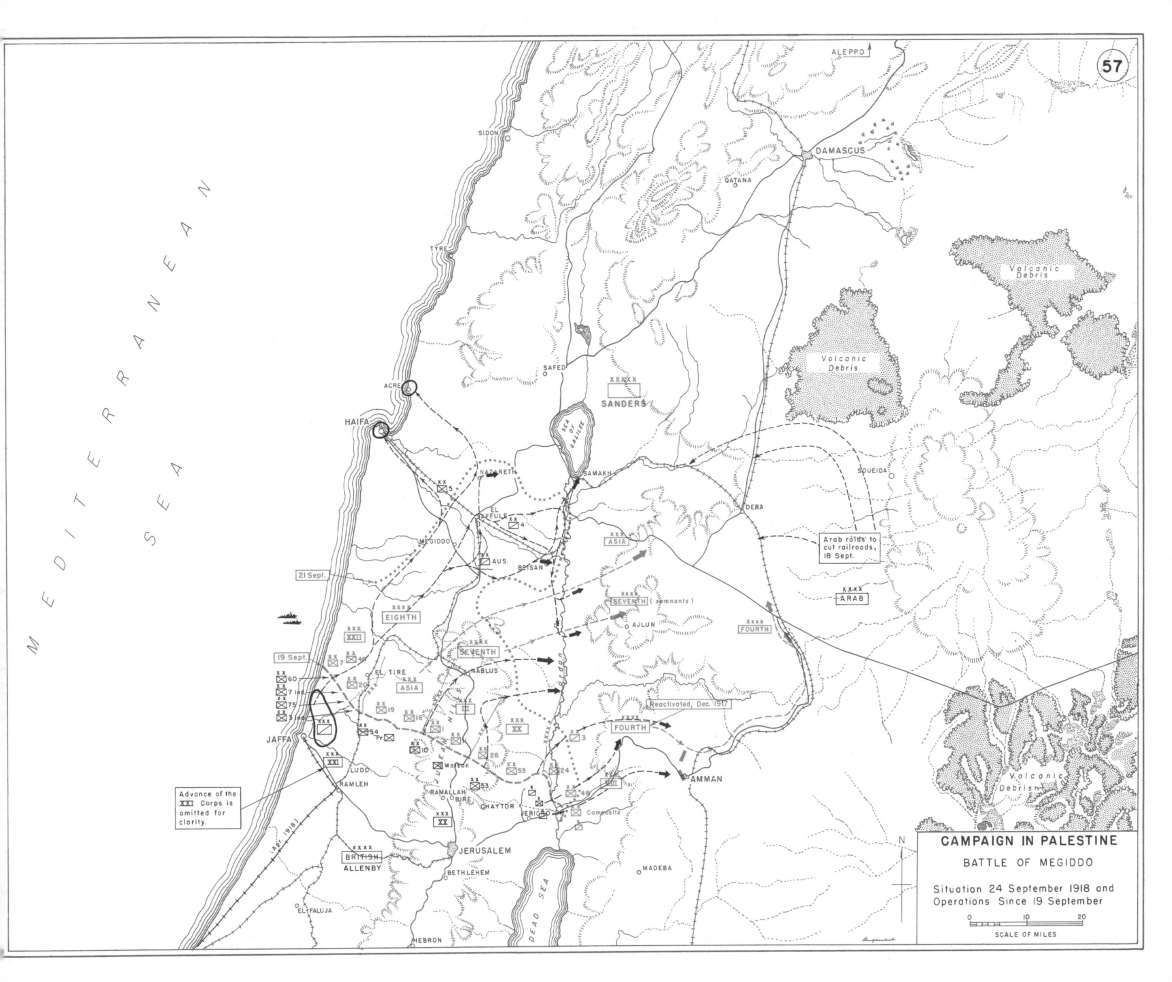

57

MEDITERRANEAN SEA

ALEPPO

DAMASCUS

SIDON

TYRE

ACRE

HAIFA

SAFED

SANDERS

Volcanic Debris

Volcanic Debris

NAZARETH

SAMAKH

SOUEIDA

EL AFFULE

DERA

XX 5

MEGIDDO

XX 4

Arab raids to cut railroads, 18 Sept.

21 Sept.

AUS.

BEISAN

XXX ASIA

XXXX ARAB

EIGHTH

XXX XXII

SEVENTH (remnants)

AJLUN

XXXX FOURTH

19 Sept.

XX 7

XX 48

SEVENTH

XX 60

XX 20

NABLUS

ASIA

Reactivated, Dec. 1917

XX 7 Ind.

XX 19

XX 16

XX 75

II

XXX XX

XXXX FOURTH

XX 3 Ind.

XX 54 Pr.

JAFFA

XX 1

XX 3

XXI

LUDD

XX 10

XX 26

VIII

AMMAN

Advance of the XXI Corps is omitted for clarity.

RAMLEH

O BIRE

Watson

XX 53

XX 324

RAMALLAH

XX 53

XX 49

CHAYTOR

JERICHO

Composite

N

JERUSALEM

MADEBA

CAMPAIGN IN PALESTINE

BETHLEHEM

BRITISH ALLENBY

BATTLE OF MEGIDDO

Situation 24 September 1918 and Operations Since 19 September

EL FALUJA

DEAD SEA

Volcanic Debris

HEBRON

0   10   20
SCALE OF MILES

In November, 1916, an Allied conference at Joffre's headquarters had decided to carry out coordinated offensives on the Western, Eastern, Italian, Salonika, and Palestine fronts during 1917, with the major effort on the Western Front. There, Joffre proposed to continue the attrition of the Somme with a massive combined British-French offensive from the Oise River (*left center*) north to Arras. This was to be followed, several weeks later, by a British-Belgian attack to clear the north coast of Belgium, where the Germans had established several important submarine bases. The Allied commanders were optimistic; except for the fall of Rumania, 1916 had gone generally in their favor. They now had definite numerical superiority on all fronts, and munitions production was increasing. They hoped that sometime during their 1917 operations the German lines would break. If not, they felt capable of grinding down the forces of the Central Powers through unremitting pressure on all fronts.

These decisions were immediately nullified by political changes in Britain and France during December, 1916. In England, the new prime minister, David Lloyd George, did not favor great battles of attrition like the Somme, preferring peripheral operations like his expanded Palestine campaign (*see map 54*). In France, political leaders, who had grown impatient with Joffre's failure to win the war, forced him into retirement and replaced him with General Robert G. Nivelle, an extrovert who had distinguished himself at Verdun. Nivelle spoke perfect English and so impressed the mercurial Lloyd George that, except for the vigorous protests of Haig and Robertson, he would have given Nivelle what amounted to complete command of the British forces. Finally, with relations badly strained, it was agreed that Haig should make his plans conform generally to those of Nivelle, but during the coming campaign only.

Nivelle's principal claim to fame was the skillful counterattack he had directed at Verdun. Now—proclaiming his belief in the effectiveness "of violence, of brutality, and of rapidity"—he boasted that he could repeat his Verdun operation on a much larger scale and obtain a complete breakthrough of the German lines in from twenty-four to forty-eight hours. Masses of heavy guns were to paralyze the enemy by a short, surprise bombardment; masses of infantry would then smash through the German trench system, opening the way for an all-out exploitation by large forces of cavalry. His operational plan provided for an initial, powerful British-French secondary attack between Bapaume and Arras, after which the French would make the main effort in the Chemin des Dames area (*left center*) between Reims and Soissons. In order to free sufficient French units for this offensive, the British were required to extend their right about twenty-five miles.

Meanwhile, the Germans withdrew from their long, unfavorable position in the Somme sector to the new Hindenburg Line (correctly, "the Siegfried zone"—a deep, complex, defensive system). This gave them a stronger front and—by shortening their line—enabled them to hold it with fewer divisions and thus form a badly needed reserve. Their organization of the Siegfried position and withdrawal to it were expertly handled, and took the Allies largely by surprise. The evacuated territory was devastated: all buildings were destroyed, all trees cut down, roads ruined, wells choked up or polluted, and booby traps, inundations, and demolitions arranged to slow the pursuit.

Nivelle's projected main attack was not particularly affected by this withdrawal, but in the sector of the secondary attack, it would take several months to close to and mount an offensive against the new German line. Nivelle contented himself with arranging for the British alone to make a strong attack near Arras. Many of the French troops who had been originally assigned to the secondary attack in cooperation with the British were added to his Group of Armies of the Reserve, which was to make his main attack. Other French forces were to make minor attacks at St. Quentin and east of Reims (*small blue arrows*).

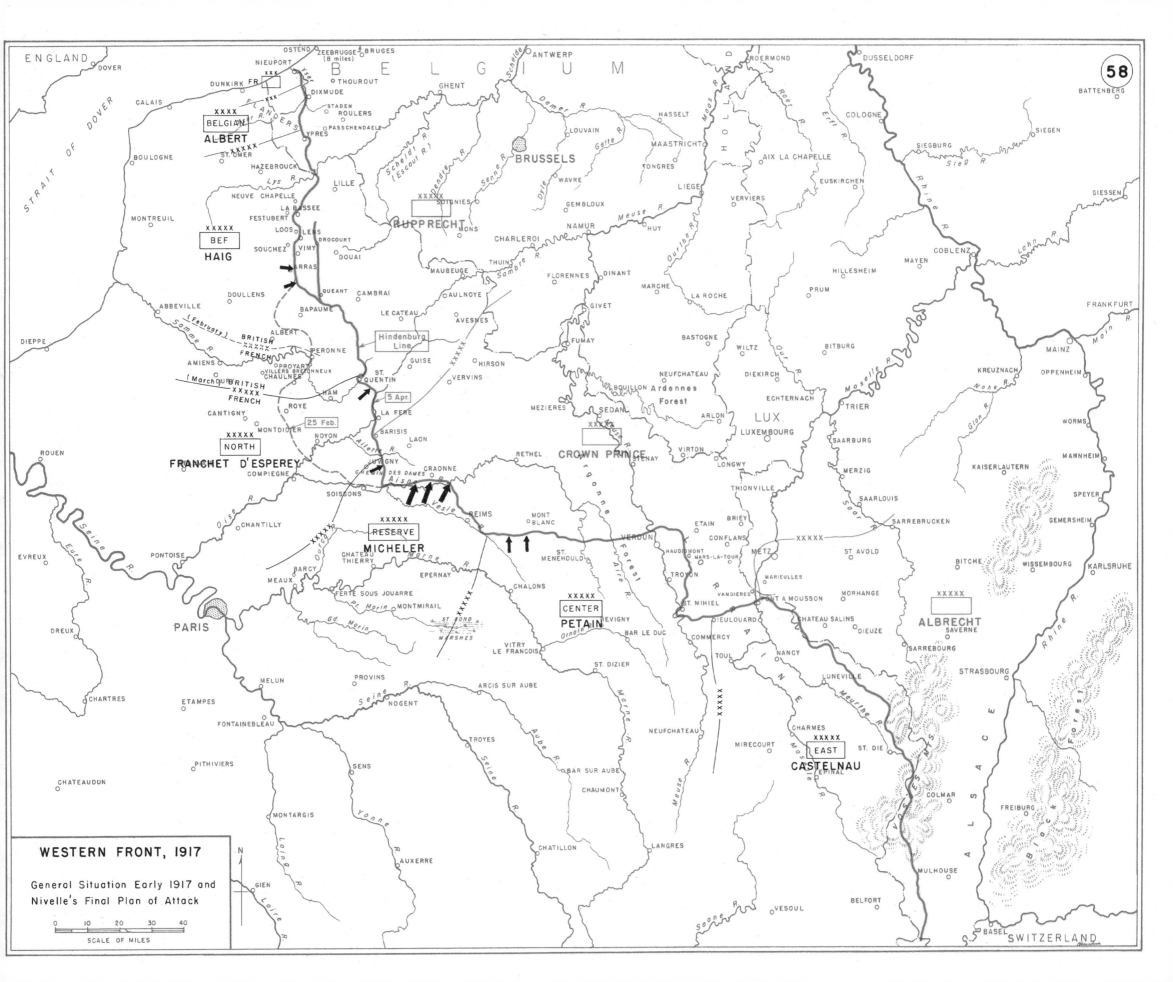

ENGLAND

BELGIUM

HOLLAND

58

WESTERN FRONT, 1917

General Situation Early 1917 and
Nivelle's Final Plan of Attack

0 10 20 30 40
SCALE OF MILES

XXXX
BELGIAN
ALBERT

XXXXX
BEF
HAIG

XXXX
RUPPRECHT

Hindenburg
Line

(February)
BRITISH
XXXX
FRENCH

(March)
BRITISH
XXXXX
FRENCH

5 Apr.

25 Feb.

XXXXX
NORTH
FRANCHET D'ESPEREY

XXXX
CROWN PRINCE

XXXXX
RESERVE
MICHELER

XXXXX
CENTER
PETAIN

XXXXX
EAST
CASTELNAU

XXXXX
ALBRECHT

PARIS

SWITZERLAND

Not the least questionable of the features of Nivelle's plan was his selection of the Arras sector (*sketch* a) for the secondary attack which the British were to launch one week before his main attack, in order to draw the German reserves northward. The German defenses here were deep and strong; about five miles behind them lay the northward extension of the Hindenburg Line, running from Quéant to Drocourt (*see map 58*). The whole area was dominated by Vimy Ridge, which the Germans considered impregnable, and which gave them excellent observation of the British lines.

Despite its strength, Haig hoped to break through this entire German defensive system. The British Third and First Armies were to attack simultaneously, the Third making the main effort, while the First protected its left flank by taking Vimy Ridge. If their attacks progressed successfully, the British Fifth Army (*off this map, south*) would join in the offensive. If a breakthrough were achieved, Haig planned to exploit it by vigorous cavalry action. Otherwise, he proposed to cut the Arras operation short in favor of a major offensive farther north in Flanders.

Masses of artillery, including many heavy guns, fired a carefully organized, five-day preparatory bombardment, employing improved ammunition with greatly increased wire-cutting capability. (Plans called for a four-day preparation, which had to be lengthened when Nivelle's inability to attack on time caused a twenty-four-hour postponement of the British attack.) A limited number of tanks were available, and these—over the objections of the tank unit commanders—were distributed among the different corps.

Having learned during the Somme fighting that attempts to hold every foot of ground during heavy attacks resulted in extremely high casualties, the Germans had developed a new system of defensive tactics known as an elastic defense-in-depth. Against it, an attacker first encountered a deep, lightly held outpost zone where a combination of dense wire entanglements and plentiful machine guns was designed to delay and disorganize him. Behind this was the first defensive position, consisting of several lines of mutually supporting strongpoints connected by trenches; behind that, a second defensive position; and, behind that, waited specially trained counterattack divisions, ready to advance and recover any lost ground. The whole system was highly flexible and permitted a great deal of opportunity for initiative and aggressiveness in what had been a purely static defense.

In the Arras sector, however, the German Sixth Army commander either misunderstood this system or willfully ignored it. Possibly because of concern over Vimy Ridge, he held his front lines in great strength and, at the same time, posted his counterattack divisions too far to the rear.

The British jumped off at 0530, 9 April, following a heavy rolling barrage. Artillery support was so heavy that the Germans in the front lines were confused and demoralized. Gains were beyond all expectations; Canadian troops capturing most of Vimy Ridge at the first rush. But the weather now turned bad, and a series of costly new assaults brought little success. The Fifth Army attacked on the 10th, and was abruptly repulsed. It tried again in early May, but made only slight gains. Elsewhere, the Germans fell back skillfully when necessary. Operations continued until late May on a very reduced scale—in part, to divert attention from Haig's preparations around Ypres (*sketch* b).

No major offensive could well be undertaken at Ypres as long as the Germans held the long spur of Messines Ridge just south of that town. A limited attack was therefore launched by General Sir Herbert Plumer's Second Army. Since normal methods of obtaining surprise were impossible in the narrow Ypres salient, which was under constant German observation, Plumer's engineers had dug nineteen mines (*indicated by blue circles on sketch* b), packed with almost 1,000,000 pounds of high explosives, under the German-held ridge. A heavy preliminary bombardment began on 21 May. At 0310, 7 June, all mines were exploded; a barrage 700 yards deep was put down on the wrecked ridge line, and nine divisions attacked with immediate success. Minor advances were made during the next few days to improve the newly won position.

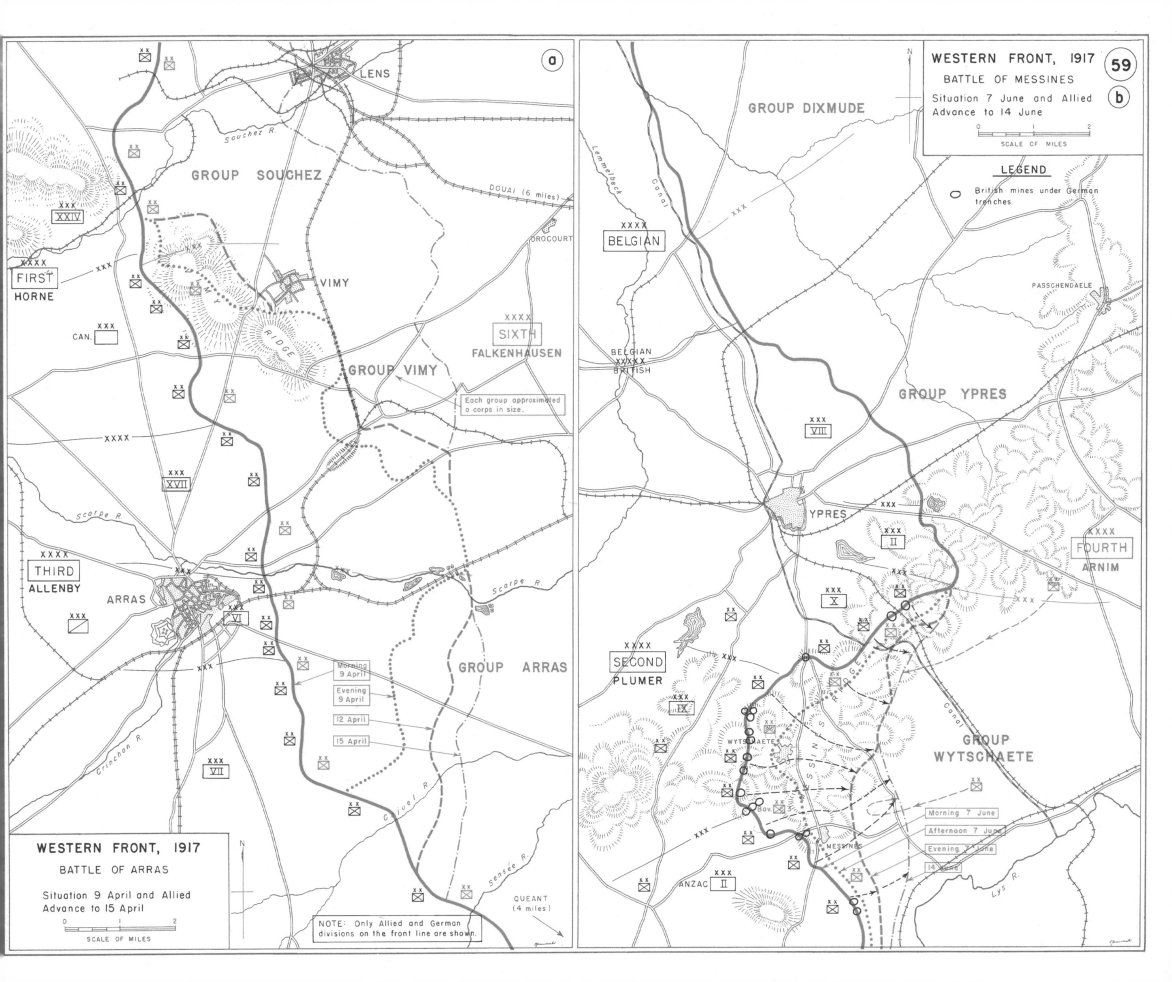

Strategically, the area that Nivelle had selected offered definite possibilities. A breakthrough here would put the French in the rear of the Hindenburg Line (*see map 58*), thus splitting the German front at a most vulnerable spot. Tactically, however, it was forbidding (*this map*). Any attack must surmount a series of steep and wooded parallel ridge lines, which the Germans had greatly strengthened. Victory here, against the new German elastic defense, could come only as the result of a skillful combination of surprise and concentrated force.

Nivelle could provide the force. The German withdrawal in the British sector had freed thirteen French divisions and 550 heavy guns. These Nivelle added to General Micheler's army group, along with the French forces originally designated to act with the British in the secondary attack. But surprise was a different matter; Nivelle himself made it impossible. For one thing, he talked too much, both in France and England. For another, detailed plans were widely circulated, even down to the front-line companies. The inevitable promptly happened: copies were captured by the Germans. When so informed, Nivelle stubbornly refused to make the slightest change in his plans.

Having confirmed the captured plans through agents and aerial reconnaissance, the Germans brought in a new army under General Fritz von Below and strengthened their lines. They planned to move their light artillery well to the rear when the French bombardment began, and to bring it forward promptly when the French infantry advanced.

Meanwhile, Nivelle found troubles in his rear. The French government had changed again, and the new minister of war mistrusted both Nivelle and his plan. In this, he was backed by Nivelle's three army group commanders, all of whom favored a more limited offensive. In a final conference, called by the President on 5 April, Nivelle still clung to his plan; rather than accept anything less, he offered his resignation. This the government lacked the courage to accept. However, Nivelle was instructed to suspend his offensive if it did not produce the rapid success he so firmly predicted. The preparatory bombardment began on 5 April; but bad weather repeatedly delayed the attack, and the bombardment had to be continued overtime, with a resulting severe drain on the French reserves of artillery ammunition. Finally, at 0600, 16 April, the main attack began. Pétain's secondary attack to the east of Reims was launched the next day. Whatever the French high command thought of their chances for success, Nivelle had inspired the rank and file. His infantry and tanks stormed forward with the old French fury.

Instantly, they met massed German machine-gun and artillery fire. Their own barrage, shifting too rapidly as they stumbled up the slippery hillsides, ran away from them. Communications collapsed. German aviators cleared the skies over the battlefield, knocking out the French artillery's aerial observation. In most places, the German first line was taken, but deeper penetrations were smashed by prompt counterattacks. French tank losses reached over 75 per cent, many of them having been caught in march column on the roads by German artillery.

Obstinately, Nivelle pushed his attack on the 17th. The weather remained stormy, but the Germans, finding the salient between Laffaux and Vailly (*top center*) under attack from both sides, began to evacuate it. Gradual, expensive gains continued at a few points along the line. On the night of 19-20 April, Nivelle ordered the Tenth Army committed between the Fifth and the Sixth, preparatory to another major attack. This produced another political-military crisis. Pétain was made chief of the general staff and thereafter limited Nivelle's operations. A final offensive on 5 May brought slight gains, but the Germans still held the high ridges that dominated the Chemin des Dames summit. On 15 May, Pétain succeeded Nivelle. In the confused wrangling that followed, the French front-line armies broke out in mutiny. This Pétain put down by mixed firmness and justice, while a thin screen of loyal soldiers held the front. By amazing good fortune, the Germans remained in ignorance of the whole affair.

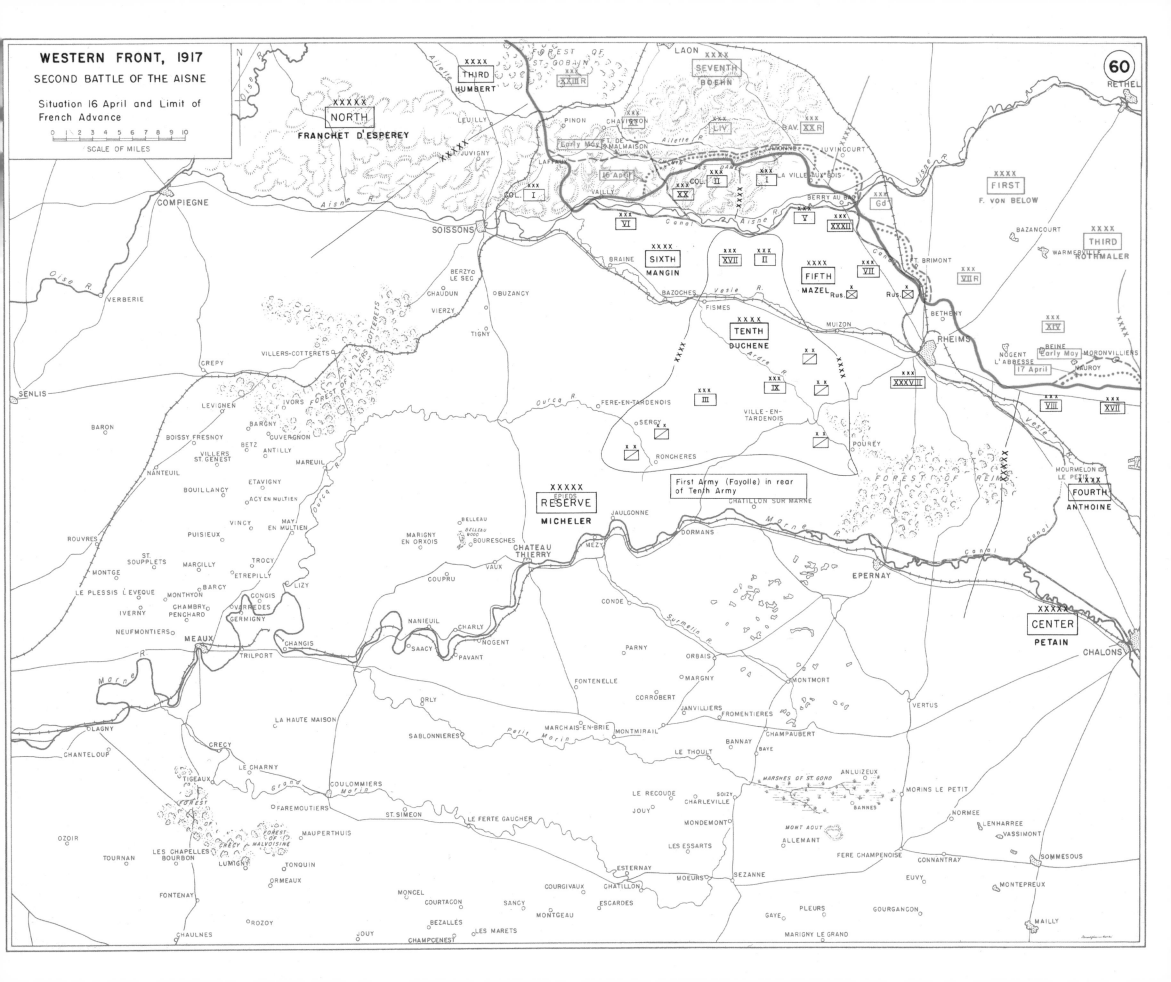

Pétain begged Haig to keep the Germans occupied while he nursed his armies, crippled by mutiny, back to effectiveness. Accordingly, Haig went ahead with his Flanders offensive. This was to consist of three phases: first, an attack by the British Second and Fifth Armies to capture the rest of the high ground east of Ypres (sketch a); next, an amphibious landing on the Belgian coast between the Yser River and Ostend (*see map 58, top left*), in conjunction with an attack eastward from the Nieuport area; finally, a general advance toward Ghent. Exaggerated intelligence reports having caused him to over-estimate the decline in German strength and morale, Haig planned an operation similar to Nivelle's recent failure and sought a sudden breakthrough that would carry the war out of the trenches into the open. Accordingly, he entrusted the main attack (*this map*) to the aggressive General Sir Hubert Gough rather than the methodical Plumer, who had commanded the Ypres area for over two years and was familiar with the terrain. Gough was to attack northeast, making his main effort on his right. Plumer would cover Gough's right flank.

If this offensive could have been launched simultaneously with Nivelle's, greater results might have been possible. Now, time was lost while men and guns were brought north from Arras and the small French First Army was fitted into line. Consequently, the Germans had six weeks in which to prepare.

Allied aircraft eventually gained control of the air over the front, but the frequent bad weather largely nullified their success. The preparatory bombardment began on 18 July; zero hour was 0350 on the 31st. Unfortunately, the heavy rains soon filled the thousands of shell holes created by the long bombardment with water, forming a major obstacle. Most of the early British gains were lost to German counterattacks. When Gough proved unable to break through, Haig placed Plumer in command of the offensive. After careful preparations, Plumer advanced on 20 September, delivering a series of limited assaults on narrow fronts, with a pause after each one to get

guns and supplies forward, and reserves held ready to meet German counterattacks. By late September, he had won three battles. Then came the winter rains and the Battle of Caporetto (*see map 43*); five British divisions had to be rushed to Italy. Mud thwarted British advances in early October, but after much suffering Haig's troops finally drove the Germans back to secure what he considered a good winter defensive position (*this map, dot-dashed red line*).

Meanwhile, seeking success before the Germans could be reinforced from the East, Haig revived an earlier plan for an attack in the Cambrai area (*sketch* b). This was to be a surprise attack without a preparatory bombardment. The artillery would open fire as the attack jumped off, using map and survey data. Tanks would be employed in mass, attacking with the infantry to break through the German position, seize bridges across the St. Quentin Canal (*lower center*), and breach the German second line behind it. Cavalry would strike through the gap thus created to isolate Cambrai and capture the wooded ridge just south of Bourlon (*center, left*) and the Sensée River crossings beyond.

At 0620, 20 November, a sudden deluge of fire dropped on the German positions, and more than 200 tanks lumbered forward, smashing gaps in the wire for the British infantry. Completely surprised and outnumbered, the Germans gave way, except around Flesquieres (*center, left*), where inept British tactics gave the defenders a chance to deal with tanks and infantry separately. But lack of infantry reserves—either casualties at Ypres or idle in Italy—finally slowed the assault; the longed-for breakthrough could not quite be achieved.

On 30 November, Ludendorff, having scraped together all available reserves, attacked both flanks of the British salient. To the south, the first German rush drove almost three miles into the original British position, but Gouzeaucourt (*lower center*) was saved by a tank counterattack, and farther north the British lines held firm. Haig, however, ordered a withdrawal (*dashed red line*) on the night of 4 December.

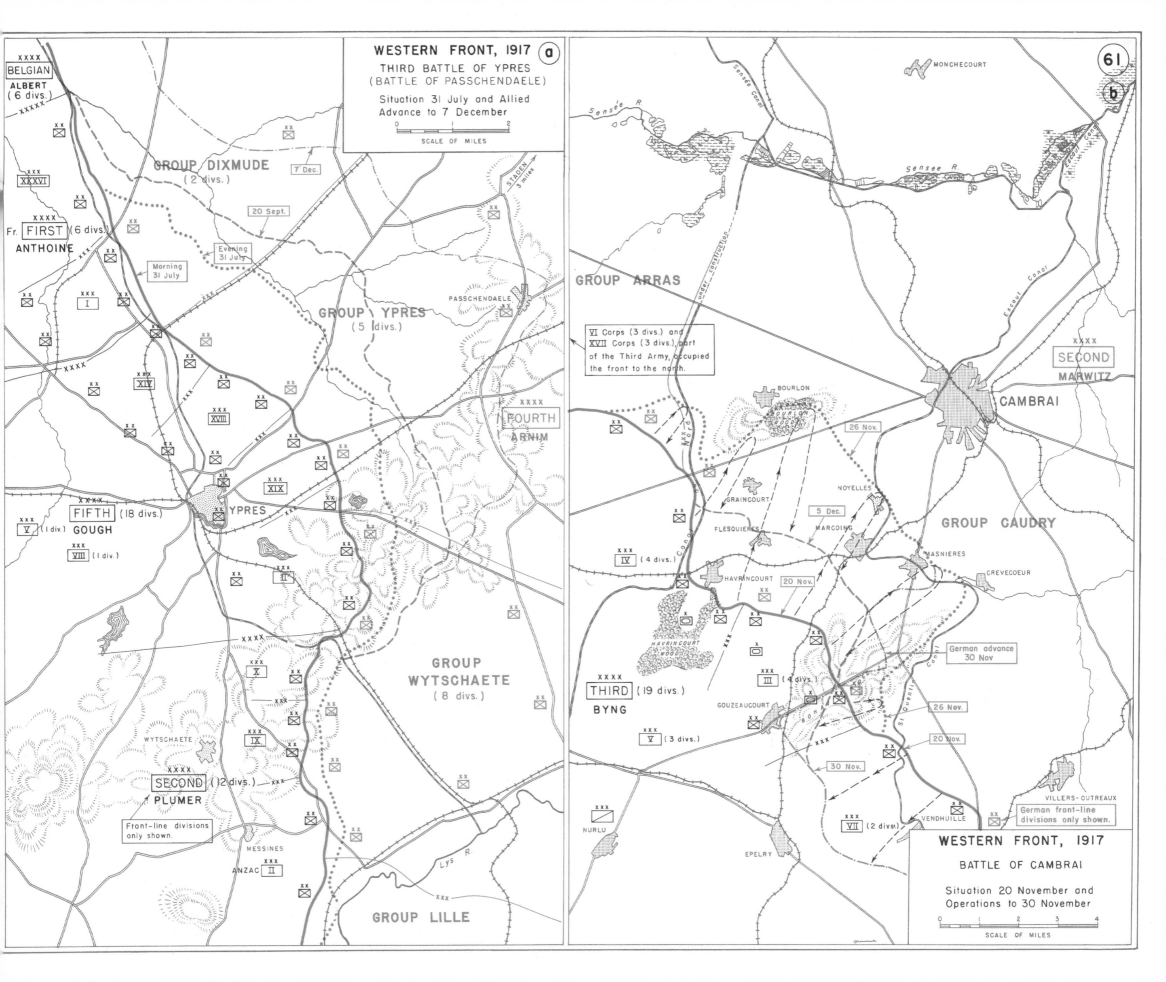

WESTERN FRONT, 1917 (a)

THIRD BATTLE OF YPRES
(BATTLE OF PASSCHENDAELE)

Situation 31 July and Allied
Advance to 7 December

SCALE OF MILES

XXXX
BELGIAN
ALBERT
(6 divs.)

XXXXX

GROUP DIXMUDE
(2 divs.)

7 Dec.

XXX
XXXVI

20 Sept.

STADEN
3 miles

XXXX
Fr. FIRST (6 divs.)
ANTHOINE

Evening
31 July

Morning
31 July

XXX
I

PASSCHENDAELE

GROUP YPRES
(5 divs.)

XXX
XIV

XXXX
FOURTH
ARNIM

XXX
XVIII

GROUP WYTSCHAETE
(8 divs.)

XXX
XIX

FIFTH (18 divs.)
GOUGH

XXX
V (1 div.)

YPRES

XXX
VIII (1 div.)

XXX
II

XXX
X

WYTSCHAETE

XXX
IX

SECOND (12 divs.)
PLUMER

MESSINES

Front-line divisions
only shown.

ANZAC
XXX
II

Lys R.

GROUP LILLE

WESTERN FRONT, 1917

BATTLE OF CAMBRAI

Situation 20 November and
Operations to 30 November

SCALE OF MILES

61
(b)

MONCHECOURT

Sensée R.

Sensée R.

GROUP ARRAS

VI Corps (3 divs.) and
XVII Corps (3 divs.), part
of the Third Army, occupied
the front to the north.

SECOND
MARWITZ

CAMBRAI

BOURLON

26 Nov.

GRAINCOURT

NOYELLES

GROUP CAUDRY

5 Dec.

FLESQUIERES

MARCOING

MASNIERES

XXX
IV (4 divs.)

CREVECOEUR

HAVRINCOURT

20 Nov.

HAVRINCOURT
WOOD

XXX
III (4 divs.)

German advance
30 Nov

THIRD (19 divs.)
BYNG

GOUZEAUCOURT

26 Nov.

XXX
V (3 divs.)

20 Nov.

30 Nov.

VILLERS-OUTREAUX

XXX
NURLU

XXX
VII (2 divs.)

VENDHUILLE

German front-line
divisions only shown.

EPEHY

Early 1918 was a time of crisis for the Allies. The French Army's morale had been badly shaken. The Italians were still recovering from Caporetto. Russia had quit the war, leaving Germany free to mass in the West. By 1 March, the United States, though it had been a belligerent for almost a year, had only six divisions in France. The British Army had been weakened by its 1917 battles, and Lloyd George refused it further replacements, claiming that Haig would merely expend them in another offensive. Under these circumstances, Haig and Pétain planned to stand on the defensive, coming to each other's assistance promptly if attacked. They attempted to organize deep defensive systems on the German model, but these were never completed because of manpower shortages and the negligence of some subordinates.

Germany also felt the pressures of war. Her allies were faltering and the Allied blockade, plus internal transportation problems, caused hunger and discontent. Submarine warfare had failed either to starve England or to halt the arrival of American troops. Therefore, Ludendorff planned to conquer a peace. He had men and heavy guns enough to mount one major offensive, but not enough to launch a simultaneous, large-scale diversionary operation. This offensive must begin as early as possible, before American strength in France increased. The first German attack would strike the British Army.

Ludendorff envisaged a breakthrough in the Somme area on both sides of Péronne (*center, left*). This accomplished, the attack would wheel to the right, advancing northwest to separate the British and French and roll up the British line. He also began preparations for two attacks near Ypres (*top center*)—partly for deception, partly in case operations there became necessary to support the main attack. The British gradually developed a fair estimate of Ludendorff's intentions, but German deceptive measures along the French front convinced Pétain that any offensive would strike the Reims–Mont Blanc sector (*center*).

Ludendorff's planning included large-scale utilization of infiltration tactics, which had been so successful in Russia and at Caporetto. Special, picked "shock" divisions were organized and given intensive training in them. The offensive would open with a relatively short bombardment, including much smoke and gas, designed to neutralize the enemy's defenses. Then the infantry would advance, keeping close behind the rolling barrage, and infiltrating between known enemy strong points. Initially, this action would be tightly controlled by higher headquarters, but once the infantry advanced beyond the range of its barrage, regimental and battalion commanders would take over, pushing as far and as rapidly as possible in a predesignated general direction. Centers of resistance were to be reported, bypassed, and later mopped up by supporting units. Fire support for the assault battalions would come from their trench mortars, attached accompanying guns, and ground-attack aircraft.

Ludendorff's preparations were impressive; German morale grew high. But his plans embodied several serious errors. He left an unnecessarily large force in the East—troops who could have at least garrisoned quiet sectors on the Western Front, thus releasing more good divisions for offensive missions. He made only feeble efforts to build up a tank force. Most serious of all, he did not adjust to the fact that he was no longer fighting Russians. In Russia, battles had ebbed and flowed over miles of open country; the Germans had always been superior in everything but numbers. France was a more difficult country, full of natural obstacles and stone villages; Allied weapons and equipment were excellent; and the Allies could use the extensive French railway system to transport troops and equipment quickly from one sector to another. Knowing this, Ludendorff's staff urged him to employ two or more limited offensives in rapid succession against different points on the British front, in order to throw the British off balance, before delivering his final blow in the Flanders area. Ludendorff, however, insisted on attempting an immediate breakthrough. The map shows (*shaded red areas*) the gains made in Ludendorff's initial offensive and in the two subsequent drives (*see text, maps 63 and 64*).

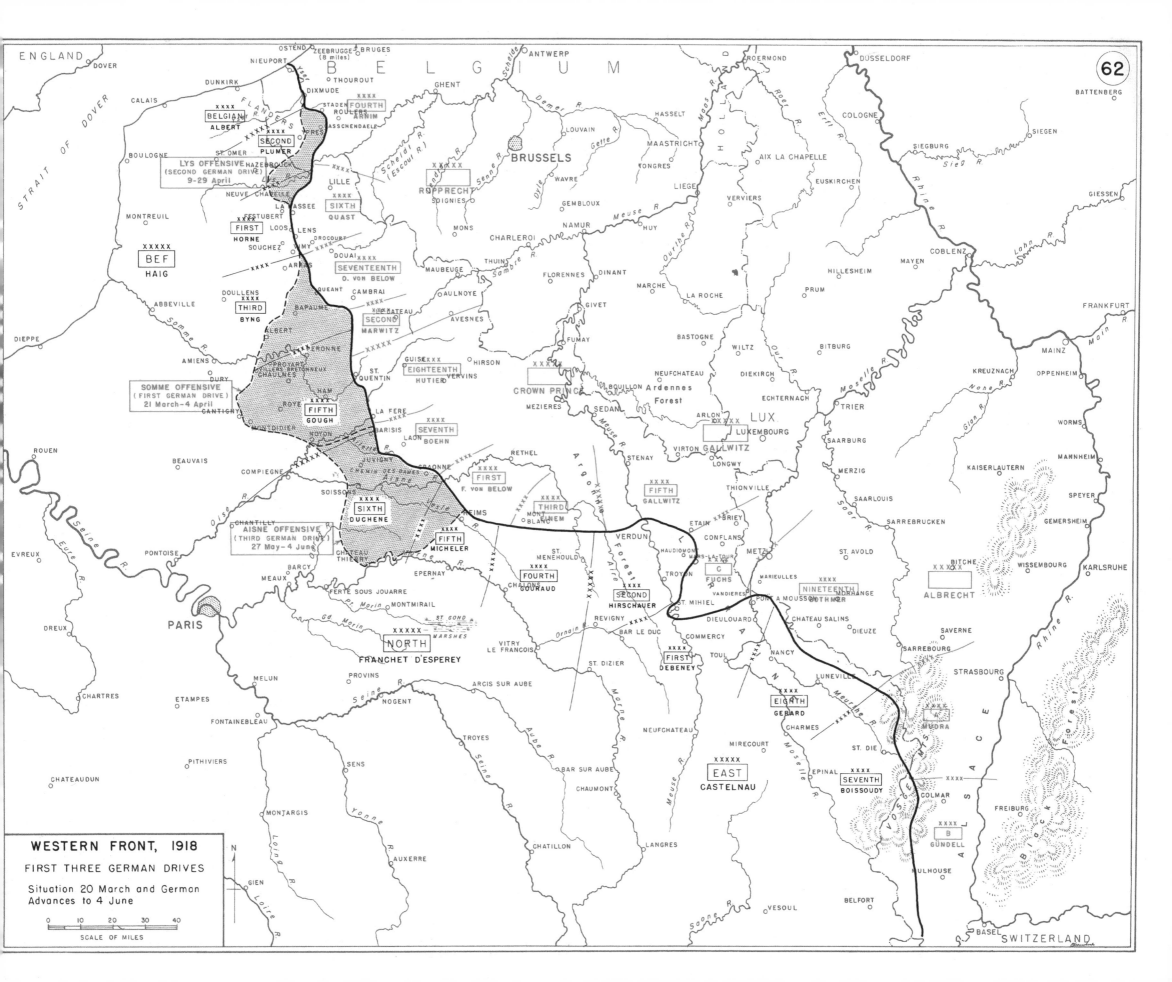

ENGLAND

BELGIUM

SWITZERLAND

62

WESTERN FRONT, 1918

FIRST THREE GERMAN DRIVES

Situation 20 March and German
Advances to 4 June

0   10   20   30   40
SCALE OF MILES

During early March, tension steadily increased on the British front (*sketch* a). Gough's Fifth Army was spread thinly along a forty-two-mile front, the southern end of which had recently been taken over from the French. The British expected an attack here and had guessed the approximate date it would strike, but Haig had only eight divisions in his reserve and refused to place more than two of them behind Fifth Army.

At 0440, 21 March, in a heavy fog, a five-hour German bombardment began. Then the highly trained battle groups of shock troops advanced. Three German armies struck the British Third and Fifth Armies. Once the British lines were broken, the Seventeenth Army was to advance to Bapaume (*center*) and then turn north toward Arras. The Second Army would capture Péronne (*center*), then push northwest through Doullens (off map, upper left). The Eighteenth Army would establish a defensive line at the Somme River, to guard the left flank of the offensive. (Note that the Eighteenth Army belonged to the Crown Prince's army group and the Second and Seventeenth to Rupprecht's—a peculiar version of the principle of unity of command, introduced by Ludendorff so that he might exercise greater personal control.)

From the start, Gough was in trouble. The trench system he had taken over from the French was unsuited to British tactics. (French defensive tactics emphasized massed artillery fire rather than infantry weapons.) By the end of 22 March, the skillful Hutier had broken through and was in open country. Farther north, the British Third Army, in its deeper defensive system, held the German Seventeenth and Second Armies to limited gains. Ludendorff now decided to exploit Hutier's success, and changed his plan: the Eighteenth Army would advance southwest across the Somme, the Second would attack toward Amiens (*off map, left center*), the Seventeenth would move northwest.

Hutier had followed Gough so closely that he captured some of the Somme River bridges. Gough's retreat uncovered the right flank of the British Third Army, forcing it to pull back. All available British reserves, including service troops, were committed; the cavalry (*not shown*) was put in to link the Fifth and Third Armies. Some French reserves arrived piecemeal, often short of artillery and ammunition, in a desperate attempt to halt the Germans, but Pétain's primary concern obviously was to form a new east-west defensive line south of the Somme to protect Paris. Haig immediately forced the convocation of a high-level Allied conference at Doullens on 26 March; this resulted in Foch's appointment as supreme commander.

On the 27th, Hutier took Montdidier (*bottom left*), actually opening a small gap between the French and British. But his troops were exhausted from the advance across the old Somme battlefield; their transport and artillery had not kept up with them. The gap was closed. A strong attack against Arras failed against stubborn British defense. Operations toward Amiens brought only slight gains, and by 4 April the line stabilized as shown (*dashed blue line*). Basically, logistical difficulties and the arrival of numerous French divisions had thwarted the Germans.

Ludendorff now shifted his effort northward to Flanders (*sketch* b). Though his immediate objectives were not clear, his basic purpose was to complete the destruction of the British Army. His own losses, however, forced him to restrict the scope of the new offensive. Using infiltration tactics, an assault on the morning of 9 April by the German Sixth Army struck the Portuguese 2d Division and gained over three miles, but was finally checked by the Lys River and stout British resistance on the flanks of the penetration. On 10 April, the German Fourth Army advanced; the attack the day before had pulled British reserves south, and another penetration was made. French units were sent up, though not immediately committed; Haig issued his famous "backs to the wall" order, demanding a fight to the last man. After 12 April, the force of the German attacks dwindled, 17 April being a day of bloody repulses for them. A surprise attack south of Ypres on 25 April took Mt. Kemmel (*upper center*). An Allied counterattack the next day failed. Plumer, his ranks badly thinned, withdrew the British line around Ypres behind the Yser Canal. On 30 April, Ludendorff halted his second offensive.

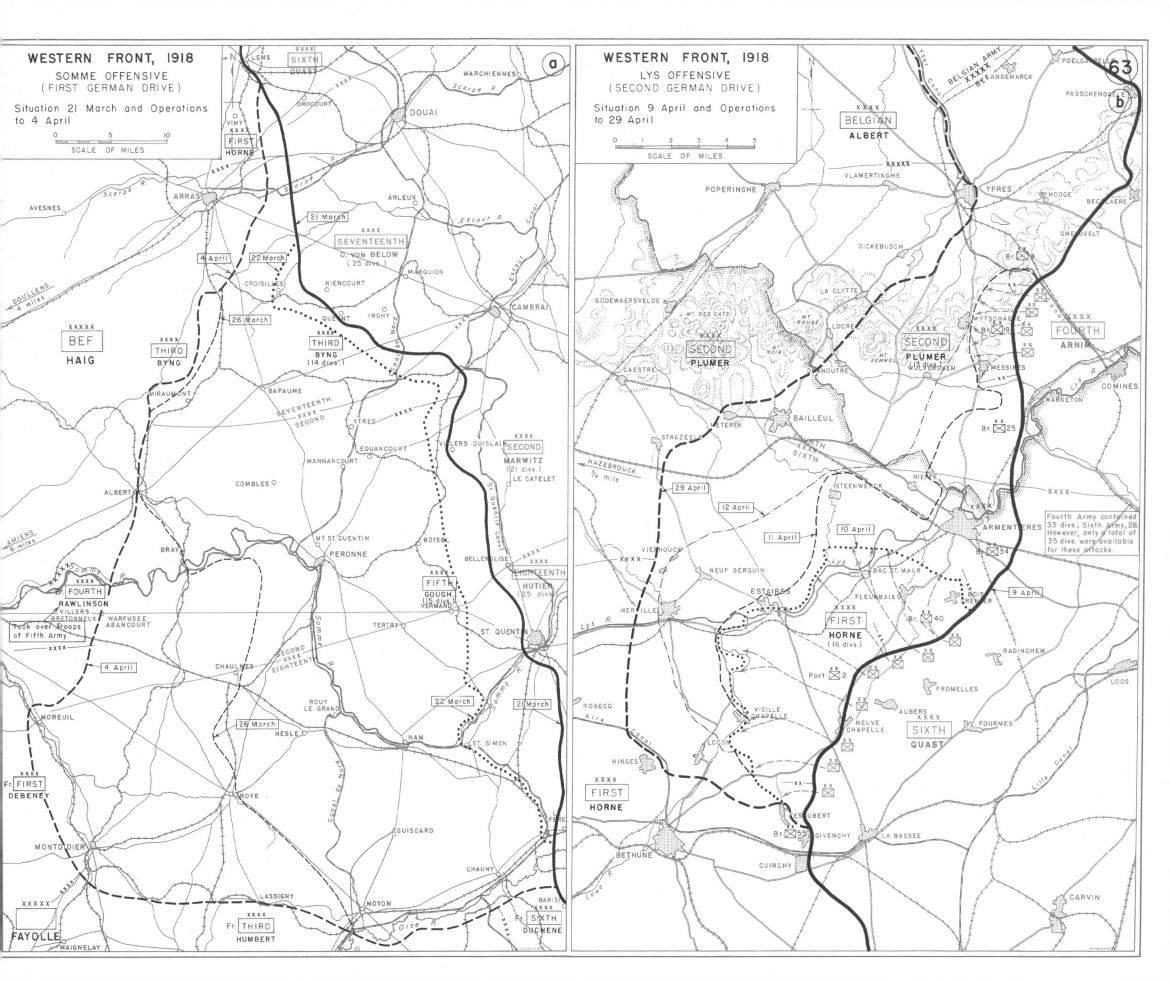

WESTERN FRONT, 1918
SOMME OFFENSIVE
(FIRST GERMAN DRIVE)

Situation 21 March and Operations
to 4 April

0   5   10
SCALE OF MILES

XXXX
SIXTH
QUAST

XXXX
FIRST
HORNE

21 March

XXXX
SEVENTEENTH
O. VON BELOW
(25 divs.)

4 April   22 March

26 March

XXXX
THIRD
BYNG
(14 divs.)

SEVENTEENTH
XXXX
SECOND

XXXX
SECOND
MARWITZ
(21 divs.)

XXXXX
BEF
HAIG

XXXX
THIRD
BYNG

4 April

XXXX
FIFTH
GOUGH
(15 divs.)

XXXX
EIGHTEENTH
HUTIER
(25 divs.)

EIGHTEENTH
XXXX
SECOND

Br. XXXX
FOURTH
RAWLINSON

Took over troops
of Fifth Army.
XXXX

4 April

22 March   21 March

26 March

XXXX
Fr. FIRST
DEBENEY

Fr. THIRD
HUMBERT

XXXX
SIXTH
DUCHENE

FAYOLLE

WESTERN FRONT, 1918
LYS OFFENSIVE
(SECOND GERMAN DRIVE)

Situation 9 April and Operations
to 29 April

0 1 2 3 4 5
SCALE OF MILES

63
b

BELGIAN ARMY
XXXXX
BEF

XXXX
BELGIAN
ALBERT

XXXX
SECOND
PLUMER

XXXX
SECOND
PLUMER
(3 divs.)

XXXX
FOURTH
ARNIM

Br. XXX 9

Br. XXX 19

Br. XXX 25

XXXX
SIXTH

HAZEBROUCK
¾ mile

29 April

12 April

11 April   10 April

Br. XXX 34

Fourth Army contained
33 divs.; Sixth Army, 28.
However, only a total of
35 divs. were available
for these attacks.

9 April

XXXX
FIRST
HORNE
(16 divs.)

Br. XXX 40

Port XXX 2

XXXX
SIXTH
QUAST

Br. XXX 55

XXXX
FIRST
HORNE

Ludendorff had now twice attacked the British. Both offensives—especially the first one—had been brilliant tactical successes, but neither had produced the necessary general breakthrough. Still, he had reason to believe that one more such major attack would wreck the British Army as an effective fighting force. Rupprecht began the necessary preparations; Ludendorff meanwhile organized a diversionary operation designed to draw all French (and, if possible, some British) reserves from Flanders.

Desiring a quick, cheap victory which would have maximum effect on the Allies, Ludendorff chose the Chemin des Dames sector (*top center*) of the Aisne front. The French position here lay along a steep ridge behind the swampy Ailette River. It was heavily fortified and naturally strong, though the presence of the Aisne and Vesle Rivers immediately behind it caused some Frenchmen to consider it a trap. Because of the formidable nature of its defenses, it was lightly held, part of its garrison consisting of English divisions which had lost two-thirds of their personnel during March and April and had therefore been temporarily exchanged for stronger French divisions. Ludendorff reasoned that, because of its strength, the French would not expect any large-scale activity in this area, and so would be vulnerable to a surprise attack. He also considered another factor: any advance here would directly threaten Paris (*off map, west*), a matter of the utmost sensitivity with the French.

The Germans had eleven divisions in line in this area; thirty more were quietly brought in under cover of darkness and hidden in the woods behind the German lines; 1,036 heavy guns were placed in concealed positions. At the same time, a variety of deceptive measures were carried out on the Flanders and Somme fronts. Foch, expecting another attack in the north, was deceived and concentrated most of his reserves around Amiens (*see map 62*), where they could counter any German attempt to split the British and French or to drive to the Channel ports.

So stringent were the German security measures that the first firm indication the Allies had of the imminent German attack came at about 1200 on 26 May, when two prisoners broke down under interrogation and stated that a heavy attack would be launched on either the 27th or 28th. Hasty preparations were begun, but the commander of the French Sixth Army (*this map*) insisted on holding his front lines in strength instead of waging an elastic defense.

At 0100, 27 May, the German bombardment began, smothering the Allied artillery. It was one of the heaviest yet employed, reaching back twelve miles to the Vesle River and extending on each flank well beyond the point selected for the attack. At 0340, still in darkness, seventeen German divisions poured across the Ailette. It was a small-scale Caporetto; the French lines dissolved. The Aisne bridges were captured intact, and by evening the Germans were up to or across the Vesle on a nine-mile front—a thirteen-mile advance, the longest day's drive in the West since the front had stabilized. Here, the attack should have stopped, but the momentum of victory swung it forward. By the next evening, Soissons (*upper center*), with large quantities of French supplies, had been captured, though an important railroad tunnel north of that town had been destroyed in time. Allied reserves arrived in dribbles, but could do little at first. Eventually, the Germans—who had never expected such a success—completely outran their supplies. Counterattacks by the American 2d Division against the nose of the salient stopped the German advance down the Château Thierry road (*center*) and eventually recaptured Belleau Wood; meanwhile, the American 3d Division repelled all enemy attempts to establish a bridgehead over the Marne near Château Thierry. (The first division-size American action had been the capture of Cantigny, near Montdidier [*see map 65*], on 28 May by the American 1st Division.)

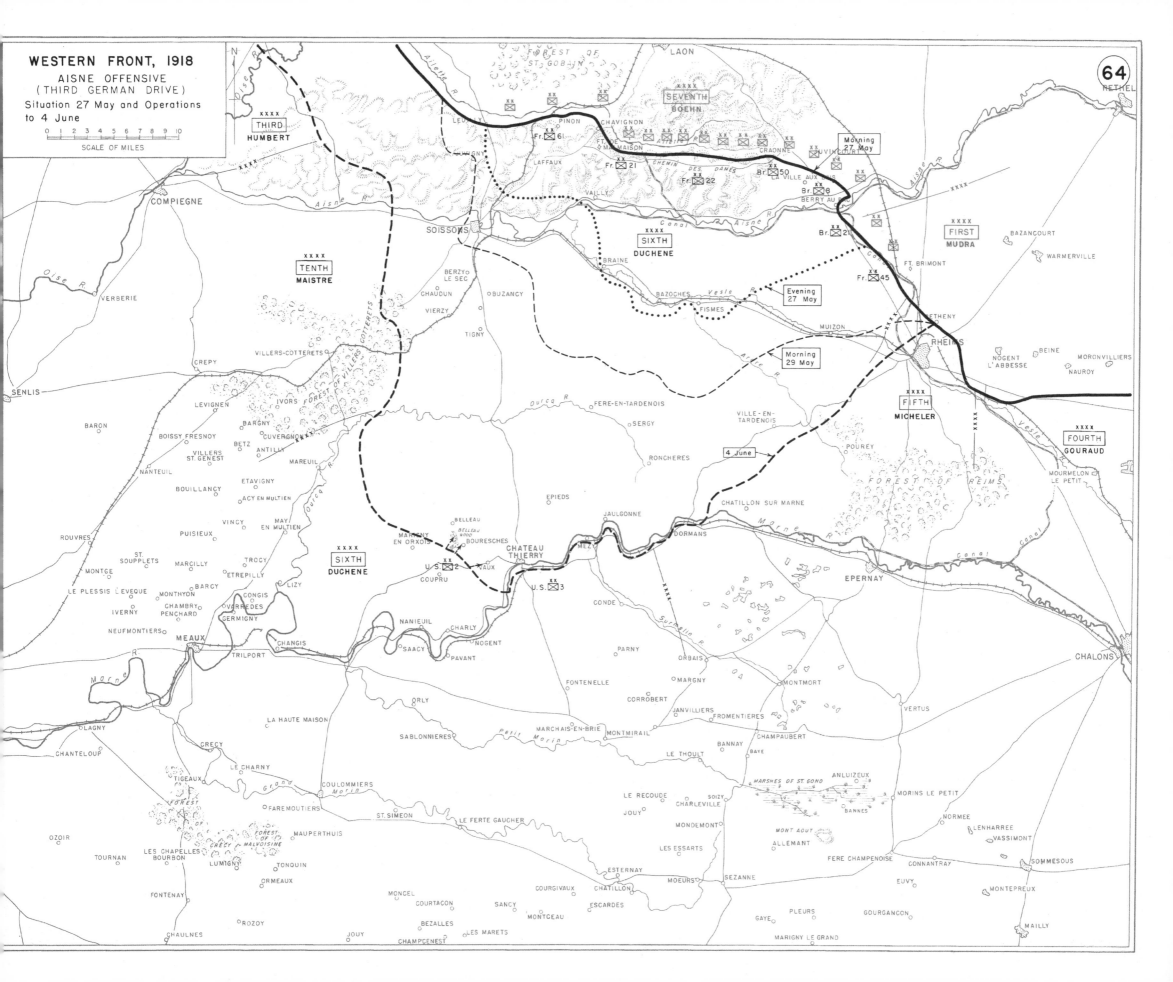

64

WESTERN FRONT, 1918

AISNE OFFENSIVE
(THIRD GERMAN DRIVE)

Situation 27 May and Operations
to 4 June

0 1 2 3 4 5 6 7 8 9 10
SCALE OF MILES

XXXX
THIRD
HUMBERT

XXXX
SEVENTH
BOEHN

Morning
27 May

Fr. 61

Fr. 21

Fr. 22

Br. 50

Br. 8

LAFFAUX

VAILLY

CHEMIN DES DAMES

LA VILLE AUX

BERRY AU BAC

XXXX
SIXTH
DUCHENE

Br. 21

Fr. 45

FT. BRIMONT

XXXX
FIRST
MUDRA

BAZANCOURT

WARMERVILLE

COMPIEGNE

SOISSONS

XXXX
TENTH
MAISTRE

BERZY O LE SEC

CHAUDUN

VIERZY

BRAINE

BAZOCHES

FISMES

Vesle R

Evening
27 May

MUIZON

ETHENY

RHEIMS

NOGENT L'ABBESSE

BEINE

MORONVILLIERS

NAUROY

VERBERIE

Oise R

Aisne R

Canal

Aisne R

Morning
29 May

XXXX
FIFTH
MICHELER

XXXX
FOURTH
GOURAUD

SENLIS

BARON

CREPY

LEVIGNEN

VILLERS-COTTERETS

IVORS

BARGNY

BETZ

ANTILLY

CUVERGNON

FOREST OF VILLERS COTTERETS

TIGNY

FERE-EN-TARDENOIS

SERGY

VILLE-EN-TARDENOIS

POUREY

RONCHERES

MOURMELON CH
LE PETIT

4 June

FOREST OF REIMS

NANTEUIL

VILLERS ST. GENEST

ETAVIGNY

BOUILLANCY

ACY EN MULTIEN

MAREUIL

EPIEDS

JAULGONNE

CHATILLON SUR MARNE

Marne R

ROUVRES

VINCY

MAY EN MULTIEN

PUISIEUX

ST. SOUPPLETS

MARCILLY

TROCY

ETREPILLY

BARCY

LIZY

MONTGE

LE PLESSIS L'EVEQUE

MONTHYON

CHAMBRY

IVERNY

PENCHARD

CONGIS

VARREDDES

GERMIGNY

NEUFMONTIERS

MEAUX

CHANGIS

TRILPORT

BELLEAU

BELLEAU WOOD

BOURESCHES

MARIGNY EN ORXOIS

CHATEAU THIERRY

MEZY

DORMANS

XXXX
SIXTH
DUCHENE

U.S. 2

VAUX

COUPRU

U.S. 3

NANTEUIL

CHARLY

NOGENT

CONDE

PARNY

EPERNAY

Marne R

Surmelin R

Canal

OLAGNY

CRECY

CHANTELOUP

TIGEAUX

FOREST OF CRECY

LE CHARNY

COULOMMIERS

Grand Morin

SAACY

PAVANT

FONTENELLE

ORLY

MARGNY

ORBAIS

MONTMORT

VERTUS

CHALONS

OZOIR

TOURNAN

LES CHAPELLES BOURBON

LUMIGNY

FOREST OF MALVOISINE

MAUPERTHUIS

FAREMOUTIERS

ST. SIMEON

LE FERTE GAUCHER

Petit Morin

SABLONNIERES

MARCHAIS-EN-BRIE

MONTMIRAIL

JANVILLIERS

FROMENTIERES

CHAMPAUBERT

BANNAY

BAYE

LE THOULT

LE RECOUDE

CHARLEVILLE

JOUY

SOIZY

MONDEMONT

LES ESSARTS

MONT AOUT

ALLEMANT

MARSHES OF ST. GOND

ANLUIZEUX

BANNES

MORINS LE PETIT

NORMEE

LENHARREE

VASSIMONT

FERE CHAMPENOISE

CONNANTRAY

SOMMESOUS

FONTENAY

ORMEAUX

TONQUIN

MONCEL

COURTACON

SANCY

MONTCEAU

COURGIVAUX

ESCARDES

MOEURS

SEZANNE

ESTERNAY

PLEURS

GAYE

GOURGANCON

EUVY

MONTEPREUX

CHAULNES

ROZOY

JOUY

CHAMPCENEST

LES MARETS

BEZALLES

MARIGNY LE GRAND

MAILLY

Lundendorff was now the worried possessor of three salients, which greatly increased the length of his front. His last drive, however—with its apparent threat to Paris—had considerably unsettled the French. On 31 May, Pétain advised the government to leave Paris, but the fiercely patriotic Premier, Georges Clemenceau, refused to budge. Dismayed by the deep German advance, members of the French government demanded the relief and court martial of Foch and Pétain. Amidst this ominous environment, Foch moved much of his general reserve from the British to the French front. He also urged the Americans to speed the arrival of their troops. Rejecting General John J. Pershing's preference for bringing entire divisions to France, he proposed transporting only infantry and machine gun units and amalgamating them into Allied divisions.

Ludendorff had planned his diversionary operation in two stages. The first—the Aisne offensive—had been only too successful. The second—an advance in the general area Soissons-Montdidier (left center)—now became increasingly important, since the only railroad into the new Aisne-Marne salient ran through Soissons and along that salient's western edge. Ludendorff hoped to eventually reach the line Montdidier-Compiègne. Preparations for this attack were rushed and open; in fact, the French at first suspected that they might be purely for the purpose of distracting Allied attention from Rupprecht's activities in Flanders. German deserters (their number had increased with declining German morale) furnished the date and the hour of the attack.

Forewarned, the French laid down an artillery counterpreparation at 2350 on 8 June, ten minutes before the German preparatory bombardment was scheduled to begin. Though both its artillery bombardment and infantry assault were consequently confused, the German Eighteenth Army still broke through the French first and second positions. On the 10th, the Germans made further advances. On the 11th, they did not attack; a French-American counterattack threw them on the defensive, though it made only slight gains. On the 12th, the German Seventh Army attacked from the Aisne-Marne salient, but made little progress.

During the subsequent month of relative inaction, a worldwide influenza epidemic struck both opponents, bearing harder on the poorly fed Germans. German morale began to crack noticeably, while American forces in France rapidly increased.

Ludendorff still clung to his plan for a decisive blow against the British in Flanders, but he felt that one final diversionary operation would be necessary to draw Allied reserves from that front. Consequently, he planned an attack on both sides of Reims (center, left) for 15 July. The German Seventh Army would take Epernay and advance up the Marne until it established contact with the German First Army, which was to take Châlons. This would pinch out the strongly fortified Reims area. The German Third Army was to cover the flank of the First. Once the preparatory bombardment was completed, the heavy artillery would proceed northward to get into position for Rupprecht's grand attack in early August.

Deserters, prisoners, and Allied aerial reconnaissance gradually disclosed Ludendorff's entire plan. Reinforcements were brought in, and Foch prepared a major counteroffensive for 18 July against the western face of the Aisne-Marne salient. Having learned the hour of the German attack, the French again employed an artillery counterpreparation, catching the German shock troops as they formed. East of Reims, the German attack collapsed against well-established defenses by 1100, 15 July. North of Epernay the defenses were weaker, and the German assault, pushed home with skill and daring, forced the Marne and established a sizable bridgehead. Only the American 3d Division held firm, fighting in three directions. Also, just southwest of Reims, the two Italian divisions which held the line there were driven back; British divisions were rushed to relieve them on the 19th. During the 16th and 17th, French resistance around the new Marne bridgehead stiffened. It became increasingly difficult for the Germans to push reinforcements and supplies across the Marne under Allied air and artillery bombardment.

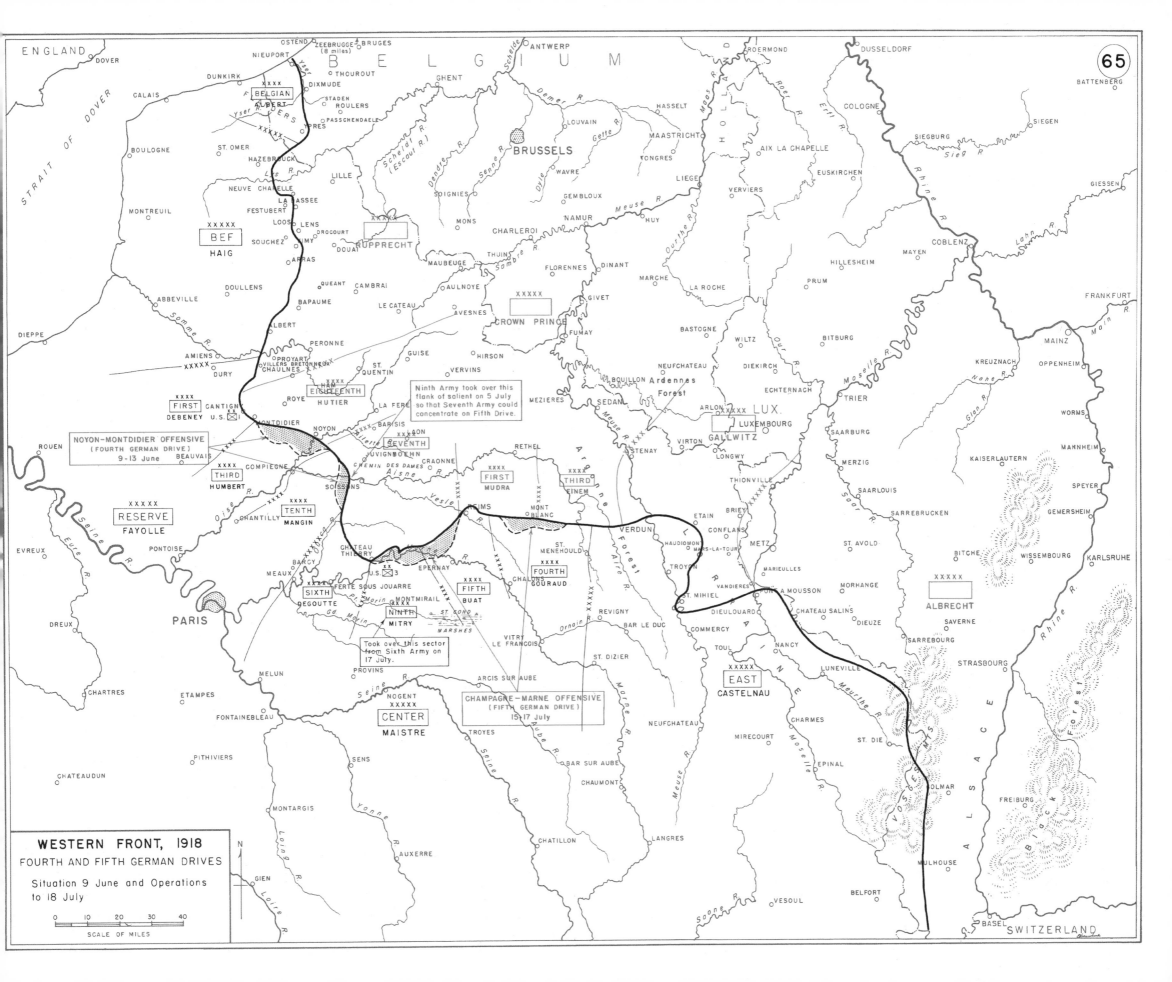

ENGLAND

BELGIUM

HOLLAND

SWITZERLAND

65

Ninth Army took over this flank of salient on 5 July so that Seventh Army could concentrate on Fifth Drive.

NOYON—MONTDIDIER OFFENSIVE (FOURTH GERMAN DRIVE) 9-13 June

Took over this sector from Sixth Army on 17 July.

CHAMPAGNE—MARNE OFFENSIVE (FIFTH GERMAN DRIVE) 15-17 July

WESTERN FRONT, 1918

FOURTH AND FIFTH GERMAN DRIVES

Situation 9 June and Operations to 18 July

0 10 20 30 40

SCALE OF MILES

As early as 20 May, 1918, Foch had begun plans for a series of massive Allied counteroffensives, only to have them upset by the German third and fourth 1918 drives. In the lull that followed the fourth (Noyon-Montdidier) drive, he kept the French forces active in minor operations to rebuild their fighting spirit. One of these attacks (*not shown*), made by General Mangin's Tenth Army, scored a creditable local success west of Soissons. Mangin suggested enlarging this operation; Foch agreed and set up a large-scale counteroffensive for 18 July. Mangin was to make the main effort, while the other armies around the Aisne-Marne salient attacked on their fronts. A minor crisis occurred when Pétain, concerned over the fifth German drive (15 July), ordered all preparations suspended, but Foch promptly countermanded that order.

As noted (*see text, map 65*), the fifth German drive (on both sides of Reims) was obviously a failure by the evening of the 17th, and the position of the German divisions holding the bridgehead south of the Marne was becoming increasingly critical.

Mangin secretly concentrated his troops at the last moment under cover of the Forest of Villers-Cotterêts. (Some American units had to move up on the run to reach the jump-off line at the zero hour.) The attack (beginning at 0435 in the west, at 0500 in the east) was a complete surprise. German troops holding the western sector were second-line "trench" units of limited combat value. Pounded by a sudden, heavy artillery bombardment, and rushed by fresh American divisions and picked French colonial units supported by masses of tanks, they gave ground rapidly or surrendered in large numbers.

Ludendorff, meanwhile, had gone to Flanders to make final arrangements for Rupprecht's great offensive. He had drawn heavily upon Rupprecht's reserves for his fifth drive, but he felt that by using some "trench" divisions in place of shock troops, he would be able to proceed as originally planned. During a staff conference on 18 July, he learned of the Allied Aisne-Marne offensive. He at once sent reserves into the Soissons area and ordered the attack on Reims stopped.

On the 19th, German resistance stiffened. The French Tenth and Sixth Armies gained some ground, but the Ninth and Fifth made little progress. That night, the Germans evacuated their Marne River bridgehead. Thereafter, they began a deliberate, skillful withdrawal to the line of the Aisne and Vesle Rivers, covering their retreat with machine-gun and artillery rear guards, while the German Air Force swept the skies over the shrinking salient. (During this period, on 20 July, Rupprecht's Flanders offensive was canceled.)

On 24 July, Foch met with Haig and Pershing and developed his future plans. The Allies now had the initiative and wished to keep it through a series of strong, closely spaced offensives that would give the enemy no chance to reorganize. The first objectives would be to free three strategic rail lines which would facilitate future operations: the Marne section of the Paris-Verdun line (to be accomplished by the current Aisne-Marne offensive); the Paris-Amiens line (to be freed by a Franco-British offensive in the Amiens sector [*see text, map 67*]); and the section of the Paris-Nancy line south of Verdun (to be carried out by an American attack on the St. Mihiel salient [*see map 68*]). These operations would be followed by others to free the coal-mining areas in northern France and force the German extreme right flank back along the Channel.

All unaware of this, Ludendorff released his own estimate of the situation on 2 August: no other Allied attacks were likely in the immediate future, though they might be expected thereafter south of Ypres, east of Reims, against the St. Mihiel salient, or in Lorraine; the Germans must pass temporarily to the defensive, while gathering forces for limited surprise offensives, designed to inflict casualties rather than to gain ground.

As indicated (*shaded blue areas*), eight American divisions took part in the Aisne-Marne offensive. It should be kept in mind that the United States infantry division of World War I had about twice the strength of contemporary French, English, and German divisions.

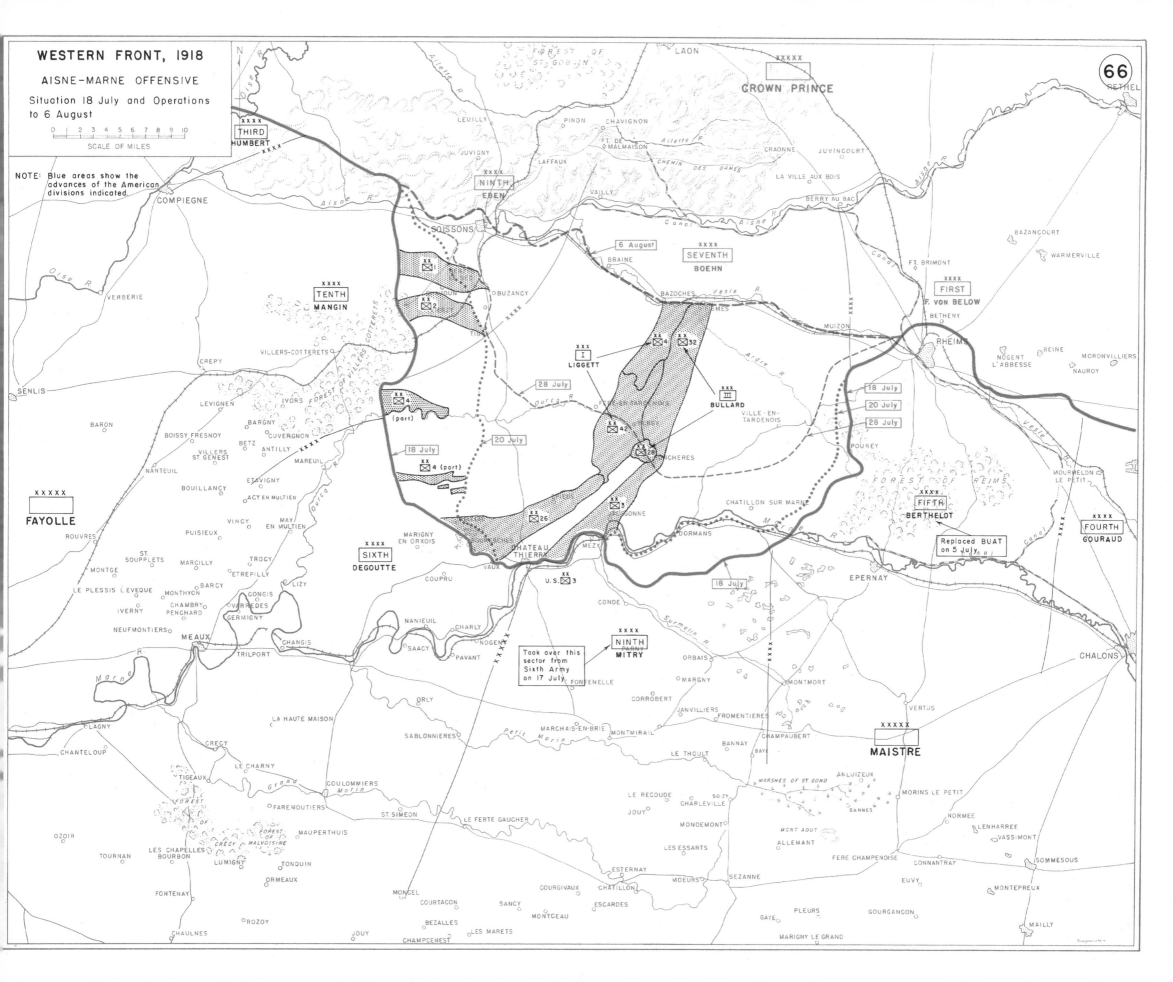

WESTERN FRONT, 1918

AISNE-MARNE OFFENSIVE

Situation 18 July and Operations to 6 August

SCALE OF MILES
0 1 2 3 4 5 6 7 8 9 10

NOTE: Blue areas show the advances of the American divisions indicated.

66

FOREST OF ST. GOBIN
LAON
CROWN PRINCE
RETHEL

XXXX THIRD HUMBERT XXXX

XXXX NINTH EBEN

LEUILLY
JUVIGNY
PINON
CHAVIGNON
FT. DE MALMAISON
LAFFAUX
VAILLY
CHEMIN DES DAMES
CRAONNE
JUVINCOURT
LA VILLE AUX BOIS
BERRY AU BAC

COMPIEGNE
Aisne R.
SOISSONS
6 August
BRAINE
Canal de l'Aisne
Vesle R.
XXXX SEVENTH BOEHN

BAZANCOURT
WARMERVILLE
FT. BRIMONT

VERBERIE
Oise R.

XXXX TENTH MANGIN

XX 1
BUZANCY
XX 2
TIGNY
BAZOCHES
FISMES
MUIZON
RHEIMS

XXXX FIRST F. VON BELOW

BETHENY

VILLERS-COTTERETS
CREPY
IVORS FOREST OF VILLERS COTTERETS
LEVIGNEN
BARGNY
CUVERGNON
ANTILLY

XX 4 (part)
XXX I LIGGETT
XX 4
XX 32
FERE-EN-TARDENOIS
Ourcq R.
28 July
XXX III BULLARD
VILLE-EN-TARDENOIS

18 July
20 July
28 July
BEINE
MORONVILLIERS
NOGENT L'ABBESSE
NAUROY
POURCY

SENLIS
BARON
BOISSY FRESNOY
VILLERS ST GENEST
NANTEUIL
MAREUIL
ETAVIGNY
BOUILLANCY

XX 4 (part)
XX 42
XX 28
FORET DE FERE
NESLES
CHATILLON SUR MARNE

FOREST OF REIMS
MOURMELON LE PETIT

XXXXX FAYOLLE

VINCY
MAY EN MULTIEN
ACY EN MULTIEN
PUISIEUX

XX 26
XX 3
RONCHERES
Marne R.
DORMANS

XXXX FIFTH BERTHELOT

XXXX FOURTH GOURAUD

ST. SOUPPLETS
MONTGE
LE PLESSIS L'EVEQUE
MARCILLY
TROCY
ETREPILLY
BARCY
LIZY

MARIGNY EN ORXOIS
XXXX SIXTH DEGOUTTE
COUPRU
VAUX
CHATEAU THIERRY
MEZY

Replaced BUAT on 5 July

IVERNY
MONTHYON
CHAMBRY PENCHARD
GONGIS
VAREDDES
GERMIGNY

U.S. XX 3
CONDE
18 July
EPERNAY
CHALONS

NEUFMONTIERS
MEAUX
CHANGIS
TRILPORT
Marne R.

NANTEUIL
SAACY
PAVANT
CHARLY
NOGENT
FONTENELLE

Took over this sector from Sixth Army on 17 July

XXXX NINTH MITRY

ORBAIS
MARGNY
CORROBERT

Surmelin R.
MONTMORT
VERTUS

CLAGNY
CHANTELOUP
CRECY
LE CHARNY
LA HAUTE MAISON
ORLY
SABLONNIERES

JANVILLIERS
FROMENTIERES
MONTMIRAIL
LE THOULT
BANNAY
CHAMPAUBERT

XXXXX MAISTRE

TIGEAUX
COULOMMIERS
Grand Morin
Petit Morin
MARCHAIS-EN-BRIE
ANLUIZEUX
MORINS LE PETIT

OZOIR
TOURNAN
LES CHAPELLES BOURBON
FAREMOUTIERS
ST. SIMEON
LE FERTE GAUCHER
MAUPERTHUIS
FOREST OF GRECY
FOREST OF MALVOISINE
LUMIGNY
TONQUIN

LE RECOUDE
JOUY
CHARLEVILLE
SOZY
MONDEMONT
ALLEMANT
MARSHES OF ST GOND
BANNES
MONT AOUT

NORMEE
LENHARREE
VASSIMONT
SOMMESOUS

FONTENAY
ORMEAUX
ROZOY
MONCEL
COURTACON
BEZALLES
LES MARETS
CHAMPCENEST
SANCY
MONTGEAU
MARIGNY LE GRAND

CHAULNES
JOUY
LES ESSARTS
ESTERNAY
MOEURS
SEZANNE
COURGIVAUX
CHATILLON
ESCARDES
GAYE
PLEURS
GOURGANCON
FERE CHAMPENOISE
CONNANTRAY
EUVY
MONTEPREUX
MAILLY

Ludendorff did not expect an Allied attack in the immediate future; nor did he anticipate that, when it did come, it would be in the Amiens area. Consequently, the Franco-British offensive there was a total surprise.

Foch wanted a British offensive in Flanders from La Bassée north (*sketch* b, *bottom center*; this sketch is an extension northward of *sketch* a) in order to liberate important French coal-mining areas; but Haig, undoubtedly remembering his 1917 experiences in Flanders, objected on the grounds that the terrain was unsuitable and the general area of less strategic importance than that east of Amiens (*sketch* a). Foch not only accepted Haig's preference, but also placed the French First Army under his command for this operation.

General Sir Henry Rawlinson carried out his preparations with the greatest secrecy. His main effort was to be made by the Australian and Canadian Corps and the left-flank corps of the French First Army. Since the Canadian Corps and one Australian division had to be moved south from Flanders, elaborate deceptive measures were necessary. A skeleton of the Canadian Corps, including its headquarters radio, was left in its original position, and the Canadian troops took over their attack positions on the Amiens front only two hours before the attack began. These measures were entirely successful. Rupprecht's attention was concentrated on the Ypres area (Ludendorff had predicted an attack there); the Germans facing Rawlinson were lax and careless.

The British attack, launched at 0420, 8 August, repeated the tactics that had been so successful at Cambrai. There was no preliminary bombardment. Just before zero hour, approximately 400 tanks (some of them speedy new Whippets) emerged from their assembly areas, reaching the front line as the rolling barrage came down, and the infantry rose and followed. On the right, the French—who had only a few tanks—opened a forty-five-minute bombardment, and then advanced.

At first, the assault was hampered by a dense ground fog, which also blinded the approximately 1,700 Allied aircraft concentrated to support it. Nevertheless, during the first day, the offensive gained up to nine miles (*lower shaded blue area*), being held up only on the flanks. Whippets, armored cars, and cavalry got among the fleeing Germans; approximately 15,000 prisoners and 400 guns were captured. Even more shocking to German commanders was the low morale, bordering on mutiny, shown by many retreating units. Still, between rallying stragglers and calling up reinforcements, they reestablished a line. On 9-10 August, the Allied attack and German defense were both disjointed and confused. Communications were fragmentary; almost two-thirds of the British tanks were out of action because of mechanical troubles, ditching, or enemy artillery fire; and the German Air Force was concentrating on the battlefield. However, also on the 10th, the French Third Army came into action on the south, and the Germans evacuated Montdidier (*bottom left*). By the 11th, the Germans were even beginning to counterattack. Haig decided that a pause was necessary on the Amiens front. This decision produced a clash with Foch, who was in favor of pushing ahead. Haig ordered his Third Army to begin probing the German lines below Arras.

The next phase of the offensive began on 21 August when the French and the British attacked. Unlike Ludendorff after his successful March 21 offensive, Foch did not intend to give the enemy time to recover. Though progress over the battle-worn area was slow and methodical, tanks and low-flying aircraft were used against strong points, and the Allies advanced.

Ludendorff now ordered a major withdrawal, and gave up the Lys salient (*see map 62*) in Flanders as well. However, on 30-31 August, the Australians crossed the Somme and took Péronne and Mt. St. Quentin (*this map, center*). On 2 September, the Canadians broke a strong position (not shown) between Quéant and Drocourt (*upper center*). Ludendorff thereupon ordered a second withdrawal (*heavy dashed red line*). His losses had been more than 100,000; morale had plummeted.

WESTERN FRONT, 1918

REDUCTION OF THE AMIENS SALIENT

Situation 8 August and Operations
to 4 September

0   5   10
SCALE OF MILES

WESTERN FRONT, 1918

TERRAIN IN VICINITY OF YPRES

0 1 2 3 4 5
SCALE OF MILES

a

b

67

Map (a) — Reduction of the Amiens Salient

LENS

MARCHIENNES

Scarpe R.

DROCOURT

DOUAI

VIMY

XXXX
FIRST
HORNE

Scarpe R.

ARRAS

ARLEUX

Escaut R.

Canal

AVESNES

DOULLENS
4 miles

Scarpe R.

XXXX

8-21 Aug.

CROISILLES

RIENCOURT

MARQUION

26 Aug.

XXXX
THIRD
BYNG

Area regained
during 21 Aug.

QUEANT   INCHY

Canal du Nord

4 Sept.

CAMBRAI

MORREUIL

BAPAUME

YTRES

XXXX

EQUANCOURT

VILLERS GUISLAIN

St. Quentin Canal

MANNANCOURT

COMBLES

LE CATELET

ALBERT

Somme R.

MT. ST. QUENTIN

ROISEL

XXXX
FOURTH
RAWLINSON

AMIENS
6 miles

8 Aug.

BRAY

PERONNE

BELLENGLISE

XXX
AUS.

Somme

21 Aug.

26 Aug.

VERMAND

XXX

VILLERS
BRETONNEUX WARFUSEE
ABANCOURT

TERTRY

XXX
CAN.

Area regained
during 8 Aug.

CHAULNES

BRITISH
XXXXX
FRENCH

4 Sept.

ST. QUENTIN

MOREUIL

ROUY
LE GRAND

BRITISH
XXXXX
FRENCH

Canal du Nord

NESLE

HAM

ST. SIMON

LA FERE

21-26 Aug.

ROYE

XXXX
FIRST
DEBENEY

GUISCARD

Oise R.

MONTDIDIER

XXX

CHAUNY

BARISIS

LASSIGNY

NOYON

XXXX
THIRD
HUMBERT

MAIGNELAY

Map (b) — Terrain in Vicinity of Ypres

POELCAPPELLE

LANGEMARCK

PASSCHENDAELE

Yser Canal

VLAMERTINGHE

YPRES

HOOGE

POPERINGHE

BECELAERE

GHELUVELT

DICKEBUSCH

LA CLYTTE

MT. DES CATS

MT.
ROUGE

LOCRE

WYTSCHAETE

GODEWAERSVELDE

MT.
NOIR

MT.
KEMMEL

WULVERGHEM

MESSINES

Lys R.

CAESTRE

DRANOUTRE

COMINES

WARNETON

HAZEBROUCK
¾ mile

METEREN

BAILLEUL

STRAZEELE

NIEPPE

STEENWERCK

Lys R.

ARMENTIERES

VIERHOUCK

NEUF BERQUIN

Lys R.

BAC ST. MAUR

FLEURBAIX

BOIS
GRENIER

ESTAIRES

MERVILLE

RADINGHEM

ROBECQ

Aire Canal

VIEILLE
CHAPELLE

Lys R.

LOOS

NEUVE
CHAPELLE

AUBERS

FROMELLES

FOURMES

HINGES

LOCON

FESTUBERT

GIVENCHY

LA BASSEE

Lille Canal

BETHUNE

Lawe R.

CUINCHY

CARVIN

The sector originally assigned the American Expeditionary Force was that between St. Mihiel and Pont-à-Mousson (*bottom right*). There were a number of reasons for its selection: first, it had long been a quiet sector, lightly held by both sides, hence suitable for advanced training; second, an offensive from this area would threaten the vital Metz-Longuyon-Sedan railroad, the Briey-Longwy iron-ore mining region, and the Saar's coal mines (*off map, right*)—also, an advance down the Moselle River would threaten the Rhine Valley; third, port congestion in northern France led to the basing of the American forces on western French seaports, such as Bordeaux and St. Nazaire, which had good, direct rail communications with the assigned area.

Pershing insisted upon a separate and distinct United States army, with its own assigned front. Its establishment was repeatedly delayed—partly because of British and French desire to keep American units under their command, partly by the crises created by the five German 1918 drives which made it necessary to put in available American units to halt the German advance. On 24 July, Foch finally accepted Pershing's plan for the reduction of the St. Mihiel salient; on 10 August, the United States First Army was activated, and on 30 August it formally took over the St. Mihiel sector. The French II Colonial Corps was assigned to it. Pershing's plans considered an advance to the general line Marieulles (*lower right*)–Mars-la-Tour–Etain. Success here would be followed by an offensive into Lorraine against Metz and the Briey mines.

But after some prodding from Haig, Foch decided that the American effort should be directed at Mezieres (*top left*), so that it might converge with Haig's push toward Cambrai (*see map 69*). Foch therefore proposed 30 August that the Americans make only a limited attack against the south face of the St. Mihiel salient; the remaining American forces would be divided between the French Second and Fourth Armies for an advance on Mézières. Pershing forcibly declined this most peculiar proposition.

Finally, on 2 September, the two commanders compro-

mised: the St. Mihiel operation would be carried out, but only to the line Vandières-Haudiomont (*this map, dashed red line*); the United States First Army would take over an enlarged sector from the Moselle to, and including, the Argonne Forest (lower left); the Americans would attack on the Argonne front immediately after the completion of the St. Mihiel operation; the French Fourth Army, reinforced by two American divisions, would attack to the west of the Argonne; these two offensives would converge on the Sedan-Mézières area.

On 8 September, Ludendorff ordered the evacuation of the lightly garrisoned St. Mihiel position. On the 11th, the garrison began removing the heaviest guns and supplies. At 0100, 12 September, a heavy bombardment began. At 0500, in a heavy fog, American forces attacked the two faces of the salient, while the French II Colonial Corps made a holding attack against its nose. A mixed American, French, British, Italian, and Portuguese air force (some 600 planes) under Col. Billy Mitchell maintained air superiority and supported the attack. Some planes were attached directly to the ground forces; others acted as an independent group in tactical support against the enemy lines; and still other groups operated in the German rear, against logistical support installations and lines of communications. Their contribution to the success was substantial. The salient was cleared in thirty-six hours with a bag of some 15,000 prisoners and over 250 guns.

Some American leaders later insisted the roads from Longuyon (*upper center*) and to Lorraine (*lower right*) were open, and a drive against either may have shaken the Germans far worse than any threat to Mézières. General Hunter Liggett, a corps commander in the St. Mihiel operation, later acknowledged, however, that American units were not functioning smoothly enough for such a complex operation.

The St. Mihiel operation nonetheless had been excellent training for American commanders, staffs, and troops alike. It also deprived the Germans of an area from which they might have been able to attack the rear of American forces engaged in the Argonne.

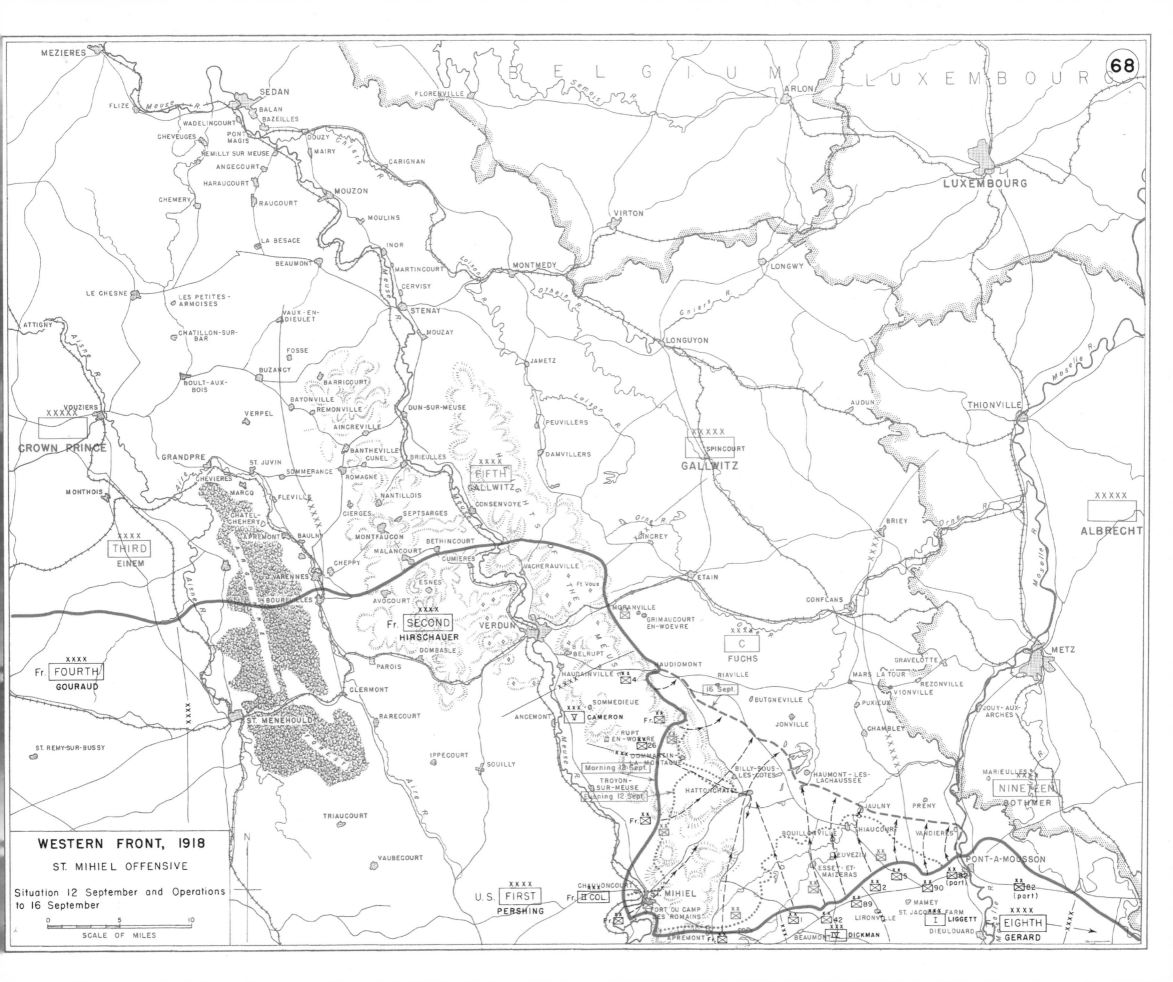

MEZIERES
BELGIUM LUXEMBOURG
68

SEDAN
FLORENVILLE
ARLON
LUXEMBOURG

FLIZE
Meuse R.
BALAN
BAZEILLES
WADELINCOURT
CHEVEUGES
PONT
MAGIS
DOUZY
Chiers R.
MAIRY
REMILLY SUR MEUSE
CARIGNAN
ANGECOURT
HARAUCOURT
MOUZON
VIRTON
CHEMERY
RAUCOURT
MOULINS

LA BESACE
INOR
MARTINCOURT
CERVISY
STENAY
Meuse R.
MONTMEDY
LONGWY

LE CHESNE
LES PETITES-
ARMOISES
VAUX-EN-
DIEULET
MOUZAY
Othein R.
LONGUYON

ATTIGNY
Aisne R.
CHATILLON-SUR-
BAR
FOSSE
Chiers R.
AUDUN
THIONVILLE

BUZANCY
BARRICOURT
BAYONVILLE
REMONVILLE
DUN-SUR-MEUSE
Loison R.
JAMETZ
PEUVILLERS
SPINCOURT
XXXX
GALLWITZ

VOUZIERS
XXXXX
BOULT-AUX-
BOIS
VERPEL
AINCREVILLE
DAMVILLERS
Moselle R.

CROWN PRINCE
GRANDPRE
ST. JUVIN
SOMMERANGE
BANTHEVILLE
CUNEL
BRIEULLES
XXXX
FIFTH
GALLWITZ
CONSENVOYE
BRIEY
ALBRECHT
XXXXX

MONTHOIS
CHEVIERES
MARCQ
FLEVILLE
ROMAGNE
NANTILLOIS
Orne R.
GINCREY

CHATEL-
CHEHERY
APREMONT
BAULNY
CIERGES
SEPTSARGES
MONTFAUCON
BETHINCOURT
XXXX
THIRD
EINEM
CHEPPY
MALANCOURT
CUMIERES
WACHERAUVILLE
ETAIN
CONFLANS

VARENNES
BOUREUILLES
ESNES
AVOCOURT
Ft. Voux
MORANVILLE
GRIMAUCOURT
EN-WOEVRE
XXXX
C
FUCHS
MARS LA TOUR
GRAVELOTTE
METZ

Fr. SECOND
HIRSCHAUER
VERDUN
BELRUPT
RIAVILLE
BUTGNEVILLE
REZONVILLE
VIONVILLE

Fr. FOURTH
GOURAUD
DOMBASLE
PAROIS
HAUDAINVILLE
XX 4
16 Sept.
JONVILLE
PUXIEUX
CHAMBLEY
JOUY-AUX-
ARCHES

CLERMONT
SOMMEDIEUE
XXX
V CAMERON
Fr.
RUPT
EN-WOEVRE
XX 26
BILLY-SOUS-
LES-COTES
HAUMONT-LES-
LACHAUSSEE
NINETEEN
BOTHMER

ST. MENEHOULD
RARECOURT
ANCEMONT
Morning 12 Sept.
TROYON-
SUR-MEUSE
HATTONCHATEL
JAULNY
PRENY
MARIEULLES

ST. REMY-SUR-BUSSY
IPPECOURT
SOUILLY
Evening 12 Sept.
Fr. XX
BOUILLONVILLE
THIAUCOURT
VANDIERES
PONT-A-MOUSSON

TRIAUCOURT
Fr. XX
VIEVILLE
HEUDICOURT
XX
XX 82
(part)

VAUBECOURT
U.S. FIRST
PERSHING
Fr. II COL.
CHAUVONCOURT
ST. MIHIEL
FORT DU CAMP
DES ROMAINS
ESSEY-ET-
MAIZERAS
XX 5
XX 2
XX 90
XX 82
(part)

Fr. XX
APREMONT
BEAUMONT
XX 89
XX 42
LIRONVILLE
MAMEY
ST. JACQUES
FARM
DIEULOUARD
XXXX
EIGHTH
GERARD

XX 1
IV DICKMAN
I LIGGETT

WESTERN FRONT, 1918

ST. MIHIEL OFFENSIVE

Situation 12 September and Operations
to 16 September

0 ___ 5 ___ 10
SCALE OF MILES

By the end of September, with all the German salients recaptured or evacuated, Foch's armies had successfully accomplished the preliminary missions he had outlined on 24 July. Furthermore, at St. Mihiel, and especially at Amiens, the Allied troops had established a definite combat superiority. Their morale was high. With the arrival of more and more American divisions, they again had numerical superiority. In the tank, they had a weapon for which the Germans were unable to develop an effective countermeasure.

A great many Allied leaders were certain that the war could not be won before 1919, and Foch continued to plan for a massive final offensive through Lorraine. But he also planned to make the best possible use of the rest of 1918. His objectives were the rail lines (*shown in blue*), by means of which the Germans supplied their armies—or would evacuate them in case of defeat. Of these railroads, the northernmost—from Cologne to Aulnoye—was the best and therefore the most vital, since it carried the greatest share of supplies. The lateral line from Strasbourg north through Metz to Bruges (*top left*) was highly important for distribution and evacuation along the whole German front. It can readily be seen that if any important junction in this system—especially Aulnoye, Maubeuge, Longuyon, or Mézières—were captured, the German situation would become exceedingly critical.

Ludendorff was fully aware of these facts. Personally, he was being rapidly worn down by his responsibilities. By 3 October, he and Hindenburg were insisting that negotiations for peace should be begun. (The Kaiser had come to the same conclusion in August.) Meanwhile, they proposed to retire as necessary, fighting delaying actions to inflict maximum delay and punishment. To accomplish this, the Germans would utilize the river and canal lines and a series of fortified positions. Their major problems would be to get their troops out of Flanders and the so-called "Laon bulge" (*center*) before the rail lines were cut. Some of Ludendorff's army group commanders had been in favor of a prompt withdrawal to the line Antwerp–Meuse River, but Ludendorff had vetoed that because it would force the abandonment of large quantities of irreplaceable supplies.

Foch now launched a series of major offensives: on 26 September, the Americans and French attacked in the Meuse-Argonne sector (*see map 70*); on the 27th, the British, between Péronne and Lens; on the 28th, the "Group of Armies of Flanders" (Belgian, British, French); on the 29th, the French and British, between La Fere and Péronne. The first two of these operations (*this map, shaded blue arrows*) should be considered main attacks; the over-all operation can best be described as a double penetration. Seven American divisions—the 2d, 27th, 30th, 36th, 37th, 91st, and 93d (Provisional)—served with the French and British in these offensives.

The remainder of the war consisted of hard, straight-ahead fighting, the Germans trading space for time in front of the British and French and holding doggedly in the rugged terrain of the Argonne against the Americans. The German retreat in most sectors was skillful, though the main British attack achieved considerable success west of Le Cateau. Up to mid-October, Ludendorff handled the situation well. Then, by 18 October, the Americans broke into the last German defensive position in the Meuse-Argonne. Between the 17th and the 23d, the British scored a breakthrough, advancing beyond Le Cateau. Nothing but further, immediate retreat was left for the Germans, but—aided by increasingly bad weather, which restricted the Allied advance guards to the roads—they succeeded in escaping any large-scale Allied envelopments. Tough little rear guards, mostly artillery and machine gunners, repeatedly delayed the pursuit. Farther to the rear, however, the German Army and government were falling apart. Ludendorff resigned on 27 October. The navy mutinied on the 29th. On 9 November, a German republic was proclaimed. The Kaiser fled the next day, and the 11th brought the Armistice, under the terms of which Allied troops occupied strategic zones in Germany (*upper right*).

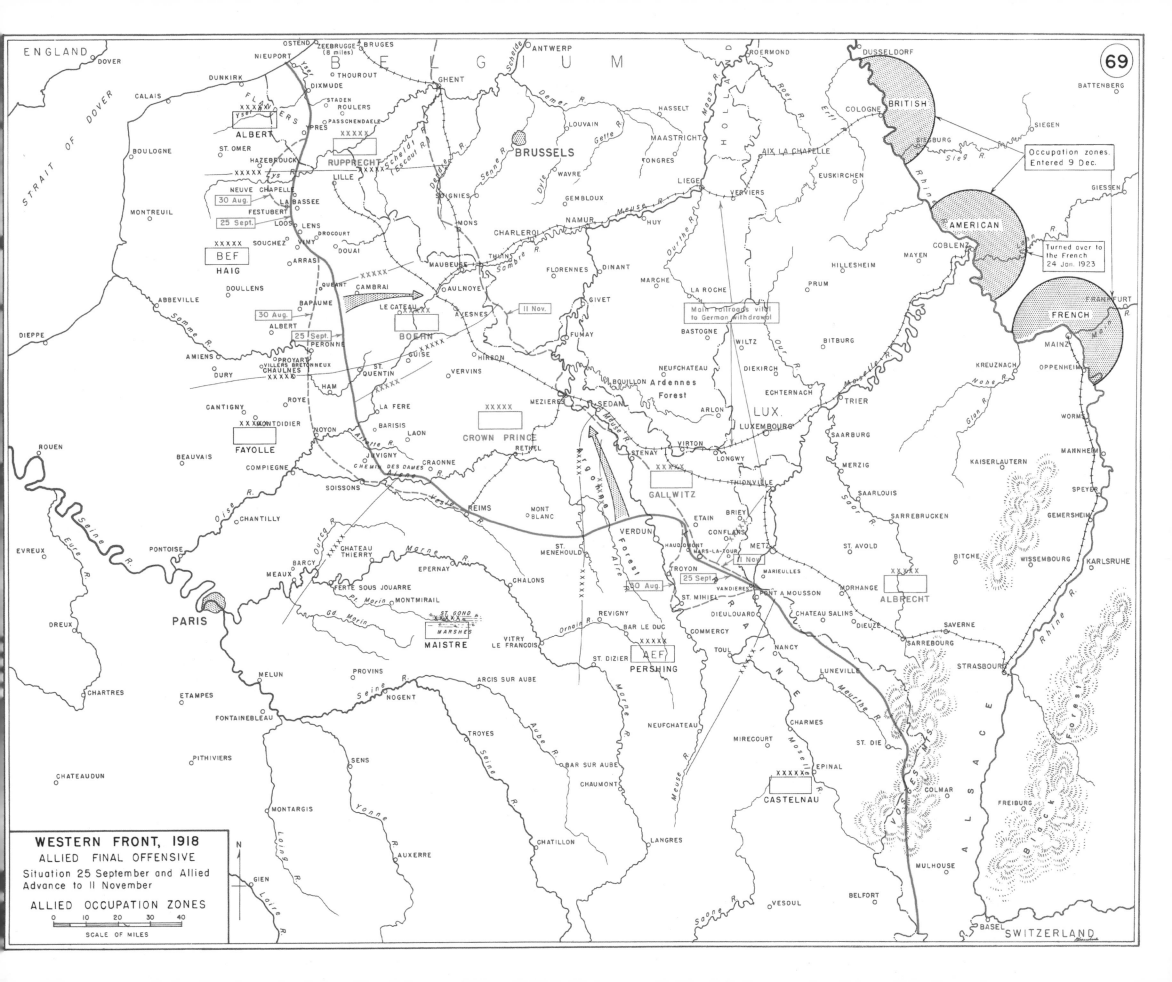

ENGLAND

BELGIUM

HOLLAND

69

BRITISH

AMERICAN

FRENCH

Main railroads vital
to German withdrawal

DUSSELDORF

COLOGNE

COBLENZ

FRANKFURT

SWITZERLAND

WESTERN FRONT, 1918

ALLIED FINAL OFFENSIVE

Situation 25 September and Allied
Advance to 11 November

ALLIED OCCUPATION ZONES

0   10   20   30   40

SCALE OF MILES

Basically, the Argonne was two roughly parallel river valleys—the Meuse and the Aire—separated by a broken ridge line which rose in commanding heights at Montfaucon, Romagne, Cunel, and Barricourt. This area was commanded on the east by the Heights of the Meuse, on the west by the hilly, tangled Argonne Forest. Across the area, the Germans had built a defensive network roughly twelve miles deep, tied together with mazes of barbed wire, mutually supporting strong points, and machine-gun nests.

The American take-over of this sector was a hurried affair, due to Foch's insistence on an immediate attack toward Mézières. Somewhat more than 1,000,000 men were shifted, during the nights of a three-week period, over inadequate road and rail nets, through the careful planning of the United States First Army Assistant G-3, Col. George C. Marshall. This hurried preparation resulted in the more seasoned American divisions remaining at St. Mihiel while the Argonne attack was initiated by troops with little or no combat experience. Pétain was of immense help in making up American deficiencies in tanks, artillery, and transport.

There was little chance for maneuver in such a situation, but feints in the St. Mihiel area persuaded the Germans that the Americans planned to renew their suspended offensive there. It seems to have been 0200 of the 26th before they learned that American units were west of the Meuse.

Pershing had planned the offensive in three phases: first, a combined advance by the Americans and the French Fourth Army on both sides of the Argonne Forest, to link up at Grandpré (*left center*); second, a further advance to the line Le Chesne (*upper left*)–Stenay (*upper center*), to outflank the German position behind the Aisne River and thus clear the way for the American-French advance on Sedan-Mézières; third, the capture of the Heights of the Meuse. The initial attack was to be a swift, massed double penetration to seize the heights of Montfaucon, Romagne, and Cunel.

The preparatory bombardment opened at 0230, 26 September; at 0525, the French Fourth Army jumped off, fol-lowed five minutes later by the Americans. Initial progress was good except around Montfaucon, where the Germans held out until the 27th, gaining time to pour in reinforcements. The Americans suffered from inexperience and a shortage of tanks. (Those that they had were rapidly used up; Col. George S. Patton, Jr., commanding a tank brigade, won the Distinguished Service Cross and was wounded here.) Replacing green divisions with veterans from St. Mihiel, Pershing continued the drive on 4 October. On 8 October, a Franco-American attack made important gains along the Heights of the Meuse (*dot-dashed red line*). By 10 October, attacking westward, the I Corps drove the Germans off the hills into Grandpré, enabling the French Fourth Army to advance up to the Aisne. Their flanks thus partially freed from enfilading German fire, the Americans resumed their grim battering, slowly gaining ground through Romagne, despite increasing German reinforcements and worsening weather. The Argonne Forest was cleared, adding to American military tradition the sagas of "the Lost Battalion" and of Sergeant York.

Meanwhile, in preparation for a renewed eastward advance from the St. Mihiel area, Pershing organized the United States Second Army under General Robert L. Bullard. General Hunter Liggett took over the First Army.

At daybreak on 1 November, Liggett—having rebuilt his communications and regrouped his forces—launched a new attack. Massed artillery and air support helped punch an opening in the last German defenses northeast of Buzancy (*left center*). On 2 November, the capture of Boult-aux-Bois (west of Buzancy) enabled the French Fourth Army to cross the Aisne. By that night, the Germans were retreating; and on the night of 6 November the Americans were before Sedan, and the vital railway was under artillery fire. The next day, the north end of the Heights of the Meuse was cleared, and Liggett was preparing an advance on Montmédy (*upper center*). On 10 November, the Second Army broke through on its front, but the Armistice halted all activity the next day.

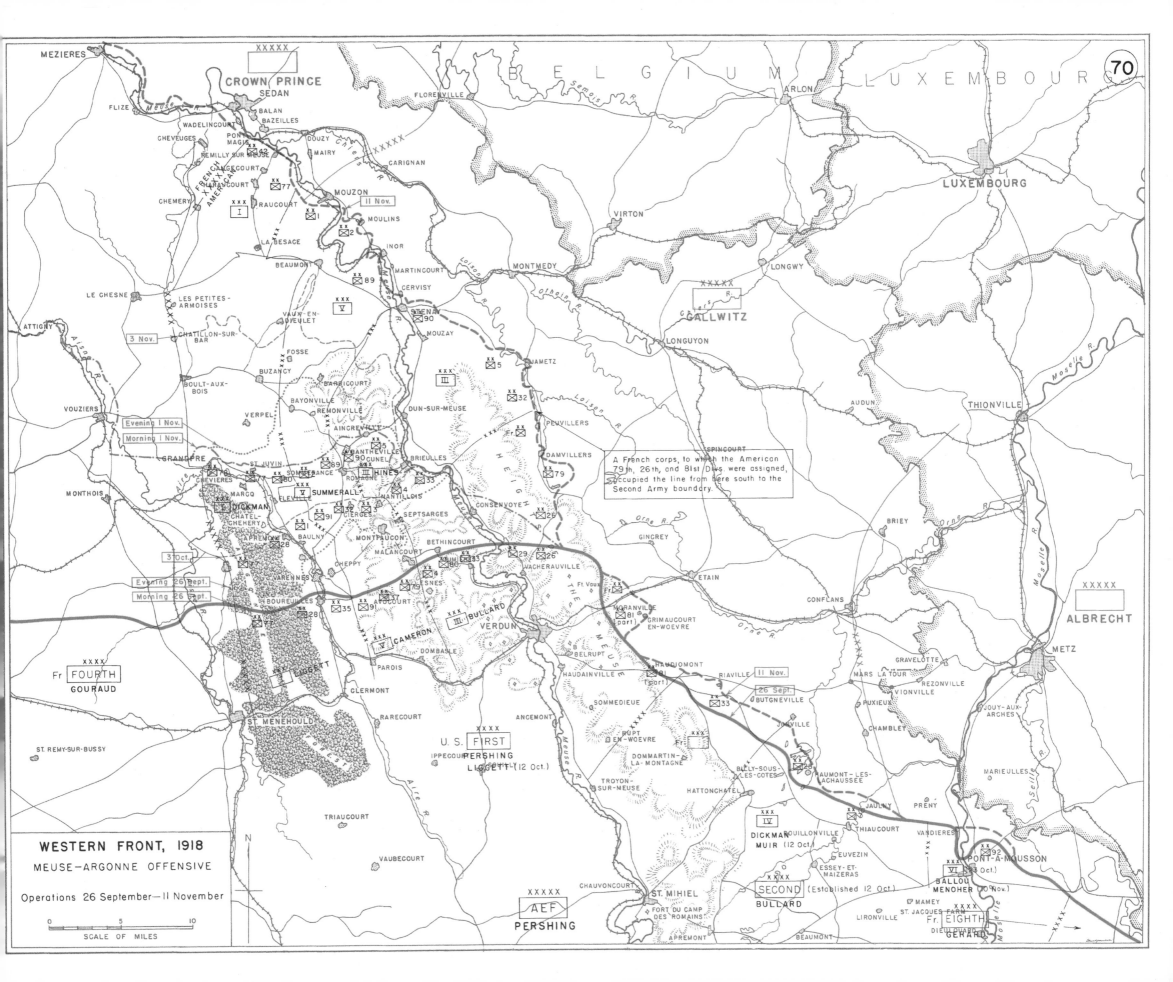

WESTERN FRONT, 1918

MEUSE–ARGONNE OFFENSIVE

Operations 26 September – 11 November

0   5   10
SCALE OF MILES

A French corps, to which the American 79th, 26th, and 81st Divs. were assigned, occupied the line from here south to the Second Army boundary.

The Allies had poured military supplies of all types into Russia during late 1916 and 1917 through the ports of Murmansk, Archangel, and Vladivostok (*blue arrows*). Large quantities remained in the port areas after the Russian collapse, awaiting shipment to the front. (At Vladivostok alone, there was about 725,000 tons, valued at over $750,000,000.)

The Bolsheviks had overthrown the Kerensky government and signed a separate peace with the Central Powers. There was a definite danger that the Germans might seize or force the weak Bolshevik government to surrender the stockpiles at the ports. Further, since the Bolsheviks were openly and contemptuously hostile to the Allies, common sense forbade allowing them to retain such military equipment. The situation in Siberia was complicated by several other factors. A large force of Czechs (deserters and prisoners from the Austrian Army, who had joined the Tsar's Army) were attempting to fight their way out of Russia along the Trans-Siberian Railway to Vladivostok. Also, the Japanese had large territorial ambitions in Siberia, which the United States considered it proper to thwart.

During July, August, and September of 1918, Allied forces landed in Russia. A sizable perimeter was established around Murmansk and Archangel under British command, though Bolshevik attacks later forced its contraction. American forces involved consisted of a reinforced regiment. In Siberia, operations were largely restricted to the line of the Trans-Siberian Railway; units of the two American regiments serving in that area operated as far west as Lake Baikal.

The immediate objectives of these expeditions were successfully accomplished: the masses of supplies were recovered, the Czechs extricated, and the Japanese kept from dismembering Siberia. Eventually, the American units were withdrawn—from northern Russia in August, 1919, and from Vladivostok in April, 1920.

World War I continued the trend—seen earlier in the French Revolutionary Wars and the American Civil War—toward Total War. Though strategy and operations remained important, the nations with superior industrial capacity and larger populations gained the victory with huge armies and vast quantities of weapons and equipment. From the clash of mass, hastily trained armies on all fronts came casualty figures that dwarfed those prior to World War I—8.5 million soldiers dead and 20 million wounded. One cannot measure the destruction solely in lives lost, however. The German, Austro-Hungarian, Russian, and Ottoman Empires broke under the strain of Total War.

War encompassed every facet of society. While most young men went to the battlefields, significant percentages of men and women stayed on the homefront churning out millions of tons of supplies. The management of these resources, both personal and materiel, placed a premium on planning that only a central government could provide. Governments became more centralized and more powerful to deal with threats to their existence. As governments adapted to the strains placed upon them, so did armies. They found new ways to organize, resupply, and fight. Unfortunately for the soldiers in the trenches, most of the innovations occurred only after massive casualties.

Many of the innovations were technological and aimed to break the deadlock of the Western Front. The resulting technology reads like a primer for twentieth century warfare: tanks, flamethrowers, light machine guns, gas, airplanes, aircraft carriers, and submarines. In addition to technology, tactical and operational methods changed considerably by the end of the war. When combined with improved infantry-artillery coordination and better tanks and aircraft, infiltration tactics provided the foundation for the German methods of 1940. Similarly, the disastrous Galipoli campaign provided important insights into the conduct of amphibious operations. Thus, World War I established the foundation for twentieth century warfare.

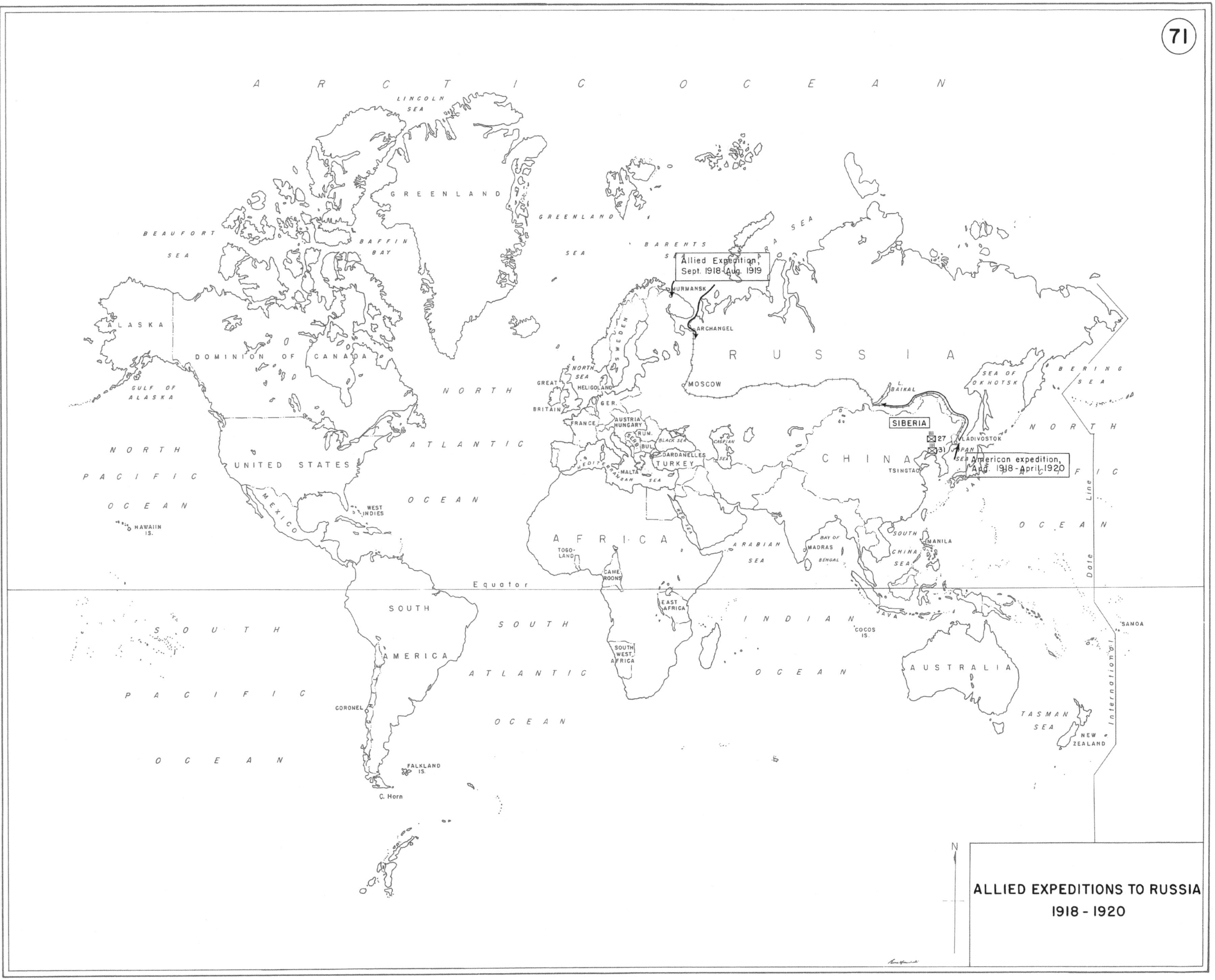

ARCTIC OCEAN

LINCOLN SEA

GREENLAND

GREENLAND SEA

BARENTS SEA

BEAUFORT SEA

BAFFIN BAY

ALASKA

DOMINION OF CANADA

GULF OF ALASKA

NORTH PACIFIC OCEAN

UNITED STATES

MEXICO

WEST INDIES

HAWAIIAN IS.

NORTH ATLANTIC OCEAN

NORTH SEA

GREAT BRITAIN

SWEDEN

HELIGOLAND

GER.

FRANCE

AUSTRIA HUNGARY

RUM.

BUL.

BLACK SEA

DARDANELLES

MALTA

TURKEY

MEDITERRANEAN SEA

CASPIAN SEA

RED SEA

AFRICA

TOGOLAND

CAMEROONS

ARABIAN SEA

BAY OF BENGAL

MADRAS

SOUTH CHINA SEA

MANILA

COCOS IS.

JAVA

RUSSIA

MURMANSK

ARCHANGEL

Allied Expedition, Sept. 1918-Aug. 1919

MOSCOW

L. BAIKAL

SEA OF OKHOTSK

BERING SEA

SIBERIA

VLADIVOSTOK

27

31

JAPAN

TSINGTAO

American expedition, Aug. 1918-April 1920

CHINA

NORTH PACIFIC OCEAN

SOUTH AMERICA

SOUTH ATLANTIC OCEAN

PACIFIC OCEAN

CORONEL

FALKLAND IS.

C. Horn

SOUTH WEST AFRICA

EAST AFRICA

Equator

INDIAN OCEAN

AUSTRALIA

TASMAN SEA

NEW ZEALAND

SAMOA

International Date Line

N

ALLIED EXPEDITIONS TO RUSSIA

1918 - 1920

RECOMMENDED READING LIST

This list does not purport to contain all the good books on the military history of the periods covered. The selections presented, however, provide the reader with worthwhile references for further study in any area he or she is likely to choose.

WORLD WAR I
BASIC WORKS: MILITARY HISTORY AND PHILOSOPHY

BERNHARDI, FRIEDRICH VON. *Germany in the Next War.* London: Edward Arnold, 1912.

CRAIG, GORDON A. *The Politics of the Prussian Army, 1640–1945.* New York: Oxford University Press, 1956.

EARLE, EDWARD M. *Makers of Modern Strategy.* Princeton, New Jersey: Princeton University Press, 1943.

GOERLITZ, WALTER. *History of the German General Staff, 1657 to 1945.* New York: Frederick A. Praeger, 1952.

GOLTZ, COLMAR, FREIHERR VON DER. *The Conduct of War.* Kansas City, Missouri: Franklin Hudson Publishing Company, 1896.

MURRAY, WILLIAMSON, MACGREGOR KNOX, AND ALVIN BERNSTEIN, eds. *The Making of Strategy: Rulers, States, and War.* Cambridge: Cambridge University Press, 1994.

PARET, PETER, ed. *Makers of Modern Strategy: From Machiavelli to the Nuclear Age.* Princeton, New Jersey: Princeton University Press, 1986.

PICQ, ARDANT DU. *Battle Studies.* New York: MacMillan, 1921.

SCHLIEFFEN, ALFRED VON. *Cannae.* Fort Leavenworth: Command and General Staff School Press, 1936.

OFFICIAL HISTORIES
France

MINISTÈRE DE LA GUERRE, ÉTAT-MAJOR DE L'ARMÉE, SERVICE HISTORIQUE. *Les Armées Francáises dans la Grand Guerre.* 10 vols. Paris: Imprimerie Nationale, 1922.

Germany

REICHSARCHIV. *Der Weltkrieg, 1914–1918.* 14 vols. Berlin: E. S. Mittler, 1925–44.

Great Britain

HISTORICAL SECTION, The Committee of Imperial Defence. *History of the Great War.* 45 vols., including maps. London: His Majesty's Stationery Office, 1927–47.

MINISTRY OF INFORMATION. *Chronology of the War.* 4 vols. London: Constable and Company, 1918.

Italy

SUPREME COMMAND, ROYAL ITALIAN ARMY. *The Battle of the Piave.* London: Hodder and Stoughton, 1919.

UNITED STATES

AMERICAN BATTLE MONUMENTS COMMISSION. *American Armies and Battlefields in Europe.* Washington, D.C.: U.S. Government Printing Office, 1938.

HISTORICAL SECTION, ARMY WAR COLLEGE. *Order of Battle of the United States Land Forces in the World War: American Expeditionary Forces, Divisions.* Washington, D.C.: U.S. Government Printing Office, 1931.

_____. *Order of Battle of the United States and Land Forces in the World War: American Expeditionary Forces, General Headquarters, Armies, Army Corps, Services of Supply, and Separate Forces.* Washington, D.C.: U. S. Government Printing Office, 1937.

_____. *Order of Battle of the United States Land Forces in the World War (1917–19), Zone of the Interior.* Washington, D.C.: U.S. Government Printing Office, 1949.

HISTORICAL DIVISION, DEPARTMENT OF THE ARMY. *United States Army in the World War, 1917–1919.* 17 vols. Washington, D.C.: U.S. Government Printing Office, 1948.

PERSHING, JOHN J. *Final Report of General John J. Pershing, Commander in Chief, American Expeditionary Forces.* Washington, D.C.: U.S. Government Printing Office, 1920.

GENERAL HISTORIES

ASPREY, ROBERT R. *The German High Command at War.* New York: William Morrow, 1991.

CHURCHILL, WINSTON S. *The World Crisis.* 4 vols. New York: Charles Scribner's Sons, 1932.

COFFMAN, EDWARD M. *The War to End All Wars: The American Military Experience in World War I.* Madison, Wisconsin: University of Wisconsin Press, 1968.

CRUTTWELL, C.R.M.F. *A History of the Great War.* Oxford: Clarendon Press, 1934.

FALLS, CYRIL. *The Great War.* New York: Putnam, 1959.

FERRELL, ROBERT H. *Woodrow Wilson and World War I, 1917–1921.* New York: Harper and Row, 1985.

FISCHER, FRITZ. *Germany's Aims in the First World War.* New York: 1967.

FULLER, JOHN F.C. *A Military History of the Western World* Vol. III. New York: Funk and Wagnalls, 1954.

GILBERT, MARTIN. *The First World War: A Complete History.* New York: Henry Holt and Company, 1994.

GUINN, PAUL. *British Strategy and Politics, 1914 to 1918.* Oxford: Clarendon Press, 1965.

HALPERN, PAUL G. *A Naval History of World War I.* Annapolis, Maryland: Naval Institute Press, 1994.

JOLL, JAMES. *The Origins of the First World War.* New York: Longman, 1984.

KENNEDY, DAVID. *Over Here: The First World War and American Society.* New York: Oxford University Press, 1980.

KENNEDY, PAUL M., ed. *The War Plans of the Great Powers* London: Allen and Unwin, 1979.

KING, JERE C. *Generals and Politicians: Conflict between France's High Command, Parliament, and Government, 1914–1918,* Berkeley: University of California Press, 1951.

STONE, NORMAN. *The Eastern Front, 1914–1917.* New York: Scribner, 1975.

TRASK, DAVID F. *The AEF and Coalition Warmaking, 1917–1918.* Lawrence: University Press of Kansas, 1993.

TRAVERS, TIM. *The Killing Ground: The British Army, the Western Front, and the Emergence of Modern Warfare, 1900–1918* London: Allen and Unwin, 1987.

TERRAINE, JOHN. *The Western Front, 1914–1918,* Philadelphia: Lippincott, 1965.

TUNSTALL, GRAYDON A. *Planning for War against Russia and Serbia: Austro-Hungarian and German Military Strategies, 1871–1914.* New York: Columbia University Press, 1993.

SCHMITT, BERNADOTTE E., AND HAROLD C. VEDELER. *The World in the Crucible, 1914–1919.* New York: Harper and Row, 1984.

BATTLES AND CAMPAIGNS

BRAIM, PAUL F. *The Test of Battle: The American Expeditionary Forces in the Meuse-Argonne Campaign.* Newark, New Jersey: University of Delaware Press, 1987.

BRUSILOV, ALEXEI A. *A Soldier's Notebook, 1914–1918.* London: MacMillan, 1930.

BULLARD, ROBERT LEE. *Personalities and Reminiscences of the War.* Garden City, New York.: Doubleday, Page and Company, 1925.

_____, and Earl Reeves. *American Soldiers Also Fought.* New York: Maurice H. Louis, 1939.

CAVALRY SCHOOL. *Cavalry Combat.* Harrisburg, Pennsylvania: Telegraph Press, 1937.

FALKENHAYN, ERICH VON. *The German General Staff and Its Decisions, 1914–1916.* New York: Dodd, Mead and Company, 1920.

FRENCH, SIR JOHN. *1914.* Boston: Houghton Mifflin, 1949.

FROST, HOLLOWAY H. *The Battle of Jutland.* Annapolis, Maryland: United States Naval Institute, 1936.

GOUGH, SIR HUBERT. *The Fifth Army.* London: Hodder and Stoughton, 1931.

GRAVES, WILLIAM S. *America's Siberian Adventure, 1918–1920.* New York: Cape and Smith, 1931.

GRAY, EDWYN A. *The Killing Time: The U-Boat War, 1914–1918.* New York: Charles Scribner, 1972.

HAMILTON, SIR IAN. *Gallipoli Diary.* New York: George H. Doran, 1920.

HARBORD, JAMES G. *The American Army in France.* Boston: Little, Brown and Company, 1936.

HOFFMAN, MAX. *War Diaries and Other Papers.* London: Secker, 1929.

_____. *The War of Lost Opportunities.* New York: International Publishers, 1925.

HORNE, ALISTAIR. *The Price of Glory: Verdun 1916.* New York: Penguin, 1962.

INFANTRY JOURNAL. *Infantry in Battle.* Washington, D.C.: Infantry Journal, 1939.

JOHNSON, THOMAS M., AND FLETCHER PRATT. *The Lost Battalion.* Indianapolis and New York: Bobbs-Merrill, 1938.

RECOMMENDED READING LIST

KEARSEY, A. *The Battle of Amiens, 1918.* Aldershot, England: Gale and Polden, 1950.

KEEGAN, JOHN. *The Face of Battle: A Study of Agincourt, Waterloo and the Somme.* New York: Penguin, 1976.

KENNAN, GEORGE F. *Soviet-American Relations, 1917–1920.* Vol. I: *Russian Leaves the War, 1956.* Vol. II: *The Decision to Intervene,* 1958. Princeton, New Jersey: Princeton University Press, 1956–58.

KENNETT, LEE. *The First Air War: 1914–1918.* New York: The Free Press, 1991.

KEYES, SIR ROBERT. *The Fight for Gallipoli.* London: Eyre and Spottiswoode, 1941.

KLUCK, ALEXANDER VON. *The March on Paris and the Battle of the Marne.* New York: Longmans, Green and Company, 1920.

KUHL, H. VON. *The Marne Campaign, 1914.* Fort Leavenworth, Kansas: Command and General Staff School Press, 1936.

_____, AND VON BERGEMANN. *Movements and Supply of the German First Army during August and September, 1914.* Fort Leavenworth, Kansas: Command and General Staff School Press, 1929.

LAWRENCE, THOMAS E. *The Seven Pillars of Wisdom.* New York: Garden City Publishing Company, 1938.

LIGGETT, HUNTER. *Commanding an American Army.* Boston: Houghton Mifflin, 1925.

MACDONALD, LYN. *They Called It Passchendaele.* New York: Atheneum, 1989.

MARCH, PEYTON C. *The Nation at War.* Garden City, New York: Doubleday, Doran and Company, 1932.

McENTEE, GIRARD L. *Italy's Part in Winning the War.* Princeton, New Jersey: Princeton University Press, 1934.

MACINTYRE, DONALD. *Jutland.* New York: W.W. Norton and Company, 1958.

MIDDLEBROOK, MARTIN. *The First Day on the Somme.* New York: Norton, 1972.

MITCHELL, WILLIAM. *Our Air Force.* New York: E.P. Dutton and Company., 1921.

MOREHEAD, ALAN. *Gallipoli.* New York: Harper and Brothers, 1956.

NEWMANN, GEORGE P. *The German Air Force in the Great War.* London: Hodder and Stoughton, 1920.

PÉTAIN, PHILIPPE. *Verdun.* New York: Dial Press, 1930.

RITTER, GERHARD. *The Schlieffen Plan: Critique of a Myth.* New York: Frederick A. Praeger, 1958.

ROMMEL, ERWIN. *Infantry Attacks.* Washington, D.C.: Combat Forces Press, 1956.

SANDERS, LIMAN VON. *My Five Years in Turkey.* Annapolis, Maryland: United States Naval Institute, 1927.

SHOWALTER, DENNIS E. *Tannenberg: Clash of Empires.* Hamden, Connecticut: Archon Books, 1991.

SPEARS, E.L. *Liaison, 1914.* London: William Heinemann, 1930.

_____. *Prelude to Victory.* London: Jonathan Cape, 1939.

TOWNSHEND, SIR CHARLES V.F. *My Campaign in Mesopotamia.* London: Thornton Butterworth, 1920.

TYNG, SEWELL. *The Campaign of the Marne, 1914.* New York: Longmans, Green and Company, 1935.

VILLARI, LUIGI. *The War on the Italian Front.* London: Cobden-Sanderson, 1932.

WOLF, LEON. *In Flanders Fields.* New York: Viking Press, 1959.

MEMOIRS, BIOGRAPHIES, AND AUTOBIOGRAPHIES

COOPER, DUFF. *Haig.* Garden City, New York: Doubleday, Doran and Company, 1946.

FOCH, FERDINAND. *The Memoirs of Marshal Foch.* Garden City, New York: Doubleday, Doran and Company 1931.

GALET, EMILE J. *Albert, King of the Belgians in the Great War.* Boston: Houghton Mifflin, 1931.

HAIG, DOUGLAS. *The Private Papers of Douglas Haig,* ed. Robert Blake. London: Eyre and Spottiswoode, 1952.

HINDENBURG, PAUL VON. *Out of My Life.* New York: Harper and Brothers, 1921.

JOFFRE, JOSEPH. *The Personal Memoirs of Joffre.* New York: Harper and Brothers, 1932.

LIDDELL HART, B.H. *Foch, The Man of Orléans.* Boston: Little, Brown and Compny, 1932.

LUDENDORFF, ERICH VON. *Ludendorff's Own Story.* New York: Harper and Brothers, 1919.

MILLETT, ALLAN R. *The General: Robert L. Bullard and Officership in the United States Army, 1881–1925.* Westport, Connecticut: Greenwood Press, 1975.

PERSHING, JOHN J. *My Experiences in the World War.* New York: Frederick A. Stokes Company., 1931.

ROBERTSON, WILLIAM. *Soldiers and Statesmen, 1914–1918.* New York: Scribner's, 1926.

RYAN, STEPHEN. *Pétain the Soldier.* South Brunswick, New Jersey: A.S. Barnes, 1969.

SMYTHE, DONALD. *Pershing: General of the Armies.* Bloomington, Indiana: Indiana University Press, 1986.

TERRAINE, JOHN. *Douglas Haig—The Educated Soldier.* London: Hutchinson, 1963.

WAVELL, ARCHIBALD. *Allenby.* New York: Oxford University Press, 1941.

SOLDIER LIFE AND TECHNICAL REFERENCES

BAYNES, JOHN. *Morale: A Study of Men and Courage.* Garden City Park: Avery, 1988.

CHINN, GEORGE M. *The Machine Gun.* 2 vols. Washington, D.C.: U.S. Government Printing Office, 1951.

ELLIS, JOHN. *Eye-Deep in Hell: Trench Warfare in World War I.* Baltimore: John Hopkins, 1976.

FREIDEL, FRANK, ed. *Over There.* Rev. ed. New York: McGraw Hill, 1990.

FUSSELL, PAUL. *The Great War and Modern Memory.* New York: Oxford University Press, 1975.

GERMAINS, VICTOR W. *The Mechanization of War.* London: Sifton Praed and Company, 1927.

GRAVES, ROBERT. *Goodbye to All That.* New York: Doubleday, 1985.

HAGOOD, JOHNSON. *The Services of Supply.* Boston: Houghton Mifflin, 1927.

JUNGER, ERNST. *The Storm of Steel.* New York: Howard Fertig, 1975.

JONES, RALPH E. *The Fighting Tanks since 1916.* Washington, D.C.: National Service Publishing, 1933.

LUPFER, TIMOTHY T. *The Dynamics of Doctrine: Changes in German Tactical Doctrine during the First World War.* Fort Leavenworth, Kansas: Combat Studies Institute, 1981.

MILLER, HENRY W. *The Paris Gun.* London: George G. Harrup and Company, 1930.

MILLETT, ALLAN R., AND WILLIAMSON MURRAY, eds. *Military Effectiveness,* Vol. I: *The First World War.* Boston: Allen and Unwin, 1988.

MORAN, CHARLES. *The Anatomy of Courage.* London: Constable, 1945.

MOSSE, GEORGE L. *Fallen Soldiers: Reshaping the Memory of the World Wars.* Oxford: Oxford University Press, 1990.

SLESSOR, JOHN C. *Air Power and Armies.* London: Oxford University Press, 1936.

SWINTON, SIR ERNEST D. *Eyewitness.* Garden City, New York: Doubleday, Doran and Company, 1933.

WILGUS, WILLIAM J. *Transporting the A.E.F. in Western Europe.* New York: Columbia University Press, 1931.

WINTER, DENNIS. *Death's Men: Soldiers of the Great War.* New York: Penguin, 1979.